Praise for the Essays of Joseph Epstein

"The modern essay has regained a good deal of its literary status in our time, much to the credit of Joseph Epstein."

—KARL SHAPIRO

"Joseph Epstein is an essayist in the brilliant tradition of Charles Lamb. He moves so effortlessly from the amusingly personal to the broadly philosophical that it takes a moment before you realize how far out into the intellectual cosmos you have been taken. He is also mercilessly free of the petty intellectual etiquettes common at this moment in our national letters. It is refreshing to hear so independent a voice."

—TOM WOLFE

"If Epstein's ultimate ancestor is Montaigne, his more immediate master is Mencken. Like Mencken, he has fashioned a style that successfully combines elegance and even bookishness with street-smart colloquial directness. And there is nothing remote or aloof about him."

—JOHN GROSS

"Joseph Epstein's essays no more need his identifying byline than Van Gogh's paintings need his signature. Epstein's style—call it learned whimsy—is unmistakable; for Epstein addicts, indispensable."

—GEORGE WILL

"Epstein's work is well in the Addisonian line of succession that Cyril Connolly saw petering out in *Punch* and the professional humorists. . . . Epstein is a great deal more sophisticated than they were, and a great deal more readable. His subjects are tossed up, turned round, stuck with quotations, abandoned and returned to, playfully, inverted, and finally set back on their feet, as is the reader, a little breathless but quite unharmed. But is essentially a merry-go-round, not a view to the death."

—PHILIP LARKIN

Essays in Biography

Essays in Biography

Joseph Epstein

AXIOS

Some of the essays in this book first appeared
in the following publications:

Commentary
The Hudson Review
The New Criterion
Sewanee Review
The Times Literary Supplement
The Wall Street Journal
The Weekly Standard

Axios Press
P.O. Box 118
Mount Jackson, VA 22842
888.542.9467   info@axiosinstitute.org

Library of Congress Cataloging-in-Publication Data

Epstein, Joseph, 1937–
Essays in biography / Joseph Epstein.
p. cm.
Includes index.
ISBN 978-1-60419-068-7 (hardcover)
1. Epstein, Joseph, 1937—Books and reading. 2. Literature—History and
criticism. 3. Authors—Biography. I. Title.

PS3555.P6527E87 2012
814'.54—dc23

2012010035

In memory of
Matthew Shanahan
(1917–2012)

Also by Joseph Epstein:

Gossip: The Untrivial Pursuit (2011)

The Love Song of A. Jerome Minkoff: And Other Stories (2010)

Fred Astaire (2008)

In a Cardboard Belt!: Essays Personal, Literary, and Savage (2007)

Friendship: An Exposé (2006)

Alexis de Tocqueville: Democracy's Guide (2006)

Fabulous Small Jews (2003)

Envy (2003)

Snobbery: The American Version (2002)

Narcissus Leaves the Pool: Familiar Essays (1999)

Life Sentences: Literary Essays (1997)

With My Trousers Rolled: Familiar Essays (1995)

Pertinent Players: Essays on the Literary Life (1993)

A Line Out for a Walk: Familiar Essays (1991)

The Goldin Boys: Stories (1991)

Partial Payments: Essays on Writers and Their Lives (1988)

Once More Around the Block: Familiar Essays (1987)

Plausible Prejudices: Essays on American Writing (1985)

Middle of My Tether: Familiar Essays (1983)

Ambition: The Secret Passion (1980)

Familiar Territory: Observations on American Life (1979)

Divorced in America: Marriage in an Age of Possibility (1974)

Contents

Image Credits

Americans

George Washington

An Amateur's View

IN *THE AMERICAN COMMONWEALTH,* his book of 1888, Lord Bryce, considering American political institutions, provides an early chapter titled "Why Great Men Are Not Chosen Presidents." Most Americans, without needing to hear the argument, are likely to agree with the chapter's premises. The *planetarkhis*, the modern Greek word for ruler of the planet, the President of the United States may well be, but we can all be assured that, whoever he is, nowadays he is almost certainly likely to be a mediocrity. "Besides," Bryce wrote, "the ordinary American voter does not object to mediocrity. He has a lower conception of the qualities requisite to make a statesman than those who direct public opinion in Europe have. He likes his candidate to be sensible, vigorous, and, above all, what he calls 'magnetic,' and does not value, because he sees no need for, originality or profundity, a fine culture or a wide knowledge." Mr. Ford, Mr. Carter, Mr. Reagan, Messrs. Bush, Mr. Clinton, and Mr. Obama—take a bow, please.

Bryce goes on to discuss the other factors inhibiting, if not absolutely excluding, the possibility of a great man becoming President of the United States: the preference for a safe over a brilliant man, the nature of American party politics, the distinct difference between a successful candidate and a successful leader, the humdrum and ceremonial nature of much of the job. "We may now answer the question from which we started," Bryce writes. "Great men have not often been chosen presidents, first because great men are rare in politics; secondly, because the method of choice does not bring them to the top; thirdly, because they are not, in quiet times, absolutely needed."

Happy with our mediocrity though we Americans may be, it is also more than a mite interesting to note that Lord Bryce felt that the presidency of the United States was nearly designed with George Washington in mind. "The creation of the office," Bryce averred, "would seem [to the members of the Second Continental Convention meeting in Philadelphia in 1783] justified by the existence of a person exactly fitted to fill it, one whose established influence and ripe judgment would repair the faults then supposed to be characteristic of democracy, its impulsiveness, its want of respect for authority, its incapacity for pursuing a consistent line of action." Washington, in this description, was not only the perfect man for the job, but the man after whom the job itself ought to be tailored.

Remarkable though George Washington was in so many ways, the ways of remarking upon both him and his extraordinary qualities are not easy. People have tried, for more than two centuries now, and with vastly uneven results. Was he an authentically great man, or instead merely the right man for his time? Was he a great military leader, or instead, General Kutuzov-like, a man whose genius lay in his sensing when not to fight? Had he a vision for his country, or for that matter anything resembling a coherent political philosophy? Was he, in the judgment rendered him by history, a fluke, a very lucky man, or was the newly fledged United States lucky beyond its wildest reckoning in having a man of George Washington's caliber to call upon in the crucial years of its revolution and the forming of its unique republican democracy?

GEORGE WASHINGTON

I hope no one thinks that I pose these questions with confident answers already in mind, for seeing Washington plain is a project at which even the best minds, of his time and ours, have strained themselves to do. Consider one of the subtlest of those minds, that of Thomas Jefferson, who served as his Secretary of State. In a letter of 1814—written nearly fifteen years after Washington's death—to a Dr. Walter Jones, who was then preparing a history of the young republic, Jefferson claimed to know Washington "intimately and thoroughly," and provided the following delineation of his character.

Jefferson did not award Washington universally high grades. He thought Washington's mind was "great and powerful, without being of the very first order." It was a mind "slow in operation, being little aided by invention or imagination, but sure in conclusion." Although Washington planned his battles "judiciously," he was "slow in readjustment" when things did not go according to plan. He was, Jefferson thought, fearless though "most tremendous in his wrath," with his integrity "most pure, his justice the most inflexible." He was "in every sense of the word, a wise, a good, and a great man," yet "his heart was not warm in its affections" and "he exactly calculated every man's value," which suggests an ungenerous utilitarianism.

As an intellectual and as a visionary, Jefferson recognized in Washington nothing of the soul mate, and of course the two men would later find themselves in different political parties. Jefferson continues: "His time was employed in action chiefly, reading little and that only in agriculture and English history." He had little sympathy for "visionary projects." What is more: "He was naturally distrustful of men, and inclined to gloomy apprehensions," such that "I do believe that General Washington had not a firm confidence in the durability of our government," which is what caused Jefferson to believe Washington thought that the United States must one day end up with the ceremoniousness of the British constitution. What

Jefferson couldn't have known was that part of the reason Washington was so highly revered was that he was thought to have gotten the best out of, without ever having been dominated by, intellectuals such as Jefferson and Alexander Hamilton.

"A riddle wrapped in a mystery inside an enigma," Churchill's fine formulation for the complexity of the old Soviet Union applies nicely to Washington, except you might take the entire package—riddle, mystery, enigma—and double wrap it inside a conundrum. Less talented than other generals, less intelligent than other politicians, not at all well educated to begin with, parochial in both his background and interests, a man with a strong sense of *amour-propre* but no complex vision, either political, religious, or economic, here was this man, George Washington, without whom, everyone who has thought at all about it agrees, the experiment in government known as the United States would, as like as not, almost certainly have failed. Consider the historian Forrest McDonald, who, in the preface to his book on *The Presidency of George Washington*, of Washington writes:

> He was indispensable to the American experiment in self-government. And yet, as his actions and the quality of his leadership as president are appraised in the following pages, the reader may wonder just what made Washington himself so special. Among others, his chief justice [John Marshall], two of his cabinet ministers [Jefferson and Hamilton], and his most trusted adviser in the House of Representatives [James Madison] will appear to have been at least as able as he was—and considerably more important in formulating the programs and policies that insured the perdurance of the federal government.

McDonald goes on to suggest that the mystery of George Washington—he calls it a "dual mystery"—may not ultimately be solvable, the man's career itself having partaken of myth, "for George Washington, in his own lifetime, was self-consciously both more than a mere man and less than a man: his people craved a myth and a symbol, and he devoted his life to fulfilling that need." Perhaps so; but then again, perhaps not.

In *Pride and Prejudice*, Jane Austen never describes Elizabeth Bennett, which allows girls and young women, when reading the novel, to believe Elizabeth looks like them. Does something similar pertain to George Washington? Do we read into him those traits we either think we have ourselves or wish we did have? "I glory in the character of Washington," John Adams, a not uncritical connoisseur of things Washingtonian—he once referred to Washington as a "muttonhead"—wrote to a friend, "because I know him to be an exemplification of the American character." The words are simple enough, but what, precisely, do they mean?

What makes an understanding of George Washington complicated is that this riddle wrapped in a mystery inside an enigma and then double wrapped inside a conundrum has also been tied with bows of celebration as gaudy as any historical package in the history of history. Washington was famous even before he was great, monumental while still drawing breath, apotheosized while still very much alive. Vast numbers of cities, a state, human beings, and finally of course the nation's capital were named after him. He was under nearly full-time request from portrait painters and sculptors. The heavy myth begins with Parson Mason Locke Weems's biography, published when Washington was still alive and perhaps able—who knows?—to squirm under its smarmy anecdotage.

Shorn of its Weemsian moral exemplum—"Father, I cannot tell a lie, it was I who chopped down the cherry tree"—George Washington's boyhood was fairly typical of the second-line Virginia gentry of which his family was a part. The family would probably have remained part of this lesser squirearchy had not Washington's father Augustine died suddenly, in 1743, when George was eleven. George was the first of his father's five children from a second marriage (Augustine had had four children from his first marriage). George was left sufficient land and personal effects to give him a start but not a secure niche in life. He would have to make his own way.

The young George Washington at first thought the way was to be made with the help of his eldest half-brother Lawrence. His father's major legatee, Lawrence Washington had been educated in England, and was intelligent, polished, and winning enough to marry above himself into the Fairfaxes, one of the first families of Virginia. George idolized his brother, who seems to have repaid this admiration with a steady flow of fine feeling between a man in his mid-twenties and a half-brother fourteen years his junior.

Lawrence thought a naval career might be the answer for George, but the boy's mother, a strong-minded woman, known neither for her wide sympathy nor generous impulses, quickly put the kibosh on that. Washington's education, about which not much is known, apparently did not go beyond the standard rudimentary subjects. (His father's early death precluded his studying, as the sons of Augustine Washington's first marriage did, in England.) He learned no foreign languages, a source of mild shame later in life. (He never visited France because, he said, he was embarrassed about requiring a translator there.) His religious training, as his biographer Douglas Southall Freeman writes, "was of a sort to turn his mind to conduct rather than creed." At fifteen he became a surveyor. Although no one ever accused Washington of being dreamy, such dreams as he had were chiefly commercial; he saw the way to wealth in the acquisition of land, which he began to acquire on his own from the age of eighteen—and continued to do throughout that portion of his life not spent either as a soldier or a political leader.

At nineteen, George accompanied his brother Lawrence to the Barbados—the only time he would ever travel outside America— where the latter went seeking a cure for weakened lungs, which he was not to find. While there, George contracted the smallpox that was to leave him pockmarked for life but also immune to that eighteenth-century killer. Lawrence himself died the following year, 1752, leaving George, not yet twenty-one but a self-starter, in charge of large portions of his estate.

Washington was becoming less a handsome than a striking, pre-possessing young man, who combined the skills of the frontier with those of the drawing room. He would grow to six foot three and weigh two-hundred pounds; he was said to be among the best horsemen of his age. He could withstand hardship but was not averse to good food, clever talk, well-made clothes. He had become a Mason, had substantial land holdings, and by the age of twenty-one was appointed a major in the Virginia militia and given a regiment to command in the wars against the French and Indians. Not at all bad for a man with less than first-rate connections in what seemed to many the closed society of Virginia.

The element of presence comes into play, perhaps heavily into play, with George Washington. He appeared to impress all with whom he came into contact. The impression Washington seemed to make on everyone was that of an attractive gravity. The initial impression of Abigail Adams, no pushover, who first met Washington in 1775, when he had been named commander-in-chief of the Continental Army, is close to the standard one. "You had prepared me to entertain a favorable opinion of him," she wrote to her husband John, "but I thought the half was not told me. Dignity with ease and complacency, the gentleman and the soldier look agreeably blended in him. Modesty marks every line and feature of his face."

If Washington was an unusually unimaginative man, he enjoyed the advantages of not having a strong imagination. Chief among them is that it allows one to take the world as it is, not to argue with it, nor wish to change it. This George Washington always seems to have done. If one takes the world as it is, it becomes a lot easier to know what to ask of it.

Consider Washington's marriage. One story has the young George in love with Sally Cary Fairfax: "The exact nature of their relationship cannot be defined," writes James Thomas Flexner. Since Sally was married, George sought elsewhere, and came up with a wealthy widow, Martha Custis, who had two children (and lost two others in their infancy) from her first marriage. Southall Freeman puts the twenty-six-year-old Washington's courtship neatly:

> The young widow, five-foot tall and pudgy, was among the wealthiest and most desirable in Virginia when the tall young Col. George Washington bowed low to her on March 16, 1758. Washington did not stay then more than a day or a day and a half [at her house], but as he looked at the lovely Martha and across the broad, rich fields of level land, he resolved to come again.

And he did, quite possibly closing the deal, Southall Freeman suggests, on his second visit. "Neither partner," the historian Richard Norton Smith writes of the marriage, "entertained illusions."

Washington would later affirm that his marriage was the one event in his life "most conducive to happiness." Yet when his step-daughter—and the Father of his Country, alas had no children of his own—was considering marriage, Washington advised her to lower her expectations, and not to

> look for perfect felicity before you consent to wed. Nor conceive, from the fine tales the poets and lovers of old have told us of the transports of mutual love, that heaven has taken its abode on earth. Nor do not deceive yourself in supposing that the only means by which these are to be obtained is to drink deep of the cup and revel in an ocean of love. Love is a mighty pretty thing, but, like all other delicious things, it is cloying; and when the first transports of the passion begin to subside, which it assuredly will do, and yield, oftentimes too late, to more sober reflections, it serves to evidence that love is too

> dainty a food to live on *alone*, and ought not to be con-
> sidered further than as a necessary ingredient for that
> matrimonial happiness which results from a combina-
> tion of causes: none of which are of greater importance
> than that the object on whom it is placed should possess
> good sense, a good disposition, and the means of sup-
> porting you in the way you have been brought up.... Be
> assured, and experience will convince you that there is no
> truth more certain than that all our enjoyments fall short
> of our expectations, and to none does it apply with more
> force than to the gratification of the passions.

This solid, if somewhat world-weary advice would seem to speak less to a marriage of endless felicity than to one built on the stronger friendship that resignation to limitations makes possible. George Washington was of the school of hard knocks. Time and again, as both a military commander and as a political leader, he insists it is a grievous error to discount the heavy role that self-interest plays in the affairs of all men. In 1778 he wrote about the need to have his troops properly paid:

> Men may speculate as they will; they may talk of patri-
> otism; they may draw examples from ancient story, of
> great achievements performed by its influence; but who-
> ever build upon it, as a sufficient Basis for conducting
> a long and bloody War, will find themselves deceived
> in the end.... For a time it may, of itself, push Men to
> Action; to bear much, to encounter difficulties; but it
> will not endure unassisted by Interest.

And again, this time to the president of the Congress:

> When men are irritated, and the Passions inflamed, they
> fly hastely to Arms; but after the first emotions are over,
> to expect, among such People, as compose the bulk of

an Army, that they are influenced by any other principles than those of Interest, is to look for what never
did, and I fear never will happen. . . . The few therefore,
who act upon Principles of disinterestedness, are, comparatively speaking, no more than a drop in the Ocean.

This, I fear, is not very inspiring; it is merely damn true.

One sees the element of self-interest in Washington's own early
military career. The sense of *amour-propre* was early, and highly,
developed in him. Throughout his career his concern for what he
called "my reputation" was always keen. "My inclinations," he early
announced, "are bent to arms." As a young man, commissioned a
major, he was sent off on a scouting expedition by the Governor of
Virginia to the Ohio territory to take a reading of the strength of
the French and the disposition of the Indians thereabouts. On this
and a second expedition to Ohio, Washington was confronted by
frontier conditions of hardship and, far from being vanquished,
rather enjoyed it; he found, too, that he dealt well, through moral
force, with Indians; and he survived at least two very close calls—
once coming near to drowning, another time when he was fired
upon at close range—neither of which seems to have lessened his
ardor for the military life.

But his military career was far from upward and onward. He suffered a loss in the French-Indian wars, and was forced to capitu-
late, though allowed to return to Williamsburg with his defeated
troops. Later he fought with the British Generals Braddock and
Forbes in various Virginia militia units, but he found his power
was often superseded, his rank diminished, by British regular army
officers. Colonial troops took second place to English ones. Washington did not take this easily. His pride was stung when, in 1754,
his rank was to be reduced from colonel to captain, with a great
reduction in the number of troops under his command. To be a
Colonial captain meant, as he put it, being outranked by "every

Captain, bearing the King's commission, every half-pay officer, or other, appearing with such a commission."

Status was at stake. British regular army officers looked down at Colonial officers, referring to them as "jockies," knocking their want of training. When a compromise of sorts—giving him a company instead of a regiment to command—was arranged, Washington found he could not live with it. "I think," he noted, "the disparity between the present offer of a company and my former rank too great to expect any real satisfaction or enjoyment in a corps where I once did, or thought I had a right, to command." He read it as an attack on his reputation, and he promptly resigned.

In *George Washington, Man and Monument*, Marcus Cunliffe, the English historian of American culture, remarks "there is something unlikable about the George Washington of 1753–1758," or the Washington between the ages of twenty-one and twenty-six. But then there tends generally to be something off-putting about young men—and now, one must add, young women—whose ambitions are not in proper alignment with their talents. (One recalls Henry James, at roughly the same age, writing home to say that he soon expects his talent to catch up with his ambition, which of course it did.) Often, too, these ambitions are unlikely to have found their proper objects. The result is that ambition in the young seems so blatant, so raw, so unconnected to anything but sheer getting ahead. Cunliffe recounts how Washington "did everything feasible to win preferment . . . —everything, that is, short of dishonor."

Honor, most commentators on Washington tend to agree, was at the heart of Washington's character. But honor, too, can be an empty thing, if not attached to something greater than itself. And too great a concern for one's honor can leave a young man puffed up with his own importance, touchier than a fresh burn, nervous about status, perpetually on the *qui vive* for insults. And so it sometimes left the youthful George Washington. The coveting of honor, like the clinging to virginity, can be overdone, if neither has a greater object in view than love of itself.

Who would have guessed that, in George Washington's case, the object would become revolution? Well, if not precisely the object, then at least the background for his ambition. Very far from a revolutionary type, Washington, when he resigned his commission, returned to Mount Vernon to cultivate his garden, to become the very model of the successful gentleman planter. It was at this time, 1759, that Washington married. Always precocious in his responsibilities, he was only twenty-seven but, as a stepfather and a landowner, seemed much older. He was the brother to whom all the surviving Washington brothers and sisters looked for advice and help. He was elected a burgess in the Virginia House of Assembly; he served as a county magistrate. He grew prosperous, larger in mind, more expansive in spirit. "Worldly success spoils many people," Marcus Cunliffe writes, "it suited Washington."

With the French no longer an enemy after the peace of 1763, Americans began to feel the cinch of English rule tighten uncomfortably. Their status as a colony began to pall upon, then gall, them. The best face that might be put on American status was that the country was in partnership with England, since most American colonists were English in their ancestry; the more realistic reading, however, was that they were the possession of England. "Is it the interest of a man," Tom Paine asked in *Common Sense*, his pamphlet of 1776, "to be a boy all his life?" Relatively mild though the taxes England placed on America might have been— on tea, on stamps, on other selected import goods—they were of sufficient irritation to rouse radicals and turn even sober men to thoughts of independence.

Inevitably, Washington's tended to be the thoughtful businessman's view of English-American relations—as witness, in a letter to an in-law in London, his *précis* of the likely consequence of the Stamp Act:

The stamp act engrosses the conversation of the speculative part of the colonists, who look upon this unconstitutional method of taxation as a direful attack upon their liberties and loudly exclaim against the violation. What may be the result of this and of some other (I think I may add ill-judged) measures, I will not undertake to determine; but this much I may venture to affirm, that the advantage accruing to the mother country will fall greatly short of the expectation of the ministry; for certain it is that our whole substance already in a manner flows to Great Britain and that whatsoever contributes to lessen our importations must be hurtful to her manufactures. The eyes of our people already begin to be opened, and they will perceive that many luxuries for which we lavish our substance in Great Britain can well be dispensed with. This, consequently, will introduce frugality and be a necessary incitement to industry.

In the movement to pull away from England, George Washington was a moderate, a middle-of-the-road man. He was one of the seven-member delegation sent by Virginia to the First Continental Congress in Philadelphia in the autumn of 1774. He is reported not to have said much—to have let Patrick Henry and others supply the rhetoric. He was delegated to attend the Second Continental Congress. At that Congress, when it was decided that a general "be appointed to command all the continental forces raised for the defence of American liberty," Washington found his name put in formal nomination and unanimously elected. (John Hancock also considered himself a candidate for the post, though Hancock had no direct experience of war.)

Although Washington's military experience was not great, it was more impressive than that of anyone else. With some trepidation, Washington accepted. After acknowledging the honor he felt conferred upon him, he added: "But, lest some unlucky event should happen unfavorable to my reputation, I beg it may be remembered by every gentleman in the room, that I this day declare, with the utmost sincerity, I do not think myself equal to the command." Note his concern, once again, for his "reputation." He offered to serve without pay, asking only that his expenses be paid. He was forty-three; eight years later, when the war for independence had been won, he would be fifty-one and seem an old man.

George Washington's quality as commanding general quickly became the subject of myth—which could only mean that it would later become the subject of controversy. No sooner was Washington made commander-in-chief than the idolization of him set in in earnest. The physician Benjamin Rush, who would later be a persistent critic of Washington, saw in him the very model of the great military man: "If you do not know General Washington's person," Rush wrote to a friend, "perhaps you will be pleased to hear, that he has so much martial dignity in his deportment, that you would distinguish him to be a General and a Soldier, from among ten thousand people: there is not a king in Europe but would look like a valet de chambre by his side." Before he had fought a single battle, Harvard provided him with an honorary Doctor of Laws degree. The Washington who was "First in war—first in peace—first in the hearts of his countrymen"—the phrasing is Lighthorse Harry Lee's—had begun. Wherever he went, adoration followed.

The historian Barry Schwartz, in *George Washington, The Making of an American Symbol*, writes that, in having been imbued by his countrymen with greatness, Washington "filled critical social needs as the colonists took their first steps toward nationhood. By identifying with him, Americans could articulate their own stake in the war and justify their personal sacrifice." Schwartz continues:

> At the same time, Washington's greatness embodied a faithful representation of something that was impersonal and objective. It gave voice to each individual's feeling that outside of him there existed something greater than

him. By choosing Washington as a symbol of this transcendent entity, Americans communicated their ideals to one another. Through him, they expressed their
sense of moral harmony, their common attachment to
a new political unity. George Washington—or, more
precisely, the idea of George Washington—was essential to America's military arousal and to her incipient
national consciousness.

Barry Schwartz is persuasive on the enormous symbolic importance of George Washington to the new republic, but, having
agreed to that, the question remains open about how good a military man Washington really was. "Washington was, by far," Prof.
Schwartz remarks, "more of an administrator than a fighter." He
sets out in detail General (as he now is) Washington's tasks, admin-
istrative and diplomatic, through his eight-year term as commander-in-chief, and they were immense and intricately complex.
Washington had, after all, to lead a unified army in a country of
thirteen different states that, despite their declaration of independence, had not come to regard themselves as at all truly unified.

Richard Brookhiser, in *The Founding Father*, notes that between
1776 and 1778 Washington's troops fought seven battles and won
only two. But because he was perpetually undermanned and
undersupplied— his negotiations with Congress to acquire the
funds to keep his army afield is an entire saga unto itself, and his
complaints about having to deal with militia rather than regular
army troops make for a chronicle of woe—Washington was forced
to devise an essentially defensive strategy through the war, and one
in which it made sense, as Washington himself put it, "to protract
the war, if possible." As Mr. Brookhiser writes: "By fighting an
aggressive defensive, which was also fluid, [Washington] raised the
cost of victory for the British to an unacceptable level. With four
thirty-thousand-man armies—one for each major theatre— Britain could have won a war of strangulation. But Britain could not

maintain four thirty-thousand-man armies three thousand miles from home"—at least not for long. Mr. Brookhiser's final evaluation of Washington's generalship seemed nicely measured: "If you are a [military] prodigy or a genius, an Alexander or a Caesar, then you bring victory from whatever you touch. Washington was not in that class. But a successful general does not have to be the best general in the world. All he has to be—or if he is not so already, all he has to become—is better than the general he faces." And this Washington proved to be.

Reading about George Washington's years at the head of the revolutionary army, one senses his enormous development. Patience, cunning, meticulous care for detail, moral ferocity, courage, a sense of the larger campaign, Washington called upon all these qualities in his command and more—including, when it was called for, ruthlessness. At one point, there was a plot to poison Washington through the bad offices of one of his Lifeguard; it was, of course, foiled and the man hanged. A cabal in Congress led by one Thomas Conway was organized to unseat him from power, on the grounds that he was not prosecuting the war aggressively enough; on his deathbed, Conway apologized for his instigations. Colleagues betrayed him—most disappointingly, Benedict Arnold, a brilliant young soldier. John Adams was often critical of him.

At one point, in the winter of 1783, at Newburgh, New York, the Continental troops, including the officers, their pay deeply in arrears owing to a financially strapped Congress, were on the edge of rebellion. Washington, always the advocate of his men in these matters, met with the mutinous-minded officer corps to calm them and counsel caution. After his best advice, which did not seem to persuade, Washington paused to read a letter he had received, supposedly from a sympathetic congressman. But before doing so, he recalled that he could no longer read without the aid of spectacles. "I have already grown gray in the service of my country," he said. "I am now going blind." The brief ad-lib remark won the day. The men felt a connection with their powerfully aloof general that they hadn't hitherto sensed. Before Washington had his spectacles in place, the rebellion was over. Recapitulating the story, Thomas Jefferson wrote: "The moderation and virtue of a single character probably prevented this Revolution from being closed [as it might have been at that moment], as most others have been, by a subversion of that liberty it was intended to establish."

Although the tributes to Washington never ceased during the war, some of them beginning to take on religious coloration, with Washington regularly styled the Moses of the American people, one senses a deep loneliness about the man. He had young men around him whom he relied upon, such as Alexander Hamilton, and others whom he loved, such as the Marquis de Lafayette, but no close friends of his own age. He seemed to view command and aloofness as connected, as if the former required the latter. Edmund S. Morgan speaks of Washington's "aloof dignity." Gordon S. Wood believes that he cultivated his aloofness. "His aloofness was notorious and he worked at it," Wood writes. Wood tells the story of the painter Gilbert Stuart attempting to relax Washington during one of his portrait sittings, but without much success. "Now sir," he pleaded, "you must let me forget that you are General Washington and that I am Stuart, the painter." To which Washington replied: "Mr. Stuart need never feel the need of forgetting who he is or who General Washington is." "No wonder," says Wood, capping the story, "the portraits look stiff."

In *Angel in the Whirlwind*, his book on the American Revolution, the historian Benson Bobrick quotes the Marquis de Barbe-Marbois, secretary to the French legation, on Washington at his daily work:

> [Washington] received us with a noble, modest, and
> gentle urbanity and with that graciousness which seems
> to be the basis of his character. He is fifty years old,

well built, rather thin. He carries himself freely and with a sort of military grace. He is masculine looking, without his features being less gentle on that account. I have never seen anyone who was more naturally and spontaneously polite. His eyes are blue and rather large, his mouth and nose are regular, and his forehead open. His uniform is exactly like that of his soldiers. Formerly, on solemn occasions, that is to say on the days of battle, he wore a large blue sash, but he has given up that unrepublican distinction. I have been told that he preserves in battle the character of humanity which makes him so dear to his soldiers in camp. I have seen him for some time in the midst of his staff, and he has always appeared even-tempered, tranquil, and orderly in his occupations, and serious in his conversation. He asks few questions, listens attentively, and answers in a low tone and with few words. He is serious in business. Outside of that he permits himself a restricted gaiety. His conversation is as simple as his habits and his appearance. He makes no pretensions, and does the honors of his house with dignity, but without pompousness or flattery. . . .

After the final defeat of Cornwallis at Yorktown on October 17, 1783, when in a rather bloodless conclusion to a long and bloody war, a British officer appeared waving a white handkerchief aloft, signaling surrender, Washington must have thought he could think of retirement at last. But of course it was not to be—not for a long while yet.

At a diplomatic dinner at Versailles, after hearing Louis XVI, in a toast, compared to "the moon, [which] fills the earth with a soft, benevolent glow," and the British ambassador compare George III to "the sun at noonday, [which] spreads its light and illumines the world," Ben Franklin rose to say, "I cannot give you the sun or the moon, but I give you George Washington, General of the armies of the United States, who, like Joshua of old, commanded both the sun and moon to stand still, and both obeyed."

Washington's own departure from his troops also took the form of a toast. The toast was given on December 4, 1783, the day he departed to resign his commission before Congress. In New York City, he met with his ranking officers in a long room at an inn known as Fraunces Tavern, and, with a glass of wine before him, said:

> With a heart full of love and gratitude, I now take leave of you. I most devoutly wish that your latter days be as prosperous and happy as your former ones have been glorious and honorable.
>
> I cannot come to each of you to take my leave, but shall be obliged if each of you will come and take me by the hand.

Immediately after all the officers had done so, Washington, in Benson Bobrick's account, "himself 'suffused in tears,' left the room and, passing through a corps of light infantry, walked silently on to Whitehall, where a barge was waiting to convey him across the Hudson to Paulus Hook. 'We all followed,' wrote one officer, 'in mournful silence to the wharf.' "

The Marquis de Barbe-Marbois concluded his account of his visit to Washington by noting that,

> if you like historical parallels, I might compare him to Timoleon who freed the Sicilians from the tyranny of the Carthaginians, and who joined to his military qualities those which make up an excellent citizen, and who after having rendered his country signal services lived as a private citizen, ambitious neither of power nor honors, and was satisfied to enjoy modestly the glory of having given liberty to a powerful nation.

Gordon S. Wood holds that "the greatest act of [Washington's] life, the one that made him famous, was his resignation as commander-in-chief of the American forces." The act was without precedent. It announced the subservience of military to civil authority in United States life. It is an act that has reverberated down through American history.

Yet when the federal convention to write a constitution met in Philadelphia in 1787, there could scarcely be any doubt that Virginia would send Washington along as one of its delegates. He was hesitant about attending—he had, after all, pledged his retirement from public life. His word, and hence his reputation, was once more on the line. But he was nervous, too, about people thinking that he wasn't behind the new government—and indeed that he might even want to form a government of his own. In Philadelphia, he was in fact elected president of the convention. Washington had his doubts about the workability of the new constitution, but, because his name was associated with it, he supported it thoroughly. "Once he had identified himself publicly with the new Constitution he became very anxious to have it accepted," Gordon S. Wood writes. "Its ratification was a kind of ratification of himself."

When, in February of 1789, it came time to elect a chief executive, there was scarcely the least surprise that Washington was unanimously elected. It is not the least exaggeration to say that no one else could have filled the job of President of the United States. With the Americans' vast distrust of political power, with a newly but barely fledged country made up of people with the strongest regional differences, not to say strong mutual antipathies, with a reigning commercial spirit of every man for himself abroad in the land, the job of president could only have been taken up by a man in whom the country felt the deepest trust. George Washington was, of course, that man.

Even then there was worry lest Washington take on monarchical powers. Everyone seems agreed that, had he chosen, he could have had even greater power than he did. It is said that such powers as a distrustful Congress allowed the presidency were based on the knowledge that Washington was the man who would first hold the job. That Washington had no children and that, consequently, no dynasty was likely was a point in his favor. The historian Richard Norton Smith refers to Washington's being "a charisma of competence," one based on utter trust. James Madison felt that Washington was the lynchpin to the new government, the only part of it that greatly pleased and excited the people.

Washington knew himself how difficult lay the terrain ahead. A year or so into the job, he wrote to an English correspondent:

> Nothing short of an absolute conviction of duty could ever have brought me upon scenes of public life again. The establishment of our new government seemed to be the last great experiment for promoting happiness by reasonable compact in civil society . . . a government of accommodation as well as a government of laws. Much has to be done by *prudence*, much by *conciliation*, and much by *firmness*. Few who are not philosophical spectators can realize the difficult and delicate part which a man in my situation has to act . . . if I may use the expression, I walk on untrodden ground.

Walk thus Washington did for eight years, for when his first term was up, he was told—by Madison among others—that his presence was required for at least another full term to make the government stable. A third term was probably his for the asking, but in the end he was glad to be quits of political power.

George Washington was a great president who did not necessarily have a great presidency. He was fortunate, for one thing, in that for almost the entirety of his time in office the country was at peace. The great achievements that occurred during his time in office—Alexander Hamilton's financial program, the opening of the Mississippi River, the removal of the threat of Indians and red-coats in the Northwest, the American role of neutrality in foreign affairs—were accomplished without his having much to do with them. But the details seem scarcely to matter. "Time only renders the character of Washington more clear," as J. T. Headley has written, "while the circumstances which developed it become more and more indistinct."

Washington legitimated the presidency in a way that no one else could have done. He set many useful precedents, not least among them limiting the Senate's role in the making of treaties and in the appointment of government officials. He graced the job with a dignity that it has not lost more than two hundred years later and under much lesser men. Without Washington, United States history would have a different shape and contour; without him, it would have had a different moral coloration.

Although he understood power and knew how to use it, unlike the case with almost every other political leader of his importance, there is no strong evidence that George Washington loved power, either for its own sake or for the perquisites that it brought him. He was a thoughtful but not a speculative man, and neither is there any serious evidence that he had a strong vision for America, a vision of stately grandeur or of human happiness. Why, then, did he accept the most arduous service his nation offered, not once but over and over again?

Because, the only answer is, of a profound sense of duty that derived from his, Washington's, moral character. "Moral character" is the name Gordon S. Wood gives to this quality in Washington, and it is the only way to account for the continual tests to which Washington put himself, throughout his life, depriving himself of the leisure and contentment of the private life for which he always longed. His retirement was short-lived, for he died in 1799, three years after he left office. He died, it is reported, stoically, in pain and with no last words of wisdom on his lips. If his life seems sacred, it is because it seems in the final analysis sacrificial, a donation to the state.

Moral character is what we continue to ask of all our politicians, and it is of course precisely what they almost always refuse to supply. Each generation of our politicians today, at the end of their careers, happily peddle their influence in large law firms, or simply set up as straight lobbyists for causes in which they can have no real belief. Washington would have been aghast—as he was aghast at the factionalization, holding party above principle, that political life in the United States began to take on in his last years in office.

Behind Washington's rigid sense of honor—and his ceaseless worry about his reputation—was really a concern that he show proper disinterest and never take advantage of his influence. This is sometimes thought to be a purely eighteenth-century quality—and Washington is himself sometimes thought to be the last great eighteenth-century political leader. He believed that honorable conduct was crucial to public life. He believed that a political leader needed to surmount the parochial interests of party. He believed that good character meant more than anything else—than special interest, than idealism, than any theoretical concerns—and worked to develop a character of the kind in himself that proved his point. Washington was not a great military mind; he was a good though not a saintly man; he was no master politician. In the end, his genius was perhaps the rarest kind of all: a genius for discerning right action so strong that he was utterly incapable of knowingly doing anything wrong. He was our founding father, and our politics has yet to turn up a better man.

Henry Adams and Henry James
Intellect Meets Sensibility

ENRY ADAMS AND HENRY JAMES were of the same generation—Adams was born in 1838, James in 1843—and the same social set (the minuscule American literary leisure class) and so were able to dislike each other in the subdued, well-mannered, yet unremitting way possible only to people who share many of the same assumptions. Not least among these assumptions was that of their own quite genuine superiority, even though Henry Adams, who made a specialty of announcing his own putative shortcomings and failure, regularly spoke of the inadequacies of their generation. That generation included William James, Oliver Wendell Holmes, Jr., John Hay, Thomas Sergeant Perry, John La Farge and (somewhat later) Edith Wharton, not to speak of various Lodges and assorted Cabots, and was, intellectually and artistically, perhaps the most impressive America has even known, representing, as it did, the only time when money, good breeding, intellect, and imagination came together in the national culture. In Henry Adams and Henry James above all the possibilities and promise of that culture—as well as its limitations—were played out to their fullest.

Like Hawthorne and Melville, Adams and James had a relationship which ought naturally to have developed into a crucial
friendship but which didn't. Why did these two men, who shared
so much in the way of friends and experience, finally not much
like each other? The pretence of friendship was always there, but
pretence for the most part it remained. Something approximat-
ing closeness between them did not emerge until near the very end
of their lives when they viewed each other as fellow survivors, not
only of their generation but of a way of life which both recognized
was finished.

One of the things Adams and James had in common was richly
textured minds, which caused them to probe everything for its ultimate complexity. But while James was the devotee of complexity,
Adams felt himself its victim. Attempting to explain why he was
not the man of action his family ancestry seemed to have destined
him to be, Adams once put it that evil never seemed "unmixed
with good" and that "what is good [was always] streaked with evil."
James loved complexity almost for its own sake. "I glory in the pil-
ing up of complications of every sort," he told his niece, adding
that "If I could pronounce the name James in any different or more
elaborate way I should be in favor of doing so."

James did not have to labor under the solid weight of expectation that bore on Adams, because he was not, after all, an Adams, a
scion of easily the most distinguished family in America, with two
American presidents in its line. (James referred to Henry Adams
as "of ancient Presidential race.") As he came to maturity, Adams
must have felt the burden of this expectation more and more; and
his self-doubt grew correspondingly. "I have steadily lost faith in
myself ever since I left college," he wrote when he was twenty-four,
"and my aim now is so indefinite that all my time may prove to have
been wasted, and then nothing [will be] left but a truncated life."
He was soon able to generalize self-doubt into a pessimism that
he spent his remaining years honing and deepening. "Meanwhile,"

HENRY ADAMS

HENRY JAMES

Adams, striking his characteristic note, wrote to another friend around this time. "I only hope your life won't be such an eternal swindle as most life is."

James's development took quite the opposite turn. Despite the world's neglect of the fiction of his major phase, despite the crushing disappointment of the reception of the New York Edition of his novels, James grew ever more confident of his own powers and of the rightness of the way he had expended them. When his brother William, who never appreciated his fiction, told Henry he ought to attempt to write more plainly in the hope of capturing a larger audience for his novels, Henry shot back that he had no great interest in producing a work on "the two-and-two-makes-four system," and as for that larger audience, it was, in his view, no more than a "big Booby," thank you all the same.

George Monteiro's edition of *The Correspondence of Henry James and Henry Adams* implies a linkage of the two men and perhaps a rivalry that he, Professor Monteiro, does not unduly press. Twenty-nine out of the thirty-six extant letters in his book are from James to Adams and Mrs. Adams, with only seven from Adams to James. In an act at the turn of the century that must to this day make his biographers weep, James burned most of his correspondence from others. The combined surviving letters between Adams and James do not make plain anything like the complex nature of their relationship. Monteiro, in his scrupulously edited volume, fills in much of the subtext to these letters in excellently informative footnotes. But between the lines and amid the ironies of the letters an odd coolness persists. Something divided these two most talented men of their generation (with William James their only intellectual rival), and it was deep and not to be camouflaged by beautiful manners or any amount of what James called "mere gracious twaddle."

Towards the end of his life, Adams acknowledged that Henry James was his "last standard of comparison." James, for his part, often made plain his rather distant envy of Adams's superior position in life. "Besides," James wrote to Sir John Clark, "he [Adams] is what I should like to be—a man of wealth and leisure, able to satisfy all his curiosities." But this envy was of a passing kind, chiefly owing to James's nearly perpetual problem, as a professional writer, of living on his own always precarious earnings. James was the grandson of an Irish immigrant who had done extremely well in real estate in Albany, New York, which may have made him an upstart in the eyes of an Adams, but in the United States two generations, then as now, were more than enough to close most social gaps.

If Adams was better connected than James—the former wrote letters of introduction for the latter, when he went off to live in London in 1876—both were on a sufficient level of equality to take little pot-shots at each other throughout their adult lives, with Mrs. Adams a strong contributor on her husband's side in this campaign. It was Clover Adams who said of Henry James that, as a novelist, he "chews more than he bites off." James said of the Adamses that they preferred Washington to London because "they are, vulgarly speaking, 'someone' here and . . . they are nothing" in England. In his story "Pandora," James has a distinctly Henry Adams-like figure, planning a party, announce to his wife: "Let us be vulgar and have some fun—let us invite the President." Adams thought that James was not very intelligent about women, while James thought Henry Adams "a trifle dry" and Clover Adams "a perfect Voltaire in petticoats." These were people who knew how to throw the most precisely aimed darts at the most delicately vulnerable places.

The two Henrys set out in life with not such very different goals. Adams declared that he wished "to look like an American Voltaire or Gibbon," then, with that characteristic tic of unconvincing modesty, added, "but am slowly settling down to be a third-rate Boswell hunting for a Dr. Johnson." James early knew that "to produce some little exemplary works of art is my narrow and lowly dream," and he, just as characteristically, would later add, "Little by little, I trust, my abilities will catch up with my ambitions." Both men were

sufficiently self-confident not to require the world's approval—
though neither, clearly, would have minded it—or to regard its
neglect as the ultimate criticism. Yet Adams was never much
cheered by the high valuation at which, in the small but important
circles in which he travelled, he was often taken, nor was James—
apart from the public débacle of the reception of his play *Guy
Domville*—for long discouraged by the incomprehension with
which the work of his major phase was greeted. As surely as Adams
was weighed down by a sense of defeat, so was James buoyed up by
a sense of expectant victory, even conquest.

In their attitudes toward the country of their birth, the two
divide once again. James was an expatriate, who at the end of his
life, to show his sympathy and support for his adoptive country in
the First World War, took British citizenship, though he retained
a genuine if critical regard for America and Americans. Adams
was an internal exile, which is another way of saying that he was
spiritually a permanent alien living in America, seeing only those
people from his own ever-diminishing social set. James found the
America of his young manhood of insufficient social density to
supply the background for his carefully tapestried art. Americans,
he discovered, were better written about in Europe, where he at
any rate found them most American of all. Adams felt unappreci-
ated, admitting, apropos of his country, when he was sixty, that "I
have certainly never been rewarded, and never received the smallest hint from anyone that I am needed."

James set out to achieve what T. S. Eliot would later claim for
him: "the final perfect consummation of an American to become,
not an Englishman, but a European—something which no born
European, no person of any European nationality, can become."
Adams was little impressed with Europe. "There is a cool ignorance
and dogmatism about this people that is hard to bear," he wrote
about the English when he was in his twenties and his father's
secretary at the Court of St. James. Later he would claim that he

couldn't get a decent meal in the Paris of the 1890s, which one wouldn't have thought all that difficult to do. Dreary as Europe was, America for Adams was even worse. In his novel *Democracy*, he featured all that was coarse and corrupt in American politics, which he described as the "dance of democracy."

Never wanting money, Adams availed himself of that opiate of the rich and the bored: travel—exotic, almost relentless travel. He claimed that "three days in any place on earth is all it will bear," and that "the pleasure is in the movement." But the boredom was never quite shaken off. "Every time I come back to what we are pleased to call civilized life," he wrote to Charles Milnes Gaskell, "it bores me more, and seems to me more hopelessly idiotic; and, as I do not care to imitate Carlyle and Ruskin and Emerson and all the rest of our protesting philosophers by trying to make a living by abusing the society of my time, nothing remains but to quit it, and seek another."

Justice Holmes, their contemporary, lends a fresh perspective on Adams and James. Holmes in later life wrote to Harold Laski that he thought James "a pretty big chap who by rejecting all that didn't come within a narrow circle of taste wrote stories that generally I found dull." To Lewis Einstein, Holmes described James as living "in rather a narrow world of taste and refined moral vacillations; but in them he is a master." Holmes's view of Adams was that "he was kind, sad, and defeated, although another man would have thought the same life [as Adams led] a success." He found his increasing sourness about life greatly dampening: "When I would step in at his house on the way back from Court and found him playing the old Cardinal, he would spend his energy in pointing out that everything was dust and ashes." Holmes did not call often.

A good sense of Adams pouring ashes over experience is to be found in his reaction to meeting Robert Louis Stevenson in Samoa. Adams, travelling in the company of his friend the painter John La Farge, met Stevenson and his wife at Vailima; he couldn't seem to get over their clothes, especially their footwear. "Mrs. Stevenson," he wrote to his friend Elizabeth Cameron, "did not now think herself obliged to put on slippers, and her nightgown costume had apparently not been washed since our visit. Stevenson himself wore still a brown knit woolen sock on one foot, and a grayish purple sock on the other, much wanting in heels, so that I speculated half my time whether it was the same old socks of the corresponding alternates, and concluded that he must have worn them ever since we first saw him." Mildly amusing though this may be, Adams, in fact, missed the great point about Stevenson, which Henry James, who soon got beyond Stevenson's bohemianism and befriended him on their first meeting, caught exactly. "He was," wrote James, "a most gallant spirit and an exquisite literary talent." But then James and Stevenson were fellow artists, while Adams, richly gifted though he was, was determined to be something larger.

In a brilliant few pages in his posthumously published, unfinished book on Henry Adams, R. P. Blackmur neatly formulated the essential distinction between these two men:

> If we may quote T. S. Eliot that Henry James had a mind—a sensibility—so fine that no mere idea could ever violate it, then we should say that Henry Adams had an intellect so fine—so energized—that no mere item of sensibility could ever violate that.

Sensibility against intellect, each with its strengths, each with its weaknesses: this is the battle that, unbeknown even to these two most percipient of men, was played out, if never quite brought into the open, between them.

One sees the force of this difference over the question of biography. When James wrote his biography of the American sculptor William Wetmore Story, a work began for money and finished in a state of deep artistic dissatisfaction, Adams wrote about the book to his brother Brooks: "Henry James can fail as often as he likes in novels, but when he fails in biography, he leaves mighty little of

William Story. In biography we are taking life." For James, the failure of all biography lay precisely in its very inability to capture life. Only fiction, for him, had any chance to do that. As James wrote to Adams apropos of the book: "the art of the biographer—devilish art!—is somehow practically *thinning*. It simplifies even while seeking to enrich—and even the Immortals are so helpless and passive in death" under the hand of the biographer.

HENRY ADAMS WROTE TWO NOVELS—*Democracy* and *Esther*—but viewed himself less as an artist than as a historian in the belletristic, and a thinker in the universal, tradition. As a thinker, he searched all his life for those key ideas, those laws really, that governed the universe. Surprise, surprise: he never found them. At the age of twenty-five, he wrote to his brother Charles:

> But my philosophy teaches me, and I firmly believe it, that the laws which govern animated beings will be ultimately found to be at bottom the same with those which rule inanimate nature, and, as I entertain a profound conviction of the littleness of our kind, and of the curious enormity of creation, I am quite ready to receive with pleasure any basis for a systematic conception of it all.

Adams in his heavy philosophical mode—in the Mariolatry of *Mont-Saint-Michel and Chartres*, in the Virgin and the Dynamo portions of *The Education of Henry Adams*, in his essay "The Rule of Phase Applied to History"—is Adams at his most disappointing. He was out of his depth in a place where very few could swim in any case. It was all misguided, a botch, a flop. Justice Holmes, who believed Adams often covered his ignorance with a pontifical manner, said that "he wrote nothing that I ever read that entitles him to pronounce science a failure and speculation futile." Towards the end of his life, Adams wrote to a correspondent: "I lost my own illusion of unity and continuity thirty years ago, and I know how fatal the rupture is to one's scheme of life. Once hit by Zeno's arrow, one is a mere mad rabbit."

James would have found the hunt for such laws quite beside the point. He was an artist, the type in its purest form. When Eliot said James had a mind so fine that no idea could violate it, he did not of course mean that James hadn't mastery over ideas. He was after all the son of Henry James, Sr., the brother of William James, and grew up around the buzz and whirr of ideas. But he had not much appetite for the abstract: he didn't think that the most interesting truths—or at least those truths that most interested him—lay in the realm of ideas. The essential truths were the truths of the heart, or those truths that only art could discover.

Henry Adams would have made a magnificent subject for a Henry James novel. The material provided by his life could scarcely have been richer. There was his distinguished birth to begin with; add to that his evident gifts, for Adams was a man almost too gifted: he could have been artist, historian, thinker, Voltaire, Chamfort, and the Duc de Saint-Simon rolled into one. ("He had remarkable abilities," said Holmes, "but never seemed to me to get to the bottom of his subjects, unless it may be in political history as to which I do not know.") Then there was the event that sheared his life in two, the death (suicide by poisoning) of Clover Adams, when Adams was forty-seven (he lived on until eighty), which put a permanent black border around the dark grey that was already at the center of his soul, but which during the years of his marriage seemed to lighten at least somewhat. There was the flirtation, in his widowhood, with Elizabeth Cameron, the wife of a Senator, a flirtation turned off by Mrs. Cameron fairly early in their correspondence. (Theirs was a relationship that continued for thirty years. Henry James remarked of it, in a letter to Henrietta Reubell, that "it's one of the longest and oddest American *liaisons* I've ever known. Women have been hanged for less—and yet men have been too, I judge, rewarded with more.") But above all there was the permanent disappointment, the story of a superior man who had early taken himself off the track, and who for unaccountable reasons had set things up in such a way that he had to view even his successes as failures, had to pour vinegar even over his caviar.

As his chronicler, James would have had no difficulty understanding Adams's snobbery, for he was enough of a snob himself to understand the motives driving so complete a snob as Henry Adams. The true spice in snobbery at the *haute cuisine* level at which Adams practiced it is, of course, anti-Semitism, and his anti-Semitism was unrelenting. His friend John Hay once remarked that it was so extreme that, when Adams "saw Vesuvius reddening the midnight air, he searched the horizon to find a Jew stoking the fire." Too, alas, true. Adams always found time to say something unpleasant about the Jews in letters to friends, of which the following, written near the end of his life, is a fairly representative sample:

> The atmosphere [in America] really has become a Jew atmosphere . . . . It is curious and evidently good for some people, but it isolates me. I do not know the language, and my friends are as ignorant as I. We are still in power, after a fashion. Our sway over what we call society is undisputed. We keep Jews far away, and the anti-Jew feeling is quite rabid. We are anti-everything and we are wild uplifters; yet we somehow seem to be more Jewish every day.

Henry James retained some of the unpleasantness of his social class in his attitudes towards the Jews, though he took up the honorable position in the Dreyfus Affair, and, next to Henry Adams, was practically a member of the B'nai Brith Anti-Defamation League. (There is some irony in the fact that these two men have been so well served posthumously in scholarship by Leon Edel and Ernest Samuels, both Jews.) James also had that supreme quality of the artist that was simply unavailable to Adams, that quality which George Santayana noticed straightaway in his only meeting with James: he was, Santayana remarked, "appreciative of all points of view, and amused at their limitations." Henry Adams had only his own point of view, and its limitations can never have been said to have amused him.

How little Adams's point of view changed over his long life, as revealed through Ernest Samuels's lucid edition of the *Selected Letters*, is at once an impressive fact and, in the end, a sadly oppressive one. Such commentators on Adams as Newton Arvin might find strands of optimism in him at various points in his life, holding that the letters allow one "to follow the *development* of his mind from phase to phase," but these are the merest unpatterned flecks on a garment of deepest brown velour. At twenty-five, Adams wrote to his brother Charles that "it suffices to say that I am seeking to console my troubles by chewing the dry husks of that philosophy, which, whether it calls itself submission to the will of God, or to the laws of nature, rests in bottom simply and solely upon an acknowledgement of our own impotence and ignorance. In this amusement, I find, if not consolation at least some sort of mental titillation." In the year before his death, Adams wrote to Charles Milnes Gaskell that "the people [the American people, he means] strike me as being less amusing with much less sense of humor than fifty years ago," but, of course, having read through his letters, one recalls that he didn't think very much of them fifty years previously, either.

What did Henry Adams want? Probably simply everything: power, appreciation, distinction, fame. But, let it be understood, he would have to have had it without the depressing fuss of struggling to acquire it on his own. Justice Holmes suggests as much when, in a letter to Lewis Einstein written more than a decade after Adams's death, he says: "If he could have been put on a pedestal, made a general without ever having gone through the school of lower grades I dare say he would have been valuable." Holmes added that, even then, he would probably still have reserved the right to call himself a failure.

With the exception of his multi-volume *History of the United States during the Administrations of Thomas Jefferson and James Madison*, which was printed by Charles Scribner's Sons, Adams brought out his other books—the two novels, *Mont-Saint-Michel and Chartres*, and *The Education of Henry Adams*—either anonymously or privately, yet complained that he had no readers. It turns out that Henry James was among his non-readers, as Adams was, with minor exceptions, among James's non-readers. Adams claimed he didn't think it was a good idea to read books by his friends, lest he compromise himself by not telling them his true opinion of them. This might be a prudent policy, but when your friends—Henry James and Edith Wharton among them—are writing some of the best books of the age, perhaps not so prudent after all. Clover Adams read James's novels, but was not enamored of them. Adams himself thought that the James and Howells mutual admiration society was a bit of a muchness: "there is in it always an air of fatuous self-satisfaction to the most groveling genius." Yet Adams did not mind praising Howells at the expense of James. Although he read *The Sacred Fount*, in another letter he referred contemptuously to his decision not to read "the Golden Fount or Mount or Count." Adams wrote to Gaskell that, though he liked James, "I don't read his books," adding with that kiss-of-death touch, "Some people like them." On one occasion, he praised William James at the expense of Henry: "As a wit and humorist I have always said that you were far away the superior to your brother Henry, and that you could have cut him quite out, if you had turned your fun that way." Later he blew a little dart at William, saying that at his death he "set up for our last thinker, and I never could master what he thought."

ENRY JAMES was no easier on Adams, of whom he wrote, in a letter to Sir John Clark, quoted by Professor Monteiro, "I like him but suffer from his monotonous disappointed pessimism." (He could not have been alone in this.) He also noted that he thought Elizabeth Cameron had "sucked the lifeblood of poor Henry Adams and made him more 'snappish' than nature intended." In a very Jamesian ironic cut he remarked about a meeting late in life with Adams that he seemed much changed for the worse, though with "a surviving capacity to be very well taken care of." James took fully a year and a half to read the copy of *Mont-Saint-Michel and Chartres* that Adams had sent him. He took nearly as long to read the copy of *The Education of Henry Adams* and then spoke rather glancingly about it, at least for James, who was known to garrulate elaborately upon his friends' books, even when he didn't think much of them.

In the first of the final two letters in George Monteiro's collection, Adams, now seventy-five, delivers a full shovel of ashes at the door of James, himself seventy. In it he speaks of "what a vast gulf opened to me between the queerness of the past and the total inconsequence of the present." James replies that he does not find it so: "I still find my consciousness interesting—under *cultivation* of the interest." He then delivers that now famous Jamesian sentence: "It's, I suppose, because I am that queer monster the artist, an obstinate finality, an inexhaustible sensibility." The relationship between Henry Adams and Henry James strikes the clear moral that, over the long haul, the advantage resoundingly goes to the man who never loses interest in life's astonishing possibilities.

George Santayana

The Permanent Transient

"If you infer the man from the books, you may go seriously wrong, because only a part of my nature has gone into my writings, and not all my writings have been published."

—GEORGE SANTAYANA to Baker Brownell,
December 26, 1939

O NE SOMETIMES SPEAKS of the proper time in life to read certain writers: no Hemingway after twenty, no Proust before forty, that sort of thing. Less attention is given to the best time of day to read a writer. The literarily omnivorous Edmund Wilson said he was unable to read the Marquis de Sade at breakfast. (I shouldn't think he would go down too smoothly at bedtime, either.) Off and on in recent years, I have found myself reading George Santayana—the eight volumes of his letters, his three volumes of autobiography, his essays, and his one novel, *The Last Puritan*—directly upon arising in the morning. Not only did the happy anticipation of returning to him serve as a reward for getting out of bed, but Santayana's detachment, a detachment leading onto serenity, invariably produced a calming effect. Reading him in the early morning made the world feel somehow more understandable, even its multiple mysteries, if not penetrable, taking on a tincture of poetry that made the darkest of them seem less menacing.

A major division among writers is the one between those who present themselves as warmly engaged with the world and those who value their cool distance from it. The problem arises, of course, from the all-too-common distinction between imperfection—let us not speak of perfection—of the life or imperfection of the work. So many writers, great-souled saints in their work, turn out to be utter creeps in their lives. As the publication of his letters show, Santayana, who never claimed saintliness and who often seems cold-blooded in his opinions, is for the most part a case of the reverse: a man much more generous than his advertised opinions.

This is but one of the oddities of Santayana's life and work. Perhaps the greatest among these oddities is that George Santayana—one of the greatest of American writers, as I have come to believe—never really thought himself an American. He was never an American citizen. Santayana's parents were Spanish. His mother's first husband, George Sturgis, a Bostonian, died young. After she left her second husband, Santayana's father, she returned to Boston where her children were brought up on the rim of the Boston Brahmin culture about which Santayana would later write so penetratingly. The boy George was nine when brought to America in 1872. A father whom he respected but did not love, and who lived out his days in Avila in Spain, and a mother colder than the norm for her own or any other day, set the seal on Santayana's early detachment. He was an outsider in his own home, a man who grew up to be not so much without a country as a man of all countries. From very early, he knew himself better furnished to observe life than to participate fully in it.

"Nature," Santayana wrote in *Persons and Places*, his autobiography, "had framed me for a recluse." He enjoyed people but seemed not greatly to have needed them. Moral independence and a taste for solitude developed in him from an early age. These qualities also gave him a fine disinterest, such that he could write about his parents:

I have no evidence as to what really may have brought these two most rational people, under no illusion about each other or their mutual position and commitments, to think of such an irrational marriage.

He claimed his parents were more like grandparents to him. (His mother was forty, his father fifty when they married.) The only person for whom Santayana felt an unqualified love was his half-sister Susana, twelve years older than he, who, he claimed, essentially raised him.

Boston seemed to the young Santayana stuffy, dry, "always busy applying first principles to trifles," a place where "the great affair, the aristocratic path to success and power, was business." His having been sent to a public day school strengthened the young Santayana's sense of isolation. Not that he would have felt more at home in the United States had he gone to a more luxurious school. Nothing would have made an American of him, for "America in those days made an exile and a foreigner of every native who had at all a temperament like mine." As for that temperament, behind its construction was a deep desire for clarity and a radical reduction, insofar as possible, of the standard human illusions. "If clearness about things produces a fundamental despair," he wrote, "a fundamental despair in turn produces a remarkable clearness or even playfulness about ordinary matters." The world, in other words, viewed straight on may be a dark and terrible place, but that doesn't mean that it hasn't much to recommend it in the way of rich variety and splendid amusements.

Santayana went on from the Boston Latin School to Harvard—to which his life between the ages of seventeen and forty-two, first as a student and then as a teacher in its Philosophy Department, was, as he must have felt, hostage. Fabled though that Philosophy Department has long been thought—William James, Josiah Royce, Charles Sanders Peirce were its most famous members—Santayana was neither comfortable in it nor awed by it. Of William James, he wrote that he was sure of his goodwill and kindness, of which I had many proofs; but I was also sure that he never understood me, and that when he talked to me, there was a mannikin in his head, called G. S. and entirely fantastic, which he was really addressing. No doubt he would have liked me less if he had understood me better; but the sense of that illusion made spontaneous friendship impossible.

THE PROBLEM WAS THAT, though Santayana wrote much philosophy, he never truly considered himself a philosopher, at least not in the professorial or professional sense. "Philosophy, after all," as he wrote to his friend Henry Ward Abbot, "is not the foundation of things, but a late and rather ineffective activity of reflecting men." He later told William James that he was initially drawn to philosophy "by curiosity and a natural taste for ingenious thinking." He viewed philosophy as "its own reward, and its justification lies in the delight and dignity of the art itself." He preferred to think himself a perennial student, which is what he wished to be. "But there are always a few men," he wrote to Abbot, in his twenty-third year, while on a Harvard traveling fellowship in Germany, "whose main interest is to note the aspects of things in an artistic or philosophical way. They are rather useless individuals, but as I happen to belong to the class, I think them much superior to the rest of mankind."

On the aspects of things, Santayana is generally amusing, invariably brilliant, and often original. While in Germany, for example, he remarks that the Germans, like other purer races, seem "to pay for the distinctness of the type which they preserve by missing some of the ordinary attributes of humanity," and he then goes on to say that "the Germans, as far as I know, have no capacity for being bored. Else I think the race would have become extinct long ago through self-torture." The Germans' — ignorance of boredom, of course, explains their love of the *Ring*

GEORGE SANTAYANA

cycle, Goethe's *Faust*, Hegel, lengthy pedantic scholarly works, interminable novels, and so many other homegrown, insuperable Teutonic cultural products.

The idea of a married philosopher, Nietzsche pronounced, is a joke. Santayana knew marriage was not for him. He wrote a comic letter to Morton Fullerton, the American journalist and polymorphously perverse lover who turns up in the letters of Henry James and the bed of Edith Wharton, asking what is one to do with the amatory instinct. Nothing very dignified, he concluded. Elsewhere he remarks that "like the Pope I shall have only nephews." So far as is known, Santayana never had a relationship with a woman that could be described as romantic. Because of this, some like to assume that Santayana was homosexual. In a conversation recorded by Daniel Cory on the subject of the homosexuality of A. E. Housman, Santayana is quoted as saying, "I think I must have been that way in my Harvard days—although I was unconscious of it at the time." Unconscious homosexuality is strikingly different, one should think, from actual homosexuality. But, as is the case with Henry James, a writer Santayana resembles in many ways and the victim of similar suppositions, there is no evidence to support the conclusion. In both instances, the Freudian penchant for what is supposedly hidden over what is in plain view has given dirty minds (which La Rochefoucauld said never sleep) much to dwell upon in the dark early morning hours.

Santayana took to teaching as a swan to ping-pong. He disliked the idea of being thought "essentially" a professor. As for teaching philosophy, he found the enterprise quite hopeless: "I can't take the teaching of philosophy seriously in itself, either as a means of being a philosopher or of teaching the young anything solid." As a teacher, his interest, he tells us in his autobiography, "was never in facts or erudition, but always in persons and ideas." He seems never to have viewed teaching philosophy as more than "a decent means of livelihood," to which he was never fully committed. Not difficult to sympathize. College philosophy is dry bones; it teaches that this is nominalism, that materialism, the other naturalism; that Plato thought this, that Aristotle thought that, and that Descartes came along and thought very differently. Not much to do with genuine thinking here. An old story about Santayana's teaching has him lecturing while looking out a window off to his right. One day a student is supposed to have asked him what he was looking for out of that window. "Europe," Santayana is said to have replied.

In 1912, Santayana's mother died, leaving him an inheritance of $10,000, which allowed him to send a letter of resignation from Harvard to its president, Abbott Lawrence Lowell. He was forty-two and had many things he wished to write. He also wanted to live in his own way, which he felt he could not do in New England nor cared to do anywhere else in America. Freedom restored, the world was now open to him; he could live where he pleased and do as he wished. One of the great side benefits of Santayana's retirement from Harvard is the increased frequency of his letters once he had settled himself in Europe.

*T*HE *LETTERS OF GEORGE SANTAYANA*, scrupulously edited by William G. Holzberger over the course of thirty years, is a model of what a splendid collection of letters should be.* Handsomely printed, thoughtfully footnoted, with a minimum of scholarly interference between the text and the reader, they form a substantial part of *The Works of George Santayana*, a continuing project published by the Massachusetts Institute of Technology Press to replace the old Triton edition of Santayana's works. In fact, they not only replace the earlier edition but are also a great improvement upon it and constitute one of the grand academic publishing projects of our time.

For a good while after quitting Harvard, Santayana was a permanent transient, a condition he found most agreeable. "I rather expect to take some small flat in London, so as to satisfy my tastes for crowds, for sitting in the park, and for eating in Italian restaurants," he wrote to Charles Augustus Strong, with whom years before he shared his graduate student traveling fellowship. (Later Santayana was allotted a room in Strong's large Paris apartment, where he spent part of each year.) "The routine of life," he wrote to

---

* *The Letters of George Santayana, Book Eight, 1948–1952*, by George Santayana, edited by William G. Holzberger; The MIT Press.

another Harvard classmate, in 1920, "is everywhere much the same, but I like to drink in congenial sights and sounds, and to haunt congenial places; and Rome is a most congenial place to me in every way." Santayana lived in Cortona and various Italian resort cities to avoid the heat of Rome in summers, and finally, in 1941, at the age of seventy-eight, settled in Rome into the Hospital of the Blue Nuns run by the Order of the Little Company of Mary. "For me," he wrote, "it is just the refuge I needed, with doctors and nurses at hand, and a nice view from my room, and moral and social quiet, although motors and trams make a good deal of noise."

Santayana traveled light, but always with a clear idea of happiness in view. For him, part of the secret of happiness lay in "the very old but forgotten maxim of not possessing things nor being possessed by them, more than is absolutely inevitable. I have made my peace with things, and find my life very acceptable." Wardrobe, furniture, even books, he kept to a minimum. He worked mornings, usually in his pajamas, went out for lunch, generally taking pages torn from a book, which he would stop to read on a bench, returning to dine and read in his hotel rooms in the evenings.

TRUE FREEDOM COMES ONLY TO a lucid mind unbound by conventional wisdom and suspicious of received opinions. This Santayana had, early, and *in excelsis*. The project of his life was to fight free from illusion, to see things straight on and as they truly are. Respecting but not subscribing to religion, he wrote to Henry Ward Abbot, "as for me, I confess I am happier without religion of the optimistic sort—the belief in a Providence working for the best. Disbelief leaves one freer to love the good and hate the bad." And to the same correspondent he wrote: "All is finite, all is to end, all is bearable—that is our comfort."

Without commitment, his position in life was entirely spectatorial. "I have never been anything but utterly bored and disgusted with the public world, the world of business, politics, family, and society. It was only the glimmer of sport, humor, friendship, or love falling over that made it tolerable." Loftiness of this height can be very grand but also, on occasion, heart-stopping. In December 1917, in the midst of the slaughter of World War I, he writes to Bertrand Russell of the war's devastations:

> As for deaths and loss of capital, I don't much care. The young men killed would grow older if they lived, and then they would be good for nothing; and after being good for nothing for a number of years they would die of catarrh or a bad kidney or the halter or old age—and would that be less horrible?

The answer, of course, is that yes, damn right, it would be a lot less horrible than dying in the prime of life from poison gas in a wet, rat-filled trench. Later, Santayana eased up on this harsh opinion, writing:

> The war *did* distress me, especially for two reasons: that I thought the Germans would win, and that I suffered at the thought of so much suffering, waste, insecurity, and perversity let loose again among people whom we had grown to think of as friendly and harmless.

Still, Santayana's view of the world *sub specie aeternitatis* can at times chill the blood.

HIS JUDGMENTS OF HUMAN BEINGS, especially fellow philosophers and writers, hum with penetration. Of G. E. Moore's *Principia Ethica,* he writes: "The book seems to contain a grain of accuracy in a bushel of inexperience." Henri Bergson, as with so many philosophers, does "not understand anything inwardly, [he does] not plunge downward towards the depths." He notes that "Emerson served up Goethe's philosophy in ice-water." He is high on Paul Valery, whom he valued for the lucidity of his thought, and feels his poems "the only original and interesting poetry being written in any language." He finds much to like in Alain, "whose philosophy is rich in casual intuitions, but without foundations or results." He claimed that "in his later years Whitehead . . . has been busy giving vague answers to questions that do not arise in a clear head." Who but Santayana had the authority to say of T. S. Eliot that he "is honest and brave, but limited," which happens to be true?

The great coming man in philosophy in Santayana's time was Bertrand Russell, about whom Santayana, in his letters and autobiography, has much to say, most of it less than enthusiastic. While allowing that Russell's "critical and logical acumen remain matchless," he feels that "he has no judgment, no good sense, no familiar affection for the reality of nature." He finds him "on the whole, a not very trustworthy thinker; he has the fault common to the political radicals of being disproportionately annoyed at things only slightly wrong or weak in others, and of flaming up into quite temporary enthusiasms for one panacea after another." He discovers in him "a strange madness whenever he touches on any human subject." Russell, for his part, wrote of Santayana: "Aloofness and facile contempt were his defects, and because of them, although he could be admired, he was a person whom it was difficult to love."

Yet for all Santayana's reservations about Bertrand Russell, when Russell was hard up, in 1937, Santayana, whose money was well managed by his nephew George Sturgis, and grew ample after *The Last Puritan* became, of all things, a bestseller, arranged to send Russell $5,000 a year anonymously to carry on his philosophical work. "The anonymity is important," he wrote to Charles Strong, "because he and his friends think of me as a sort of person in the margin, impecunious, and egotistic; and it would humiliate Bertie to learn that I was supporting him."

Santayana's charitableness was unrelenting. In the same year, 1937, he agreed to help Ezra Pound, again on the condition of anonymity,

for he "wish[ed] to see only people and places that suggest the normal and the beautiful: not abortions or eruptions like Ezra Pound."
He regularly sent money to relatives in Spain, provided lavish wedding gifts, helped out impoverished scholars. He paid the dubious
Daniel Cory, his amanuensis and a man of far from perfect reliability, a generous salary for decades, and left him the copyright to his
works upon his death. None of these is the act of an aloof man.

Santayana may not have been aloof but he remained detached,
especially from the world's little attentions. He turned down
honorary degrees, offers to lecture, invitations to serve on honorific committees. He ceased reading English newspapers, on the
grounds that "it would be pointless for me to be abreast of many
confused and sad events, when I cannot become involved in them."
In his seventies, he wrote to a correspondent that "it is interesting
to have lived so long that one hears people talk about one as if one
were dead," adding that "the G. S. now talked about in the US is a
personage almost unknown to me." His detachment he felt gave
him his edge: "Sometimes an astronomer can survey things better
if he does not become a planet."

Yet one sometimes wishes Santayana's detachment were even
more complete. "Philosophical detachment," he wrote to Sidney
Hook, "does not signify political indifference." He might write of
"the illusions of the Left, the fabulations of the Right"—products
of human fancy both—and declare his intention never "to belong
to any party." But Santayana had something like a sure instinct
for lining up on the wrong political side and for making incorrect
political prognostications. "No," he wrote to his nephew George
Sturgis in 1937, "I don't think there will be a great war soon." At the
time of the Russian Revolution, he wrote to Bertrand Russell that
"I rather like Lenin (not that fatuous Kerensky); he has an ideal he
is willing to fight for, and it is a profoundly anti-German ideal." To
Sidney Hook, in 1934, he wrote:

> I love order in the sense of organized, harmonious, con-
> secrated living; and for this reason I sympathize with
> the Soviets and the Fascists and the Catholics, but not
> at all with the liberals. I should sympathize with the Na-
> zis, too, if their system were, even in theory, founded
> on reality.

He found nothing to cavil about over Mussolini and Franco. Fortunately, he eschewed political activism of any kind. When Italy entered World War II on the side of the Nazis, he writes: "I went and had an orangeade in a quiet café around the corner." Of the war itself he notes: "what is happening interests me like ancient history, and illustrates the same truths."

What is it about the study of philosophy that tends to make brilliant minds stupid when it comes down to what are known as actual cases? Consider Martin Heidegger, Bertrand Russell, Jean-Paul Sartre, and Ludwig Wittgenstein, the four great names in twentieth-century philosophy: the first was a Nazi, the second died certain that America was responsible for all the world's evil, the third was a Stalinist long after any justification for being so could be adduced, and the fourth lived on the borders of madness most of his life. Contemplation of the lives of the philosophers is enough to drive one to the study of sociology.

IF SANTAYANA FAILS THE POLITICAL TEST, sad to report that he also fails the Jew test, and this with crawling colors. Not many writers in Anglophone literature, from Shakespeare on, have passed it: Dickens, Trollope, Henry James, Edith Wharton, T. S. Eliot, Hemingway, Fitzgerald, and so many other English and American writers managed to save a cold place in their hearts for the Jews. (Two great writers who didn't, who portrayed Jews imaginatively and sympathetically in their writing, were George Eliot and Willa Cather.) In Santayana's letters, whenever the word "Jew" comes up or a Jewish philosopher or critic is mentioned, one doesn't have to wait long for an ugly dig to follow. Why did he close his heart to a minority people long oppressed and harassed by peasants, brutes, and tyrants and join the chorus of the ignorant in besmirching the Jews? Professor Holzberger, in his introduction to *The Letters*, attempts to mount a defense for Santayana's anti-Semitism, but it doesn't come near persuading.

Santayana viewed Judaism as a worldly religion, and his own preference, as a non-practicing connoisseur of religions—he styled himself, late in life, a pagan—was for those religions centered in poetic myth, religion as supreme fictions. He even claimed to dislike his philosophical hero Spinoza's "*tame* ideal of man," which he thought derived from his Jewishness. He (Spinoza) "is entirely impervious to the traditions that appeal to me most—the Greek, the Catholic, and the Indian . . . he doesn't sympathize with the human *imagination*."

But it is the coarseness of Santayana's remarks about Jews, coming from an otherwise so refined intelligence, that is so unsettling. In his references to them in the letters, Jews are pushing or money-hungry—often both combined. They are communists. He refers to the "Jew critics of New York." Anti-Semitism always puts one in bad company, and so Santayana writes to Ezra Pound:

> As to the Jews, I too like the Greek element in Chris-tendom better than the Jewish; yet the Jews, egotisti-cally and fantastically, were after a kind of good—milk and honey and money.

He writes: "The Jews . . . aren't in the least like Abraham or King Solomon: they are just sheenies." Late in life, at the age of eighty-five, he softened a bit on the subject, allowing that "my best pupils were Jews, as was my only modern 'master' in philosophy, Spinoza. But many are not happy, and that is a pity." Santayana's inability to understand, or show minimal sympathy to, Jews is a sad failure of imagination, all the sadder on the part of a man who prided himself on the power of his imagination.

Is the foregoing little more than political correctness, Jewish version? Isn't one supposed to allow for the fact that Santayana, in his crude comments on the Jews, is only speaking for the standard views of his social class and historical period? Perhaps, except that Santayana above all writers wished to live beyond social class and outside his historical period. "Experience and philosophy have taught me," he wrote, "that perfect integrity is an ideal never fully realized." But his brand of low-grade anti-Semitism goes, as the attorneys say, to character, and in this realm those of us who find so much to admire in Santayana's other writings wish he had not revealed himself, this most uncommon of men, as just another common Jew-hater.

THE SANTAYANA ONE FINALLY ADMIRES is the writer who cuts through nonsense to get at the straight truth of things, the Santayana who is a free-thinker and skeptic. This is the Santayana who remarks that "reformers do not like one another" and that "humanitarians have an intense hatred of mankind as it is," which is of course why they are always so hard at work trying to change it. A character in *The Last Puritan* says of the people of Boston that they "had a second-class standard of firstness." Santayana was always there to remind one of what genuine firstness is—something one is likely to forget in a time of debased intellectual and cultural life. Another character, the hero Oliver Alden's aunt, remarks that "You individually can't raise the lowest level of human life, but you may raise the highest level," which Santayana, in his formal writings, was all along trying to do.

A number of sustained stories of relationships run through these letters. One is with Santayana's graduate-school friend Charles Augustus Strong. Many of their several letters are given over to their disagreements about what, in academic philosophy, constitutes "essences"; I was myself unable to decipher the different positions of each man and found the discussion on this subject between them constituted the only *longueurs* in all of Santayana's letters. More interesting is the Santayana line of criticism of Strong's personal quirks, which are not few and which he writes about to Daniel Cory. About Cory he writes critically to others:

> He is by instinct a lady-killer . . . but has become less attractive (and deceptive) with middle-age and cannot do the elderly gentleman as well as he did the young intellectual. . . . He would have made a capital actor, is a most amusing mimic, and has a bohemian temperament, spends money when he gets it, and never thinks of the future.

Cyril Coniston Clemens, a cousin of Mark Twain and the founder of the International Mark Twain Society, hounds Santayana with honors he does not accept and offers he finds it easy to refuse.

Santayana found old age entirely agreeable, more so than youth or middle-manhood. "I was a little old man when I was a boy," he writes, "and am an old fat boy now that I have completed my seventy-fourth year." He would live on to eighty-nine. He published his one novel, upon which he had worked for no fewer than forty-eight years, to acclaim and commercial success. He worked nearly up to the end, reasonably content with what he had accomplished: "Personally," he wrote to one of the anthologists of his work, "I don't feel at all neglected, never having expected popularity nor permanent fame . . . I never wished to be a professional or public man. Nor do I want disciples: I want only a few sympathetic friends, and I have them."

After Santayana's middle eighties, the world closed in on him, as it does on everyone who arrives at that stately age. Parts wear out; the body breaks down. His hearing was all but gone, his eyesight badly dimmed, his teeth shot. He lived much of his life in pajamas.

He grew fat; his physician suggested that he lose fifteen pounds, to which he responded by remarking, with characteristic irony, that the man obviously wanted him in perfect health just in time for death.

When death came he seemed as ready for it as anyone could be. "Think what an incubus life would be if death were not destined to cancel it, as far as any fact can be cancelled," he wrote in *Persons and Places*. He cherished his tranquility and didn't in the least mind his solitude. He worked on reducing his five-volume *Life of Reason* to one volume: "To think how many foolish and rash things I shall be able to leave from an old effusion of mine rather excites me." When he completed his last book, *Dominations and Powers*, he wrote that "I have no particular reason for remaining alive, although I shall certainly not be bored if I go on living." He left instructions for Daniel Cory not to believe any stories told by the nuns who took care of him that he underwent a deathbed conversion, for that, he assured Cory, wasn't going to happen. He died, of stomach cancer, on September 26, 1952, and was buried in unconsecrated ground in the Tomb of Spaniards in Verano Cemetery in Rome.

George Santayana is among the small handful of true artist philosophers—Plato, Nietzsche, Schopenhauer are in this select category—who write beautifully and whose finer-grained meanings are never so straightforward as philosophers who write without artistry. "Each real artist," he wrote in one of his last letters, "has a message of his own. No one else is obliged to share it nor (except as part of politics or ethics) even to exclude it from sympathy." If Santayana may be said to have an overarching philosophical message, it is to strip oneself of all possible illusions—a task that can never be entirely completed—while understanding, as best one is able, the powerful attraction of illusions to others. The person who can do that, as Santayana consummately could, deserves to be called philosopher.

Adlai Stevenson

The Man Who Couldn't Say Yes

"MADLY FOR ADLAI**"** read a campaign button from the two Eisenhower-Stevenson Presidential campaigns, and it has since become apparent that those who wore it meant it. One might like Ike, but if one was for Stevenson, one was for Adlai madly. Not since William Jennings Bryan had a Presidential candidate found so devoted a following; not since Theodore Roosevelt or Woodrow Wilson had a national political figure so thoroughly captured the fancy of American intellectuals. The quality of this appeal was extraordinary, as, in many ways, was Stevenson's whole career. He possessed the very reverse of "charisma," a term first hauled into the arena of political discourse to denote the magical capacity of leaders to mold large crowds, or even whole nations, into a passionate community of the faithful. Hitler had charisma; Ghandi had it; Churchill and Franklin Delano Roosevelt each had a touch of it. Stevenson's magic was of a different order; his appeal was of a subtler kind. In what did it consist? Except for those fortunate few to whom politics is an unending string of moral certitudes, this remains a puzzle, as does Adlai Stevenson himself.

He did manage to evoke an astonishing degree of adoration. The aura of special feeling that enveloped John F. Kennedy only after his death in Dallas surrounded Adlai Stevenson for a substantial stretch of his adult life. Alongside the warmth and determined elegance with which his friends and admirers have written about Stevenson, the eulogies to President Kennedy read as though spoken by a clergyman who did not know the deceased while he lived. Nor can there be any doubt that Stevenson's personality had a profound effect on the people who knew him; he seemed to elevate all of them and somehow make them feel good. As for the rest of his admirers, it is already a cliché to say that he struck a chord of affection in people in a way few other American political figures have ever managed to do. As Hans J. Morgenthau, not a notably sentimental man, wrote: "His promise was ours, and so was his failure, and the tears we shed for him we shed for ourselves."

Adlai Stevenson's personality was always at the center of his political career and now the career is beginning to recede and the personality to take over altogether. Stevenson was a politician—his admirers would insist on the word "statesman"—whose influence appears to have outweighed his achievements. What he had to say seems in many respects to be a good deal less striking than the way or the time he chose to say it. Because of these and other factors, interest in Stevenson as a political figure has begun to evanesce. Yet the meaning of his political career seems to offer so many clues to the riddle of American political life, to raise so many important issues and problems, that it is worth examining that career more closely before Adlai Stevenson is permanently laid to rest in the Westminster Abbey of the American liberal consciousness.

Aᴅʟᴀɪ Sᴛᴇᴠᴇɴѕᴏɴ was born in 1900 into a family that, if it was not excessively wealthy, seemed to want for very little. They summered at Charlevoix, Michigan, then the Midwest version of Newport, Rhode Island, and Adlai's sister was able to study in Switzerland under Carl Jung. Stevenson was said to have had an almost Confucian regard for his ancestors, and in his case such family piety was not without justification. His paternal grandfather, the first Adlai Ewing Stevenson, was Vice President of the United States during Grover Cleveland's second administration; his grandmother, Letitia Stevenson, played a prominent part in the founding of the Daughters of the American Revolution. But the most important influence on the young Stevenson, according to friends and biographers, was the memory of Jesse Weldon Fell, his maternal great-grandfather. Fell is credited with having suggested the idea for the Lincoln-Douglas debates; he was Lincoln's floor manager at the 1860 Republican Convention; and he later served as an Associate Justice of the US Supreme Court as well as the executor of Lincoln's will.

Stevenson's boyhood in Bloomington, Illinois, seems to have been tranquil. Since his father was active in national Democratic politics and for a brief time served as Secretary of State of Illinois, the pleasures of small-town life were occasionally heightened by an important political visitor. In 1912, his father introduced Stevenson to Woodrow Wilson, who was later to become one of his political heroes. In the same year, the tranquility of Stevenson's life was interrupted, catastrophically. At a party, a gun he was playing with went off and killed a female cousin—an incident that doubtless would have unstrung a less finely balanced boy. (In later years, commentators with a taste for psychoanalysis attempted to make something of this sad incident, but without much success.) In school Stevenson seldom rose above a Gentleman's C, favoring the social and extracurricular life. After a rather mediocre record in the public schools of Bloomington and Springfield, he failed the College

ADLAI STEVENSON

Board examinations for Princeton. In preparation for a second try, it was arranged for him to attend Choate, where "habits of efficiency and industry" were instilled along with an "understanding of the enduring values and of the spirit of public service."

Finally admitted to Princeton, Adlai Stevenson proceeded to achieve the kind of success there that F. Scott Fitzgerald dreamed about. Moreover, he achieved it in the best patrician manner: quietly, casually, without seeming to strive for it. He became an officer of Quadrangle, one of the school's most desirable eating clubs; managing editor of the *Daily Princetonian*; and a member of the prestigious Senior Council (class of 1922).

Princeton had a lasting effect. It can plausibly be argued that a good part of the Stevenson style, as well as many of his important political decisions—or, as the case may be, indecisions—derived from Princetonian notions of good form. Princeton also enabled Stevenson to set out his first lines to the cultivated and politically powerful East. His Eastern connections, like a letter of credit, were later there for him to draw on when needed. In the spring of 1946, when Edward R. Stettinius, Jr. resigned as head of the American delegation to the UN, Hermon Dunlap Smith, Stevenson's longtime friend, launched a campaign to secure the post for him. Since Truman promptly appointed Warren Austin to the job, that effort came too late, but the manner in which it was begun is of some interest. "The group I was able to approach," Smith wrote in a memoir of his late friend, "was augmented by the fortuitous circumstance of my going east to my twenty-fifth Harvard reunion, where, in the locker room of the Essex Country Club, I solicited the support of three classmates who represented an incredible combined circulation and influence: Roy Larsen, executive of *Time*, *Life*, and *Fortune*; John Cowles, of the Cowles newspaper-magazine family; and Ralph Henderson of *Reader's Digest*." This is not what the boys at ward headquarters would call grassroots support.

After Princeton, Stevenson attended Harvard Law School but he did so with less than enthusiasm, for his mind was not yet set on a definite career, and he found Harvard not at all to his tastes: "Everything is concentrated, work, play, exercise." Toward the end of his second year there, upon the death of a relative who had been the publisher of the Bloomington *Pantagraph*, a newspaper owned in part by the Stevensons, Adlai returned home to work as an editor and to look after his family's interest in the paper. Two years later, however, he returned to law school, this time at Northwestern University, where he took law more seriously, earned his degree, and passed the Illinois Bar. In the summer of 1926, before settling down to practice law, he set off on one last journalistic fling. Having secured the credentials of a foreign correspondent for the Chicago *Herald-American*, he sailed with two friends for the Soviet Union. He hoped to acquire a scoop of sorts by interviewing Grigori Vasiliev Chicherin, then Foreign Minister of the USSR and an extremely inaccessible man. Though he failed to get his interview, he was to remark in later years: "I've always been very thankful for that trip. After what I saw there, I could never believe, as so many did in the early 1930s, that Soviet Russia's way was a good way for any state to go."

Upon returning from the Soviet Union, Stevenson, through a Princeton connection, became a law clerk in the old and prestigious Chicago firm of Cutting, Moore, and Sidley. He moved into a bachelor apartment along the city's fashionable Gold Coast, and from there conducted a life commensurate with his social position and by now well-developed gregariousness. He was said to be putting in a 50-hour week at his law firm, but there was time in the summer to play tennis, shoot, and ride in the lush suburb of Lake Forest; during the winter, there were the Harvard-Yale-Princeton Club, squash, and a regular round of dances and parties. In 1928, Stevenson married Ellen Borden, the daughter of a wealthy Chicago real-estate man. After a honeymoon in North Africa, the couple moved into another apartment along the Gold Coast. Single or married, Stevenson's life during these years was extremely circumscribed and cushy, spent almost entirely among the wellborn and the well-to-do.

NEITHER THE KIND OF LIFE he was leading nor his first-hand experience of the Soviet Union was calculated to prepare Stevenson for any involvement in radical politics. And the 1930s, whatever they may have meant to most Americans, were to be an extremely good decade for Adlai Stevenson. He was neither unaware of, nor insensitive to, the ravages of the Depression, but he was not hit hard by it personally. He retained his interest in the Bloomington *Pantagraph*, and after his mother's death he came into real-estate holdings. While his active social life continued after his marriage—vigorous sociability was to be a hallmark of his life—he now also began to take an interest in civic affairs around Chicago. He became interested in Jane Addams's Hull House, of which he was later to become a member of the board of trustees, and he joined the Chicago Council on Foreign Relations, of which he was later to become president. After Roosevelt's election in 1932, Stevenson, along with a great many other young lawyers, found himself caught up in the excitement of the New Deal, and a few months later he went to Washington to work as a special assistant to the General Counsel of the Agricultural Adjustment Administration. (A fellow staff member at the AAA, who was later to prove of consequence in Stevenson's career, was Alger Hiss.) For a brief time, he was also with the Federal Alcohol Administration.

Returning to Chicago in the fall of 1934, Stevenson was appointed government member of the code authorities of two different industries—wine and flour. The following year he was made a partner in his law firm. Branching out now, he became president of the Legislative Voters League in Illinois, finance director of the Democratic National Committee during the 1936 Presidential election campaign, and Illinois chairman of the National Council of Roosevelt Electors. He was beginning to acquire a modest but solid reputation.

After turning down several offers from Washington, all for jobs considerably more glamorous than those he had held earlier, Stevenson did return to the capital in 1941 to serve as personal assistant to Secretary of the Navy, Frank Knox. Knox had been impressed by Stevenson for some years, especially by the latter's work as chairman of the Chicago chapter of the William Allen White Committee to Defend America by Aiding the Allies—a job which required courage in the heavily isolationist Middle West. Stevenson was similarly impressed by Knox, who had ridden with Teddy Roosevelt's Rough Riders, who was strongly opposed to the New Deal, and who in his late sixties nevertheless accepted a strenuous bipartisan political assignment that he must have known was destined to shorten his life. Talk began of Stevenson's running for the Senate in 1942, but Pearl Harbor put an end to that. He continued to work for Knox until the latter's death in 1944, with time out only for a brief stint as head of an emergency mission to Sicily and Italy for the Foreign Economic Administration.

By now, Stevenson had begun to develop a reputation as an expert on international affairs. Less than a year after leaving Washington, he was called back once more, this time to work with Archibald MacLeish, then the Assistant Secretary of State with responsibility for postwar international organizations. During this period, Stevenson served as press spokesman for the American delegation to the United Nations Conference in San Francisco. Later, he was a member of the American delegation to the UN Preparatory Commission meeting in London, and when Secretary of State Stettinius fell ill, Stevenson was appointed chief of the delegation. This was the first government assignment which allowed him to shed his anonymity, and everyone who witnessed his performance agreed that he handled things impressively.

YEARS LATER, with what had by then become characteristic resignation, Stevenson would say that he was "doomed" to a political career. For the time being, however, he chose to forestall that doom. After his stint with the American UN delegation in London, he turned down, among other offers, embassies in South America, the chairmanship of the Securities and Exchange Commission, and an Assistant Secretaryship of State. Personal considerations may have played a part in Stevenson's reluctance to continue in government service: he was now forty-seven years old, his three sons were growing up, and it was an open secret among his friends that his marriage was going badly. More likely, he was thinking about the Senate. He certainly made what sounded like senatorial noises when he spoke, inevitably on foreign policy, to various organizations around Chicago— the Council on Foreign Relations, the University of Chicago audience for his 1946 Walgreen Lectures, the Jewish Welfare Fund Campaign. Asked about his ambitions for the Senate, he told a Chicago reporter: "There is no sense being disingenuous about these things. My mind is open. Naturally, I'm interested." This may be the closest he ever came to candor about his interest in political office.

As it turned out, of course, Stevenson was placed on the 1948 Democratic slate as the party's gubernatorial candidate. The reason he was denied the chance to run for the Senate was that the Republican incumbent, one C. Wayland ("Curly") Brooks, had a distinguished war record, and the Illinois Democratic machine felt that a senatorial candidate was needed who could match Brooks battle for battle. The man it came up with was Paul H. Douglas, who in his fifties had enlisted as a private in the Marines. It did not matter that Douglas was an expert on state financing and was said to be interested in the governorship; nor did it matter that Stevenson's one abiding interest was foreign affairs and that his only governmental experience had been at the federal level. The smart money had spoken, and Stevenson, after agonizing over the decision in a manner that was to become habitual and greatly intensified in later years, finally chose to listen.

This was Stevenson's first encounter with the Democratic machine in Illinois, and it illustrates, all too unhappily, R. H. S. Crossman's contention that "American liberalism . . . is still sundered, both emotionally and practically, from the everyday world of machine politics." Stevenson never felt altogether comfortable among the

Democratic Party pros, and his relationship with the Democratic machine was characterized by a kind of political schizophrenia. On the one hand, he required the machine's support on a number of occasions; on the other hand, his career seemed to hold out the hope that maybe one day the machine, with all its parochialism and lack of idealism, might be smashed. That hope was, of course, to prove naïve.

Stevenson campaigned for governor on a bipartisan platform of good government against a Republican incumbent who had finally scandalized even the scandal-hardened Illinois voters once too often. He won by the largest plurality in the history of the state.

On balance, Stevenson proved a good governor. True, he failed to achieve the three items to which he himself had assigned special priority: a revised constitution, a network of bills to improve the quality of criminal justice in the state, and a Fair Employment Practices Commission. But he did make every effort to cut down on the corruption endemic in Illinois, and in good measure he succeeded. Only three minor scandals occurred during his governorship—the most flamboyant involved the discovery that horsemeat was being used to adulterate hamburgers—and these, comparatively speaking, were mere pigeon droppings in the Augean stables of Illinois politics. Before he agreed to run for office, Stevenson extracted from the party pros the promise that he would be entirely free to make his own major appointments, including, if he so chose, Republicans and independents; and he did in fact bring men of exceedingly high caliber to state government. He also doubled state aid to education, streamlined the state's financial system, improved the quality of its welfare programs and mental institutions, and launched an extensive road reconstruction program.

Stevenson's real distinction lay in what he refused to do. He registered more vetoes of appropriations bills than any Illinois governor before him. To the extent that he felt he had the political muscle to do so, he refused to go along with the state's patronage system, and the most decisive damage he did to this system was to remove the state police force from political control and to subject it to the merit system. His most notable refusal came with his veto—during the ascendancy of Senator Joseph McCarthy—of the Broyles Bill, an extremely moronic piece of legislation that would have imposed an anti-Communist loyalty oath on all candidates for public office, all public officers, and all state employees, including teachers. Stevenson vetoed the measure on precisely the right grounds:

> I can see nothing but grave peril to the reputations of innocent people in this perpetuation of rumors and hearsay. . . . I must, in good conscience, protest against any unnecessary suppression of our ancient rights as free men. . . . We will win the contest of ideas . . . not by suppressing those rights, but by their triumph.

The major casualty of Stevenson's years as governor was his marriage; late in 1949 Ellen Borden Stevenson sued for divorce on grounds of incompatibility. The Chicago *Daily News* noted: "Mrs. Stevenson never made any secret of the fact that she considered a political campaign disrupting of home life and that she found political banquets boring." The failure of his marriage lent support to the view of Stevenson as a tragically lonely figure, for it now appeared that he had paid for his devotion to public life with the shattering of his private life. From this point on, an aura of the sad conflict between the public and the private life clung to his career, investing it with an extra dimension of poignancy.

PRECISELY WHEN STEVENSON began to be considered for the Presidential nomination is not easy to determine. In his *Memoirs*, President Truman contends that Fred M. Vinson, then Chief Justice of the Supreme Court, was his first choice. After Vinson demurred, Truman began canvassing the country for possible candidates. His criteria were straightforward enough:

> Now if we can find a man who will take over and con-
> tinue the Fair Deal, Point IV, Fair Employment, parity
> for farmers and consumers protective policy, the Dem-
> ocratic Party can win from now on. It seems to me that
> the Governor of Illinois has the background and what
> it takes. Think I'll talk to him.

On the night of January 23, 1952, Truman and Stevenson met for about two hours. According to Stevenson's account of the meeting, he told Truman he was honored by his consideration, deeply honored, but that he was not interested in the nomination at this time because he very much wanted to complete the ambitious program he had launched in Illinois. In Truman's account, Stevenson was "apparently flabbergasted" by the offer. The story of their meeting was leaked to the press, and the following day there was speculation that Truman had in fact offered Stevenson his support for the nomination. Shortly thereafter *Time* picked up on the rumor in a three-page cover story on Stevenson. In February an independent group was organized as the "Illinois Committee, Stevenson for President," whose hope, in the words of Walter Johnson, one of its co-chairmen, was "to set fire to the Stevenson talk around the country." These were but the first steps in what would prove to be one of those rare occasions when a Presidential candidate was really drafted by his party—it had happened only twice before, with James Garfield in 1880 and Charles Evans Hughes in 1916. And it was to be the first such draft in which private citizens without official assignment exercised a major influence. In a sense, it was all out of Stevenson's hands.

But only in a rather restricted sense. Later, Stevenson remarked that both the Democratic nomination and the office of the Presidency were "unwanted" by him and that he felt "no sense of adequacy." In fact, he could have stopped the draft movement on his behalf any time he chose. All he had to do was follow General Sherman's example and say he would not run even if nominated. Despite his protestations, his feelings of inadequacy, his proclaimed ambitions for Illinois, Stevenson refused to make a statement of this kind; he said everything else *but* that. He said he was a candidate for reelection in Illinois and could not in good conscience "run for two offices at the same time." He said he would discourage anyone from trying to gain the nomination for him, and he attempted to do so, writing to Walter Johnson: "I do not want to embarrass you and I am grateful for your good will and confidence but my attitude is utterly sincere and I desperately want and intend to stay on this job [the governorship], with your help I hope." Right up to the point of his actual nomination he insisted he *could* not run for the Presidency, but he never said he *would* not.

In retrospect, it seems a bit much to believe that the sole reasons for Stevenson's hesitancy were his sense of inadequacy and his desire to be re-elected governor of Illinois. One underrates him as a politician if one does not assume that he also must have sensed that the Democrats had very little chance of electing a President in 1952. They had been in power for twenty years; an unpopular war was being fought in Korea; the Truman administration was beset by charges of corruption; and finally there was the extraordinary popularity of Dwight D. Eisenhower, who looked, as he later proved, unbeatable. In the summer of 1964, Stevenson was to remark to Lillian Ross of the *New Yorker*: "Both times I ran it was obviously hopeless. To run as a Democrat in 1952 was hopeless, let alone run against the No. 1 War Hero."

L ARGELY OWING TO THE EVENTS surrounding the 1952 Convention, Stevenson became subject to the charge of indecisiveness, a charge that greatly bothered him. "The more decisive you are in not seeking an exalted office," he told Miss Ross, "the more they say you're indecisive." Even today many of his friends and admirers are sensitive about this point. Yet all attempts to explain away Adlai Stevenson's indecisiveness pretty quickly run aground;

more interesting are the attempts to explain it. Beyond doubt, it was connected with Stevenson's relationship to power, which was ambiguous at best. Hans J. Morgenthau has cited Stevenson as the very opposite of the Machiavellian politician whose first concerns are the attainment and the maintenance of power; he considered him one of that rarer breed, in the tradition of the biblical ideal of the good ruler and of Plato's philosopher-king, who is willing to subordinate his "pursuit of power to transcendent intellectual and moral values." After Stevenson's death, Morgenthau wrote about his last years as UN ambassador:

> What could already be discerned in 1952, 1956, and 1960 now became almost pathetically obvious: the conflict between intellectual and moral awareness and the pursuit of power, spoiling both.

Plato remarked that the philosopher-king was always hesitant to accept power, but Stevenson carried hesitancy to the borders of the ludicrous. He was the exact antithesis of Bismarck, who, upon being sent with relatively little training to serve as Prussia's delegate to the German Federal Diet in 1848, commented: "I shall do my duty. It is God's affair to give me understanding." In his acceptance speech to the 1952 Democratic Convention, Stevenson evoked the Lord in very different terms:

> I have asked the Merciful Father—the Father of us all—to let this cup pass from me. But from such dread responsibility one does not shrink in fear, in self-interest, or in false humility.
>
> So, "If this cup may not pass from me, except I drink it, Thy will be done."

Among those who took exception to these remarks was General Eisenhower, whose initial regard for Stevenson was such that he claimed he would never have gone into politics if he had known that Stevenson would be the Democratic nominee. The General listened to the speech while he was on a fishing trip with friends. "Then it *happened*," Eisenhower later recalled to Emmet John Hughes. "He got to that part . . . about having debated with himself about the nomination—and 'wishing that this cup might pass' from him. Right there I snapped off the TV set and said: 'After hearing that, fellows, I think he's a *bigger* fake than all the rest of them.' "

Notwithstanding the General's reaction, Morgenthau is certainly justified in attributing a keen appreciation of the responsibilities of power to Stevenson. Stevenson had an equally keen propensity for self-dramatization, of which the acceptance speech in Chicago was but one example. Another came after he had won the nomination: back in Springfield, he went off by himself to spend an hour of contemplation in Abraham Lincoln's home. Again, after the drubbing he took in the 1956 election, he told John B. Oakes of the *New York Times*:

> The responsibility of being Chief Executive of this country is humbling and frightening. I have often wondered how a man can presume to seek from his party so exalted a position. . . . To say to your party, . . . "I am the best man to be President," seems to me inconsistent with the grandeur of the office, and I've never quite made the reconciliation in my mind.

One might, of course, argue that such remarks betray less of self-dramatization than of self-deprecation, and there is no doubt that the latter quality was very much an element of Stevenson's personal style. But it went along with a very precise idea of his own worth. When scanning the list of potential candidates for the Democratic Presidential nomination in 1960, he found himself hard put to come up with anyone who was better suited than himself. Adlai Stevenson was a strange mixture of arrogance and humility.

Not even the Messiah could have beaten Eisenhower in 1952. Stevenson's only hope lay in the possibility that the General, through a series of monumental blunders, would defeat himself. On more than one occasion, Eisenhower came close to obliging. No one will claim that the 1952 Presidential campaign set new marks for heightened political discourse. As Richard Hofstadter was later to write, "Stevenson's hopeless position might more readily have been accepted as such if the Republican campaign, in which Nixon and McCarthy seemed more conspicuous than Eisenhower, had not struck such a low note as to stir the will to believe that such men must be rejected by the public." Many came to see Adlai Stevenson as the best of men in the worst of times.

His attraction to his followers went deeper than the immediate political context. For one thing, his urbanity seemed especially appealing, and—in contrast to the terse style of Harry Truman and the bumbling clichés of General Eisenhower—well suited to America's preeminent position in the postwar world. That Stevenson was a patrician who also could sound like an intellectual when the occasion called for it was even better. His wit endeared him to many, even while it may have cost him more votes than any single stand he took during the campaign. There was also a nostalgic element to his candidacy; Stevenson's obvious and fundamental decency, as well as his insistence on appealing to reason, had something of the 19th century about them. Finally, he was, as Irving Howe pointed out, "The first of the liberal candidates in the post-Wilson era who made no effort to align himself with the plebeian tradition or with plebeian sentiments." And therein, perhaps, lay the greatest single attraction of all—Adlai Stevenson seemed simultaneously to be in politics and above politics. His insistence on good form, which was not only a matter of style but also a matter of temperament, set him apart from the hustlers and operators, the wheelers and dealers, who have given American public life its dominant tone. In part, it was also what finally brought Stevenson down.

In 1952, there were still reasons for optimism. Despite repeated Republican claims that Stevenson was a "captive candidate," no one in recent times has gone into a Presidential election owing fewer political obligations. While it is difficult to believe that Stevenson's indecisiveness about accepting his party's nomination was a deliberate strategy, it nevertheless had a definite strategic advantage. Owing his nomination to no one, not even to the incumbent President, Stevenson could afford to be his own man.

Despite this enormous freedom, Stevenson's 1952 campaign did not signify much of a substantive change in Democratic politics. During the Convention, Walter Lippmann noted: "Governor Stevenson's position is unique in that he alone is not certain to alienate any of the major factions of the party." Nor was Stevenson about to do so in the course of the election campaign. It was not his way to swim too far out of the mainstream; however distant he may have felt from Democratic machine politics, he did not really make any waves within the party.

IN REVIEWING THE 1952 CAMPAIGN, one is easily led to the conclusion that in an America with a saner political life Adlai Stevenson might have led an eminent government of enlightened American Tories—a government characterized by a mature conservatism, a serious regard for the importance of tradition as well as change, and a strong sense of decency. One is tempted further to fantasize that such an administration might have included George F. Kennan as Secretary of State, George C. Marshall as Secretary of Defense, and Douglas Dillon as Secretary of the Treasury. Stevenson's own rather special conception of the role of tradition in the Democratic Party does no damage to this fantasy:

> The strange alchemy of this [tradition] has somehow converted the Democrats into the truly conservative party of this country—the party dedicated to conserving all that is best, and building solidly and safely on

these foundations . . . . Our social security system and
our Democratic party's sponsorship of social reforms
and advances of the past two decades are conservatism
at its best. Certainly there can be nothing more conservative than to change when change is due, to reduce ten-
sions and wants by wise changes, rather than to stand
pat stubbornly, until like King Canute we are engulfed
by relentless forces that will always go too far.

There was little in the 1952 campaign to contradict the image of
Stevenson as the mature conservative. His campaign resembled his
governorship in being distinguished less by any strong originality
than by what he refused to do. Most admirably, he refused to be
cowed by Senator McCarthy and Richard Nixon. In a speech on
"The Nature of Patriotism," delivered before the American Legion,
Stevenson said:

The tragedy of our day is the climate of fear in which we
live, and fear breeds repression. Too often sinister threats
to the Bill of Rights, to freedom of the mind, are concealed under the patriotic cloak of anti-Communism.

One is reminded of the extent of this climate of fear when one
rereads another of Stevenson's speeches, "The Hiss Case." To reinforce their charge that Stevenson was soft on Communism, Nixon
and the McCarthyite wing of the Republican Party used against
Stevenson the fact that in the spring of 1949 he had testified on
behalf of Alger Hiss. Stevenson's testimony, Lord knows, had been
innocent enough. All he had said was that during the time he had
worked with Hiss—in 1933 in the Agricultural Adjustment Administration, between 1945 and 1946 at the State Department, and in
the fall of 1947 at the UN—his reputation, as far as Stevenson
knew, was "good." He had not testified on Hiss's innocence or guilt,
and indeed he never doubted the verdict of the jury that convicted
Hiss. In "The Hiss Case," Stevenson struck back at McCarthy, at

Nixon, and at Eisenhower, who, despite his pretensions of running a Crusade, stood by while this sort of muck was being spread on his behalf. Angry and really lashing out for the first time in the campaign—the speech was delivered less than two weeks before the election—he said in his peroration:

> For I believe with all my heart that those who would beguile the voters by lies or half-truths, or corrupt them by fear or falsehood, are committing spiritual treason against our institutions. They are doing the work of our enemies.

Although Stevenson was a staunch enough anti-Communist, he was also perhaps the first major American political figure of the 1950s to talk about the Soviet Union as if its leaders and people were of human, rather than demonic, proportions. By informing the American people of the inevitable attraction of Communism to the underdeveloped countries, he fulfilled his pledge to talk sense to them. He did no less by informing them of the hard truth—hard for a people whose tastes in such matters were attuned to complete and unconditional victory—that for the present coexistence was the only feasible foreign policy for America.

Most other aspects of Stevenson's campaign were quite conventional. Surely it was conventional for him to select Senator John Sparkman of Alabama as his running mate, and for the standard reason of balancing the ticket with someone palatable to Southern voters. Apart from Stevenson's greater efforts to placate business, his domestic program called for no more than a continuation of the New and Fair Deals. It would be good to be able to report that on civil rights he spoke as forcefully in the South as in the North, but, alas, he did not. In "The New South," a speech delivered in Richmond, Virginia, he extolled the virtues of the South, with special praise for its political genius, before finally getting around to Topic Number One, segregation. When he did get around to it, it was on tiptoe, referring to it ever so delicately as "the problem of minorities—a problem which I have had occasion to think about a good deal, since my own state also has minority groups." In one passage he even explained the "problem" away and predicted its imminent demise:

> The once low economic status of the South was productive of another—and even more melancholy—phenomenon. Many of the lamentable differences between Southern whites and Negroes ascribed by insensitive observers to race prejudice, have arisen for other reasons. Here economically depressed whites and economically depressed Negroes often had to fight over already gnawed bones. Then there ensued that most pathetic of struggles: the struggle of the poor against the poor. It is a struggle that can easily become embittered, for hunger has no heart. But, happily, as the economic status of the South has risen, as the farms flourish and in the towns there are jobs for all at good wages, racial tensions have diminished.

Attacking this fragile statement would be like taking a sledgehammer to an egg.

But let us instead pause for a moment to consider the phrase "hunger has no heart" in the above passage. Stevenson's speeches are filled with such elegant little touches. Before he was drafted as a Presidential candidate, he told a friend that the only way he would possibly run would be on his own terms, with everything he said and did bearing his own imprimatur. That imprimatur consisted largely of his style. Stevenson had the usual corps of speechwriters—though unusual in distinction, including as it did John Kenneth Galbraith, Arthur M. Schlesinger, Jr., and Bernard DeVoto. Although he tended to deprecate it publicly, he obviously had a high regard for his own prose style, and is said to have detested the idea of ghostwriting. The various writers on his campaign staff have conceded that those speeches Stevenson did not write himself he more or less made his own by editing them generously, or even by rewriting them.

It was on the basis of his speeches in 1952 that the cult of Adlai Stevenson went national. In large part, their appeal was due to Stevenson's deliberate intention to eschew pomposity and condescension. He had set out, it will be recalled, "to educate and elevate the people." What is more, it is doubtful he ever said anything he wholly disbelieved. "For years," he wrote in the introduction to the collection of his *Major Campaign Speeches*, published after the election, "I have listened to the nauseous nonsense, the pie-in-the-sky appeals to cupidity and greed, the cynical trifling with passion and prejudice and fear; the slander, fraudulent promises, and all-things-to-all-men demagoguery that are too much a part of our political campaigns." His own speeches avoided all these traps, but they also avoided greatness; they were certainly better said than read; and they do not, as some have claimed, stand alongside those of Edmund Burke, John Stuart Mill, Disraeli, Abraham Lincoln, or even Woodrow Wilson as political oratory of the highest order. Read today, Stevenson's campaign speeches have an oddly familiar ring, and this familiarity has little to do with one's having heard them before. For the Stevenson style, refreshing though it may have been when first brandished in the early 1950s, has come to seem quite stale.

More is involved than the mandarin flourishes, though these are certainly in frequent evidence. If "hunger has no heart," Stevenson, never one to let a good thing go, would later remark of Communism that it cannot "satisfy the hungry heart." He seemed incapable of enunciating the word "world," preferring on various occasions "this shattered globe," "this blood-soaked, battered globe," "this small vulnerable planet," or even "our little spaceship, earth." In an elegant aside, Stevenson could say of the migrant labor problem that "it certainly invites our compassionate attention." He could be a master of the rhetorical fast switch, seeking support for a foreign policy "which recognizes the principle of compromise and rejects the compromise of principle." With this statement we are, of course, only a short hop from "ask not what your country can do for you—ask what you can do for your country," and the Great Society cannot be far behind. As Richard Goodwin noted after Stevenson's death: "It is hard to overstate the extent to which he helped shape the dialogue and hence the purposes of the New Frontier and then the Great Society." One of the reasons Stevenson's style seems so stale today is that it has become the dominant official liberal rhetoric.

The style, it is said, is the message. But in the case of Adlai Stevenson, the style seemed sometimes to persist in the absence of any clear message whatsoever. He preached sanity; he preached reason; his very person seemed to exert a pull toward decency in public affairs. Yet there is little evidence in any of his speeches or writing that he had a very precise idea of how American society was, or ought to be, organized. His understanding of the American political process was less than perfect, as can be seen from his predilection for the bipartisan approach to so many of the issues of his time. One might almost say that Stevenson tried to set up shop as a modern, disinterested Pericles, but that he failed to realize that the America of the 1950s was a long way from the Golden Age of Athens. Unjust though it is to dismiss Stevenson as a utopian liberal, as some have done, his general view of politics was indeed hopelessly utopian to the extent that it did not allow him to take into account the great role of vested interest in American life, and it prevented him from realizing with sufficient clarity that some conflicts among men are not reconcilable by reason alone. Nor did he ever succeed in overcoming a kind of gentlemanly distaste for the practice of politics itself. In the 1960s, assessing the political career of his son, Adlai III, he said: "I don't know whether he's got the stomach for the crudities of politics."

THE OUTCOME OF THE 1952 ELECTION could not have done much to improve Stevenson's own stomach for politics. Toward the end of the campaign, he apparently came to believe that he stood a chance of winning. Senator Sparkman has told how, on election eve, on their way to deliver a final television broadcast, Stevenson began to discuss possible members for their prospective cabinet. And the historian Kenneth Davis reports that in a private pool among his immediate campaign staff Stevenson predicted he would win by an electoral college vote of 381 to 150. When the returns were in, Eisenhower had defeated him by a vote of 442 to 89.

But Stevenson's admirers put the 1952 election defeat—and all his setbacks—to good use. In their view, losing only seemed further to ennoble him. Americans are said to be preoccupied with success; but they also have a taste for failure if it takes place on a grand enough scale. As a testament to this rather special taste, Stevenson received a great many letters congratulating him on his campaign. As he noted, "Thousands even wrote gracious, flattering letters, after the election, explaining why they did *not* vote for me."

One letter to Stevenson—printed in *The New Republic*—came from John Steinbeck, and the fulsomeness of its praise might have brought a blush to the cheek of Mao Tse-tung. "You have given us a look at truth as a weapon," Steinbeck wrote, "at reason as a tool, at humor as a method, and at democracy as a practical way of life. We would be crazy if we let you go." Urgently pleading that Stevenson remain in public life, Steinbeck ended on a note which brought the Adlai myth into full flower:

> We offer you the highest gift of the people—work beyond your strength, responsibility beyond your endurance, loneliness to freeze you, and despair and vilification. Quite contentedly, we propose to take from you most of the sweet things of a man's life—privacy and companionship, leisure and gaiety and rest. We offer to cut your heart out and serve it up for the good of the

nation. And the terrible thing is—I don't think you can
refuse. Your greatness is the property of the nation, but
to you it is a prison.

After his defeat, Stevenson remained the leader of his party,
and in that job he was eminently successful. By extensive speaking engagements, he eliminated the debt acquired by the Democratic National Committee during the campaign and his efforts
were instrumental in bringing about the Democratic election
triumph of 1954, which enabled the party to attain a majority in
both houses of Congress as well as a number of new governor-
ships. When the subject of the 1956 Presidential election arose, he
expressed the inevitable hesitancy about running again—there was
talk about his returning to private life. Yet later, when he found
himself opposed by Estes Kefauver, and thereby forced to run in
primaries, Stevenson was openly resentful, intimating to friends
that he felt the party in effect owed him the nomination.

After finally deciding to run in 1956, Stevenson also decided that
this time he would stage a much different campaign. He had become
convinced "through rather sad experience," as he put it, "that real
issues cannot be developed, nor even effectively presented, during
a political campaign. They must be sharpened and clarified largely
through the legislative process between elections." At first it seemed
that Stevenson was in a stronger position in 1956 than he had been in
1952. He was no longer hampered by any admiration for Eisenhower,
an admiration that had been one of his stated reasons for his reluctance to run in 1952. Nor was he any longer hindered by having to
defend an incumbent Democratic administration; this time he could
go on the attack against the party in power. Finally, there seemed to
be in Stevenson a new determination to win. "I'm not going to run
again for the exercise," he said. "I've had all that kind of exercise I
need. Another race like the last one and I will *really* have had it."

In point of fact, 1956 turned out to be worse than 1952 in every
respect. In a wretched piece of luck for Stevenson's candidacy,

Eisenhower suffered a heart attack in September 1955, thus forcing Stevenson into a moratorium on criticism of the sick President. Then Stevenson found himself not only strongly opposed by Kefauver in the primaries, but also by Harry Truman at the Democratic Convention. Announcing for Averell Harriman, Truman called Stevenson a "conservative," charging him with following the "counsel of hesitation" and with lacking the "kind of fighting spirit we need to win." Far from having the nomination thrust upon him as in 1952, Stevenson now had to engage in a certified struggle to achieve it.

Fatigued from his efforts during the primaries and the Convention, Stevenson was vastly over-scheduled for the regular campaign. This took its toll. His indecisiveness, formerly reserved for grand decisions, now intruded upon petty matters. Crowds of supporters and important politicians would be kept waiting at airports, while Stevenson's plane circled aloft, the candidate within endlessly touching up his speech. Among his campaign staff, according to James A. Finnegan, his campaign manager, the politicians insisted on acting like intellectuals and the intellectuals like politicians. The result was that on substantive issues Stevenson tended to be vague, ambiguous, sometimes even contradictory. Thus he came out for a reduction in the draft, when it would have been more in keeping with his attacks on John Foster Dulles's reliance on massive nuclear retaliation to call for a build-up of conventional forces.

Admirers who would salvage something from the debacle of 1956 point to Stevenson's proposal to end nuclear testing, which, they hold, came to fruition with the nuclear test-ban treaty of 1963. An element of truth resides in this, but one must add that Stevenson was more than a little unclear about how to effect a cessation of testing. At different times, he spoke about America's undertaking the action unilaterally, about its leading the West into taking such an action collectively, and about its taking the initiative in persuading the Soviet Union to enter into a joint treaty.

A certain amount of sheer carelessness was involved in the 1956 campaign. Stevenson attacked the Eisenhower administration for extending financial help to the Peron regime in Argentina—when, in fact, it was the Truman administration that had done so. But the lowest point of the campaign was saved for the end. On election eve, in Boston, Stevenson made an issue of Eisenhower's health:

> I must say bluntly that every piece of scientific evidence we have, every lesson of history and experience, indicates that a Republican victory tomorrow would mean that Richard M. Nixon would probably be President of this country within the next four years.

On the next day, Stevenson was defeated even more crushingly than in 1952. He won 73 electoral votes to Eisenhower's 457.

EVEN TODAY, many people view Stevenson's two defeats as symbolic of America's rejection of the intellectual in public life. Such a view, however, is far from accurate. It is extremely doubtful whether Stevenson's two Presidential campaigns augured a distinct change in the substance of American politics but it is beyond doubt that they inaugurated a new *tone* in public life. Writing after the 1958 Congressional elections, Karl E. Meyer called this change "The Triumph of the Smooth Deal." By Smooth Dealer—a term meant to be descriptive rather than pejorative—Meyer had in mind those civilized moderates who came to national prominence from 1952 on. These were men who were not ashamed of their breeding, who had a certain amount of gentlemanly learning, and who were notable less for their passion than for their reasonable, if somewhat bland, manner. Joseph Clark, Eugene McCarthy, Frank Church, Clifford Case, Henry Jackson—the difference between the Republicans and the Democrats among them seemed negligible—such men began to appear in the Senate and as governors in ever greater number after Stevenson's emergence on the national political scene.

Meyer was premature in hailing the triumph of the Smooth Deal in 1952, for its ultimate victory came only in 1960 with the election of John F. Kennedy, the smoothest of the smooth. Ironically, this final triumph also meant the gradual eclipse of Adlai Stevenson. Arthur Schlesinger, Jr., who switched over from Stevenson to Kennedy in 1960, marked the watershed. Comparing the two men in *A Thousand Days*, Schlesinger noted:

> Kennedy was in the school of Roosevelt. He did not wish cups to pass from his lips. He displayed absolute assurance about his capacity to do the job; and he had a hard and sure instinct about how to get what he wanted. . . . One watched the changing of the guard with a mixture of nostalgia and hope.

An even greater irony is involved in the fact that John F. Kennedy and Adlai Stevenson, the two political figures most intensely admired by American liberals, were far from attractive to one another. Their first confrontation, if it could be called that, came at the 1956 Democratic Convention, when Kennedy opposed Estes Kefauver for the Vice-Presidential nomination. Although it was customary for the Presidential nominee to name his running mate, Stevenson chose not to do so in 1956, preferring instead to allow the Convention delegates to make the choice on their own. Kennedy, of course, lost a close contest to Kefauver, and it seems doubtful that he appreciated Stevenson's stance above the battle. Whatever its other virtues, the Kennedy family has never been noted for its keen appreciation of disinterestedness.

A confrontation of a more direct kind began to take shape with the approach of the 1960 Presidential election. Kennedy wanted Stevenson's support. "He is the essential ingredient in my combination," he remarked to Schlesinger in May of 1960, "I don't want to have to go hat-in-hand to all those Southerners, but I'll do that if I can't get the votes from the North. . . . I want to be nominated by the liberals." It was not yet clear whether Stevenson himself wasn't seeking the nomination—or, to be more precise, a draft for the nomination. In December 1959, he had declined to say he would refuse a draft. "I hope I will always do my duty to my party and country," he commented, somewhat ambiguously.

After the Oregon primaries, Kennedy stopped off for a visit at Stevenson's Libertyville farm. He asked Newton Minow if he should offer Stevenson the post of Secretary of State in exchange for his support, but Minow told him this would be a mistake. Stevenson described his meeting with Kennedy as satisfactory, though he later wrote Schlesinger that Kennedy "seemed very self-confident and assured and much tougher and blunter than I remember him in the past." Toughness and bluntness were not complimentary terms in the Stevenson lexicon, and on more than one occasion he made it clear to friends that he thought Kennedy a brash young man. For his part, Kennedy found the meeting with Stevenson less than satisfactory. Stevenson told him he intended to remain true to his pledge not to come out for any candidate before the Convention, adding that he would not participate in any stop-Kennedy movement, or do anything to encourage the various draft-Stevenson movements then underway around the country. On the plane back to Boston, according to Schlesinger, Kennedy said to William Blair, Stevenson's longtime associate, "Guess who the next person I see will be—the person who will say about Adlai, 'I told you that son-of-a-bitch has been running for President every moment since 1956'?" Blair answered correctly, "Daddy."

As the Convention drew nearer, Stevenson's friends split in their advice. Some told him to announce for Kennedy, others to announce his own availability for the nomination. He would do neither. The ambiguity of his position grew daily; it reached extravagant proportions in the course of an interview on the television program, *Face the Nation*. Asked whether there was any way he could be made to say he was a candidate, Stevenson replied, "If they want me to lead them, I shall lead them. I have indicated that many times. I don't see why it is so complicated . . . for one to say he will not seek nomination, who has enjoyed the greatest honors that his party can accord to anyone, not once but twice, to step aside and say, 'Now it is time for someone else,' and likewise to say that if called upon I will serve."

Adlai Stevenson's inability to get his tongue around the phrase "I want it" finally made the nomination unavailable to him. At the Convention, he hedged and squirmed and quoted Robert Frost and made sad little jokes—and must have felt something go dead inside him as he realized he was saying too little too late. It was becoming clear that there was no stopping Kennedy. At the eleventh hour, Stevenson nonetheless tried to do just that by telephoning Richard J. Daley, whom he had helped elect as Mayor of Chicago and who now headed the Illinois delegation. Daley at first avoided answering. When he finally did, Stevenson said that he hoped that the Illinois delegation wouldn't take the fact that he had not actively sought the nomination to mean that he didn't want it, or that he wouldn't campaign against Richard Nixon with everything he had. (The latest poll of the Illinois delegation was 59½ for Kennedy, 2 for Stevenson.) According to Theodore H. White, Stevenson then asked "whether he had no support period, or whether he had no support because it was the delegates' impression he was not a candidate. Daley replied that Stevenson had no support, period."

WITH KENNEDY'S ELECTION AS PRESIDENT, Stevenson's life began its final—and saddest—phase. Relations between the two men seem permanently to have soured. It is said that Kennedy lost all respect for Stevenson's political acumen because of the latter's behavior before and during the 1960 Convention, and shortly before the election Stevenson told William Attwood, now editor-in-chief of *Look*, "How could I ever go to work for such an arrogant young man!" Nevertheless, he campaigned vigorously for

Kennedy, and it is clear that he wished to be asked to serve as Secretary of State. But that was out of the question: Kennedy intended to supervise his own foreign policy; and besides, he owed Stevenson nothing. It was evident that he preferred someone whose gifts were more clerical than rhetorical; a good gray type like Dean Rusk was adequate.

Yet Kennedy obviously needed to find a place for Stevenson, who was therefore sounded out on the jobs of attorney general and ambassador to the UN, and said he preferred the latter. The UN ambassadorship was especially padded for Stevenson: it was raised to Cabinet rank and Arthur Schlesinger, Jr., Stevenson's longtime friend, was made liaison between the White House and the UN Mission in New York. "I have satisfactory assurances from the President-elect and the new Secretary that I shall have an adequate voice in the making of foreign policy," Stevenson announced after accepting the appointment. At first it seemed that service at the UN was in every way ideal for Stevenson. He would be above the petty squalor of domestic politics and deal exclusively in international relations, the field he loved most; he would work for world peace, the goal that had long been the name of his desire.

After less than three months in the job Stevenson learned that the US was planning to sponsor an invasion of Castro's Cuba by Cuban exiles trained and armed under the direction of the Central Intelligence Agency. He was said to have been dismayed by this news, to have thought the plan an egregious mistake, but since the decision had already been made, he agreed to defend it as best he could. From this point on he was not kept very well informed about the invasion. He thus denied on the floor of the UN that the United States was responsible for the attack on three Cuban airfields on April 15, thereby swallowing the CIA cover story that the attacking planes were manned by pilots defecting from Castro's air force. After the Bay of Pigs invasion of April 17, he found himself unable to deny the charge, leveled by the Cuban delegate at the UN, that the invasion was "by a force of mercenaries organized, financed, and armed by the government of the United States." All he could offer in rebuttal was the lame reply that no American troops were directly engaged. He had in effect lied to the UN and been caught at it. He felt that his integrity was partially destroyed, and that his stature had been cruelly exploited. Yet any impulse he might have had to resign was tempered by the fact that Kennedy himself had been badly misled by the CIA and his own military advisers.

But the Bay of Pigs was only the first in a long chain of humiliations endured by Stevenson at the UN. There was, to name but one other, the annual indignity of having to lead the fight to keep Red China out of the UN—this must have been especially painful since Stevenson had previously been a prominent advocate of a reexamination of our China policy. To humiliation was added insecurity. One of the after effects of the Bay of Pigs debacle was Kennedy's radical revision of the Chief Executive's decision-making machinery, a revision that involved greater influence for the White House staff and tighter State Department controls over foreign policy. Many saw in this a diminution of the status of Stevenson's Cabinet rank. Henceforth his UN speeches were read in advance by State Department men, who saw fit not only to question their substance but also—much to his irritation—to tamper with their style.

Increasing both the insecurity and the humiliation, there was the vigorous gossip being pedaled back and forth between the White House and the UN Mission in New York. Stevenson found out that Kennedy referred to him as "my official liar." Many of the less than flattering remarks Stevenson made about Kennedy were somehow getting back to the White House. In his biography Kenneth Davis reports that Stevenson told his sister: "It's something like Orwell's *1984*, if you please. Big Brother is watching you. Informers seem to be everywhere."

This and other aspects of his experience at the UN led Stevenson in 1962 briefly to consider running for the Senate in Illinois against

Everett Dirksen. Chicago's Mayor Daley had queried him about the possibility. When Stevenson mentioned it to Kennedy, the latter initially acted as if he couldn't care less, though later, when the idea of Stevenson's leaving the Kennedy administration got a bad press, Kennedy did announce that he was "delighted" Stevenson had decided to stay on at the UN. But Stevenson was said to be hurt by Kennedy's initial response; his vanity seemed to rise as his personal prestige fell.

It was the Cuban missile crisis that most undermined Stevenson's prestige and confidence and served to cloud even further his relationship with Kennedy. When informed of the presence of Soviet missiles in Cuba, Stevenson sent a note to Kennedy stating that the US could not "negotiate with a gun at our head," but adding that it must be made clear "that the existence of nuclear bases anywhere is negotiable." At the White House meetings called to determine the US reaction to the Missile Crisis, Stevenson argued his case for the political moves the US ought to be prepared to make in addition to its military plans. He suggested the US be prepared to withdraw from Guantanamo and that the Jupiter missile bases in Turkey and Italy might also be used for negotiation. He was at once attacked by the hard-liners in the room; and later, in writing out his views, he eliminated the Turkish and Italian bases as bargaining counters, but retained Guantanamo.

After this, it seems that Stevenson was not altogether trusted to present the American case about the missiles to the UN. Kennedy called in John J. McCloy to aid Stevenson in New York. Arthur Schlesinger maintains that he did so to give the UN presentation a bipartisan flavor, but this appears less than credible. It is belied by, among other things, the account Schlesinger offers of the instruction he received from Robert Kennedy before leaving to join Stevenson. "We're counting on you to watch things in New York," Kennedy told Schlesinger. "We will have to make a deal at the end, but we must stand absolutely firm now. Concessions must come at the end of negotiations, not at the beginning." Stevenson, however, was very staunch at the UN, especially when he said to Ambassador Zorin:

> You are in the courtroom of world opinion. You have denied they [the missiles] exist, and I want to know if I understood you correctly. I am prepared to wait for my answer until hell freezes over. And I am also prepared to present evidence in this room—now!

Many people remember this as Stevenson's finest hour at the UN. He himself had doubts, for he did not fancy himself as UN District Attorney, and he was fearful his prosecutor's tone had destroyed his objectivity in the eyes of the Russians.

SHORTLY AFTER THE MISSILE CRISIS, Stevenson underwent a new personal crisis, when an article, written by Charles Bartlett and Stewart Alsop and published in the *Saturday Evening Post*, accused him of having advocated a Caribbean Munich. Since Bartlett was known to be a personal friend of the President, it was natural for Stevenson to believe that Kennedy had planted the piece. He told Schlesinger that if Kennedy wanted to get rid of him, he needn't go about it in so tortuous a manner. In Schlesinger's account, Kennedy denied having anything to do with the article, claiming—with plausibility—that if he wanted to get rid of Stevenson he could find a less obvious way of doing so. Kennedy told Schlesinger to tell Stevenson to keep cool, and that the whole matter would die down in forty-eight hours. He also issued a statement expressing full confidence in his UN ambassador. "If not a forty-eight hour wonder," Schlesinger notes, "the furor died away in the next few days." But it is hard to believe it ever died in Stevenson's mind.

Perhaps the most telling effect of the off-and-on battering Stevenson's ego suffered under the Kennedy administration came in connection with Stevenson's trip to Dallas in the fall of 1968. While there, he was booed, spat upon, and struck over the head.

"Are these human beings or are these animals?" he asked about the Dallas mob that attacked him. Afterward he warned Schlesinger against Kennedy's visiting Dallas four weeks hence, as planned. "I was reluctant to pass on Stevenson's message," Schlesinger has written, "lest it convict him of undue apprehensiveness in the President's eyes. In a day or so Adlai called again to ask whether I had spoken to the President and expressed relief when I said I had not." The point worth making here is not that Stevenson could have prevented Kennedy from going to Dallas—it is unlikely that he could have done—but that Stevenson's confidence was at this stage so badly shot that he was rendered incapable even of warning the President that his life was in danger.

Stevenson's personal relations with Johnson were considerably smoother than with Kennedy. When Johnson became President, he made it clear he wouldn't hear of Stevenson's resigning. His flattery was persistent and vociferous. Yet, under Johnson, Stevenson had even less influence on foreign policy than under Kennedy. If during his time with Johnson, Stevenson rethought any of his old ideas on foreign policy, he kept the fact to himself. The word on him from his days with the Kennedy administration was that he was "soft" on Communism, and he was not about to do anything to lend credence to this charge. To his friends he might quibble about various aspects of Johnson's handling of foreign affairs, but he resented the charge that he was saying anything on the floor of the UN that he didn't really believe.

Lillian Ross has left an account of Stevenson's social life during his last years that seems—though it undoubtedly was not intended as such—a veritable portrait of self-destructive vitality. He had always been extraordinarily active, but now, according to friends, he was overeating, his drinking had increased, and he played tennis with a ferocity that was madness for a man in his middle sixties. His death in London on July 14, 1965, came as a shock; but that he died of a heart attack should have surprised none of his friends. Harry

Ashmore, a member of his campaign staffs and a friend, noted that it was somehow appropriate that Stevenson died in London, for London, the most civilized city in the world, became him. But it is depressing to recall that he was there to make an appearance on the BBC program, *Panorama*, an appearance the State Department hoped would reduce the force of the teach-ins against American involvement in Vietnam then being conducted at Oxford. Style and substance have rarely been further apart.

A SPECIAL FEELING continues to surround Stevenson's name even after his death. His claim to be remembered as more than a period politician surely rests on the striking effect he has had on a large segment of the American electorate. Stevenson is inextricably tied up with the aspirations of a great many Americans for a better world in which America will have an honorable place— and rightly so, for these were also Adlai Stevenson's aspirations. He was a fundamentally decent man in a political climate where decency was a rare commodity. Yet these same qualities, because unalloyed with any strong political vision or original political program, finally ended in crippling him. Plutarch's epithet for Aristides the Just might stand as Adlai Stevenson's own:

> But Aristides walked, so to say, alone on his own path in politics, being unwilling, in the first place, to go along with his associates in ill-doing, or to cause them vexation by not gratifying their wishes; and, secondly, observing that many were encouraged by the support they had in their friends to act injuriously, he was cautious; being of the opinion that the integrity of his words and actions was the only right security for a good citizen.

This was the same Aristides whom the citizens of Athens were supposed to have ostracized because they finally grew tired of always hearing him called The Just.

Henry Luce

Missionary among His Own People

ENRY LUCE DIED on February 28, 1967, but the mention of his name managed to ignite passions all over the United States—and the world—long after his death. One is hard put to find another man outside of politics so much surrounded by controversy. In the pantheon of American businessmen and conservatives, Luce's portrait hangs high: about as high, one imagines, as it hangs in the rogues' gallery of most American intellectuals and liberals. As founder and general impresario of the world's largest publishing empire, Luce's power, though probably immeasureable, was obviously great—so great as to make it almost impossible to sustain a neutral attitude toward him. Many people would agree with the remarks of Gardner Cowles, editorial chairman of Cowles Communications and *Look* magazine, on the occasion of Luce's death: "Henry Luce was a true journalistic genius. There has been no one in journalism for whom I had more admiration and respect. His influence will be felt for generations." Others share the opinion of Norman Mailer, who some years ago insulted an editor of *Time* by suggesting that anyone who worked for a mind so exquisitely and subtly totalitarian as Henry Luce's was not likely to have any ideas of his own.

Since Luce was a figure of indisputable magnitude in American life, his death generated editorials and biographical sketches in all the major papers, including the obligatory full-page V. I. P. obituary in the *New York Times*, and cover stories in both *Newsweek* and his own *Time* magazine. Journalistically, it was an event calculated to numb the senses. As occurs increasingly in these days of so-called "widespread communications," the more one read, the more one's picture of the man blurred, the more one's sense of his remarkable career seemed to fade. It was as if someone had set out to prove that he who lives by journalism shall eventually be obscured by journalism.

As a model of this kind of obfuscation, *Time*'s cover story on Luce is difficult to surpass. At the death of their Editorial Chairman, as Luce styled himself in his last years at Time Inc., one expected the editors to haul out their very best obituary prose and lay a gracious wreath of it at the graveside. But they outdid themselves and produced a full-blown work of landscape architecture. When they had finished, no one—Henry Luce perhaps least of all—would have recognized the terrain. The Luce of the *Time* cover story emerged as "courtly" and "compassionate," with the "magisterial presence of a Koussevitsky" and blue eyes that could "twinkle as merrily as Mr. Pickwick's." He was a "contemporary intellectual" and a "wise general," whose "infinite idealism," along with his "conscience and commitment," led him to extol "the Roman ideal of virtue as dedication to social and civic duty." Presumably, it was the composite of these qualities which made his publications a "valued and trusted voice of America throughout the free world." "He ran the course," one might say—*Time*'s editors, alas, did say—"He kept the faith."

Henry Luce's own self-appraisal was more nearly accurate, more candid, and therefore more admirable. "I am," he once said, "a

Protestant, a Republican, and a free-enterpriser, which means I am biased in favor of God, Eisenhower, and the stockholders of Time Inc.—and if anyone who objects doesn't know this by now, why the hell are they still spending 35 cents for the magazine." Not that this statement tells the whole story of Henry Luce either. He was a complex human being, difficult as that fact sometimes is to remember, and cannot simply be reduced to his beliefs, nor made to fit the streamlined simplicities of a *Time* cover story.

Oddly enough, for one who had made room for himself at the top so early—he was a self-made millionaire at the age of thirty— and who managed to stay at the top so long, Luce showed remarkably little in the way of personal presence. His few public appearances were inevitably disappointing; his official utterances lacked the vibrancy and flashiness associated with the language of his magazines; his writings, when not altogether banal, were dull and often pompous; and he looked rather more like a well-to-do jeweler or the owner of a Buick agency than what he was: a man of enormous, even towering, stature in the field of magazine publishing.

Then, too, there was Luce's reputed shyness, which, if one thinks of Northcliffe, Beaverbrook, or Hearst, is very much at odds with the traditional style of the Press Lord. He was not given to wide self-advertisement. In fact, very little has been written about Henry Luce as a personality. Such knowledge as we have of his personality comes mainly from the biographies, novels, or memoirs of people connected with him in one way or another. To a degree unusual in a man of his position, he appears to have been more content to wield the spotlight than to bask in it.

THE BARE FACTS OF LUCE'S BIOGRAPHY are well known; they form one of the more substantial chapters in the onward-and-upward annals of American business. Henry Luce was born in 1898 to missionary parents at the Presbyterian mission-compound in Tengchow, China. In preparation for the Hotchkiss School in

America, he spent one year at the Cheefoo School in China, where birching, caning, and fagging in the English style were in vogue. At Hotchkiss, where he first met Briton Hadden, his future partner, he edited the school's *Literary Monthly* and prepared for Yale. At Yale, where he was a member of Phi Beta Kappa and Skull & Bones, he contributed stories, poems, and essays to the *Literary Magazine*; he also became editor of the Yale *Daily News*, Hadden being chairman of the board. After a brief stint in the army (no overseas duty), he returned to Yale and graduated. Subsequently, he spent a year at Oxford reading history, worked as a legman for the late Ben Hecht on the Chicago *News*, and then joined Hadden on the Baltimore *News*. In 1922, both men quit their jobs on the paper to bring to fruition their longstanding idea of a weekly news magazine, which they thought of calling *Facts*. After the struggle to raise funds, the first issue of the new publication, now of course known as *Time*, appeared on March 3, 1923. The magazine ran in the red until 1927, but thereafter both circulation and profits continued to rise. The idea had caught on; the partners had it made.

So much for the beginnings. In 1929, Briton Hadden died of a streptococcus infection, leaving Luce in control of *Time*. Under Luce, *Time* begat *Fortune*, the two begat *Life*, and other off-spring—*Architectural Forum*, "The March of Time," *House and Home*, *Sports Illustrated*, Time-Life Books, etc.—followed in fairly orderly progression. As his fortune and influence grew, Luce became a kind of black eminence. Although it was rumored that he was somewhat disappointed at not being asked to serve in the Eisenhower administration, he apparently felt confident enough of his power to require no formal certification of it through political office. Instead he settled comfortably into the role of friend to Presidents and Prime Ministers, adviser to statesmen and bishops; praised and revered in some quarters, hated and feared in others, he became a genuine force in American life.

But a force for what?

Henry Luce's long career divides into three main spheres of activity: there was Luce the businessman; Luce the ideologist, or propagandist, for a specific set of ideas and ideals; and Luce the editor-journalist. Luce the businessman is the least controversial. After all, a popular maxim among businessmen is that "You can't argue with success." Although one might think that there is nothing quite so worthwhile arguing with, the saying nevertheless has a certain inner logic to it. What it actually means, of course, is that you cannot argue with the statistics of success, with the ineluctable finality of the profit-and-loss statement. By his own confession, the businessman's ethic is an intensely practical one, concerned with consequences rather than methods and principles. To quote another favorite business maxim, this one with a slight Yiddish lilt to it, "It's what you got left over that counts!" By this standard, the businessman's sole standard, Luce was a genius.

At his death, what Henry Luce had left over was considerable—a small empire, in fact. Here are a few of the raw statistics:

- During the week of Luce's death, Time Inc.'s four major magazines—*Time*, *Life*, *Fortune*, and *Sports Illustrated*—and their international editions together printed 14,331,458 copies.
- Time Inc.'s revenue for 1966 was $503 million, its net earnings $37.3 million. The current market value of the corporation's 6.9 million shares was $690 million, of which Luce himself, as the largest single stockholder, owned 16.2 per cent at a market value of $109,862,500.
- Time Inc.'s diversification program was of a model kind. According to the *New York Times*, the staggering rate of the appreciation of its market value "is a measure of the success and profitability of the company's magazines, its expansion into other businesses, such as book publishing, radio and television broadcasting, pulp and paper manufacturing, and a variety of other interests,

including developments in the graphic arts, information storage and retrieval, and marketing information."

And all the above started with the relatively piddling beginning capital of $86,000 which Luce and Briton Hadden managed to borrow in 1922.

There is no doubt that Luce was the business genius of the two young founders of the enterprise, even though one of the small intramural controversies at Time Inc. has to do with the exact nature of each of their contributions. One story has it that since both Luce and Briton Hadden were journalists by training, they planned to alternate annually in the jobs of editor and business manager, and that initially they flipped a coin to determine who would serve as first editor. The coin may well have been tossed, but it is clear from Noel Busch's biography of Briton Hadden* that the latter worked exclusively as managing editor during *Time*'s first three years while Luce, apart from writing the Religion Department, confined himself to being the magazine's full-time business manager. If Hadden was even one-tenth the editorial genius Busch makes him out to have been, then it is yet another testament to Luce's business acumen that he kept the financial management of *Time* in his own hands and left the "creative" side largely to Hadden.

The young Henry Luce strikes one as a somewhat drab, prematurely middle-aged man when compared to Briton Hadden. The latter was peculiarly a child of the American 1920s. Like Scott Fitzgerald, he was an athlete *manqué*; like Harold Ross, he was a bit of a philistine; like H. L. Mencken, he cultivated and parlayed his eccentricities into a legend. While the conception and original prospectus for *Time* was the joint product of the two partners; the magazine's early editorial form and contents would appear to have been largely Hadden's work. He invented the notorious *Timestyle*, with its

---

* Briton Hadden. *A Biography of the Co-founder of Time*, Farrar, Straus & Cudahy, 1949.

double-barreled adjectives and inverted syntax. Unquestionably, he brought great zest and zaniness to his work. He was not, for example, above writing fake letters to the editors to stir up false controversy, or—with Luce's approval—of putting the name "Peter Matthews" (after the two apostles) on the masthead as a blind for the editor of the Religion Department.

On the business side, Luce was in firm command. In order to save the costs of telegraphing copy to the printer in Cleveland, cut down office expenses, and centralize distribution, Luce moved *Time*'s headquarters to Cleveland in 1925. (Later, of course, it was moved back to New York.) Financially, that move put the magazine over the hump and eventually into the black. Hadden, a Brooklyn boy, almost went out of his mind in the Middle West, so uncongenial did he find the region's pace and people. Sinclair Lewis's *Babbitt* had been published only three years before, and one of Hadden's few delights was Babbitt-spotting on the streets of Cleveland. The Middle West caused Luce no pain. Not only was he rather comfortable among the Babbitts; there is reason to believe that he was turning into something of a high-level Babbitt himself. "I have no use for a man who lies in bed after nine o'clock in the morning," he is supposed to have said. "In Cleveland," Noel Busch writes, "the Luces occupied a conventional suburban house, moved in country-club circles, and took a lively and enthusiastic part in the life of the community."

After Hadden's death, Luce continued for some time to concentrate on business affairs. At the beginning of the Depression in 1930, he launched *Fortune*, a magazine dedicated to the thesis that "business is obviously the greatest single denominator of interest among the active leading citizens of the USA. . . . the distinctive expression of the American genius." Another side to Luce's interest in business, one perhaps more interesting than the pronouncements of any prospectus, is revealed in the fact that the original name for *Fortune*— dropped, one imagines, because it was simply too naked—was *Power.*

CLARE BOOTH AND HENRY LUCE

In 1932, Luce bought a trade publication called *Architectural Forum*, and brought it into the growing Time Inc. empire. At the time, he was fascinated by architecture, and he was growing wealthy enough to indulge his interests. He could soon afford to indulge other people's interests; in 1935, at the insistence of Mrs. Clare Boothe Brokaw, who was to become the second Mrs. Luce, he bought *Life*, the old humor magazine, and entered the field of photojournalism. The early *Life* was Luce's only serious business failure—the failure consisting of having underestimated the magazine's immediate and immense popularity. Between its first issue in 1936, and 1939, the year the magazine began to show a profit, circulation far outdistanced advertising revenues, and it cost Luce roughly $5 million to keep *Life*, in the words of *Time*'s editors, "from dying of success." Meanwhile, the rest of Time Inc. kept on growing. In 1939, with *Life* now out of the red, Luce announced a reorganization of his corporation; from now on, each of his publications would have its own editor and publisher. He himself took on the title of Editorial Director, declaring he had had "plenty of fun (and profit) as an entrepreneur," but was now ready to slip back into the role of journalist.

B EFORE TURNING TO LUCE the journalist-editor, it is necessary to discuss the ideological baggage he brought to that career. Luce the ideologist, in turn, is closely connected to Luce the businessman, for it is evident that without his business success Henry Luce would have had neither the platform nor, probably, the confidence necessary to the ideologist. It seems that nothing does so much to bolster the ideological instinct of Americans as success in business, especially among magazine publishers.

"America's great achievement," Henry Luce once said, "has been business." A sense of self-significance, largely derived from his own success in business, was unmistakable in Luce, and most openly manifested itself in his high regard for a free enterprise economy. The six points of "Editorial Bias" in the original prospectus for *Time* included: "(2) A general distrust of the present tendency toward increasing interference by government." This, to be sure, is little more than a safe shibboleth of the 1920s, but Luce retained his personal belief in the point throughout his life. After John F. Kennedy lunched with Luce and the editors of *Time* and *Life* in New York, the late President (according to Arthur Schlesinger, Jr., in *A Thousand Days*) remarked:

> I like Luce. He is like a cricket, always chirping away. After all, he made a lot of money through his own individual enterprise so he naturally thinks that individual enterprise can do everything. I don't mind people like that. They have earned the right to talk that way. After all, that's the atmosphere in which I grew up. My father is the same way. But what I can't stand are all the people around Luce who automatically agree with everything he has to say.

If success in business brought out the ideological instinct in Henry Luce, his strong religious impulse served to deepen it. He was, of course, the son of missionaries; he grew up in the atmosphere of a mission; and he attended Yale at a time when that university was characterized, according to Santayana, by a kind of muscular Christianity and undirected moral enthusiasm.* Such a background helps to explain Luce's lifelong habit of quoting Scripture. In *Witness*, Whittaker Chambers, for years an employee of Time Inc., recalls that before his ordeal at the Hiss-Chambers trial he was fortified by Luce with a quotation from the Gospel of St. John.

In 1965, Luce personally reviewed Teilhard de Chardin's *The Future of Man* in the pages of *Life*, and found that author's mystical Christianity to be congenial to his own views. Those views were so unshakable that they were immune to the impact of modern theological debates, which Luce appears to have followed with great interest. On the "God is Dead" controversy, for example, he struck

---

* "It seemed to me at Yale," Santayana wrote in his autobiography, "as if enthusiasm were cultivated for its own sake, as flow of life, no matter in what direction. It meant intoxication, not choice. You were not taught to attain anything capable of being kept, a treasure to be laid up in heaven. You were trained merely to succeed. And in order to be sure to succeed, it was safer to let the drift of the times dictate your purpose. Make a strong pull and a long pull and a pull all together for the sake of togetherness. Then you will win the race. A young morality, a morality of preparation, of limbering up. 'Come on, fellows,' it cried, 'Let's see who gets there first. Rah, rah, rah! Whoop-her-up! Onward, Christian Soldier!' "

a characteristically peremptory tone in a letter to a friend: "The real question about God is, of course, 'whose God?' After all the argumentation is done, I believe that God revealed in the Scriptures is, quite simply, God; and therefore, not only living, but the creator and source of all life." Speaking to his assembled employees, he once remarked that the evolution of the modern journalist—a figure Malcolm Muggeridge has likened to a piano player in a brothel—began with the medieval troubadours. "Be ye troubadours of the Lord," he thereupon invoked his staff. There can be little question but that for Luce, journalism was at least in part a form of missionary work.

THE QUALITIES OF THE BUSINESS IDEOLOGUE and the missionary are nicely combined in an essay Luce wrote just before America's entry into World War II. Titled "The American Century" and published in February 1941, that essay also provides some strong clues about the place of America in Henry Luce's personal cosmology. Born an American, but having spent the first fifteen years of his life in China without once setting foot in this country, Luce had every opportunity to construct a fantasy-image of the United States. His attitude toward the nation resembles that of a convert to his new-found religion; his interest in America was almost proprietary and his patriotism bordered on the chauvinistic. "I was never disillusioned with or by America," he once wrote, "but I was from my earliest manhood dissatisfied with America. America was not being as great and as good as I knew she could be, as I believed with every nerve and fiber God Himself had intended her to be."

Never one for small talk, Luce was fond of thinking in grandiose terms. "The American Century" is ostensibly devoted to the issue of whether American foreign policy in the early 1940s should be isolationist or interventionist, but the essay soon turns to the subject of America's destiny. Luce was an interventionist, but the reasons for his position are curious. Surprisingly enough, the specter

right wing
vision

totalitarian overtones - germanic?

of Hitler has no real prominence in his essay; at no time does Luce broach the possibility that America might have limited aims in the war, such as helping to destroy Nazism. According to Luce, the purpose of the war is "to defend and even to promote, encourage, and incite so-called democratic principles throughout the world." Not that there weren't sufficient problems at home—though in Luce's mind all of these seemed to reduce themselves to the name Franklin Delano Roosevelt:

> We start into this war with huge government debt, a vast bureaucracy, and a whole generation of young people trained to look to the government as the source of all life. The party in power is the one which for long years has been most sympathetic to all manner of socialist doctrine and collectivist trends. The President of the United States has continually reached for more and more power, and he owes his continuation in office today largely to the coming of the war. Thus, the fear that the United States will be driven to a national socialism, as a result of cataclysmic circumstances and contrary to the will of the American people, is an entirely justifiable fear.

The important point to grasp about World War II, the argument of "The American Century" continues, is "simply that the complete opportunity of leadership is *ours.*" Noting that Americans have seemed unable to accommodate themselves spiritually and practically to the fact that their nation is the most powerful in the 20th-century world, Luce writes that "they have failed to play their part as a world power—a failure which has had disastrous consequences for themselves and for all mankind. And the cure is this: to accept wholeheartedly our duty and our opportunity as the most powerful and vital nation in the world and in consequence to exert upon the world the full impact of our influence, *for such purposes as we see fit and by such means as we see* fit." (Italics mine.) Even though, "Under Franklin Delano Roosevelt we ourselves have failed to make democracy work successfully," it is evident that "Our only chance now to make it work is in terms of a vital international economy and in terms of an international moral order."

Toward the end of the essay, Luce points to four areas in which the vision of the American Century can be realized. The first is economic: "It is for America and for America alone to determine whether a system of free economic enterprise—an economic order compatible with freedom and progress—shall not prevail in this century." The second is technological: "Closely akin to the purely economic area and yet quite different from it, there is the picture of an America which will send out through the world its technical and artistic skills." Thirdly, there is the purely Christian ideal of the Good Samaritan: "It is the manifest duty of this country to undertake to feed all the people of the world who as a result of this worldwide collapse of civilization are hungry and destitute—*all of them, that is, whom we can from time to time reach consistently with a very tough attitude toward all hostile governments.*" (Italics mine.) Finally, there is that loose equipage of convictions known as "Americanism": "But all this is not enough. All this will fail and none of it will happen unless our vision of America as a world power includes a passionate devotion to great American ideals."

Luce was apparently able to reconcile his optimistic conception of America's role in the world with his profound adherence to Presbyterianism, according to which man is a lowly sinner to whom worldly success can be of no avail. Infusing all his activities with religious fervor, he seemed to be the very embodiment of what Max Weber called the Protestant ethic. It is fascinating, but ultimately futile, to speculate about the inner turmoil that may have attended his outward serenity. We may leave it at the following comment by T. S. Matthews, who was with *Time* for twenty-four years, six of them as principal editor:

As a fervently patriotic American he had an almost religious faith in competition and a striving belief that it was a man's duty, like his country's, to win. He must have been daily (and nightly) torn by the struggle with these apocalyptic beasts [his religion and his patriotism], these irreconcilable and mutually hostile convictions. Although his devotion to the Presbyterian creed was not always apparent during office hours, and was certainly not allowed to shackle his progress as a press tycoon, it was there, it was a part of him, and it made both himself and his success more interesting. I finally decided that what most drew me to Luce and made me feel that we had something in common—and has kept me fond of him even when I didn't like him—was his guilty conscience.

Shortly after the publication of "The American Century," Quincy Howe, the radio commentator and journalist, called Luce "the most influential editor in the United States." Here are Howe's reasons for this high estimate:

Because Henry Luce is primarily a great *editor*, his genius lies more in anticipating public trends than in actually leading the public one way or the other. For the great editor is an advance sounding board of public opinion rather than the crusader who molds public opinion. The great editor does not create a trend; he anticipates it. The importance of Mr. Luce's article does not lie in the fact that it is going to persuade a reluctant public to share its author's convictions. Its importance lies in the fact that Mr. Luce has that sixth sense—of which he himself may be quite unaware—of thinking a few weeks ahead of the public. There, rather than in his gift for writing, for publicity, for organization, lies the secret of his success.

editor's task

Spotting trends in public opinion is, it seems to me, only a small part of the editorial task; what is more important, what defines a magazine editor's excellence, is how he deals with a given trend. The great editor's real ability, I should say, lies in extracting and clarifying the true issues embedded in the amorphous welling of mass public opinion; in introducing new and useful ideas to his readers; and in *directing* public opinion toward rational thought and action, or even in the service of a cause.

If one applies these standards, can one still consider Henry Luce a great editor? The answer to this question involves a close look at Luce's magazines, especially *Time*, to determine whether they have guided public opinion or merely reflected it. In taking such a look one must be prepared to question what Dwight Macdonald has described as one of the enduring tenets of the liberal myth, the conviction that the main trouble with our press is that it is a mere mouthpiece for the reactionary views of its owners. Luce qualifies beautifully as a reactionary; most of his ideas were terribly dated, and there is no evidence that he ever changed his mind about anything fundamental. And yet his magazines—especially *Time*, the crown jewel in his empire—have not grown more reactionary as they have grown older and more powerful. If anything, it has been the other way around. If *Time* can be said to have had an ideological line all through the years, that line, upon investigation, turns out to have been neither so straight nor so firm as one might have imagined. There have, in fact, been multiple lines—a labyrinth, a veritable maze of lines.

Time has always been strongly opinionated. The biases of the magazine are sometimes excused on the ground that Luce never advanced any pretenses about its objectivity. This is true, but only in part. While the original prospectus for *Time* claimed the "the editors recognize that complete neutrality on public questions and important news is probably as undesirable as it is impossible . . . ," it also stated, "No article will be written to prove any special case."

No one can deny that *Time* frequently pleaded a "special case" in line with Luce's convictions. *Time*, as T. S. Matthews said, was not only Luce's invention but his property. As business head of the corporation, he had the final say on every important business decision; and his role as editorial director was an analogous one. When Luce announced his retirement in 1964, he declared that editorial decisions would now be made by others. Yet Herbert R. Mayes, a personal friend and a former president of the McCall Corporation, records the following exchange with Luce:

> "But if the editors now decide to support candidate A for President, and you are for candidate B, which candidate will the magazine support?"

> "That's simple," Mr. Luce responded after a long interval of a tenth of a second. "They will support candidate B."

UP TO THE DAY OF HIS DEATH, then, Henry Luce exercised a pervasive influence over *Time*. This is not to say that he dictated his personal line on every item that appeared in the magazine, from a review of a biography of Marcel Proust to the latest Jerry Lewis movie (though one may well wonder how many peripheral items were written to please the Boss). But every substantive stand that *Time* ever took was, above all, the stand of Henry Luce. In a way that applies to few other recent publishers, Luce turned his magazines into his personal diaries.

Not all of Luce's opinions were of equal intensity. But when he held a strong conviction in one area it tended to affect strongly his views in other spheres. He evidently embraced the Arab proverb, "The enemy of my friend is my enemy and the enemy of my enemy is my friend." This tendency is vividly illustrated by Luce's strong approval of Dwight Eisenhower and *Time*'s coverage of the 1952 Presidential election campaign.

There is reason to believe that Luce bore Stevenson no very great malice until the latter was chosen to oppose Eisenhower in 1952. In a *Time* cover story on Stevenson before he had become a Presidential candidate, he is cited as a governor dedicated to "a more hopeful and dynamic proposition: that the US is not a static pattern but an experiment, among other things—in good government." Once a candidate, however, he became prey to the furies of Lucean journalism. Thus, after the 1952 Democratic convention the readers of *Time* were informed that Stevenson had "never so much as slapped the wrist of the Cook County Democratic organization, the most corrupt and powerful of existing big-city machines." In a later cover story on Richard Nixon—"a good-looking, dark-haired young man, with a manner both aggressive and modest . . . a fine TV manner, an attractive family, a good war record, deep sincerity and religious faith, a Horatio Alger-like career," etc.—one discovers that Stevenson's English is "more polished than plain." In the September 1, 1952 issue of *Time* Eisenhower is depicted as offering "the kind of shrewd analysis . . . which the US seldom hears from its officials . . . ," while Stevenson is up in Wisconsin, spending "hours loafing." Cover stories on Eisenhower carried caption lines such as "E pluribus unum" and (a quote) "Free government is the political expression of a deeply felt religious faith"; a Stevenson cover, however, posed the question: "Does he speak for the American people?" The answer was, by and large, "No."

The bias of the 1952 campaign coverage extended all the way down to photography. Ben H. Bagdikian points out that in the thirteen issues published during the campaign, *Time* printed twenty-one photographs of Eisenhower, all generally attractive: shaking hands, smiling that winning smile, looking altogether earnest and mellow and wise. During the same period there appeared only thirteen photographs of Stevenson; two of them were thirty years old, and of the remainder four showed him in such unfelicitous poses as eating, drinking, and frowning. (This, incidentally, lends credence to the rumor that when going out on an assignment *Time* photographers ask only one question of the editors: "Good guy or bad guy?")

Luce's Republicanism even affected *Time*'s depictions of the American mood, which generally turned out to be more serene under Republican than Democratic administrations. In the issue of March 10, 1952, here is how Americans are described as paying their taxes under the Truman administration:

> This week, once again, the American taxpayer . . . was working over his income tax return. He did not do the job happily. . . . The blow, in full and crushing measure, now lands each March 15 on the chin of a fellow named John Q.

But by April 18, 1955, under the Eisenhower administration, taxpayers seem to have become not only accustomed to, but almost joyous about, their lot:

> 60 million Americans have by this week signed their 1954 income tax forms. . . . They did this, wonderful to tell, without riots or protest. . . . It has become more and more unfashionable to criticize the income tax level.

The same kind of bias, though more subtly expressed, can be found in the following two descriptions of airport scenes. Given the fact that they are ostensibly describing the same rather commonplace act of debarking from a plane, they could hardly be more different in tone:

> As the plane landed, the familiar bony face, the hawk nose, the mustache, the Homburg, were framed in a cabin window. The plane, the President's *Independence*, rolled to a stop at the Military Air Transport Service terminal in Washington, and the most controversial [a word simply meaning "unpopular" in *Time* language]

figure in international politics [Dean Acheson] came down the ramp. (January 8, 1951)

A tall, sunburned man in a straw hat climbed out of a small plane at the Syracuse airport last week, and with a trim, grey-haired woman hurrying along beside him, made for the airport waiting room. No one recognized Mr. & Mrs. John Foster Dulles as they crossed the crowded lobby, sat down at the lunch counter, and ordered ice-cream sodas. (August 13, 1951)

The Homburg versus the Ice Cream Soda—who would hesitate to choose between them? The Acheson story ends on a particularly strident note, asking whether the then Secretary of State constitutes so great a political liability as to be a "national danger."

Sometimes, *Time* has found targets that deserved its enmity; the magazine's early stand against Senator Joseph McCarthy is certainly to Luce's credit. In the issue of October 22, 1951, the junior Senator from Wisconsin was roundly attacked; indeed, he was even worked over pretty well on the cover, which carried the caption: "DEMAGOGUE MCCARTHY, Does he deserve well of the Republic?" (The answer to *Time*'s cover questions, it seems, is almost invariably negative.) Not only in this particular issue, but at almost every opportunity *Time*'s editors scorned McCarthy's destructive antics as, among other things, a "national disgrace." But *Time*'s memory is short; what is said one week may bear little relation to what was said in the past or will be said in the future; the current issue is *the* issue. Thus, while *Time* thoroughly excoriated McCarthy and McCarthyism in October 1951, a cover story on Acheson, nine months earlier, had stated that "A lot of the charges that the State Department had housed party-liners and homosexuals had obviously stuck"; and, "The Acheson group [in State] (which included, among others, Alger Hiss) had held various attitudes toward Russia, none of them unfriendly." And ten

months *after* the exposé of McCarthy, a cover story on Richard
Nixon made no mention whatever of the latter's use of McCar-
thyite smear tactics to defeat Jerry Voorhis for Congress and, later,
Helen Gahagan Douglas for the Senate.

As one might suspect from the above attacks on both McCarthy
and Acheson, Luce's own attitude toward the dangers of Communism was not unambiguous. He could be open-minded enough to
remark to Emmet John Hughes: "I don't *care* how my editors add up
their facts and omens. I just don't *feel* the Soviets bringing on world
war. In the '30s I *felt* it—surely—with the Nazis. The Communists?
Damn it, no." At other times, he could reveal a remarkable lack of
sophistication in this area. In *Witness*, Whittaker Chambers tells of
an evening he spent with Luce and an unnamed European. When
the subject of Communism and the Hiss case entered the conversation, Luce demonstrated his naiveté by saying to Chambers: "By
any Marxian pattern of how classes behave, the upper class should
be for you and the lower classes should be against you. But it is the
upper class that is most violent against you. How do you explain
that?" Shortly afterward, there occurs one of the most moving passages in Chambers's book. In it Luce shows that at times he could
achieve a depth of humaneness seldom to be found in his publications. The passage occurs after the European has left:

> Alone, we sat facing each other across a low table. Nei-
> ther of us said anything. He studied my face for some
> time as if he were trying to read the limits of my strength.
> "The pity of it is," he said at last, "that two men, able
> men, are destroying each other in this way."

On the Soviet Union generally, Luce tended to reflect rather
than direct public opinion. Like almost everyone else, *Time* was
glad to have Stalin's troops on our side in World War II; in the
1950s, like almost everyone else, including many American intellectuals, the magazine was rather crudely anti-Communist; in the

1960s it cooled its anti-Communist zeal—once again, like almost everyone else.

Luce's and *Time*'s line, then, cannot be described as simply anti-liberal. If one wished to "keep score" one could say that Luce and the liberals found common ground on the following causes: the fight against Fascism, the United Nations, world law, and the civil-rights movement, at least in its more respectable manifestations. They were opposed in their assessments of Franklin Delano Roosevelt and Dean Acheson, both of whom Luce fervently despised, and of Harry Truman, whom he simply could not abide. In the *Time* story of Truman's firing of General Douglas MacArthur (April 23, 1951), there appears a passage that is less interesting for what it has to say about the two combatants than for what it has to say about the sympathies and temperament of Henry Luce:

> Seldom had a more unpopular man fired a more popular one. Douglas MacArthur was the personification of the big man, with the many admirers who look to a great man for leadership, with the few critics who distrust a big man's dominating ways. Harry Truman was almost a professional little man, with the admirers who like the little man's courage, with the many critics who despise a little man's inadequacies.

B̲UT THE ONE SUBJECT on which Luce seemed to depart completely from reality was China. "Luce was stubborn and headstrong," T. S. Matthews has written, "but facts and logic could usually persuade him; on this issue alone he went beyond the bounds of reason." His view of China doubtless owed something to his love for the country in which he had been born and brought up, something to his loyalty to Chiang Kai-shek, and something to his capacity for wishful thinking. It has even been suggested that he shared the dream of his missionary parents and wished to Christianize

China. That, of course, is a dubious speculation, but after the Communists gained control of the country, Luce's attitude toward China did resemble that of a man advocating a Holy War. Not only was he blind to the brutalities and ineptitude of his friend Chiang Kai-shek, but he almost seemed to take a positive delight in the better organized—and hence larger-scale—brutalities and ineptitudes of China's Communist leadership:

> Two out of every three able men in Canton are unemployed. In other cities the problem is swelled by thousands of rural refugees, who have lost their means of support in the land reform. Whole classes of merchants and professionals like lawyers, brokers, and jewelers are idle: their functions have simply vanished. In Shanghai, Tientsin, Hankow, Chungking, Foochow, and Swatow, thousands of shops and factories have gone bankrupt. Shopping centers in almost every big city in China now seem lifeless and deserted.
>
> That, last week, was China under the rule of a mob of Communist soldiers, politicians, and intellectuals. (June 18, 1951)

In the Luce-*Time* view, the proper policy of the United States toward China was to stir up more of the above: "China's Red masters may be in for plenty of trouble," the magazine reported in the summer of 1951, "(and if the US chooses, it can increase that trouble)." Luce never openly advocated an invasion of China; it seems he hoped that one day the Communists would simply throw up their hands and go away. As late as January 1967, he was apparently still hoping. In a cover story entitled "China in Chaos" and dealing with the power struggle among the Chinese leaders and the activities of the Red Guards, *Time* reported: "To many observers in both the West and the East, it seemed as if China were reaching the final stages of the legendary dance of the scorpion—just before it stings itself to death." "The Great Revolution," the story added, "had clearly begun to devour itself." Anyone who has ever proposed that the reality of a Communist government in China be acknowledged was bitterly put down. In 1953, when the *New Statesman* suggested that the Chinese Communists be given a seat on the Security Council, so that "the cement that holds the Stalinite empire so rigidly together might begin to flake away," *Time* rejoined that the *New Statesman* "inhabits a pink cloud all its own."

A S ONE MOVES AWAY FROM POLITICS, *Time*'s "line" becomes harder to discern. In its coverage of the arts, for example, the magazine has been fairly catholic in its interests and tastes. Sometimes, it is true, the Books section has been used to support the political views of the magazine—as when a recent review of *The Autobiography of Bertrand Russell* turned out to be little more than an attack on Russell's present politics. But it is also true that *Time*'s cultural departments have occasionally differed from the rest of the magazine in permitting the individual voice of a single writer to emerge—as in the days when James Agee was writing movie criticism and when Louis Kronenberger was the magazine's drama critic. One reason for this is that critical judgment in the arts is by its very nature resistant to a collective line and to collective journalism. Luce's indifference to most areas of culture may well be another reason; insofar as one can discover, he had no great interest in secular literature, visual art, music, or drama. He may have allowed his critics their own points of view for the simple reason that he did not believe in the power of art to move men's minds.

Yet no artist is honored by a *Time* cover story unless he meets one of two criteria: he must either be financially successful or make extraordinarily good copy (preferably both). In literature, recent *Time* cover-story subjects have included such disparate types as Herman Wouk (1955), James Gould Cozzens (1957), Boris Pasternak (1958), Yevgeny Yevtushenko (1962), James Baldwin (1963), and Phyllis McGinley (1965). Slowly developing talent and hard-won achievement in the arts have never been among *Time's* excessive concerns; flashiness and the flat dead level of the "interesting" have always been. In the mid-1950s the Luce publications thus latched on with great excitement to the antics of the Beat Generation. Even now they are said to employ a woman who serves as their connection to the American avant garde, such as it is, and whose job is to ferret out and report on the more exotic goings-on in the artistic underground.

To return now to our original question: was Luce a great editor-journalist? Was he a missionary or Muggeridge's "piano player in a brothel"? Did he guide public opinion or merely reflect it? The answer is necessarily a mixed one. While the spirit of the missionary ran deep in Luce, it was frequently in conflict with the spirit of the businessman-journalist, which (China always excepted) more often than not won out. Luce's stand in the 1964 Presidential election is a case in point. One of his deepest commitments, surely, was to the Republican party, but he failed to support Barry Goldwater. It may well have been that Goldwater's Republicanism was too much even for Henry Luce, though the two men probably agreed on a number of fundamental issues. But it may also have been the case that the businessman-journalist in Luce, sensing which way the wind was blowing, managed to still the voice of the journalist-missionary. Again always excepting China, Luce seems to have had a nice sense of how far he could go without discrediting his magazines in the eyes of the general public. Whatever his missionary impulse, Luce always managed to keep that piano handy.

THOUGH HENRY LUCE WAS SOMETHING LESS than a complete tyrant who imposed a monolithic line on *Time*, a subtle totalitarian influence has nevertheless been at work on the magazine for years. To discover that influence, one must turn to the editorial practices and organization of *Time*. As Luce and Briton Hadden recognized more than forty-five years ago, the intended audience of *Time* lacked the "time" properly to inform itself of what was going on in the world—and time, as they say, is money. But they also recognized that it wasn't enough simply to inform people; they had also to be entertained. These insights led to *Time*'s standard practice of dramatizing the news, making of every little item a short story whose point and purpose cannot be mistaken. "I am," Luce once allowed, "all for titillating trivialities. I am all for the epic touch. I could almost say that everything in *Time* should be either titillating or epic or starkly, super-curtly, factual."

But to titillate and apply the epic touch—let that "starkly, super-curtly, factual" go for a moment—required talent, as Luce and Hadden were well aware, and talent of a kind that was likely to be expensive. *Time*'s first foreign news editor, an Englishman named Thomas J. C. Martyn, was hired at a larger salary than that of either of the magazine's two founders. Luce's magazines were among the first on which the editorial budget was not slighted. He might exhort his employees to be "troubadours of the Lord," but the rewards which Time Inc. conferred upon its editors were by no means confined to the afterlife.

"You get what you pay for," to quote another business maxim, and the talent that has gone through the mill at Time Inc. has been of a very high order. The phenomenon of intellectuals who have worked for Henry Luce constitutes an interesting chapter in the 20th-century history of that class. Besides Agee and Kronenberger, the roll call of Luce's employees at one time or another included Stephen Vincent Benet, Archibald MacLeish, John O'Hara, J. K. Galbraith, Theodore H. White, Alfred Kazin, John Chamberlain, Daniel Bell, Whittaker Chambers, Dwight Macdonald, John Hersey, William Schlamm, and Robert Cantwell.

Hadden's biographer, Noel Busch, is by no means a hostile critic of *Time*, but he makes a similar, if more moderate, assessment when he states that "writers of strongly personalized talent rarely found the medium much to their taste." It is interesting to note that, despite Time Inc.'s various stylistic innovations and all the talent that has been lodged there over the years, perhaps the only genuine work of art produced under the corporation's auspices has been Agee's *Let Us Now Praise Famous Men*. Written originally for *Fortune*, it never appeared there, because it was considered altogether too uneven and complex for that magazine's readers.

Few of the writers who have gone to work for *Time* started out with the assumption that they would spend many years there. One imagines that they planned to write "on the side" while taking home those hefty Luce paychecks, and dreamed of an early day when the recognition and rewards due their own work would allow them to quit *Time*. But, as is often the case with writers who in an analogous fashion decide to turn out potboilers to finance their masterpieces, it seldom worked out that way; they tended to get caught up in the system.

T. S. Matthews and Whittaker Chambers are characteristic instances. Matthews came to *Time* from the *New Republic*. Starting out as a part-time book reviewer who for the most part worked at home, he ended up, twenty-four years later, as principal editor: "My work week was then about seventy hours, packed into five days." Chambers also started out as a *Time* book reviewer. Over the years he rose to Senior Editor, and at one time he was in charge of thirteen sections of *Time*. He called it an invaluable experience, though "it was somewhat like working directly behind a buzz saw, chewing metal faster than the eye can follow and throwing off an unremitting shower of sharp and shining filings." During this period, Chambers and an assistant "ended our week at four o'clock in the morning after having worked for thirty-six hours, almost without stopping and wholly without sleep. We kept up the pace by smoking five or six packs of cigarettes and drinking thirteen or fourteen cups of coffee a day."

How was Luce able to get such Sisyphean labors from his employees? There was, of course, the money—for example, within nine years Chambers saw his salary raised roughly six-fold, to the extraordinary (for 1948) figure of almost $30,000. But money wasn't the whole story. Even those who came to *Time* with stark cynicism were likely to be infected by the seriousness with which the magazine took itself. Surely no one could have been more cynical about the magazine at the start than T. S. Matthews. As he writes in his autobiography:

> The contrast I felt between the *New Republic* and *Time* was a contrast between scholarly, distinguished men and smart, ignorant boys. The *New Republic* did not exist primarily to call attention to itself; it had the nobler motive (or so it seemed to me) of trying to recall Americans to their better senses. The *New Republic* was a failure. And what was *Time* up to? As far as I could see, *Time* simply wanted to succeed, to get bigger, to get all the readers it could collect by exhibiting its bumptious, impertinent, adolescent self. After it grew up . . . but I couldn't imagine *Time* growing up.

Twenty-odd years later, however, there was Matthews, dead on his feet after a seventy-hour week at *Time*.

DWIGHT MACDONALD tells a revealing anecdote. He worked on *Fortune* for six years during the 1930s, and in his spare time began editing a little literary magazine. Thinking to impress his boss with his new cultural enterprise, he sent a copy up to Luce. Far from being impressed, Luce felt betrayed. "But Henry," Macdonald said, "you can't expect *Fortune* to be my only interest. I give it a good day's work from nine to five, that's what you pay me for, and it's my business what I do in my spare time." Luce didn't see it that way. "This is," he told his employee, "a twenty-four hour profession, you never know when you may get an idea for us, and if you're all the time thinking of some damn little magazine. . . ."

This attitude of Luce's undoubtedly contributed greatly to Time Inc.'s success, especially in the case of *Time*. That he was able to secure such great devotion from so many able men is especially impressive in view of the fact that his employees had to forgo much of the pleasure that ordinarily attends a journalist's work. The reasons for going into journalism are usually four in number: (1) ego satisfaction in one form or another; (2) aesthetic satisfaction; (3) money; and (4) a chance to alter the world in some small way. By implementing the editorial practice known as "group journalism," a practice devised by himself and Briton Hadden, and one integral to *Time*, Luce in one swoop did away with reasons (1) and (2).

Group journalism is what it says it is: writing produced not individually but cooperatively by a team composed of writers, researchers, correspondents, and editors. *Newsweek*, which took over the practice from *Time*, has described it in its ideal form:

> Group journalism is a demanding craft which at its best can (and often does) produce journalism of the highest order. Theoretically no one man is master, not even of the coverage of such specialized subjects as medicine, fiscal affairs, or science—no one man, except, that is, for the man at the top of the pyramid; and he, in turn is (or should be) strongly susceptible to the advice, background, and judgment of those under him. Thus reporters and correspondents often file vast and meticulously researched reports on a given subject, only to see their labors appear in print as a concentrated distillation of a few hundred words.

In practice, group journalism achieves nothing so much as to put the journalistic coverage of an event at several removes from the direct experience of it. Let us assume for a moment that *Time* is planning to do a cover story on the Union of South Africa. The mighty and smooth wheels of group journalism will roll in the following fashion. The magazine's African correspondents will file reports on the country, its research staff will get up all sorts of additional statistical and other factual matter. All the material will then be placed on the desk of the editor assigned to write the story. As like as not, this editor will never have been to South Africa, so his job will call not merely for expository skills but for certain powers of invention. One of his tasks will be to lend authenticity to the story—in other words, to belie the fact that it is being written in New York. Our imaginary writer will have to depict South Africa's *veld* and mining towns, neither of which he has ever set eyes on; he will have to describe the faces of politicians on the basis of photographs, and the Afrikaans accent of the Prime Minister, which he has never heard; he will have to insert all manner of facts and statistics, of whose real significance he is ignorant. When he has finished, the country of South Africa will doubtless have taken on a few new dimensions, and everything will be at one substantial remove from reality.

The story will now go to the Senior Editor in charge of international news, who will no doubt want to sharpen it up a little: state the issues somewhat more forcibly, describe at greater length the desolation of the compounds in which the Blacks live, interlard the story with a few more statistics. The story is now at another remove from actuality and ready for the perusal of the Managing Editor. Though the copy should be in pretty good order by this time, the Managing Editor might be in a mood to add a touch or two of his own (give the Prime Minister another wart, lend his smile a slight twist). If the subject is one on which *Time* has a "line," the story will now be sent upstairs—formerly to Luce, now perhaps to Hedley Donovan, his most trusted associate and currently Editor-in-Chief—for further tinkering and yet another distancing from first-hand experience.

At some time during all this; the story will be sent back to Research. Those facts which have been wrenched out of all shape will have to be modulated somewhat; outright errors will have to be corrected; the various editors' imaginations will have to be forced into some accommodation to the hard information. Finally, the piece will be printed and read and no doubt enjoyed by almost everyone except those who happen to have been in South Africa and know what it is really like; such people are likely to experience a strange, rather queasy feeling.

It is one of the unmistakable signs of writing produced by group journalism that it violates one's personal knowledge of what it describes. Edmund Wilson has made much the same point:

> *Time*'s picture of the world gives us sometimes simply the effect of schoolboy mentalities in a position to avail themselves of a gigantic research equipment; but it is almost always tinged with a peculiar kind of jeering rancor. There is a tendency to exhibit the persons whose activities are chronicled, not as more or less able or noble or amusing or intelligent human beings, who have various ways of being right or wrong, but—because they are presented by writers who are allowed no points of view themselves—as manikins, sometimes cocky, sometimes busy, sometimes zealous, sometimes silly, sometimes gruesome, but in most cases quite infra-human, who make speeches before guinea-pig parliaments, issue commands and move armies of beetles back and forth on bas-relief battle-maps, indulge themselves maniacally in queer little games of sport, science, art, beer-bottle-top collecting or what not, squeak absurd little boasts and complaints, and pop up their absurd little faces in front of the lenses of the Luce photographers, and add up to a general impression that the pursuits, past and present, of the human race are rather an absurd little scandal about which you might find out some even nastier details if you met the editors of *Time* over cocktails. . . .

It should be added that *Time* is not altogether insensible of some of the defects of group journalism. A former editor informs me that, whenever possible, *Time* writers are now sent out on a whirlwind tour (often at lavish expense) of the place they are assigned to write about. But this does not and cannot change the decisive fact that they are allowed no point of view of their own. Nor are their manuscripts ever really free from all sorts of editorial infringement by their superiors. So entrenched is the practice of group journalism at *Time* that Henry Luce himself was prepared to submit to it. T. S. Matthews tells a story of a piece Luce had written about a speech by Charles Lindbergh on isolationism; the piece was, for *Time*, highly unorthodox. In the editorial process, the lead had been lopped off and the rest largely rewritten. "Well," said Luce, upon reading his mangled copy, "quite a lot of it got by."

"How can *Time* get very close to reality," Dwight Macdonald has written, "when every story has to be tailored and tortured into a little drama, with an angle, a climax, an arresting lead, and a 'kicker' at the end?" As a B-movie contorts human experience, snuffing out its complexity and tidying up its loose ends for an audience which has, after all, come primarily to be entertained, so does *Time* magazine: the B-movie of current events and personalities.

But B-movies are usually harmless, because they do not deal with real people and events; *Time* does, and is often harmful. P. G. Wodehouse has said, "*Time* is about the most inaccurate magazine in existence. They will write just about anything to be picturesque and amusing." During Wodehouse's internment by the Germans in World War II, *Time* had him, he says, "'throwing a cocktail party in the jolly old pine woods at Le Touquet' as the German army was sweeping toward Paris." "Can you imagine the bastards inventing an idiotic story like that?" he asked. "Apparently everyone believed the story because it has been picked up time and again. It did me a lot of harm twenty years ago, and is still repeated often. It is embedded in the world's folklore—thanks to the inventiveness of one of *Time*'s editors."

One wonders whether this is what Henry Luce had in mind by the "starkly, super-curtly, factual." Which brings us to the subject of the anonymity of *Time* writing, which not only makes it easy to be irresponsible but serves other functions. For one thing, it gives an evenness of tone and style to each week's issue, a uniformity to the whole product. It also lends specious authority to what is being written about, as if the magazine were produced not by insignificant human beings but by an omniscient machine. At present, there is no distinct *Timestyle* in the sense that there was one in Briton Hadden's day, and for some time afterward. "Backward ran sentences until reeled the mind," Wolcott Gibbs noted of that style; now the sentences run forward, though the mind might still reel. "The overwhelming fact about *Time*," as Marshall McLuhan has written, "is its style. It has often been said that nobody could tell the truth in *Time* style." But the truth is one thing, the demands of the product another. What Luce and Hadden in their original prospectus for *Time* called the "complete organization of the news" has actually turned out to be a consummate packaging job. It may be the most artful packaging job in the history of publishing, giving its readers the illusion that by investing a few hours of time they can acquire knowledge of everything of interest that has happened in the world during the past week. "*Time*," according to McLuhan, "is a nursery book in which the reader is slapped and kicked alternately. It is full of predigested pap, spooned out with confidential nudges. The reader is never on his own for an instant, but, as though at his mother's knee, he is provided with the right emotions for everything he hears and sees as the pages turn."

As *Newsweek* reported in its cover story on Luce:

> By last week, in fact, there were at least 50 journals throughout the world that trace their origins to some extent to the ideas first incorporated in *Time*. They run the gamut

from the prestigious West German *Spiegel* and France's *Express* to the smudgily similar but eagerly read magazines that appear in some half-dozen newly independent African nations.

Perverse, but apparently true, the Oxford Don, the Brooklyn mechanic, the Lebanese merchant, the writer of this article, and (with a little training) the African tribal chief are all eager to store up a little information each week about Coptic art, leather lungs, Carnaby Street, NATO, what's doing with Liz and Richard Burton, etc., etc.

What does all this information add up to? The answer, of course, is nothing; it all adds up to absolutely nothing. But for Henry Luce's employees the question was not so easy to avoid. After six years as editor of *Time*, T. S. Matthews asked himself:

> And what did I accomplish in those six years? Nothing tangible, visible, or lasting, as far as I could see. . . . I was sometimes told that I had 'changed the tone' of Time—which I am quite sure I didn't—or at least had left some ephemeral impress on the magazine. I could never see any signs of that myself, much as I should have liked to see them.

Ezra Goodman, for years *Time*'s Hollywood correspondent, tells of a colleague who answered the question in less articulate fashion. "Every morning before leaving for work," Goodman reports, "he would throw up."

How did HENRY LUCE view his own accomplishments? In judging himself he usually bowed to the spirit of business and the specter of public opinion. ". . . All our publications, all our activities, are successful," he once said. "They are successful not only at the box office, but they are successful also in the opinion of a large part of mankind. This is a considerable consolation for our efforts over the years."

But Luce also had another standard for assessing men and their achievements. Of Douglas MacArthur he once remarked to Emmet John Hughes: "You may not like him, but he meets the test of greatness. He *fills* the living space around him. He cannot be trespassed upon, or toyed with, or subtracted from. Whatever ground he stands on, it is *his.*" He probably would have liked to be judged in the same way, and it is a measure of his influence that by and large he was. Writing in *Newsweek*, Hughes said of Luce: *"He* plainly filled the space around him. He made the ground he stood on truly—sometimes defiantly—*his.* And so his life served its sovereign and precise purpose: to make some difference to history." The *New Yorker's* TV critic, M. J. Arlen, suggested that television could stand more men of the stature of Luce:

> One thing you could say for Henry Luce—when you picked up one of his magazines, especially *Time*, you really felt his presence. Think of it—all those pages, pictures, words, long series on snakes and Art, and whatever happened to the Holy Roman Empire, and you felt that presence of this one man.

And in the *Saturday Review*, Herbert R. Mayes went so far as to suggest that Luce would have made a "superb President," adding: "I am content, however, that he gave himself to publishing."

There was in Luce all that energy, all that religious zeal to do good, and it all came to so little. Through the agency of his magazines, he confused more issues than he clarified, harmed more people than he helped, and contributed more to the Gross National Product than to American culture. Commenting on Luce's death, Lyndon Johnson, then President of the United States, declared: "The magazines which bear his stamp are an authentic part of life in America." Since Luce's ardent dream for an "American Century" has soured for so many—even this well-intended accolade is ambiguous. *Time* marches on even after the death of Henry Luce, but when one views his life one is haunted by a line from Shelley's "Ozymandias," a line which in one of his rare introspective moments, Luce himself might have uttered: "Look on my works, ye Mighty, and despair!"

Ralph Ellison

Indivisible Man

T HE NOVELIST RALPH ELLISON grew up, poor and black
and (past the age of three) fatherless, in Oklahoma City
under the reign of Jim Crow. After working at various ser-
vile jobs, he was able to scrimp up enough money to go off—riding the rails, hobo-fashion, to get there—to Tuskegee Institute in
Alabama. His first ambition was to become a composer of classical
music; he also played trumpet. At Tuskegee he was stymied by lack
of funds and a homosexual dean of students who made life difficult
for him. He did encounter a few gifted teachers at Tuskegee and
a librarian who befriended him and introduced him to the great
modernist writers: T. S. Eliot, André Malraux, James Joyce, and
William Faulkner were the main figures in his literary pantheon.

Departing Tuskegee without a degree, Ellison moved to New
York in the middle of the Depression, where he fell in with men and
women connected to the Communist party. He was befriended by
Langston Hughes and Richard Wright, both of whom turned his
ambitions away from music, and a passing interest in sculpture,
and onto literature. He wrote journalism and criticism for *The*

New Masses and other party publications. But literature for Ellison meant the novel. After publishing a number of short stories, he worked for more than seven years on *Invisible Man*, which he published in 1952, at the age of 39. *Invisible Man* was the one novel he would complete in his life, a book that was immediately recognized as the powerful and subtle and richly complex work that it is. The novel lent him renown of a kind that he was able to live off for the remainder of his life (he died in 1994, at the age of 81).

The fame of *Invisible Man* brought Ralph Ellison lucrative university jobs (with little teaching required), gave him an allure as a candidate for membership on boards of various nonprofit organizations from the early National Council on the Arts to the founding of public television to the Williamsburg Foundation. In good part, his attractiveness to the people who made such appointments was that, during the most feverish days of the civil rights movement, he refused to conduct himself as angry or in any way as a victim. Instead Ellison relentlessly insisted on the complexity of Negro (a word he used as an honorific) experience in a pluralist America he hoped would continue along an integrationist path.

Ralph Ellison had all the accoutrements of literary and intellectual success—those boards, lots of honorary degrees and other awards, high lecture fees and other emoluments that fall into the laps of the famous—but his was far from a happy life. Because of his stand on racial matters, he was often under attack by militant younger blacks, who accused him of being a sellout, calling him an Uncle Tom; in their view he was, as sixties radicals liked to say, part of the problem.

Then there was the blasted question of the second novel, the novel to follow *Invisible Man* that, like Godot, was long awaited but never arrived. (Some of the parts were assembled after his death by his literary executor and editor, a man named John F. Callahan, to form a disappointing book called *Juneteenth*.) *Invisible Man* was Ralph Ellison's first extended work of fiction; *Invisible*

RALPH ELLISON

Novel might cruelly be said to be his second. His inability to complete this book had to have been a crushing weight on Ellison, as an artist and as a man.

So what looked from the distance to be a charmed life was, viewed from closer up, a complicated, in some ways even a quite sad, life. Possibly the saddest thing to have happened to Ralph Ellison came after he died, when the assignment of writing his biography was given to Arnold Rampersad. The author of two previous biographies—one of Jackie Robinson, another of Langston

Hughes—Rampersad is an academic (a teacher at Princeton, now at Stanford), a writer one thinks of as reverential and hence quite uncritical toward his subjects. But in *Ralph Ellison*, far from being reverential or uncritical, he is unrelenting in the persistence of his pinpoint attacks on his subject's character and politics and highly critical of much of his writing, only rarely giving his subject the least hint of the benefit of any possible doubt.

The tip-off for the kind of book Rampersad has written comes in its blurbs, four of five of which are provided by writers who comprise the main body of the African-American intellectual establishment in America: the literary critic and historian Henry Louis Gates Jr., the biographer (of W. E. B. Du Bois) David Levering Lewis, the philosopher Cornel West, and the novelist Toni Morrison. (Where, one wonders, was Maya?) In his play *Purlie Victorious*, Ossie Davis has one of his characters say to another, "You are a disgrace to the Negro profession." This, really, is the charge, the organizing principle behind Arnold Rampersad's attack on Ralph Ellison: he was a disgrace to the Negro (now African-American) profession. Ellison would, of course, have understood, for there were few things he disliked more than the notion of black establishments and an African-American profession.

Here, without the tedium of his repeated charges, is Rampersad's bill of complaint against Ralph Ellison: He was an ungrateful son, a bad brother, a cheating and otherwise often cruel husband, an unreliable friend. He was a spendthrift (on himself), a cheapskate (when it came to other people), a snob, an elitist, an ingrate, ill tempered; also condescending, disloyal, a sloppy, sometimes mean, drunk. Did I neglect to mention that he was a misogynist, pretentious, and without elementary sympathy for the young? And, oh yes, he was a boring teacher—though, for some unexplained reason, he failed to sleep with his students. Other than that he was not at all a bad guy.

Rampersad's is a full-scale biography, running to 672 pages including scholarly apparatus, and has the dead, heavy feel of the definitive work on Ralph Ellison. The book is filled with useful information—in the Oklahoma City of Ralph Ellison's youth, blacks could buy clothes in shops owned by whites but were not allowed to try them on (nor, one assumes, return them if they were ill-fitting)—and is richly detailed about its subject's personal life. Ellison's correspondence, diaries, income tax forms, financial life generally have all been carefully scrutinized by his biographer. Just about everyone still alive who knew Ellison has been interviewed for this book. (I was not, though my single, utterly delightful meeting with Ralph Ellison, a four-and-a-half hour lunch he stood me to at the Century Association in New York, an occasion I shall never forget.) Rampersad has put together what at times feels like a day-to-day chronicle of the life of a writer who, increasingly as the years passed, did less and less writing.

The theme of *Ralph Ellison* is set out on the book's second page:

> Clinging fearlessly and stubbornly to the ideal of harmonious racial integration in America, [Ellison] found it hard to negotiate the treacherous currents of American life in the volatile 1960s and 1970s. Although he always saw himself as above all an artist, and published a dazzling book of cultural commentary in 1964 [*Shadow and Act*, A collection of essays], his later successes were relatively modest. For some of his critics, his life was finally a cautionary tale to be told against the dangers of elitism and alienation, especially alienation from other blacks.

Everything in this indictment is true. Ralph Ellison did consider himself, above all, an artist; he did believe in the ideal of integration of the races in America, with blacks never losing the valuable cultural experience that was theirs alone; he was an elitist, insofar as he believed in the importance of pursuing the best in Western and American Negro folk culture above all others; and finally, in the realm of art, he saw no reason to favor, or even lend particular sympathy to, black writers simply because they happened to be black. Such are the counts on which Rampersad puts Ralph Ellison on trial. The question is, Do any of them constitute real crimes, or do they bring honor to the man who has been put into the dock by his prosecutorial biographer?

Ellison, in fact, thought himself primarily an artist and, as such, felt that his art came before his politics. In this, he joins a long tradition of writers. Ivan Turgenev, who felt as Ellison did, wrote: "I pay attention to politics only in so far as a writer is called upon to depict contemporary life must." Of course, Ellison knew that the Jim Crow laws in the South were intolerable, for he grew up under them; he knew, too, that, though things in the North were better, race prejudice remained very much a going concern there, too. He could be quite properly ticked, sometimes to the point of rage, when he felt himself the victim of racial discrimination.

At the same time, Ellison felt it important to keep a careful distance from full engagement with political action, and never sought to be a spokesman for his people. He loathed the notion of blacks as pure victims, which gained currency during the 1960s; he abominated the heightened racial rhetoric of Stokely Carmichael, H. Rap Brown, and other of the young radical civil rights figures, rhetoric that is, alas, still occasionally put into play today.

Although Rampersad does not do so in any large-scale way, the figure whose career Ralph Ellison's might be most profitably compared to is that of James Baldwin. As a young man, Baldwin wrote against the protest novel; as an essayist, he commanded a prose style that seemed neither black nor white, but instead was authoritative, elegant, above race, in the best sense. (Baldwin's fiction, much overrated, was described, accurately, by Truman Capote as "balls-achingly boring," though this hasn't stopped it from being enshrined in the Library of America.) But Baldwin soon found another, more popular, way. As described by Rampersad, "he was attracting celebrities and many younger blacks alike with a combination of militancy and supplicating eloquence, his sensual hugging of America and yet his rejection of it." Rampersad quotes, without comment, a standard Baldwin utterance: "I don't want to be fitted into this society. There's no difference between being fitted into this society and dying." Those may be fighting words, but they are also foolish and not in the least helpful ones.

Ellison did not think much of James Baldwin, who he thought was trying "to inflate his personal problem to the dimension of a national problem." (Saul Bellow, always mindful of the possibility of malice extended to a fellow scribbler, once told me that Baldwin's problem was simple: "He wanted to be Martin Luther Queen.") The rhetoric of public rage and the tactics of easy demagoguery never impressed Ellison, who held a low view of those who specialized in it, which included Malcolm X, LeRoi Jones (later, in his anti-Semitic phase, known as Amin Baraka), and the youthful advocates of the Black Power movement. Ellison saw the latter as "a disruptive force that depended on insult, rage, and antagonism." He never says so directly, but it is clear that Rampersad would have preferred it had Ellison dropped his critical scruples and got on the bus by showing a simpler, more direct solidarity with fellow blacks, no matter what their foibles.

Ralph Ellison was an artist and an independent intellectual and he didn't want anyone to tell him what stands to take or how he ought to interpret his own experience as a Negro, an American, or a writer. When the critic Irving Howe wrote an essay in the early 1960s suggesting that Ellison and (the not-yet-militant) Baldwin ought to write in the tradition of Negro protest, Ellison wrote a scorchingly brilliant reply that removed what remained of the scant hair on Howe's head: "The greatest difficulty for a Negro writer," Ellison wrote, "was the problem of revealing what he really felt, rather than serving up what Negroes were supposed to feel, and were encouraged to feel."

For these same reasons, Ellison was an early opponent of sociology, with all its studies of how American blacks lived and felt and believed. This enmity toward the social sciences plays throughout his career; he rejected the Moynihan Report, arguing that Daniel Patrick Moynihan "looked at a fatherless family, and interpreted it not in the context of Negro cultural patterns, but in a white cultural pattern." His case against social science generally was that it treated people "as abstractions and ignored the complexity of actual experience." The artist is always interested in the exception that proves no rule.

Ellison insisted on the complexity of his own experience as a Negro, feeling that no one from outside that experience was in a position to interpret it. So strongly did he believe this that he even wrote a strongly negative review of Gunnar Myrdal's *An American Dilemma*, even though the book was a strong argument against the injustice of American social arrangements to African-Americans.

Arnold Rampersad does not entirely ignore such problems and issues in Ellison's life and in America itself. But the greater impression his biography leaves is of Ellison as a man of almost uniformly wrong, and therefore ultimately pernicious, opinions. Most of these opinions, as we shall see, violate the canons of political correctness.

Here are the opinions, or absence of acceptable opinions, for which Rampersad holds Ellison at fault:

- He gave insufficient credit to the influence of the writers of the Harlem Renaissance on his own career.
- He had a low view of all-black colleges.
- He held to a line of "liberal cosmopolitanism," which meant that he remained committed to the grandeur of high modernism in art and cultivated friendly contact with whites.
- In a letter about Vermont to his friend Ida Guggenheimer, he failed to mention "the tragic fate of the Algonquin and Iroquois nations."
- He tended to be optimistic in matters of race. Sometimes he spoke as if there were things more important than race: "Here's to integration," he wrote in later years

to one of his teachers at Tuskegee, "the only integration that matters: integration of the personality." He even claimed that "my problems are not primarily racial problems, that they are the problems of a writer."

- The developing countries, those in Africa prominent among them, meant little to him, or at least he failed publicly to voice his concern about them; he never even had an African in his and his wife's home.
- He "refused to blame [the poverty and squalor of Pakistan and India] on European colonialism."
- He was not for affirmative action, even thought it in fact likely to be deleterious to young blacks.

The list goes on:

- He didn't care for the dark, often drug-driven Miles Davis, John Coltrane, Charlie Parker strain in jazz, preferring the music of Duke Ellington and Louis Armstrong.
- He didn't think Norman Mailer much of a writer, and thought that he and the Beats were "all trying to reduce the world to sex."
- He never opposed the Vietnam War, having felt indebted to Lyndon Johnson for his civil rights legislation and for his personal courtesy to him, Ellison.
- His response to the death of Martin Luther King "would remain muted."
- He preferred to be called "Negro."
- He argued for the need for a solid black middle class.
- Once a member of the Century Association in New York, he put forth no fellow blacks and opposed the membership of women when it was up for a vote: "No women, and especially young black women," were among his inner circle of friends.
- The only black artist that he praised without qualification was the painter Romare Bearden.

And to complete the checklist, though he was generally liberal, "exuberant gay culture offended him."

With such ghastly opinions as these, is there anything that could redeem Ellison? Redemption isn't Rampersad's game; instead he sets out to nail his subject more firmly to the cross by filling us in on all his personal peccadilloes. A man on the wrong side of so many right opinions cannot, surely, be very decent generally; how else would he come to hold such wretched opinions if, in the first place, he did not suffer grave flaws in character?

Rampersad highlights those flaws. He portrays Ralph Ellison as a thoughtless son. He is always the operator; apropos of a woman with whom Ellison had an affair, Rampersad notes that "he was already a cautious man [whose] instinct was to avoid risk." Speculating on the bust-up of Ellison's first marriage, his biographer writes: "Perhaps his coldness and cruelty—the result of his own lifetime of suffering—had worn her down." He was early on to "the shrewd cultivation of whites on which Ralph, eager to succeed and optimistic about human nature, would build much of his success."

From here it is a short hop to the fact that, in his winning the National Book Award for *Invisible Man*, Ellison "was lucky in having three young, progressive Jewish writers on the [judging] panel." Rampersad is excellent at finding quotations from others to use against Ellison. Gore Vidal and Fred Dupee (a once-famous teacher in the English Department at Columbia) thought Ralph was "pompous and overbearing." He used his friendship with John Cheever to get himself elected to the American Academy of Arts and Letters. He wanted to live the WASP life, at least as he imagined it; here Rampersad quotes William Styron saying that "Ralph had a deep-seated need to be a member of the establishment." He and his wife had close friendships with Robert Penn Warren and Richard Wilbur and their wives—not, apparently, a good thing. He really didn't know many blacks, Rampersad contends, though he allows that Ellison's two closest friends, Albert Murray and Nathan Scott, were black.

At the most trivial level, Rampersad describes Ellison wearing a fedora in a photograph on the cover of the *Atlantic* "covering his baldness." At the most serious, and vicious, he writes that "each terrible event [referring to the riots and assassinations of 1968] meant, perversely, more prestige and money for Ralph" in honors and speaking fees. This biography is, in short, a lynching, and the coarse rope used to hang the victim is political correctness.

This endless picking away at Ralph Ellison's ostensible flaws, political and characterological, is finally put to the service of a literary criticism meant to supply the reason for Ellison's inability to complete a second novel: "His inability to create an art that held a clean mirror up to 'Negro' life as blacks actually led it," Rampersad writes, "especially at or near his own social level, was disabling him as a writer. As a novelist, he had lost his way. And he had done so in proportion to his distancing himself from his fellow blacks."

This is unpersuasive, for various reasons. The first is that Ralph Ellison knew African-American culture with a depth of understanding available to few others, and he demonstrated this in a number of brilliant pieces in his two essay collections (*Shadow and Act* and *Going to the Territory*). He did not cut himself off from blacks, but merely kept his distance from those whose calling card was the race card. He was cold to Toni Morrison, Rampersad reports; he chose not to eulogize James Baldwin at his funeral. But what if he simply hadn't much regard for either Morrison or Baldwin, as a person or as a writer? One has only to read Ellison on jazz and gospel music to realize how little cut off he was from African-American culture.

If one has to arrive at a reason for Ellison's failure to complete a second novel, my own best guess is that the enormous critical success of *Invisible Man* was too tough an act to follow. *Invisible Man* was a novel that not only won all the prizes of its day, but in 1965, in a poll of critics and writers, was voted the most distinguished American novel written since World War II. It is probably still entitled to that accolade. Although the book reads less power-fully today, having perhaps too heavy an anchor in the time of its creation, when the American Communist party was still a force and Jim Crow was a bird found aloft everywhere in American life, *Invisible Man* remains a dazzling achievement.

Poor Ellison worked away on his always-almost-nearly-com-pleted second novel for more than 40 years. Bits and pieces of it appeared in little magazines; a large portion of it was said to have burned in a fire in his house in the Berkshires, though Ellison tended to exaggerate the extent of his loss; the number of its pages was reported (by Ellison) to be in the thousands. But the fact is, it was not close to finished—he could not give shape to all his scrib-blings on the book—and perhaps not really finishable.

Perhaps it is not a good idea to write a great book the first time out. Kingsley Amis made this mistake in writing *Lucky Jim*, which he never topped, but Amis went on to write a long line of less good novels. But American literary ambition operates differently than English: Can You Top This? is the name of the game as it is played here. Thomas Heggen, who wrote *Mr. Roberts*, and Ross Lock-ridge Jr., who wrote *Raintree County*, two enormous commercial successes, each killed himself because he couldn't finish a second work. "The greater the ambition," remarked Stanley Crouch apro-pos of Ellison's inability to complete a second novel, "the greater the failure." The torture of this great failure for Ellison must have been always present, souring all his private achievements.

Reading Rampersad's highly tendentious biography has had, at least on this reader, the reverse effect its author intended: It has convinced me that Ralph Ellison was an even greater man than I had thought. His greatness consisted of his never suggesting, when so many people would have been pleased to hear him do so, that America was a racist country and every black person in it born a victim; of his relentlessly insisting that we all make our own way, each with the unpredictable combination of gifts and talents and temperament that culture and race and nationality bestow; of his love for the black culture in which he was born and his deep understanding of its true richness; of his unflagging assertion that separatism, racial or any other kind, is always a mistake; of his keeping cool during a time of frenzy and easy rage while being insulted by many of the people who should have admired him most of all.

Arnold Rampersad understands none of this, which is why, my guess is, his *Ralph Ellison* figures to be a strong candidate to win next year's Pulitzer Prize for biography.*

---

* I am pleased to report that Professor Rampersad's book did not win a Pulitzer Prize.

Isaac Rosenfeld

With Love and Squalor

ENTION ISAAC ROSENFELD'S NAME, even to people
with literary interests, and they are likely to confuse
it with that of Isaac Rosenberg, the English poet who
died on the western front in France in 1918 at the age of twenty-
eight and whose poem "Break of Day in the Trenches" some say is
the greatest to come out of World War I. The other Isaac, Rosenfeld, was an American who died in 1956, at the age of thirty-eight,
alone, in an apartment in Chicago, leaving a small body of all too
perishable work and a large sad feeling of promise unfulfilled.

While he was alive and for a brief time after his death, Isaac
Rosenfeld enjoyed something like cult status among New York
intellectuals. In certain circles—at *Partisan Review* and at *Commentary*, down in Greenwich Village—if you were simply to say
"Isaac," everyone would have known of whom you spoke. He was
thought a golden boy, full of ideas and glitteringly fresh ways of
expressing them. He had come from Chicago and was two years
younger than his friend Saul Bellow, than whom he was, at the outset, thought to have had much greater prospects. "It should have

been Isaac," Bellow is supposed to have said upon learning that he had won the Nobel Prize.

Isaac Rosenfeld was an intellectual prodigy. He babbled not in numbers, as they used to say of the poets, but in ideas. Friends from his early Chicago days recall him discoursing on Schopenhauer while still in short pants. Bellow, who invented very little in his fiction, had an unfinished novel about Isaac Rosenfeld, a portion of which he published as a story called "Zetland: By a Character Witness," in which he writes about the Rosenfeld figure: "He was wonderful. At fourteen, when we became friends, he had things already worked out and would willingly tell you how everything had come about. . . . He was a clever kid. His bookishness pleased everyone." In a story called "The World of the Ceiling," Rosenfeld, in an obviously autobiographical reference, writes: "I was a very serious young man, interested only in philosophy and politics, with a way of wrinkling my face in thought which I had copied from a portrait of Hegel. I had no girl friends, no frivolities. I had a *Weltanschauung*."

The sons of immigrant parents, Isaac Rosenfeld and Saul Bellow grew up in the same neighborhood, Humboldt Park, part of the old Chicago Jewish west side, which fed into Tuley High School. Along with a handful of others at Tuley, they formed an outside group specializing in inside information about politics, music, the avant-garde, the great philosophical questions. The Depression was in full force, and for such boys books were their chief form of currency. In those bleak times there was little hope of career advancement, which, for young intellectuals, allowed the mind to concentrate on more serious things than merely getting ahead. "In my time," Rosenfeld wrote in his journals, "the young looked upon life as an adventure. Today, they regard it as an investment."

Intellectuals of the Depression generation have long since been replaced by that much narrower species known as public intellectuals, men and women who have columns or appear on television talk shows, affiliated with one of the two political parties, pushing one line or another. But the engagement with ideas possessed by intellectuals of Rosenfeld's day was both wider and deeper. An intellectual was then little more than the stock of his ideas, and these ideas extended well beyond anything so pedestrian as national politics. Dwight Macdonald once said—and he was doubtless speaking for most New York Intellectuals at the time—that he considered the two major American political parties as little more than Tweedledum and Tweedledumber. To be of interest politics had to be international, carrying a whiff of revolution, as did art; other ideas, to capture the imagination, needed to be universal in scope.

The deep engagement with ideas of the generation of the New York Intellectuals was not without its drawbacks. The main question, of course, is not about the value of this engagement per se, but about the quality of the ideas themselves. Marxism in politics, Modernism in art used to be the unspoken banner under which the old and immensely influential *Partisan Review* set sail. Ideas—political, artistic, psychological—were in the air, like so many viruses, bringing down unlikely victims. Today one is still astonished by the degree of commitment to Freudianism, now that it has been so largely discredited, of a man as subtle and as pledged to the complicated rendition of life and literature as Lionel Trilling, but deeply committed to it Trilling was.

The New York Intellectuals, that group of forty or so regular contributors to a small number of magazines—"intellectual marines," Auden wrote, "landing in little magazines"—chiefly interested themselves in ideas expressed through the form of literary criticism and essays. Although the collectivity called New York Intellectuals has by now been the subject of many books, and come to be viewed as an influential movement in American intellectual life, rather like the Transcendentalists in early 19th-century New England, many of the main figures among them are now sliding out of memory. Philip Rahv, William Phillips, Lionel Abel, Paul Goodman, Robert

Warshow, Meyer Schapiro, Leslie Fiedler, Harold Rosenberg, Elizabeth Hardwick, Diana Trilling—these are names now known only
to people of a certain age or of specialized interests.

Yet at the peak of their influence, during the decades after the
Second World War, the New York Intellectuals had great power.
Small though the circulation of their magazines was, these magazines were read with great care by the editors of *Time*, *Life*, *Newsweek*, the *New York Times*, and other organs of wide circulation.
Susan Sontag could publish an article in *Partisan Review* on the
subject of Camp, the homosexual style of deliberately comic, exag-
gerated vulgarity, and soon the word began popping up in *Vogue*
and *Harper's Bazaar*. In *Commentary* in 1958, Dwight Macdonald wrote a scorching attack on James Gould Cozzens's *By Love
Possessed* from which Cozzens's reputation, to this day, has never
revived. In letters to his friend Theodore Solotaroff, Philip Roth
reported that he found it difficult to write his first novel because he
was besieged by worry about what Irving Howe and Alfred Kazin
might think of it (not all that much, it turned out).

If THE NEW YORK INTELLECTUALS could be daunting to those
outside their magic circle, they could be positively vicious to
one another. Norman Podhoretz, himself a junior because younger
member of the group, referred to them as the Family. They were a
family, though, more in the pejorative than in the approbative sense:
envious, disputatious, always sniping at and cutting one another
down. I once told Saul Bellow that Irving Howe and Philip Rahv
were conducting a dispute on the nature of revolution in the letters
columns of the *New York Review of Books*. "Two old Jews arguing
in the back of the synagogue," he replied. "And what do they turn
out to be arguing about: Lady Astor's horse." In his journals, Isaac
Rosenfeld recounts Harold Rosenberg saying to Lionel Abel that,
over a long friendship, they rarely talked about anything personal.
Given the go-ahead to do so, Abel said: "I think you're wasting

your time writing nonsense and marginal stuff. You've never written anything central or important. And how can you stand Mae [Rosenberg's wife]? If you ask me, I think you should divorce her." In my one meeting with Alfred Kazin, every time he opened his mouth to speak of a fellow writer, a black toad came out. Jean Stafford, who was a peripheral member of the New York Intellectuals, once suggested to her husband A. J. Liebling that they attend a party of the group. "I don't want to go," said Liebling. "There'll be sheenies who are meanies."

Not that the New York Intellectuals were all Jewish, though Edmund Wilson used to call *Partisan Review* the "Partisansky Review." Mary McCarthy, Dwight Macdonald, James Agee, James Baldwin were not Jewish; and even the Jews among them weren't all that Jewish: Philip Rahv and William Phillips and Irving Howe changed their names from, respectively, Greenberg, Litvinsky, and Horenstein. Bellow and Rosenfeld had more Yiddishkeit than most. Bellow's translation from the Yiddish of Isaac Bashevis Singer's "Gimpel the Fool" had a lot to do with putting Singer's work before an American audience; and Rosenfeld and Bellow together translated a parody version, in Yiddish, of T. S. Eliot's "The Love Song of J. Alfred Prufrock": "I grow old, I grow old, and my bellybutton grows cold."

Bellow and Rosenfeld were further distinguished from the New York Intellectuals in their aspirations to be artists. Delmore Schwartz, who began as a poet of great but eventually unfulfilled promise, was the only other central figure among the New York Intellectuals not to think of himself as primarily a critic.

Where Rosenfeld and Bellow meshed with the New York Intellectuals is in the importance they placed on ideas. The red thread of a handful of ideas can be traced through Saul Bellow's career, most of them futile if not ridiculous, but which he evidently required, as they say, to function. Bellow's early life was given over to Trotskyism; then came the wild sexual theories of Wilhelm Reich, with its apparatus of the orgone box, literally a box (wood on the outside, lined with metal, called an Orgone Energy Accumulator) in which one sat to contemplate the cosmos and gather sexual energy; this was followed by the airy anthroposophical notions of Rudolf Steiner; and Bellow's career ended with a vague neo-Platonism learned at the feet of Allan Bloom, with souls mingling and meeting in the beyond. What helped redeem Bellow from this roiling pot of message was the recognition, set out to comic effect in his novels, of how preposterous so much of it could be. Intellectual among novelists and novelist of the intellectuals though Bellow was, no figures are more foolish in his novels than are intellectuals themselves, not least those who strikingly resemble their author, whose ideas are often badly buffeted by the world's harsh reality.

ISAAC ROSENFELD was, if anything, even more committed to ideas than Bellow. How deeply committed he was we now know with a certainty, owing to the publication of an earnest book about Rosenfeld by Steven J. Zipperstein, a professor of Jewish culture and history at Stanford. Zipperstein's is a sad, in many ways an unremittingly depressing book. How could it be otherwise? His subject is a writer who died so early in his life, with so much left undone. The story is one of a genuine talent that didn't develop, of passion misplaced and misplayed, of a life lived in great squalor, both intellectual and domestic.

"A secondary talent of the highest order" is the way a character in Wallace Markfield's roman á clef *To an Early Grave* describes Leslie Braverman, the character in the novel unmistakably based on Isaac Rosenfeld. "A secondary talent of the highest order" is, alas, an accurate assessment as far as it goes, but it doesn't quite capture what was essential in Isaac Rosenfeld. Although nothing he wrote is completely satisfying, everything had a touch of splendor about it. What remained after his death was a novel, *Passage from Home* (1946), published when he was twenty-eight; a book of stories,

Alpha and Omega (1966), published posthumously; and two different collections of reviews and stories: *The Age of Enormity* (1962, edited by Theodore Solotaroff) and *Preserving the Hunger* (1988, edited by Mark Shechner).

Rosenfeld, as Zipperstein's book makes clear, was more than the sum of his writings. No one who encountered him seems to have been untouched by the meeting. A small man, pudgy, bespectacled, striking a distinct note of schlepperosity in his clothes and grooming, he nonetheless captured attention wherever he went. Everyone who met him came away with an Isaac story. "I'll turn your insults into anecdotes," says the narrator of *To an Early Grave*, "your mishugass into myth."

In his memoirs, Irving Howe remembered Rosenfeld as a "Wunderkind grown into tubby sage. . . . Owlish and jovial but with sudden lifts of dignity, loving jokes even more than arguments, he had a mind strong at unsystematic reflection, though he never quite found the medium, in either fiction or essay, to release his gift." Rosenfeld made Howe feel "the world was spacious," and he "envied his staggering freedom." Yet, Howe concluded, "little remains of this flawed, noble spirit: a minor first novel, some fine critical miniatures, and a legend of charm and waste, a comic intelligence spent upon itself."

Alfred Kazin, in his memoir *New York Jew*, recalled Rosenfeld's mad restlessness. "He lived not like a writer but like a character in search of a plot. Every day, he woke up determined to be a new man, to recast everything, to try a new role, to be attractive, promiscuous, and wise." Kazin remembers Isaac sitting in his Reichian orgone box "as if he were waiting for a telephone call that was not coming through." Rosenfeld was a Reichian all his adult life.

Steven Zipperstein's is a more complex portrait. He feels that more is entailed in Isaac Rosenfeld's life than the story of early genius flaming out and ending in dismal failure, which is the standard view. He finds that Rosenfeld's talent was growing stronger as his life neared its end, that he may have begun to get his life in order and to live up to his promise. He thinks that the real meaning of Rosenfeld's life is to be found in his attempts to resolve the conflict between head and heart that should be at the center of everyone who sets out to live the life of the mind. "I came to see," Zipperstein writes, "that [the subject of this book] was more a reflection on a writer's sense of what it meant to be immersed in, and also deeply suspicious of, a life given over to books."

Rosenfeld's Lives is not, strictly speaking, a biography, but instead something closer to a study, with such biographical detail supplied as is required to understand its subject. Sometimes one longs for more in the way of detail; we learn, for example, that Isaac Rosenfeld left what sounds like a good job on the *New Republic*, but are not told why he left; late in his brief life, we are told that Rosenfeld was tooling around Chicago in a red convertible, but the year or make of the car isn't supplied. Still, Zipperstein's broad brushstrokes do render a strong portrait of Isaac Rosenfeld of a kind that, with a little imagination, allows one to fill in much that has been left out.

Saul Bellow is more than a supporting character in Zipperstein's account. Bellow and Rosenfeld, who "as always, each measured success with reference to the other," though ostensibly friends, were also natural competitors. For Zipperstein the problem is "how to write about failure, particularly played out against the backdrop of Bellow—one of the century's most fertile writers—and his achievements?" A tack that Zipperstein does not quite follow is to ask why these two writers, with such similar backgrounds, went on to such wildly different careers. What qualities did Bellow have, outside pure literary talent, that Rosenfeld lacked?

The first difference between Rosenfeld and Bellow is that Rosenfeld was the more passionate personality. He lived more freely, took more chances, was wilder in every way. Rosenfeld was a true bohemian, in spirit and in fact. "I have an idea," Bellow wrote, "that he found good, middle-class order devitalizing—a sign of meanness, stinginess, malice, and anality." ("Anality," a character in a Kingsley Amis novel exclaims, "my ass.") Bohemianism, in Rosenfeld's case, meant endless parties, around-the-clock disorder, talking the nights away, untrained dogs, neglected children, relentless gossip, domestic squalor of a very high order. Rosenfeld became a Greenwich Village character, ran with Paul Goodman and such tertiary and now forgotten writers as Milton Klonsky and Willie and Herb Poster. Jews have not been known to do well as bohemians; Modigliani, one recalls, living the bohemian life in Paris, died at thirty-five.

Bellow, on the other hand, was an imperfect *petit bourgeois*, always setting up house. How else account for his expensive hobby of marriage, an act he committed no fewer than five times, hope ever winning out for him over experience? Ever the guilty parent, the inadequate husband, Bellow, such was his yearning for a settled domestic life, was always ready, as the song goes, to pick himself up, dust himself off, and start all over again.

Rosenfeld married once, to a beautiful Greek-American named Vasiliki Sarantakis, who was quite as bohemian-scruffy in her instincts as he. They had two children together, a boy and a girl, and appear to have early settled into an easy promiscuity (Vasiliki, according to Zipperstein, at least once with Bellow) that appears to have brought both much misery. Artists not infrequently marry women or men who help stabilize their lives; in Rosenfeld's case, something closer to the reverse obtained. Ever the player, he used to speak of marriage as a "base of operations."

If Rosenfeld did anything to advance his career, his biographer hasn't been able to find it. He left jobs—on the *New Republic*, the *New Leader*—that might have helped promote and ultimately elevate his own reputation. He abandoned numerous novels; carried away by intellectual enthusiasms, he set out to write books on Tolstoy and on Gandhi, also never finished. All these projects joined, in Zipperstein's phrase, the "small mountain of incomplete manuscripts" that he couldn't sustain.

Bellow, meanwhile, was an immensely careful caretaker of his career. Perhaps the most famous phrase Isaac Rosenfeld ever wrote was his description of the young hero of *Passage from Home* as "sensitive as a burn." When it came to his own work, Bellow was touchier than ten burns, all on the face. Every less than ecstatic review of his novels was remembered. He discovered insults that were never launched. When John Updike corrected his grammar in a review, he chalked it up to anti-Semitism. In the mid-1970s, he told me that, by keeping his own counsel, he was defeating Norman Mailer and Robert Lowell in the literary PR wars. On another occasion, when someone accused him of being a less than ideal father, he told me that his novels consumed all the energy he had, with nothing left over for anything or anyone else, though this didn't stop him from acquiring more wives and more children.

The competition between Isaac Rosenfeld and Saul Bellow was in the end a competition that was no competition. Bellow had his novels and the world's many prizes, Rosenfeld had his failures and manifold regrets. "I see Saul once in a while—in fact, quite often—but still don't get along too well with him," Rosenfeld wrote to their high school friend Oscar Tarcov. "I'm jealous of him and I think he is of me: I'm ready to admit it, but I don't think he is. . . . He's poured everything into his work, which seems to be all he lives for. He's really very sad and the 'literary figure' and the self-consciousness don't hide it." Bellow, for his part, wrote to Tarcov, "I still resent his not too well-hidden hope that I will fall on my face. If we're ever to be friends again, that's got to stop."

PERHAPS THE CHIEF REASON that Rosenfeld failed while Bellow succeeded is that Rosenfeld genuinely believed in ideas, and, fatally, acted on those beliefs, whereas, in the realm of ideas, Bellow was in the final analysis a kibitzer, however charming a one. Rosenfeld lived his ideas, which can be a terrible mistake if the ideas themselves are defeating—and his were, damnably so. His fatal gift was his aptitude for and attraction to abstraction. "I have a severe case of analysitis," he said of his too deep involvement with Reichianism. "Away with this rubbish. I want to find myself. Me! Not a reaction formation, an oral sadistic neurosis, a fixation, by myself! This person I buried somewhere under all this rubbish." Yet his gift for abstraction could aid him in writing criticism often enlivened by brilliant formulation. Here, for example, is the concluding paragraph from his essay "Kafka and His Critics":

> Only now, with a knowledge of the end, can the beginning, the first of Kafka's symbols, his first parable, be explained. The order of interpretation is circular: the tautology of art has been achieved, but also its truth, and the evidence in support of its truth—a complete description of the condition of man. Kafka begins, where he ends, with an understanding of the limitation of human freedom, and an effort to transcend that limitation to the achievement of as much peace as one can reach in mankind.

Rosenfeld was not himself much interested in limitations; the better part of his life, in fact, was spent in the pursuit of extending boundaries in the hopeless search for happiness. He wasn't so naïve as to believe that happiness was available on a full-time basis. He believed instead that life provided radiant moments in which it revealed its grandeur and beauty, and it is these moments that must be sought and cherished.

Such a moment occurs in *Passage from Home*, where the novel's young protagonist is taken by his grandfather to a meeting of Hasidim, which transforms the normally petty and grasping older man into a new and different person. "Though unable to understand, I had shared the experience of that ecstasy, and I, too, felt grateful for it." In an early story, "Joe the Janitor," a young man working as a janitor at the University of Chicago comes upon musicians in one of the campus courts playing the Tchaikovsky overture from *Romeo and Juliet*. Swept up by the music, he breaks into tears, and thinks: "Life is precious, let me hold to it, oh let me live forever, yes forever, dear sweet life. Let me always feel myself, know that I am I to the ultimate change in nature, past death, past grass, past stone."

The yearning, the hunger for such moments, appears not merely to have dominated much of Isaac Rosenfeld's fiction but also his life. "The hunger must be preserved at all costs," he wrote in his journal. His intellectual heroes tended to be men who in their own lives sought transcendence: Nietzsche, Tolstoy, Gandhi among them. Reichianism was the ultimate psychology of transcendence, combining Freudianism and Marxism and going beyond both, sup-posedly by establishing a hegemony over repression—and thereby bringing about in one swoop the end of the superego and the state. A place that Rosenfeld came increasingly to look for his own tran-scendence was sex: hence the interest in Reichianism, hence the relentless Village chasing. Sex wasn't everything to Isaac Rosenfeld, Zipperstein contends, but it counted for a lot. "All my troubles," he wrote in his journal, "are with women."

When Rosenfeld moved from Chicago to New York, he did so with the notion of studying philosophy, which he did at New York University. But he soon gave this up, believing that what he had to say was better said through fiction. "He became convinced," in Zipperstein's words, "that fiction was the best route to philosophi-cal knowledge."

This turned out to be a mistake, at least for Rosenfeld's own fic-tion, which tends to be heavily weighted in favor of the parable, the fable, the symbol-laden tale. In art, as we know, there are no rules, except the one I have just set out: that there are no rules. But in superior stories themes tend to arise naturally out of tales, whereas in Rosenfeld's stories, the theme seems to be steering the story from the outset. One feels Rosenfeld straining for the comic gravity of

Kafka—"There lives the Jewish Kafka," Delmore Schwartz is supposed to have quipped when passing Rosenfeld's Village apartment on Barrow Street—but without success. Attempting to set sail, like Melville, another of his heroes, in his fiction he remained landlocked. *Luftmensch*, or air-man, though Rosenfeld was in his daily life, he couldn't really quite manage to get his fiction off the ground. "More and more," Zipperstein writes, "concrete reality disappeared in his prose: what remained were his increasingly abstruse reflections about it." Only toward the end of his life, in his story "King Solomon," did his comic gifts begin to shine through, specificity of detail coalescing with the ambition of theme.

As a critic, the young Rosenfeld could be very authoritative. Of the highly regarded British novelist Henry Green he wrote: "The over-evaluation of Henry Green in some of our literary circles is a typical American relapse into provincialism, an instance of our tendency to credit a work as a great achievement on the insufficient ground that its sensibility is finer than our own." Not bad for a man just turned thirty who was himself a provincial.

As early as 1951, he nailed Ernest Hemingway:

> His reputation must soon decline, and while the excellent aspects of his style, at least in the earlier novels and some of the stories, the clear, clean writing that he does at his best, will retain their value, the deep moral significance that some critics (e.g. [Malcolm] Cowley) have found or pretended to find in his attitude toward life has already begun to look like a hoax.

He is always interesting, sometimes touching on the profound, especially on the brilliance of Sholem Aleichem's Yiddish, in which he finds "a kind of consciousness in verbal form, call it historical paranoia or call it truly mystical, that interprets the whole creation in terms of a people's deepest experience and intuition."

Rosenfeld could also be provocative. In 1949, he wrote the most controversial article ever to appear in *Commentary*, "Adam and Eve on Delancey Street." The subject was kashruth, or keeping kosher, which Rosenfeld argued was tied up with—was perhaps the primary reason for—Jewish repression of sexuality. "As our food taboos are also sexually repressive, serious damage occurs," he wrote. "Kashruth should be permitted only to Hasidim. Where a natural enthusiasm and use for joy are lacking, the ideal of a Kosher Home becomes an insidious ruin of life."

An essay in a Jewish magazine calling, in effect, for the abolition of Jewish dietary laws—talk about starting a bonfire in an oil field! "The article," Professor Zipperstein writes, "offended many . . . and led to an effort to censure *Commentary*, even close it down." The dean of Yeshiva University wrote to the Anti-Defamation League complaining about the essay. Rabbi Milton Steinberg, the leading Conservative rabbi in New York, excoriated the essay every chance he had and did his best to separate *Commentary* from the American Jewish Committee, then its sponsor, because of it. A press release went out describing Rosenfeld's essay as "not only smut, but actually anti-Semitism worthy of the best efforts of Streicher and Goebbels." Liberals rallied around the magazine's decision to publish the essay. The immediate result, Zipperstein reports, is that Rosenfeld was excluded from publishing in *Commentary* for the next eighteen months, no small punishment, since writing for the magazine was then one of his chief sources of income.

"Adam and Eve on Delancey Street" demonstrates, in a heightened manner, the mischievousness of intellectuals. Rosenfeld wrote the essay without any basis in scholarship or religious learning. He was floating an idea, riding one of his favorite hobbyhorses, casting another ballot against sexual repression, which he thought one of the great blockages on humanity's way to a better life.

"For all of Rosenfeld's presumption in how sexuality indelibly shapes life," Zipperstein writes, "he also believed that sex was but one

of a large medley of human actions and by no means the most important one." Yet it is hard to think of another that loomed so large in
both his life and his writing, unless it be the notion, taken originally
from Marx, of alienation. For the intellectual, and especially the Jewish intellectual, alienation came, according to Rosenfeld, naturally.

Many of Rosenfeld's admirers see this cultivation of alienation
as a badge of honor. "The defining feature of Rosenfeld's modernity," wrote Mark Shechner, "was his revulsion against the modern
world, and his refusal to collaborate with it." Theodore Solotaroff
lauded him for keeping "himself in the clear, taking risks of insta-
bility and independence, or uncertainty, sterility, and failure." Zipperstein cites Bellow as praising "him for turning his back on the
fat gods and . . . his refusal to welcome the new order of things as a
victory of the spirit."

So there Rosenfeld was, accepting alienation as his natural heritage, lashed to Reichian sexual theories of character analysis, ill at
ease in the present yet finding no succor in the past—all this and
more in the way of excess intellectual baggage, did not leave him
much room to respond directly to life. In his journals, Rosenfeld
might mock Paul Goodman and others for being lashed to their
theories, but it is difficult to see how he was less so. In his journals
he views the then young editors of *Commentary*, Nathan Glazer,
Irving Kristol, Robert Warshow as "locked in offices, locked in stale
marriages and growing quietly, desperately ill." Yet in the end it was
Rosenfeld who died young, some would say of a broken heart.

STEVEN ZIPPERSTEIN, after living long with and looking closely
at the sadness of Isaac Rosenfeld's life, is still enraptured by him
and wants even now to revive his reputation. Toward the end of
his book, he pictures him as he might have been had he lived a longer life. He imagines that he might have emerged, "as did [Paul]
Goodman, an elder sage of this [the 60s] movement." He feels that
the times, which accepted the abstruse fiction of Thomas Pynchon,

would have been more receptive to Rosenfeld's fiction. He believes that "as we experience once again, coolly or in panic, the modern dilemmas of contactlessness, the inability to grasp the life around us, the numbness and uncertainty toward terror and vulgarity that it embodies—that Rosenfeld's consciousness of contemporary mind and feelings is once again pertinent."

Is it really? In an autobiographical fragment that Zipperstein quotes, Rosenfeld writes that when younger, "I was surer, I had life. I felt a holiness and beauty in the world. I understood everything, and my own experience as well. I was called upon to be great." He also wrote, three years before his death, to Oscar Tarcov: "What a life! I remember the dreams, plans, ambitions, and energies I used to have—and they make me feel insignificant now. I hope you're not such a middle-aged schmuck like me." Isaac Rosenfeld was thirty-five years old when he wrote this. He felt cornered, trapped, out of luck, and he turned out to be right. What he failed to understand was that his own ideas ensured his defeat.

Saul Bellow

A Long, Unhappy Life

"One has to have a less than admirable character to be a fiction writer."

—SAUL BELLOW

THE MOST PENETRATING LITERARY CRITICISM I know of the novelist Saul Bellow was made in my presence by my dear friend Edward Shils one afternoon in his apartment in Hyde Park. Edward had been reading, in manuscript, a portion of James Atlas's biography of Bellow. He put down Atlas's pages, and, with his fondess for extended metaphors, said to me:

> You know, Joseph, Mr. Atlas will only grasp the true nature of Saul Bellow when he understands that our friend Saul, had he been allowed to sit for two hours in the lap of the Queen of England, would, when told by the Queen that she must now attend to her official duties, though she much enjoyed their visit, freshly emerge from the Queen's lap with two observations: first, that the Queen had no understanding whatsoever of the condition of the modern artist, and, second, that she was an anti-Semite.

Edward and Saul went back a ways. In 1962, two years before the publication of *Herzog*, Edward arranged for Saul to be made a member of the faculty of the Committee on Social Thought at the University of Chicago. That same year Saul wrote to his friend John Berryman, "I love Edward Shils." Edward had contributed much to the composition of *Mr. Sammler's Planet*, chiefly to the cosmopolite character of Arthur Sammler, or so people who have seen the novel in manuscript have told me. When Edward told Saul that he did not require many friends, Saul wrote back, "you have a friend in me, I assure you."

Saul, with whom I used to play racquetball, introduced me to Edward in 1972. By that time their relationship had already begun to fray. These men were two of the greatest put-down artists in the country, and, of course, they regularly practiced their art, if still behind the other's back, upon each other. For a spell, I was an amused recipient of this slightly toxic banter. Of a Wednesday morning I might get a call from Saul, asking what I had been doing. When I mentioned having dinner the night before with Edward, who was something of a gourmand, Saul asked, "Ah, does he still have a leather palate?" Half an hour later, Edward would telephone, and, after I told him I had just spoken with Saul, remark: "Have you ever noticed that Saul is the kind of Jew [Edward was himself Jewish] who wears his hat in the house, and when he wants to talk seriously seats himself in a kitchen chair turned backwards to do so?" When Saul stayed at Monk's House, Virginia and Leonard Woolf's country retreat in East Sussex, and complained in a letter about the heating and other arrangements, Edward said: "Why did he go there in the first place? But that's our Saul; houses, women, if it's for nothing, he takes it."

Saul felt Edward did not treat him as an equal, and thought he was sitting in judgment on him and finding him wanting. He was, I fear, right about the latter. Edward thought little of Saul's choices of female company and was less than admiring of his taste

SAUL BELLOW

for low-life. He thought him a lazy teacher, who didn't get anywhere near the most out of his graduate students, and in later years he did what he could to foil Saul's attempts to get jobs on the Committee on Social Thought for his former lady friends. "I refuse to allow him to use the Committee," Edward told me, "as a rest home for his old *nafkes.*" In the 1980s, he mocked Saul's forays into the anthroposophy of Rudolf Steiner. "If there's a bad idea out there—Trotskyism, Reichism, Steinerism—leave it to our friend Saul to swallow it."

Things grew worse between them. I had ceased to see Saul, for reasons that shall be made plain presently. Edward, who was five years older than Saul but looked much younger, began to refer to him as "the old gentleman." Edward once showed me a note Saul had written him describing him as "wicked," a word choice that caused him to chuckle. Then, in his early eighties, Edward was struck by cancer. After two long bouts with chemotherapy, nothing more could be done. As Edward lay on his deathbed, Saul called to ask if he might come over, presumably to patch things up. "I have no wish to ease the conscience of that son of a bitch," Edward said. "Tell him no." Saul took it in the way he took most rejections throughout his life—by taking literary revenge. In his next (and last) novel, *Ravelstein*, he created a monstrous character named Rakhmiel Kogon, unmistakably based on Edward Shils, to whom he imputed useless learning (Edward's learning was genuine and highly useful), a musty smell (which Edward didn't have), and homosexuality (which was as far from Edward's nature as possible).

N ONE OF THE DRAMA of this relationship or others appears in *Saul Bellow: Letters*. Perhaps this is owing to the nature of collections of printed letters, in which people appear as correspondents with some regularity, are vouchsafed confidences, and then drop away, never to be heard from again. Or, if heard from, written about in a radically different way: Edward Shils, for example, goes from being loved to being described as "an unlanced boil," but the reader will have no notion of what took place in the intervening years to so alter feelings between the two men.

Unfortunately, this ample collection of Saul's letters has been lazily edited by Benjamin Taylor, a member of the faculty at the New School in New York. Taylor does little more than translate phrases in foreign languages and sometimes provide a bare-bones biographical note about Bellow's lesser-known correspondents. But he ties up no loose ends and fails time and again to establish context or make clear what is going on beneath the surface. At one point, Bellow tries to calm John Berryman over a scandal that has caused his name to be besmirched in New York (what scandal we are not told) by mentioning that he himself had three years earlier been involved in a great scandal (the particulars of which also go unmentioned) that has long since been forgotten. This happens all too often.

Professor Taylor has no doubt that Saul Bellow is a great writer. In his introduction, he mentions a meeting between Samuel Beckett and Bellow that he likens to the famous—and inconsequential—meeting between James Joyce and Marcel Proust at the Majestic Hotel in Paris in 1922, without any apparent awareness of the discount in quality on both ends: Beckett was no Joyce, nor was Bellow's talent close to that of Proust. Taylor seems confident, too, that Bellow was a deeply sensitive man who felt that the import of life was to be found in love, possibly because Bellow was always proclaiming his sensitivity and was one of those men to whom the word "love" came very easily. (A boyhood friend, later in life, once said of Bellow that he betrayed everyone who ever loved him.) Taylor thus misses, in his introduction, and in his editing, touching upon the two main questions about Saul Bellow: How good a writer was he? And why was there so gaping a discrepancy between the large moral claims made in his fiction and his own erratic personal behavior?

I am myself mentioned thrice in *Saul Bellow: Letters.* In the first instance, in 1978, Bellow, complaining about the paucity of opportunities for freely open conversation in Chicago, writes: "Joe Epstein I like and respect but I don't open my heart to him because he doesn't have the impulse . . . to open up. Besides he's more fair-minded than we [he is writing to *The New Republic* editor Leon Wieseltier] are, or more circumspect when he discusses our bogus contemporaries." In 1984, I am one of the reasons that he asked to have his name dropped as one of the sponsors of Midge Decter's Committee for the Free World for, among other reasons, my giving a speech in which he claimed I misrepresented his views. (I didn't, and a more energetic editor than Professor Taylor could easily enough have discovered that.) In 1991, I have progressed to

being "a second rate Jewish writer from Chicago," who has written a short story with a protagonist resembling him, a story that is
"gross, moronic, and clumsily written."

I was never a central figure in Saul Bellow's life, so it would be
beside the point to chronicle how I went from a person liked and
respected to a second-rate writer of gross and moronic stories. But
for a while we were fairly close. To provide some notion of my
closeness to him during the time of our friendship, between 1972
and roughly 1980, he called to inform me the morning he had been
awarded the Nobel Prize for Literature. He emphatically told me
that, after three failures in marriage, he would never remarry. Then
one morning I learned that he had married Alexandra Tulcea, a
mathematician at Northwestern. I was twenty-two years younger
than he, and in our racquetball games—sometimes at the Evanston YMCA, sometimes at the Riviera Club in the Loop, where he
was a member—I used to worry slightly about his having a stroke
from over-exertion, and could too easily imagine a photograph in
the Chicago press bearing the caption, "Nobel Prize-winner dies in
racquetball court. Man in shorts at left unidentified."

I was friendly with Bellow during the period in which he was
writing *Humboldt's Gift*, sections of which he read to me aloud in
his apartment, asking for corrections, of which I hadn't many to
offer. I remember feeling greatly complimented when he told me
that I had retained a fundamental love of literature that made me a
much better reader than all critics and reviewers. In his letters, he
attributes this same love to Philip Roth, whose own literary pro-
ductions I once heard Saul and Harold Rosenberg cut up with all
the delicacy of a Cook County coroner for the corpse of a homeless man found drowned in Lake Michigan.

ONE OF THE SIDESHOW AMUSEMENTS of *Saul Bellow: Letters* is to read him writing intimate things to people whom I
have heard him verbally maim in conversation or later crush in his

novels. In early letters to a Chicago attorney named Sam Freifeld, with whom he grew up, he describes their relationship as that of blood brothers; in *Humboldt's Gift*, he describes this same Freifeld as a flasher. Bellow was a literary Bluebeard, killing off his ex-wives in devastating portraits in his novels. His fourth wife, Alexandra, whose unworldliness he limned so tenderly in *The Dean's December*, he treats in *Ravelstein*, after their divorce, as a figure of pure evil, as if she were the twin sister of Eva Braun. Vengeance, the Italians say, is a dish best served cold; Bellow garnished the dish with viciousness and served it on the pages of his novels.

Saul had two valves on his emotional trumpet: intimacy and contempt. He could be immensely charming and funny; he once described me in the racquetball court as "quicker than a sperm." But one of the first things one sensed upon meeting him was his extreme touchiness. A slip in conversation, or worse in print, praising the wrong writer, and you figured to be whacked, to use the Mafia phrase, told to practice anatomically impossible acts upon yourself, and mocked ever after to others. The distinction between sensitivity and touchiness is a crucial one; so many people who think themselves sensitive are merely touchy, and Saul was among them. His touchiness was increased by a streak of paranoia. Erich Heller one day told me that Saul declared him an enemy because he, Erich, had written less than enthusiastically about the future of the novel. "I never mentioned his name in my essay," Erich said, "but he took it as a personal attack." Saul considered the novel a family business.

A veritable Jewish porcupine of touchiness, Bellow also suffered from Irish Alzheimers: he remembered, that is, chiefly his grudges. As late as 1991, he is still claiming that Norman Podhoretz "tried to do me in" with his 1953 review of *The Adventures of Augie March*. (Podhoretz's criticisms, it turns out, are not all that dissimilar from criticisms of the novel that Bellow would later himself make in letters in which the novel is mentioned.) He has a strange on-again-off-again relationship with Alfred Kazin, whose sexual braggadocio he used to mock in my presence. Yet he never entirely broke off this relationship with a man he despised. Like many people capable of great cruelty, Bellow could also be a heavyweight sentimentalist.

ONE OF THE THINGS *Letters* does reveal is Bellow's unfailingly high quality as a correspondent. He was a deft letter-writer, with a lovely gift for comic phrasing and a talent for epistolary intimacy. Scarcely a letter in this volume is without an amusing phrase or arresting insight or interesting formulation. As he grows older, and as the demands on him as a literary celebrity increased—"I haven't been good at managing celebrity," he writes to an old high-school classmate—Bellow had less time for his correspondence. The letters written in the last decade or so of his life almost invariably contain an apology for being so tardy in responding.

Apart from his go-fuck-yourself letters, which are not few, Bellow's letters are generally amiably cozening, giving each of his correspondents the notion that he is only capable of this level of candor and intimacy with him or her. This gift for intimacy was very seductive; he made you feel among the elect, one of the good and sensitive people with whom his troubled soul could find succor; you were not among the rabble, the swine, the creeps, the *nudniks*, the shits, until of course, eventually and almost inevitably, you irredeemably were.

The one protection from this was death. Bellow was, as the letters show, also sentimental about the dead. I recall his mockery to me of Philip Rahv: "an old bull gone weak in the knees," he called him. In one of his early letters, he refers to him as "Commissar of Grumps." But as soon as Rahv died, he became, for Bellow, one of those giants who no longer walks the earth.

The element of con in much of Bellow's correspondence has to do with his always managing to come across as the large-hearted, sensitive, great-souled fellow, the expansive spiritual sport, the artist in a crass culture, more than a touch naïve perhaps, but a sweetheart, really. In so many of these letters, he appears to have cornered the market on virtue. My guess is that most people reading his letters will swallow it—their editor certainly seems to have done so—taking Bellow for the poor sensitive guy, much set upon by an ignorant world filled with stupid people, he persistently portrays himself as being.

The letter, in some ways, was Bellow's true métier. Perhaps the most memorable passages in all his fiction are those letters that his character Moses Herzog writes to Adlai Stevenson, Nietzsche, God, and others. "I sometimes think I write books in lieu of letters," Bellow wrote to Sophie Wilkins, Karl Shapiro's wife, "and that real letters have more kindness in them, addressed as they are to one friend." Sophie Wilkins, a writer named John Auerbach, and Martin Amis are the few among his correspondents that he did not turn on—or felt had turned on him—or at some point spoke mockingly about behind their backs, and with whom he appears genuinely to have let himself go. Richard Stern, Bernard Malamud, Leon Wieseltier, Philip Roth, and a number of other people to whom he wrote affectionate letters, he mocked, at least in my presence.

I F ONE WERE HIS ENEMY, it was death in the afternoon, for he was a bull who could gore one beyond repair. When one's sympathies are aligned with his, his attacks can be great fun to read, and many are impressively penetrating. "Hannah [Arendt] was rash," he writes, "but she wasn't altogether stupid (unlike her friend Mary Mc[Carthy])." To Mary McCarthy's future biographer, he writes: "For a decade or more she hated me, quite frankly. I could not return her feelings with the same intensity but I did what I could." As for Hannah Arendt, "that superior Krautess," well, "she was monumentally vain, and a rigid *ashkente* [Yiddish for ball-buster, Professor Taylor informs us]. Much of her strength went into obstinacy, and she was the compleat intellectual—i.e. she went always and as rapidly as possible for the great synthesis and her human understanding, painfully limited, could not support the might of historical analysis, unacknowledged prejudices, frustrations, her German and European aspirations, etc. She could often think clearly, but to think simply was altogether beyond her, and her imaginative faculty was stunted."

He refers to Christopher Hitchens as one of those "Fourth-Estate playboys, thriving on agitation," and one of "these *Nation*-type gnomes that . . . drink, drug, lie, cheat, chase, seduce, gossip, libel, borrow money, never pay child support, etc. They're the bohemians who made Marx foam with rage in *The Eighteenth Brumaire*." Of Gore Vidal he writes: "He has a score to settle with the USA. Anywhere else, he might have been both a homosexual *and* a patrician. Here he had to mix with rough trade and also with Negroes and Jews; democracy made it impossible to be gentleman invert and wit. Also the very source of his grief has made him rich and famous." He wrote a recommendation for a Guggenheim grant for James Baldwin early in his career, yet in one of his letters remarks on his laziness and sponging. Later he calls Baldwin's novel *Another Country* "abominable." He writes to Cynthia Ozick that, in one of her essays, she has been too kind to George Steiner, "who is, of all pains in the ass, the most unbearable because of his high polish and his snobbery." In 1972, he blackballed William Phillips for membership in the Century Club because, as he wrote to the admissions committee, "he betrayed, and intellectually and artistically bankrupted, the magazine [*Partisan Review*]," turning it over to "the hysterical, shallow and ignorant academic 'counter-culture.'"

Bellow consistently praises John Cheever, to whom he suggested their affinities but above all their common membership in the club of artists. Unlike Henry James, who could never lie about art, one gets the sense when Bellow is writing to fellow authors that, for the most part, he goes easy on them; he praises Cheever's *Falconer* well beyond its actual quality. He tells Bernard Malamud that he is "the real thing," but then to others harshly criticizes his novel *A New Life* and emphasizes his limitations. After Malamud's death he writes to Philip Roth that "he did make something of the crumbs and gritty bits of impoverished Jewish lives. Then he suffered from not being able to do more." Let pass that in *The Fixer*, a great Russian novel written by an American Jew, Malamud wrote a better novel than Bellow ever came close to writing.

Of the quality of Isaac Bashevis Singer's fiction—he had helped put Singer on the literary screen by doing a splendid translation, published in *Partisan Review*, of Singer's great story "Gimpel the Fool"—Bellow never speaks, but more than once notes that Singer does not think much of him, though he does not say why, nor does Professor Taylor fill in this blank for us. Part of the reason may have been that Singer was a pure storyteller, and as such, less than likely to be enamored of Bellow's unplotted, maundering fictions. Bellow has no use for the "representatives of the affluent revolution": Allen Ginsberg, Nadine Gordimer, Grace Paley, E. L. Doctorow. He told me that Norman Mailer was little more than a clichémeister, and claimed that, during the Vietnam War years, he was defeating Mailer and Robert Lowell in the literary PR derby by keeping his own counsel. His views on Nabokov are mixed, and at one point, he writes that he would like to rewrite *Lolita* from the young girl's point of view, which is an amusing notion.

BUT NOT NEARLY SO AMUSING as would be a novel about Saul Bellow written in collaboration by his first four wives. He married five times, and had four children, one with each but his fourth wife. I have heard it said that it is a mistake to acquire a third cat, for if one has three, then why not five or six? Perhaps the same rule applies to marriage. One of the not so leitmotifs of these letters is the revolving-door wife game. Anita, Sondra, Susan, Alexandra, Janis—in and out the room the women come and go, and they ain't talking of Michelangelo, but of alimony, child support, betrayal, rage. The most shocking news on the domestic front comes near the end of *Letters*, when, at the age of eighty-four, after complaining about the continuing pain in his legs, the effects of toxic poisoning on his nervous system, the installation of a heart defibrillator, shortness of breath, failures of memory, loss of balance, and an inability to walk more than a block, he announces that he and his forty-four-years-younger-than-he wife are to have a baby. Don't, as the Jews say, ask.

Saul Bellow was a notorious heterosexual. By this I don't mean that he was an extraordinary sexual athlete, for of course I can have no knowledge of that, though in James Atlas's biography the poet Sandra Hochman, who kitchen-tested him, is quoted as saying that "he was the put-it-in-and-take-it-out type . . . [and] didn't know a clitoris from a kneecap." No, he was a notorious heterosexual in the sense that he was almost continuously flirtatious. I remember riding in a bus with him in Chicago, talking about something fairly serious, and, when an attractive woman boarded the bus, he was gone, conversation over. My wife, who was a photography editor at *Encylopaedia Britannica*, once called him for a photograph for the *Britannica Yearbook*, and recalls his coming on to her over the phone. He notes in a letter of 1998 that, apropos of Bill Clinton's White House dalliance, political power can have a strong aphrodisiacal effect; to which one might add his own literary fame—with a certain kind of woman—had much the same effect.

Why did a man of such habits also acquire the far more serious, not to say expensive, habit of marriage? Time and again he placed his head, three-quarters profile, a soft Borsolino hat atop it worn at rakish angle, in the domestic lion's mouth. One might have thought the sinews of his neck would have been cut clean through, or at least the wounds from the teeth marks would have made him more cautious. But after each divorce, with its emotional bruises and financial penalties, Bellow, like a man hit by a bus, got up, shook himself off, and got back on the curb, where he awaited the next bus, the Heartbreak Avenue Express.

Why the need for so many marriages is a secret Saul Bellow has taken with him. Perhaps he longed for domestic stability. Perhaps he thought a wife could give him the uncritical adoration and emotional support he craved. Perhaps he feared falling into the bohemian life, the life of the Village, that took its toll on so many of his contemporaries, not least on his high-school friend Isaac Rosenfeld. Perhaps, *contra* Picasso and Balanchine, he did not need new wives for inspiration but ex-wives to attack in new novels. At one point, at the age of sixty-five, he writes to a man named Hymen Slate in Chicago, in one of the few ill-made sentences in all his letters, that, once he had determined to devote himself entirely to his writing, his only other drive, the sexual one, dropped away, and: "My erotic life was seriously affected, too, in that I diverted myself with a kind of executive indiscriminateness—without a proper interest in women."

"A proper interest in women"—it is far from clear that Bellow ever had that. One is unlikely to find it in his fiction. He created no memorable female characters. Neither, one needs to add here, have Philip Roth or John Updike or Norman Mailer, whose female characters exist chiefly to service their author's sex fantasies. The great novelists—Balzac, Tolstoy, George Eliot, Willa Cather, Marguerite Yourcenar—were androgynous in their powers of creation. Recent male American novelists almost universally fail this test.

Bellow's marriage chronicles might be mildly amusing but for the fact that children were always placed between him and his angry wives. One of the things his letters do reveal is that Bellow made serious efforts to remain a decent father, though the job couldn't have been made easier by the rage in which he left ex-wives. Bellow's distress at his failure at fatherhood feels real enough, and supplies some of the few genuinely poignant elements in these letters. "I am, with all my faults, a responsible papa," he declared. When his youngest son, Daniel, is to marry at the age of thirty-two, Bellow writes to Sophie Wilkins that, despite his extreme fatigue, he attended the wedding: "I didn't want the kid accusing me of disappearing on *all* important occasions." One's heart goes out to these children at the same time that one realizes that one of the unacknowledged blessings in life is not to have a famous father.

His problem with his children was yet another item, a substantial one, on the long bill of complaint that sometimes seems to have comprised much of Saul Bellow's life. He compliments Robert Penn Warren on his dealing with his troubles in a manly way, and remarks that "as the youngest child I learned to make the most of mine." The artist as victim might serve as the rubric for many of these letters, or even as subtitle to the entire collection, for a large quantity of his letters are given over to self-absorption, self-pity, and complaint. "But the world has been too much with me," Bellow writes at one point. True, he brings a high style and polish to his complaining—he is the George Steiner of complaint—but complaint it remains.

WHAT MAKES ALL THIS COMPLAINT seem so incommensurate is that Bellow was really a very lucky man; and such misfortune as he encountered he brought on himself with what he at one point terms "my numerous and preposterous marriages." He was fortunate in that the world lined up to offer him all its rewards and prizes—Nobels, Pulitzers, National Book Awards, medals from PEN, the American Academy of Arts and Letters, honorary degrees, and the rest of it—without his ever having written an entirely successful novel.

This last judgment is quite as much Bellow's as mine. While always touchy about any criticism of his novels—he charged John Updike and Hugh Kenner's criticism of his fiction up to anti-Semitism—in his letters Bellow stakes out no grand claims for his books. He is appealing, in fact, in coming across as someone still learning his craft right up to the end. As late as 1994, he writes to an old college classmate: "Life has by now prepared me to write an essay called 'How Not to Write a Novel.'" All he lays claim to is the earnestness of his struggle and the seriousness of his intentions. His elevated intentions were never in doubt. But did he fulfill them?

Did Saul Bellow leave any masterpieces? Is there any one book on which his reputation ought to stand? Or is it the collectivity of his fiction, his *oeuvre*, on which he should be judged? Some people will prefer one book over another: If one loathes all that happened in the 1960s, *Mr. Sammler's Planet* is probably your favorite Bellow novel. (Bellow called the book "an essay," but it needs to be said that he took politically courageous positions in the so-called culture wars, and this novel is one of the best-aimed missiles fired during its duration.) For those whose tastes run to comic irony, *Herzog* figures to be their book. Others might prefer one of the novellas; *Seize the Day* would probably be the top candidate here. (In a freshman class I taught many years ago at Northwestern, a student said that he liked *Seize the Day* well enough, but frankly didn't understand why its hero, Tommy Wilhelm, just didn't get a job, thus tendering a criticism I have never been able to answer.) But there will be nothing like a consensus, and I think I know why.

The reason is that Bellow could not construct persuasive plots. "My stories aren't very successful," he wrote to Pascal Covici, his editor at Viking. "I suppose I lack a sense of form." For all his rich gifts, his powers of invention were limited. He wrote *romans à clef*, with the keys not all that hard to find to unlock and reveal the people on whom his characters were based. Having to draw so strictly on life often got him into difficulty, sometimes as a writer, inhibiting his imagination by locking him into fact, and sometimes with readers, some of whom he saddened by these methods.

I N 1974 MY FRIEND HILTON KRAMER was in Chicago to review a show at the Art Institute. I arranged a dinner for Hilton, Saul, and me at the Whitehall, a dining club of which I was then a member. The dinner, I thought, went well—excellent food, a flow of good talk, lots of laughter. Only later, when I read the published version of *Humboldt's Gift*, Bellow's novel about the poet Delmore Schwartz, did I realize that Saul got rather more out of the dinner than Hilton or I.

In the novel, Hilton is a character named Magnasco—no first name is given—whom Von Humboldt Fleisher, the Delmore Schwartz character, in his paranoia, believes is having a love affair with his wife. (This paranoiac episode happened, if you'll pardon the expression, in real life.) When Humboldt/ Delmore turns up at Magnasco/Hilton's hotel—called the Earle but in fact the Chelsea—certain in his paranoia that his wife is with Magnasco/Hilton, the latter calls the deskman who in turn calls the police. Later Magnasco/Hilton hires a detective, which eventually results in Humboldt/Schwartz being sent off to the loony bin at Bellevue.

The sin here, in a bohemian culture, is calling the police on a poet, no matter how mad he might be. The Bellow character, Charley Citrine, had earlier advised Magnasco to "leave town for awhile." But Magnasco/Hilton had, Citrine reports, "long prepared for his career," and was about to get a tryout as a reviewer for the *New York Herald-Tribune*, so, rather than put off his plans, he calls the cops. "When I met Magnasco," Bellow has his narrator Citrine write, "he proved to be overweight, round-faced, young in calendar years only, steady, unflappable, born to make progress in cultural New York." In other words, Hilton is portrayed as another heartless hustler on the make, ready to do anything to stoke his career.

Hilton was, naturally enough, hurt by this portrayal, especially since it was a lie. He had called Bellow when Delmore Schwartz threatened him; in fact, at one point Schwartz told Hilton he was in the lobby of the Chelsea awaiting him and that he had a gun; and it was Bellow, thirteen years older than Hilton, who told him not to be a fool but to call the police straightaway. But there was little Hilton could do about Bellow's false account—as bad as calling the police on a poet is suing a novelist—which made him look so bad. The only people who would know that the Magnasco character was supposed to be him were a small handful of intellectuals in and around New York. Still, it was a mean act: another instance of Bellow doing someone in, first because of the needs of his wobbly plot, and, second, because, in denying the truth of the matter, he made himself look good.

Bellow was always playing with fire in drawing withering portraits of friends, acquaintances, ex-friends, and especially ex-wives. In one of his letters, he reports a nightmare in which one of the people he contemned under thin fictional cover in *Herzog* is suing him. But with his final novel, *Ravelstein*, the acetylene torch truly seared the back of his pants. "I've never written anything like *Ravelstein* before," Bellow wrote to Martin Amis, "and the mixture of fact and fiction has gotten out of hand." In the less than clear sentences that follow, he writes that "Allan [Bloom, the University of Chicago teacher who is the undisguised model for the character Ravelstein] had enemies who were preparing to reveal that he had died of AIDS. At this point I lost my head. . . ." Professor Taylor ought to have stepped in here with a lengthy footnote to recount, and if possible clarify, the import of what Bellow is saying, but, with his hands-off editorial policy, he doesn't.

What was at issue is the exact cause of Allan Bloom's death, which, so far as I know, has yet to be made finally clear. In *Ravelstein*, Bellow kills him off with AIDS. Bloom's friends all insist that the effects of the disorder of the nerves called Guillain-Barré led to Bloom's death by heart and liver failure. Werner Dannhauser, Allan Bloom's closest friend, asked Bellow to lessen the emphasis on Bloom/Ravelstein's private life, which would, one gathers, have meant playing down his homosexuality and expunging his death by AIDS. Bellow writes to Dannhauser that he tried to do so, but it didn't work. By "it didn't work," one assumes Bellow meant that his plot required that Allan Bloom die of AIDS.

Bellow did, apparently, tone things down but not decisively. Then, later, after the book was out in the world, he told a reporter from *The New York Times*: "For a long time I thought I knew what Allan died of, and then I discovered other things that didn't jibe with that, so I really can't say now. I don't know that he died of AIDS really." So there it stands, a mess, created by a man willing to sabotage a putatively dear friend to contrive what he thought an appropriate ending for a novel.

Despite all the prizes and critical praise, one comes up against the possibility that Saul Bellow wasn't truly a novelist. He could do extraordinary, even marvelous, things: draw a wondrous cityscape; describe a face at the MRI level of detail; capture the comedy in self-presentations; soar in great lyrical, and even more in intellectual and metaphysical, flights. The problem was that he couldn't quite seem to land the plane. His endings never quite fit, which is to say, work. He couldn't do the first, essential thing that novelists with vastly less talent than he know in their bones how to do, which is to construct convincing plots.

Highly intelligent people without an interest in the lives of intellectuals and artists—and intellectuals and artists were always his main subjects—can't read Saul Bellow, even though these artists and intellectuals puff away, Nestor-like, on the meaning of the universe, the dissolution of the soul, the death of art, and other such elevated topics. (Bellow once told me that when he published a novel "50,000 people buy it in hardcover, 5,000 read it, and 500 care.") In the end, of course, his subject was almost always himself: "By now," he wrote to Cynthia Ozick in 1987, "I have only the cranky idiom of my books—the letters-in-general of an occult personality, a desperately odd somebody who has, as a last resort, invented a technique of self-representation." Perhaps he wasn't a novelist at all but a high-octane riffer, a philosophical schmoozer, an unsurpassed intellectual kibbitzer, one of the great monologists of the age. But he was no storyteller. Which explains why one doesn't have much taste for rereading him and why, there is good reason to believe, future generations are likely to have even less taste for reading him in the first place.

Bernard Malamud

The Hard Road to Truth

SAUL BELLOW USED REGULARLY to refer to himself, Bernard Malamud, and the considerably younger Philip Roth as the Hart, Shaffner, and Marx of American literature. The comment, as often with Bellow, is a loaded one: Loaded with suspicion about the acceptance of Jewish writers in America, with contempt for those critics and readers who tended to lump the three distinctly different writers together, and with resentment for his being reduced to the status of a writer of chiefly ethnic interest.

Certainly, the three writers are easily enough distinguished. Saul Bellow was the virtuoso of the sentence, the comical physiognomical detail, the brilliant cityscape, the high philosophical schmooze, and less than strong on plot. One doesn't read Bellow for the story; at the end one is never quite sure what the story was. One reads him for Bellow himself, in the same way that one didn't go to a Yehudi Menuhin concert to hear Mozart but to hear Menuhin. Philip Roth has always been a writer most happy when *épaté*-ing Jews, Gentiles, and whoever else happens to be free at the moment; in his fiction, sex is always waiting in the wings, ever ready to present itself center stage, which sooner or later it generally does. He is the man, as he put it in *Portnoy's Complaint*, who has attempted to put "the Id back in Yid."

The fiction of Bernard Malamud is quite a different dish of *kreplach*. His fiction possesses greater gravity than that of either Bellow or Roth. His themes—guilt, redemption, the urge for the beginning of a newer, fuller life—are more in the line of the great 19th-century Russians. In *My Father Is a Book*, a memoir of her father, his daughter Janna Malamud Smith compares Bernard Malamud's fiction to that of another Russian, the painter Marc Chagall. "Like the painter born a generation earlier," she writes, "the writer also, at a greater remove, carried tales of the *shtetl*, had familiarity with Yiddish folk literature, found freedom in fables, and could capture in a short story a seemingly naïve moral complexity in which studiedly simple words evoked deep feeling."

"How much feeling have you got in your heart?" Malamud claimed was the question that a serious writer must always ask of himself. He seems to have had a vast quantity. Much of Malamud's feeling was acquired through his own difficult upbringing. Born in 1914 to Russian immigrant parents, he lived upstairs of their Mom and Pop grocery store in Brooklyn. Max and Bertha Malamud's life in America was the reverse of an immigrant success story: Everything his father touched turned to sawdust; his mother, diagnosed as schizophrenic, died at 41, in a mental hospital, when Malamud was 15. When he was 13 he returned one day from school to find her on the kitchen floor, her mouth foaming from poison she had just swallowed. His younger brother later turned up schizophrenic, and he, too, died, in a mental hospital.

Such was Bernard Malamud's early life: scarred by mental illness, poverty, sad immigrant ignorance, with a major economic depression looming in the background. Malamud's wife Ann said that her husband's "leitmotif" was that "Life is sad." The title of one of his darkest stories, "Take Pity," could stand as a rubric over much of

BERNARD MALAMUD

his fiction. A relentless worker, Malamud revised and polished and burnished his stories and novels. He believed in revision as a form of truth seeking: find the precise words, cut away all that is extraneous, put enough pressure on each sentence, and with luck the truth, filtered through the powerful lens of storytelling, will emerge.

Along the way, Malamud developed an unmistakable style, a use of language sometimes referred to as Yinglish, a combination of English words and Yiddish syntax and sentiment. "Where would he drag that dead cat, his soul?" runs such a line from the story "The Girl of My Dreams." From the same story: "He stared unbelieving, his heart a dishrag." A character in "Take Pity" says: "Kiddo, this is a mistake. This place [a grocery store like Malamud's father's] is a grave. Here they will bury you if you don't get out quick."

A magical realist *avant la lettre*, Malamud combined fantasy with realism in writing that was both comic and heartbreaking. Black Jewish angels show up, and just as mysteriously disappear. Census-takers are treated to stories of human tragedy. A man very far down on his luck prays: "My dear God, sweetheart, did I deserve that this should happen to me. . . . Give Fanny back her health, and to me for myself that I shouldn't feel pain in every step." Characters have faces "whiplashed with understanding." A woman has a left eye that "also looks sadder than her right eye." A character in the story "A Choice of Profession" to himself says, "It's not easy being moral"—which may be the chief message of all Bernard Malamud's fiction.

Malamud's wife and children—along with his daughter, he had a son—quickly enough grasped that his work came first. Janna Malamud Smith didn't title her memoir *My Father Is a Book* for no reason. She reports that the moral instruction offered *chez Malamud* was: "Read, value art, seek education and experience, attend to others, shelter the vulnerable, and try to treat each person fairly. The underlying big message was, 'Work to overcome yourself.' " Disciplined work was Malamud's religion.

So much was Malamud at his desk that Roger Straus, his publisher at Farrar, Straus, thought a biography of him wasn't merely impossible but ridiculous. "Everything was up here, in the head," Straus said, "nothing down there. . . . As a life it was unexciting." Malamud's biographer Philip Davis, who quotes Straus saying this, gets around the publisher's objections by living up to his biography's subtitle and producing "A Writer's Life." This is above all a book about a man working at his writing: About the frustrations, the subtleties, the rewards of working at storytelling. "My own view," writes Professor Davis, a literature don at the University of Liverpool, "is that any biography that seeks to 'see in' and thus do justice to Malamud should learn from the fiction, from its methods as much as its contents, and then direct its readers back to it."

Malamud thought half-a-page not at all a bad day's work. He wrote in longhand, leaving space for his inevitable rewriting. He began each morning reworking what he had written the night before. He viewed every sentence as a sculpture. He had longhand pages of a completed story or chapter of a novel typed by his wife or a hired secretary.

"Then," according to his daughter, "he would rewrite. And rewrite. Usually two or three times, occasionally into the double digits of drafts. His sentences and paragraphs were hard won, the result of considered thought and constant revision. He understood that his success had come from 10 percent talent and 90 percent hard work."

Professor Davis writes out of deep admiration for Malamud's fiction, which doesn't blind him to his human flaws: clogged feeling, an artist's selfishness, vanity. He senses (correctly, I believe) that Malamud's reputation is in decline, his popularity waning, and he writes to change this unjust condition. He seeks, as he writes, "more recognition and more readers for Malamud in the future."

"Too often where Malamud is still remembered," Davis writes, "it is for a handful of great short stories; but, wonderful as many of those stories are, I want most of all to make the case for the novels." The problem with this case is that it is tied directly to the very reasons for the decline of Bernard Malamud's reputation. Malamud's last three published novels, *The Tenants* (1971), *Dubin's Lives* (1979), and *God's Grace* (1982), were books that didn't really come off. Reviewers felt this, and so did the best of all critics, ordinary readers. People who loved—not in this instance too strong a word, I think—Malamud's earlier novels and brilliant stories were beginning to give up on him, thinking he had lost the magic that was earlier his. I was myself among them.

I wonder if, perhaps, a more accurate description of the trajectory of Bernard Malamud's career than Philip Davis's wouldn't be one that attempted to explain how so good a writer as Malamud wrote three such off-the-mark novels late in his artistic maturity? If I am correct about this falling-off, Malamud's last good novel—I happen to believe it is a great novel—is *The Fixer* (1966).

For the young Bernard Malamud, as for the children of so many immigrants of that time, education was the only way out. Fortunately, he was good at school, even more fortunately, he had a few teachers who saw something extraordinary in him. He went to Erasmus Hall High School in Brooklyn, one of the superior public schools of its day. He socialized easily enough with his middle-class schoolmates, but at night it was back to the dreary apartment above the hopeless grocery store. In a nice detail, Janna Malamud Smith notes that her father acquired his first bathrobe and slippers at the age of 26.

City College of New York, the famous CCNY, home of nascent Trotskyites, Shachtmanites, and Stalinists, was Malamud's next stop, though he seems not to have been greatly caught up in politics. After CCNY, he worked as a substitute high school teacher and also taught night school; he did a master's degree at Columbia. He moved to Washington, where he earned a meager living as a census taker. During this period, he published some prose sketches in the *Washington Post* and also sold a few radio scripts to the Bulldog Drummond detective series. After a lengthy courtship, he married Ann de Chiara, whose Italian parents weren't pleased with her choice; his own father, meanwhile, ceased to speak to him for marrying a Gentile, and only relented years later when presented with the news of a grandson.

Ann Malamud helped Bern, as she and his friends called him, send out some 200 letters seeking a college teaching job. The only one that struck a positive response was that sent to Oregon State College in Corvallis, where he was hired to teach freshman composition. This most Brooklynite of men, intellectually intense, passionate for art, must have seemed anomalous, to put it gently, at what was then a school that specialized in agriculture. One of his students, reminiscing, reported: "I think he felt Oregon was a foreign country." Malamud's father, in good New York fashion, seemed to confuse Oregon with Oklahoma. Malamud himself tried to colonize Corvallis through culture, helping to form a foreign film society, a Great Books discussion group, an arts theatre. He taught creative writing courses in the evenings to local residents.

The years he spent in Oregon, 1949–1961, despite all the cultural deficiencies of the college and the town, were to prove decisive for Malamud's literary career. He wrote his first published novel *The Natural* (1952) in Oregon; during this period some of his most memorable short stories were printed in *Partisan Review*, *Commentary*, and *The New Yorker*, later to be collected in *The Magic Barrel* (1958); he completed *The Assistant* (1957), his novel based on the honorable sadness of his father's life in his hardscrabble Brooklyn grocery store. He began to win the awards—a Yaddo fellowship, the National Book Award, a Rockefeller Foundation fellowship that permitted him and his family to live for a year in Rome—that brought him to national prominence.

Soon after leaving Oregon State for a much cushier teaching job at Bennington, he wrote *A New Life* (1961), a brilliant comic novel about a wild Jewish loser teaching English at a cow college in the northwest who gets a new start in life when he runs off with the wife of his department chairman. *A New Life* sounds like a novel with a strong anchor in autobiography. It is, and it isn't. Malamud was no S. Levin, as the book's hero is named: he wasn't, like Levin, a former alcoholic, nor did he run off with anyone's wife, as does Levin. But, here as elsewhere, what Davis's biography helps us understand is how Malamud made use of his life's experiences: it deepens one's appreciation of his stories and novels by demonstrating how he transmuted his experience into art.

Malamud's experiences were not wide—he often expressed the wish that they had been—but he wrung everything out of them for his own artistic purposes. Unlike other writers—Bellow comes notably to mind here—Malamud didn't put close facsimiles of actual people in his novels in order to repay old (sometimes imagined) injuries by destroying them in print. Of contemporary writers, Malamud may have relied on invention, on pure imagination, more than any other. His stories are filled with invented widows, relentless matchmakers, miracle-working rabbis. Two of his novels, *The Natural* and *The Fixer*, are entirely imagined, even though the latter is based on the imprisonment in czarist Russia of Mendel Beilis, a Jew who was superintendent of a brick factory, falsely charged with the ritual murder of a Christian child.

Life changed decisively for Malamud when he moved to Bennington College in Vermont. Bennington was one of those radical schools of the 1940s and 1950s—Bard, Antioch, Reed were some of the others—where, as a wag (me, actually) once put it, students spent the months of January and February off campus as members of the opposite sex. Bennington was different from these other schools in having all female students. Bennington girls were thought to be rich, neurotic, and libidinous as all outdoors. Bennington was hard on family life, and it would prove to be so for the Malamuds.

Malamud completed *The Fixer* during his first five years at Bennington. In the novel a relatively simple man named Yakov Bok, a Jewish handyman, spends three years in a czarist prison cell alone with his imagination, trying to work through the questions of human existence, not least among them why there is so much suffering and injustice in the world. *The Fixer* is a book that requires the utmost attention on the part of its readers, but richly repays it. Malamud believed that suffering can make one wiser, and so Yakov

Bok, through lonely hard-won lucubration, becomes. "There's no such thing as an unpolitical man," the hitherto unpolitical Bok concludes, "especially a Jew. You can't be one without the other, that's clear enough. You can't sit still and see yourself destroyed."

The Fixer is a book of the sort for which the Nobel Prize was designed. The novel didn't win it, but it did win a Pulitzer and Malamud's second National Book Award. The reviews were ecstatic. *The Fixer* was made into a movie directed by John Frankenheimer and starring Alan Bates. Malamud was earning serious money. Studies of his fiction began to appear in academic journals. Bernard Malamud was now regarded as a major writer.

And yet, somehow, he never regained his stride. Earlier, he had said, "I have not given up on heroes. I simply use heroic qualities in small men." Nor did he like it when his characters were thought *schlemiels*, bumbling losers, without dignity, meant only to suffer. The reason so many of his characters are put to such suffering, he claimed, was that "in suffering the self is contemplated as it had never before been contemplated." A student of Malamud's during a summer session he taught at Harvard recalls his teacher's distaste for what he, the student, calls "the Delmore Schwartz syndrome, the Herzog syndrome, certainly the Portnoy syndrome." He told this student, apropos of writing stories, "Have the insight to recognize the neurotic patterns, and the integrity to break them."

Soon after the 1960s were underway, Bernard Malamud lost his way and gave up writing about the kind of small-scale heroes that gave his fiction its magic. The sixties generally was not a good decade for him. He had a love affair with a Bennington student nearly 30 years younger than he; and Malamud, being the earnest man he was, took the affair with great seriousness. He must also have felt under the false commandment for writers to change, expand, grow, cut loose, let 'er rip.

In his novel *The Tenants*, written during the last part of the sixties, Malamud took on the subject of race. A black and a white novelist are the last tenants in a building about to be torn down, and their rivalrousness, as writers and over a woman, is at the center of the book. But the black writer doesn't ring true, the woman in the novel feels tonally wrong; the novel just doesn't come off.

Neither did *Dubin's Lives*, Malamud's account of the affair of a married biographer with a woman 33 years younger than he. Played as comedy, this might have been a rich novel. But Malamud couldn't have played it any straighter. Now that, through the offices of Davis, we know about Malamud's love affair with his student (Malamud's daughter, too, writes about it in her book), *Dubin's Lives* reads like an *apologia*, though not a very persuasive one. "Middle-age," William Dubin thinks, "is when you pay for what you didn't have or couldn't do when you were young." *Dubin's Lives* reads as a self-pitying novel, heavily laden with clichés about youth: "With this girl I know the flowering pleasure beneath innocence, of the natural life," Dubin thinks. And: "One recovers of youth only what he can borrow from the young." How sad—not the plight of the book's hero but the descent of Bernard Malamud, that most conscious of artists, into unconscious pathos.

God's Grace (1982) was Malamud's last published novel. A fantasy, it is about life after nuclear war between the Djanks and the Druzhkies (the Yanks and the Russkies, one supposes) has killed every human being but a paleontologist named Calvin Cohen who was in a bubble at the bottom of the sea with a chimpanzee when the weapons were fired. Once on land, Cohen encounters other chimpanzees and apes and sets out to reestablish a new community of the peace-loving on earth.

"There is nothing so fatal as a good vast subject," says a character in Sybille Bedford's novel, *A Legacy*, and so this one proves for Malamud. A writer whose wonderful stories so often suggested fable now writes a fable without a wonderful story to go with it. Four years after this novel Malamud died, at age 72, of a worn-out heart, but he seems to have died as a literary artist long before.

The received opinion about Bernard Malamud is that he was best as a writer of short stories, and this opinion is probably correct. He himself defined the short story as "dramatizing the multifarious adventures of the human heart." Not many writers—Chekhov, Isaac Babel, Isaac Bashevis Singer—did it better. In his stories, no matter how dark his subject, his comic genius came alive, and when it did, so did his characters, whereas in the longer form of the novel his innate glumness too often seemed to win out.

Philip Davis calls Malamud "great" because he understood the struggle of limited men who discovered themselves in limitless difficulties, and chronicled their struggle to play—one does not speaking of winning—through against impossible odds. Malamud was such a man, and his struggle with his art turns out to be no less poignant a story than one he himself might have written.

Dwight Macdonald
Sunburned by Ideas

AT A 1980 SYMPOSIUM at Skidmore College set in motion by a normally portentous essay by George Steiner about the death of culture in America, Dwight Macdonald, long established as a slashing critic of popular culture and politics, sitting on a panel on "Film and Theatre in America," seemed to have little of interest to say. He was seventy-four years old and a fairly serious boozer who had written almost nothing of interest for more than a decade. He seemed the intellectual equivalent of the boxer who has taken way too many shots to the head. His death by congestive heart failure was two years away. Reacting against the tendency in the discussion to take current-day movies and plays seriously, Macdonald emitted—one almost hears him muttering—a remark that could stand as the epigraph for his long career in intellectual journalism: "When I say 'no' I'm always right and when I say 'yes' I'm almost always wrong."

Dwight Macdonald was the intellectual par excellence, which is to say without any specialized knowledge he was prepared to comment on everything, boisterously and always with what seemed an unwavering confidence. He was the pure type of the amateur, and gloried in the status. And why not? "What's wrong with being an amateur," one easily imagines him saying. "Look where the professionals have got us."

Perhaps this is too much in the spirit of put-down. But then this was also Macdonald's reigning spirit, and possibly it is contagious. Answering a reader who accused him of taking a snide tone in an article on the Ford Foundation in *The New Yorker* in 1954, he put the blame for the article's tone on himself, writing: "after all, I've done a lot of 'snide' writing in my time, [and] am indeed rather an SOB, on paper at least."

I once greatly admired Dwight Macdonald, and I esteemed precisely that unforgiving, relentless SOB side of him above all. As a graduate of Mencken University, with a major in what I took to be anti-BS and a minor in radical politics, I thought Macdonald, when I first came across his writing in the late 1950s, next in succession to H. L. Mencken himself. To read Macdonald on the barbarity of General George S. Patton, the goofy gadgetry of Mortimer J. Adler's Syntopicon to the *Great Books*, the depredations upon the King James Bible committed by its new English translators was to hear melodious bells go off and have the sky fill with fireworks.

Macdonald got away with much that he did through style. The trick of this style was to be sharp and intimate simultaneously. He wrote to a correspondent that the secret to successful lecturing was to speak as if talking to no more than three or four people, and he seemed to write the same way. His general tone was that of the unconnable addressing the already highly skeptical. He never condescended to his readers, but assumed that they were on his intellectual level. A brilliant counterpuncher, specializing in mockery of his opponents, he wrote unshapely essays in which the best things were often to be found in ungainly asterisk footnotes. His witticisms seemed truth-bearing. The first sentence of his article on the Ford Foundation ran: "The Ford Foundation is a large body of money completely surrounded by people who want some."

ORN IN 1906, the son of a father who was a lawyer and a mother with social pretensions, Dwight Macdonald was by background upper-middle class. He was a prep school boy (Exeter) and an Ivy League man (Yale), whose first job out of school was in the executive training program at Macy's. Yet straight out of the gate he was a rebel, antagonizer division. At Exeter, at fourteen, he and a friend formed a group called The Hedonists, whose motto was "*épater les bourgeois*." Although as a young man he held many of the prejudices of his social class—racism, anti-Semitism—a strong belief in religion was not among them. "Literature and knowledge, wisdom and understanding, intellect, call it what you will, is my religion." These would be the gods he worshipped all his life.

"I have a prose mind," the young Dwight Macdonald wrote in college. "I want to write serious criticism." At first, though, he was swept away by the vigor of businessmen, whom he found "were keener, more efficient, more sure of their power than any college prof I ever knew." Upon discovering he had no mind for business, he took up a notion he found in reading Spengler: that there were Men of Truths and Men of Action, and he was clearly among the former. Even then he liked to have an idea—not yet an ideology— in support of any move he made.

Macdonald's next step was to a job at *Time* magazine, which he got through a Yale classmate. Henry Luce, one of the two founders of *Time*, was himself a Yalie, and for many years Yale functioned as a farm team of sorts for Time, Inc. Macdonald began by writing finance and business stories, and soon was transferred to *Fortune*, Luce's new magazine, devoted to chronicling the high romance of industry and commerce. He spoke well of Luce personally— though often mocking him, once referring to him as "Il Luce"— but Time, Inc. was a persistent force for evil in the culture drama that played in Macdonald's head. "For fourteen years," he wrote of his friend James Agee, "like an elephant learning to deploy a parasol, Agee devoted his prodigious gifts to Lucean journalism."

Feeling himself stifled by working for *Fortune*, Macdonald, with two Yale classmates, Fred Dupee and George L. K. Morris, began, as a moonlighting venture, a magazine called *Miscellany*, a bimonthly that lasted nearly two years. Through Dupee he was put in touch with Philip Rahv and William Phillips, who had recently removed the magazine *Partisan Review* out from under the Stalinist sway of the John Reed Club, and were looking for financial supporters to keep it alive. Along with Dupee and Morris, Macdonald became one of the magazine's five principal editors.

Macdonald had been drifting leftward. "Marx goes to the heart of the problem," he wrote to a college classmate in 1936. To the same man he wrote: "I'm growing more and more intolerant of those who stand—or rather squat—in the way of radical progress, the more I learn about the conservative businesses that run this country and the more I see of the injustices done people under this horrible capitalist system." Earlier he had noted that "my greatest vice is my easily aroused indignation—also, I suppose, one of my greatest strengths. I can work up a moral indignation quicker than a fat tennis player can work up a sweat." Over the years his similes, if not his temperament, would improve.

By the time he was thirty, Macdonald was fully formed, intellectually and emotionally. Politically, he was anti-Stalinist and anti-statist yet also anti-capitalist. In the 1936 presidential election, he voted for Earl Browder, the Communist candidate. For a few years he was a member of the Trotskyite Workers Party. But he had only to join a group to find it objectionable and thus left the Workers Party in 1941. Trotsky himself had referred to him as a "Macdonald-ist." (In an article left in his dictaphone machine before his death, he described a Macdonald piece as "very muddled and stupid.") Macdonald always took the high road—that "moral indignation" again—preferring clarity over complexity in politics and keeping a palette restricted to two colors, black and white, with very little interest in gray shadings or texture of any sort. His unwillingness to grant America the least virtue led him to make some impressively idiotic statements, notable among them: "Europe has its Hitlers, but we have our Rotarians."

He settled into a lifelong bumptiousness. His tone and spirit were heavily polemical. This was not helped by his drinking, which did not tend to make him more courtly. The ultimate art form of the *Partisan Review* crowd may have been the go-screw-yourself letter, which they were always sending one another: choice examples of Macdonald's use of the form are found in *A Moral Temper,* a new collection put together by his biographer Michael Wreszin. These were letters written not to disable but to maim. In a milder variant on the form, Delmore Schwartz wrote to Macdonald:

> I always defend you among academics and the genteel (two of your curse words ...) by saying: Yes antagonism for its own sake is his appetite and neurosis, and none of his political predictions come true, but he is a master of expository prose ... and he opens himself up to all kinds of being and beings, Open House Macdonald ought to be his name.

Macdonald shot back: "In future, do me a favor and either keep silent or join the Enemy" and went on to chide Schwartz for not having "the guts to speak out on anything."

A Moral Temper is filled with amusing and interesting material, some of it unknown to me, who has long felt glutted with accounts of the New York Intellectuals. I knew that Macdonald's wife Nancy had served as business manager—the unknown soldier of most little magazines—of *Partisan Review*, but I didn't know that for a good spell much of the daily drudgery of bringing out the magazine fell to the Macdonalds, in whose Tenth Street Village apartment it was actually produced. At one point Macdonald wished to do away with Dupee and William Phillips as members of the editorial board and replace them with Harold Rosenberg and Clement Greenberg.

Macdonald felt that the magazine, bogged down in "Rahv's cautious negativistic policies," had become no more than a periodical anthology, publishing the best things sent to it, which may have had its uses, "but it's not the sort of magazine I would want to give any large amount of time to right now."

What Macdonald wanted was a more directly political magazine than *Partisan Review*. He was himself becoming ever more radicalized. He had turned into a mad letter writer, sending off little blasts to John Dewey, James B. Conway, Freda Kirchwey, and others, among them a letter to Edmund Wilson upbraiding him for not publicly attacking Malcolm Cowley for his Stalinism and Van Wyck Brooks for his insistence on patriotism from American writers.

Finally, in July of 1943, Macdonald resigned from *Partisan Review*, remarking that "the divergence is mainly political." He also had cultural objections to the drift of the journal. He felt that in its cultural coverage the magazine "has become rather academic," where he favored "a more informal, disrespectable, and chance-taking magazine, with a broader and less exclusive 'literary' approach." He claimed that his was the only Marxist point of view on the editorial board.

But the true stumbling point was disagreement about the right position to take on World War II. Macdonald was against siding with the Allies in the war. His Marxist outlook, combined with a newly burgeoning pacifism, persuaded him that the war was little more than one among capitalist imperial powers, excluding the Soviet Union, which, as an anti-Stalinist, he viewed as a totalitarian nation. He thought the war a mistake because it didn't confront the issue of social class and wasn't really a war about democracy. He was an advocate of what was then known as a "Third Camp" position, between fascism and Stalinism, which would be truly revolutionary socialism. Only an intellectual, as Orwell said in another connection, could be so stupid.

ALL AN INTELLECTUAL HAS, it sometimes seems, is his integrity. This he guards as a Boston virgin guards her chastity. What integrity means for most intellectuals is proper alignment of their opinions. Perfect consistency bestows that condition devoutly to be sought, ideological purity. "Ideas and principles were what was important to Dwight, not the politics—nor the historical context," wrote Michael Wreszin in his biography. He is correct in saying that Macdonald did not tailor his writing "to fit an effective political agenda." What mattered more for him was establishing a right alignment of opinion such that he could never be accused of contradiction, inconsistency, impurity—God forfend, selling out.

No little magazine was perhaps more pure than *Politics*, which Macdonald and his wife founded soon after their departure from *Partisan Review*. I had not come into cultural consciousness in time to read *Politics*, but I do recall buying in 1962 a remaindered copy of *Memoirs of a Revolutionist*—later, in paperback, retitled *Politics Past*—which contained much of Macdonald's political writing from the magazine. Even his stylishness cannot survive what now seems the aridity of most of the subject matter: political journalism disappears faster than passion in a bordello on the equator. One can only wonder in bemused astonishment at the perversity of political thinking that, in May 1947, can lead an intelligent person to write: "If we admit there are only two alternatives in world politics, USA or USSR, and if we find it impossible, from the standpoint of our own values and hopes, to choose either, where are we?" In need, I'd say, of a mental gyroscope.

Yet there was something gallant, even heroic about the one-man (and wife) stand entailed in putting out *Politics*. Macdonald did it on the savings from his relatively lucrative salary at *Fortune* and his wife's small trust fund, which brought in $4,000 a year. He stayed on the case of his contributors, whom he couldn't have been paying very much, to produce quality prose. He tells the young Irving Howe that an article he wrote for the magazine on Walter Reuther is "lousy." He eliminated straight literary criticism from the magazine and gave great prominence to criticism of popular culture, which he viewed as helping to barbarize the country. He took potshots at such "lib-labs" and "Stalinoids," as he called them, as Henry Steele Commager, Carey McWilliams, and I. F. Stone. He published the odd, sometimes important piece that might not have found a place elsewhere: Simone Weil on *The Iliad*; Bruno Bettelheim on the concentration camps in Germany. Paul Goodman, Daniel Bell, C. Wright Mills were among the American contributors to the magazine; Andrea Caffi, Victor Serge, and Macdonald's dear friend Nicola Chiaromonte were the leading European contributors.

But at the heart of everything was Macdonald, a three-armed Italian policemen, directing the heavy traffic in competing ideologies, isms, and political schisms. "Negativism remained Dwight's single weapon," his biographer wrote, "a purity in *Politics* and in politics, too, that had its comforts but offered little in the way of genuine political activism."

Brutal in argument though he could be, foolish about other people's reactions to him though he was ("What I don't know about human relations," he confessed during the tumult of leaving his first for his second wife), confident though he was that he was in possession of the truth, there was, in his private life, more give, more of a sense of fairness and largeness of spirit to Dwight Macdonald than his hard-edged writing conveyed. He could command objectivity; he didn't always take things personally.

Although his *bien pensant* friends professed not to understand his liking for William F. Buckley, Jr., and although he attacked the *National Review* for its stylelessness, Macdonald always defended Buckley as a nice man, or, as he told F. W. Dupee, "a hard guy to hate." When late in life someone told him that Borges was a right-winger, he replied, "Who gives a fuck? When you're that good it doesn't matter anymore."

Politics ran between 1943 and 1949. Burnout for its editor set in roughly midway. The magazine went from a monthly to a bimonthly to a quarterly, and sometimes issues came out wildly late or missed appearing altogether. To the financial strain—"Everything I get involved in seems to be a way of not making money, or of losing it"—was added political dubiety: "I have lost my faith in any general and radical improvement in modern society whether by Marxian socialism or pacifist persuasion and ethical example," he wrote to a subscriber in 1949. In an item in its issue of July 1944, Macdonald wrote, "I have always had a sneaking admiration for the editors of a tiny mimeographed journal called *Proletarian Outlook* who once asked the usual leftist question, 'What is to be done?' and answered it unexpectedly: 'Nothing, absolutely nothing.' . . . and the editors showed they were in earnest by folding up their paper." In 1949, to the dismay of his small band of loyal readers—T. S. Eliot among them—Macdonald did the same with *Politics*.

Sectarian Macdonald might from current perspectives seem, but he was not so far out of the main currents of the intellectual life of his time. He was always anti-Stalinist. In 1949 he wrote to William Phillips that "I'm fairly sure Hiss is guilty." He had his doubts about the whole radical perspective on life generally: "Don't you feel," he wrote to Joan Colebrook, with whom he was having an affair, "that we've all been on the wrong track all our lives—by 'we' I mean myself and the milieu I've lived in so long here in NYC." To a reader of *Politics* he noted: "I no longer see any political (or . . . historical) reality in such all-or-nothing doctrines as revolutionary socialism or pacificism."

F REED FROM SECTARIAN POLITICS, Macdonald turned to cultural criticism. This entailed an examination of contemporary cultural products for what they might yield in the way of insight into the presuppositions and inner workings of the larger society in which they were produced. Cultural criticism gave him what fame he would enjoy as a writer and made him a larger figure than he had hitherto seemed, or perhaps even dreamed. In the 1960s, he was briefly employed to do ten-minute bits on movies for NBC's "Today Show." Outside academic life, among critics in the 1950s, 1960s, and early 1970s perhaps only Edmund Wilson was better known. In large measure, this was owing to the magazines for which he had begun to write—*The New Yorker* and, later, *Esquire*, for which he wrote about movies.

In culture, Macdonald was a traditionalist, which meant an elitist, while remaining politically a man of the left. An "anarcho-conservative" was one of the labels he used to describe his own position in this middle period. When tension between the two appeared, the conservative in him tended to win out over the anarchist. He never went for the Beats in America nor the Angry Young Men in England. He despised the watering down of culture—which supplied the powerful animus to his attacks on the Great Books, the revised Bible, and the new *Webster's*—and in devising his own theory of culture made use of the conservative Albert Jay Nock's *Memoirs of a Superfluous Man.*

The quickest way to Dwight Macdonald's heart—with, that is, a dagger—was to call him "our best journalist." Paul Goodman did so, when reviewing *Memoirs of a Revolutionist* in *Dissent*. Macdonald took this to mean that he was fundamentally unserious. "For what is a journalist?" he shot back in a letter to the editor. "Alas, an ignorant and superficial fellow, a kibitzer (rather than 'a man determined to a goal of action and truth')." Macdonald felt himself a thinker, subtle, discriminating, penetrating.

As a writer, he was a sprinter, not a marathon man, and while his dream was the book, his form was the essay. Over the years in his letters he refers to plans to write books on modern dictatorship, misconceptions about capitalism, Communism and fascism, the steel industry, Edgar Allan Poe, an intellectual autobiography, mass culture, and the Kennedy assassination. Enchanted cigarettes, Balzac called such books, works that exist ever so beautifully only in a writer's mind as

the smoke of fantasy forms before him. Macdonald got furthest perhaps on a book on mass culture, but what he produced, a sixty-five-
page essay titled "Masscult & Midcult," shows that he probably didn't
have a full book on the subject in him.

Along with "The Responsibility of Peoples"—his essay about
collective guilt after World War II—"Masscult & Midcult" is Macdonald's most ambitious intellectual effort. A rerun of the old
highbrow, middlebrow, lowbrow triad developed by Russell Lynes,
the essay is a characteristic performance. Written with not a little
dash, it struggles to cut deep without quite being able to do so,
despite an early Adorno quotation and much waving about of the
flag of classical modernism: two Picassos rampant upon a field of
Finnegans Wake.

"Masscult & Midcult" has two chief concerns. The first is to
make the case that mass entertainment is "an instrument of domination." The second is that Midcult, or the middlebrow, will infect
true High Culture, and its values "instead of being transitional—
'the price of progress'—may now themselves become a debased,
permanent standard." Some good things get said along the way.
Of the Lords of Kitsch, as he calls them, Macdonald says "never
underestimate the ignorance and vulgarity of publishers, movie
producers, network executives, and other architects of Masscult."
He declares "a tepid ooze of Midcult is spreading everywhere,"
which seems to me also correct, though this was predictable with
the rise of higher (half-) education.

Yet one wishes Macdonald had taken on tougher cases in this
essay. He attacks *Our Town, The Old Man and the Sea,* Archibald
MacLeish's play *J. B.,* and Stephen Vincent Benét's poem *John
Brown's Body* as examples of Midcult, when it would have been
much more interesting to consider instead, say, *The Death of a Sales-
man, The Naked and the Dead, Cat on a Hot Tin Roof,* and the
poetry of Mark Van Doren. The essay also posits a prelapsarian time
for culture, with patron-aristocrats cultivating beautiful gardens of

art while the happy peasantry enjoyed the purest of folk art. The existence of this ample art-sensitive aristocracy is surely a fiction; and the lower classes of golden olden days, one does well to remember, had such charming divertissements as bearbaiting, dogfights, and gin drinking to keep their minds off the plow.

As for the old leftist question, "What is to be done?" Macdonald's best answer is that we recognize that we really have two cultures, high (or authentic) and the rest (inauthentic), "that have developed in this country, and that it is the national interest to keep them separate." He closes by noting: "Let the majority eavesdrop if they like, but their tastes should be firmly ignored."

Two cultures we now have—have had, shall always have—but I wonder if we need be much concerned about the elitism of high culture, chiefly because it is a democratic elite. In the United States, most of the people who both create and respond to high culture do not derive from the upper- or even the upper-middle classes. They have come instead in greater numbers from the lower-middle and middle classes. Nor have most of them gone to the putatively best schools. Many of the people I know who are in on the secret of the superiority of high culture have come to it by accident, almost magically, through the luck of encountering an important teacher, book, recording, or exhibition. Luck of all good luck, a spark ignited the flame of a passion that didn't burn out.

Things can be done through education to insure that some sparks continue to go off and that flames, once ignited, may be sustained. But railing against mass culture is so much howling in the wind. Smashing the pretenses of middlebrow culture that wants to pass itself off as more serious than it is is something else again, and always worth doing, and this in his time Dwight Macdonald did as well as anyone in the business.

But the question is whether he did anything more. A search of his writings reveals nothing original about his critical opinions. He discovered no new writers or filmmakers, nor revived the reputations of any whose reputations were in need of revival. He slashed James Gould Cozzens's bestselling novel, ignoring his earlier, more impressive work, yet fell for the elevated clichés of Norman Mailer. As a critic of culture, Macdonald fired away out of the secure cockpit of received intellectual opinion. He shot a spitball at Cozzens, for example, for being on record as admiring Somerset Maugham. Would he be shocked, I wonder, to be told that Somerset Maugham is a better writer than Virginia Woolf?

With the exception of a rather disappointing piece on Buster Keaton written near the end of his life, he wrote no extended appreciations of a writer nor any other artist. No one ever accused Macdonald the critic of fairness, evenhandedness, disinterestedness. His was chiefly a polemical mind, quick, sharp, smart, but without much in the way of texture, balance, concern with complexity.

I N *ARMIES OF THE NIGHT* (1968), his account of the anti-Vietnam War protest march on the Pentagon, Norman Mailer describes himself, Robert Lowell, and Dwight Macdonald as "America's best poet, best novelist, and best critic." This is a judgment of all three men that hasn't held up, but it is one made in the first place more on political than literary grounds—as, in 1968, almost all cultural judgments tended to be.

By the time of *Armies of the Night*, Macdonald was all but finished as a writer. As early as 1961 to John Lukacs, who was always encouraging him to be better than he was, he wrote:

> John, I am simply not in a state of mind to discuss seriously what I should be writing. This impasse, this long drawn-out depression, must end sometime. I am aware that it exists and that what I am now writing is not what I should be doing.

He was doing factual pieces for *The New Yorker*, but they seemed not to give him—or his readers—much pleasure. "Fact is, I'm sick to death of doing *New Yorker* fact pieces. . . . Exposition bores me. Let them Look It Up themselves, I say."

Macdonald's biographer describes but does not attempt to explain his writing block. Depression is mentioned; so is heavy drinking and the ineluctable fact of getting older. The general explanation for writing block that I prefer is absence of fresh ideas, which I suspect applies in Dwight Macdonald's case. In one of his letters, he makes the point that the best method for commercial writing—the edge of the hack—is not to care about your subject. But Macdonald was never that kind of writer. Without passion, for him, all interest was drained.

Politics temporarily saved—or, depending on one's point of view, permanently sunk—him. Always anti-Stalinist, sometime in the 1950s, with Stalin now dead, he crossed the line to become anti-anti-Communist. At one point, he was scheduled to replace Irving Kristol as co-editor with Stephen Spender of *Encounter*, the excellent English monthly. Doubts about Macdonald's reliability set in and instead he was offered the job at excellent pay as roving correspondent for the magazine. He wrote a piece called "America! America!" a standard attack on United States materialism (those tail fins on the cars, all those television sets, and—would you believe it?—none of the feeling of community one finds in Tuscany), that was rejected by *Encounter*, with much anger on Macdonald's part. When it was later revealed that *Encounter* had had financial support from the CIA, he wrote that he was an "unwitting" accomplice of the CIA's "dirty work" and had been "played for a sucker." (If Macdonald were writing this piece, an asterisk would now appear, directing readers to a footnote that would read: "Any attempt on his part to return the money is unknown.")

In 1967, he switched his column in *Esquire* from movies to politics. The Free Speech Movement at the universities had let loose the young middle-class masses, the Vietnam War had the country in a state of full-time agitation, first Lyndon Johnson and then that great punch-up Bozo doll Richard Nixon were in the White House—bliss it was in that dawn to be alive, but to be an aging left-winger looking for new life was very heaven.

Dwight Macdonald was, after all these years, saying "Yes" again. "This is becoming our Peloponnesian War," he wrote about Vietnam. He was on the side of the draft-card burners, withheld a fourth of his own income taxes in protest against the war, bracketed Lyndon Johnson with Hitler and Stalin, wrote "I am ashamed to be an American." All cultural standards were out the window, as he praised his friend Mary McCarthy's pro-North Vietnam book (though he himself opposed siding with the Viet Cong, for reasons both moral and prudential) and Barbara Garson's play *MacBird*, which laid the blame for Kennedy's assassination on his vice-president. He attended a White House Festival of the Arts, boorishly asking other guests to sign a petition expressing dismay over the country's policies in Vietnam and the Dominican Republic. At the protest march at the Pentagon, he was disappointed not to have been arrested. A case, not uncommon on the bourgeois left during the 1960s, of pure subpoena envy.

"You must come up right away, Dwight," F. W. Dupee reported enthusiastically over the phone from Columbia University. "It's a revolution. You may never get another chance to see one." Here was Macdonald saying "Yes" again, more yeses this time out than Mrs. Leopold Bloom. He wrote a letter soliciting funds for the Students for a Democratic Society, and declared the Columbia ruckus "a beneficial disturbance." He was puffing on the good stuff—smoking, that is to say, pot—and dabbling with other drugs. At the New Haven trial of the Black Panther Bobby Seale, he showed up wearing two buttons: a pink one for gay rights and another with Eldridge Cleaver's political aperçu, "If you're not part of the solution you're part of the problem." Abbie Hoffman became part of his social set. Going, you might say, going, and gone:

how sympathetic in general I am to the Young, they're the best generation I've known in this country, the cleverest and the most serious and decent (though I wish they'd READ a little—also I hate that obscenity bit, Up Against the Wall Motherfucker turns ME off, nor do I like—though must accept wryly—that "shit" has become an ordinary word of parliamentary discourse, nothing obscene or vulgar intended, they just use it the way we would say "nonsense.") [Well, not quite gone.]

In a very poor piece he wrote for *The New York Review of Books* attacking Tom Wolfe, he showed himself jealous of a younger writer who had swept the boards of all the kind of attention his own writing used to garner. His attack on Wolfe reads rather like an attack on himself. He mentions the books Wolfe had promised but failed to write. He claims that Wolfe's subjects are of only ephemeral interest and his writing won't last. He nails him for producing an anthology on the New Journalism: "Those who can, write; those who can't, anthologize." The irony of this remark is that the only book of Macdonald's that is likely to have a continuing life is *Parodies*, a brilliant anthology he published in 1960.

A CCORDING TO HIS BIOGRAPHER, Macdonald died thinking himself a failure. Perhaps at the end each of us does, but Macdonald had the further goads in this direction supplied by drink and depression. (He was in psychotherapy for the last decade of his life.) Karl Kraus defined a journalist as "no ideas and the ability to express them." Not true of Macdonald, who could be said to have been sunburned by ideas. It's the quality of his ideas that is troublesome. How tired and thin, received and even rather coarse they now seem, beginning with the notion that being radical, which Macdonald liked to remind his readers means "goes to the root," suggested greater penetration than calmer, more centered thinking. While he rightly understood that his mind worked best when rubbing up against the particular and the concrete instance, he allowed lots of ideas—Trotskyism, anarchism, pacifism, even nudism—to violate him by destroying his common sense and balanced perspective.

Aesthetically, Macdonald's central idea seems to be that form and content were indivisible. Style and man, he liked to quote Buffon saying, they are one and the same. One understands the attraction of such a notion, the sweet symmetry of it, but adherence to it would force one to disqualify every bad writer in the history of thought, beginning with Immanuel Kant and running through at least John Dewey.

Another of Macdonald's core ideas was that the job of the intellectual was to keep up the critical pressure, especially on his own country, which, by definition, can never be good enough. The word *intellectual* was purely an honorific for Macdonald and with dissent understood to be the first priority of intellectuals. This of course neglects the possibility of the reflective intellectual, on the model of Tocqueville. Macdonald wanted terribly for intellectuals to matter in history, but seems to have failed to notice that whenever they have—during the French and Russian and (to lower the scale a bit) Cuban revolutions—it has always meant disaster.

Macdonald's other ideas were equally thin. He was big on community, that longstanding intellectual cliché and utopian abstraction, for which no vivid actual examples exist. A creative disorder man, he felt the country was in better shape when disturbance, and not order and harmony, was dominant. The status quo, for him, was always the enemy. When his friend Delmore Schwartz died, he recognized that there was a large self-destructive element in Schwartz—who had an overweening ambition combined with true mental illness—but that didn't stop Macdonald from making the hoary claim that America is not kind to its poets and that Schwartz was, somehow, a victim of mass society.

This same mass society had for a time greatly elevated Macdonald, and such was his fame that in the late 1950s serious people began comparing him to Mark Twain and H. L. Mencken. Writing to Ian Watt about this, Macdonald not immodestly claimed, "I've always been more tough-minded, less open to illusions than Mark was—and my laughter is not so bitter as his was, in his last phase." (There is also the fact that Mark Twain was a thwarted artist, and Macdonald a pure critic.) He disliked Mencken's style, but allowed that "like Mencken, I really enjoy being disappointed and outraged."

But one of the principal differences between Mencken and Macdonald, along with the former having had greater energy, more impressive intellectual production, and stronger influence upon his time, is that Mencken had a surer understanding of the reality of everyday life in America. More crucial, his skepticism ran much deeper. Nowhere was this skepticism greater than about ideas, for which Mencken had the greatest distrust. He was always blowing the whistle on con men—professors, would-be revolutionaries, and anyone else who claimed he had the answers to the impossible questions. Dwight Macdonald far more often blew the trumpet, welcoming their arrival. In a small time way, he was himself, unconsciously, even one of the con men. Poor guy, he just couldn't stop saying "Yes."

Gore Vidal

What Makes Vidal Run

IN THOSE JOURNALS in which they appear, Gore Vidal's essays are the intellectual equivalent of the comics. Intellectual journals are not noted for providing many laughs, but laughter is Gore Vidal's specialty—what he plays for and what he is about. The chief ploy in a Vidal essay is to point out that the emperor has no clothes and then to go a step further and remove the poor man's skin. The spectacle can be most amusing, assuming, of course, that it is not one's own carcass that is being stripped. But two questions present themselves: How serious is Gore Vidal? And how seriously ought he to be taken?

As it should in a familiar essayist, Gore Vidal's personality permeates all he writes. More than merely permeating his essays, his personality is, as we nowadays say, very much up front. His grudges, his biases, his social origins, hints about his sexual adventures, the bits of gossip he has to divulge—all come into play. Often it is less what he has to say than what he says by the way that is of greatest interest. While he claims to detest the cult of personality in writing, perhaps no other contemporary writer plays to it as thoroughly as he. Along with his lacerating wit, his fluent prose, and his wickedly funny mimicry, it is part of the attraction.

Another part of the attraction is that Gore Vidal, in this nation of the sons and grandsons of immigrants, is moderately well born, passing, among Americans, as something of an aristocrat. The reason that we know this is that he keeps telling it to us. His maternal grandfather was Senator T. P. Gore of Oklahoma; his father was said to have been the best all-around athlete ever to have attended West Point, as well as Franklin Delano Roosevelt's first Director of Aeronautics; he himself was a friend of Mrs. Roosevelt; and his stepfather, whom he shared briefly with Jacqueline Kennedy, was Hugh Auchincloss. Far from resenting their upper classes, Americans tend to be quite balmy about them. As a celebrity intellectual, a habitué of the television talk shows, Gore Vidal is the equal in fame to his political opposite number, William F. Buckley, Jr. Quite apart from one's politics, a good accent and what is taken to be an aristocratic point of view are no deterrent in these democratic United States.

GORE VIDAL has also been not only a highly productive but a considerably successful writer, though his success has perhaps not been quite of the kind he would have wished. While his fiction more often than not achieves the commercial status of bestsellers, it has not been taken as seriously as he should no doubt like. But he is generally considered to be a master of the essay. ("America's finest essayist," says the New Statesman.) Novelist and essayist are not altogether separate creatures, however. Aristocratic yet radical heroes out of tune with their times—Julian the Apostate, for example, or Aaron Burr—these are the figures Gore Vidal the novelist is drawn to; it is also the kind of figure upon which Gore Vidal the essayist has modeled himself. If his standing in the view of the world is not so high as he might like, in his own view it is very high indeed. Self-love, in him, does not go unrequited. In a recent interview, he has compared himself as a critic to Edmund Wilson; Vidal

GORE VIDAL

is used to placing himself among good company. But mightn't this be, one wonders, an act not of social but of intellectual climbing?

As a critic, Edmund Wilson was preeminently the connoisseur. His great art was that of an introducer and importer of literature, which, without a trace of condescension, he would lay out before his readers: explaining how a piece of literature works, why it is important, what its place is in the grand scheme of things. As with so many writers who have spent their careers chiefly on the attack—Dwight Macdonald, say, or John Simon—Gore Vidal, unlike Wilson, has no convincing language of praise.

In two of the essays in his collection, *Matters of Fact and Fiction*, Vidal does come to praise rather than, as usual, to bury—and neither essay quite convinces. The first is "The Great World and Louis Auchincloss," in which Vidal sets out to make the case that Louis Auchincloss's talent as a novelist has gone insufficiently recognized because, in the 1950s, "he did not appear to deal with anything that really mattered, like the recent war, or being Jewish/academic/middle class/heterosexual in a world of ball-cutters." Louis Auchincloss himself has written: "I was perfectly clear from the beginning that I was interested in the story of money: how it was made, inherited, lost, spent." This is a very great subject, and Vidal's case for the novelist who has chosen to take it up is compelling up to a point—the point at which one reads Auchincloss's novels. If one has, then Vidal's essay is likely to seem an instance of what the English call over-egging the pudding. Although he is a novelist of seriousness, Louis Auchincloss's novels suffer from what is perhaps the upper-class fault of too great a reticence. He is interested in money, all right, but he does not tell us enough about the mechanics of it. Too often, moreover, his novels degenerate into the stale, and rather cardboard, drama of the depredations of new money upon old money. But in Vidal's telling, the neglect of Louis Auchincloss is tantamount to our neglecting the direct novelistic descendant of Henry James and Edith Wharton in our midst.

The other writer Vidal praises is Italo Calvino. Here his task more closely resembles that which Edmund Wilson regularly took upon himself—a bit of "cultural cross-fertilization," as Wilson used to call it—introducing the little-known work of a writer of one country to the readers of another. Vidal goes through the Wilsonian steps, telling us what is special about Calvino's talent, specifying what he does that no other novelist does, patiently tracing his development by summarizing each of his novels. But then, when he comes to the crux of the matter, the point at which Calvino appears to have struck out for new literary ground in a new "marvelous creation," Vidal backs away. "I shall spare myself the labor," he writes, "noting, however, that something new and wise has begun to enter the Calvino canon. The artist seems to have made a peace with the tension between man's idea of the many and of the one." Here, at just the point where Edmund Wilson would have rolled up his sleeves and set to work, Vidal departs the premises.

As a literary critic, Vidal is much to be preferred on the attack, where he can work his ploy of the emperor-has-no-clothes. The three best essays in *Matters of Fact and Fiction* are essays of this kind: "French Letters: Theories of the New Novel," "The Hacks of Academe," and "American Plastic: The Matter of Fiction." All three have to do with the so-called "post-modernist novel," the first with its theoretical underpinnings, the second with the criticism devoted to it, and the third with the American products themselves, the fiction of Barthelme, Barth, Gass & Company. The first essay is appropriately serious—fewer detours for snideness, fewer one-liners; the second two essays are straight-out devastating. The effect is that of a literary massacre; when Vidal is finished, in the words of one of Truman Capote's killers in *In Cold Blood*, there is hair and flesh all over the walls. If one happens to come to these essays already in agreement with Vidal—as I did—then one can only salute him for a job supremely well done.

ONE OF THE TESTS OF A CRITIC, however, is how persuasive he is when one does not come to his work already in agreement. Does he persuade one to change one's mind, or at least to reconsider one's own position? In "The Top Ten Best Sellers," Vidal had the nice notion of reviewing the best-selling fiction of the spring of 1973. The result is, predictably, a romp. Alas, one of the novelists on the list happens to be a serious one, perhaps the most serious novelist now at work, Alexander Solzhenitsyn. (It could have been worse; one of Gore Vidal's own novels could have been on the list;

or one by Saul Bellow, a novelist he is on record as admiring. The best-seller list can be more complex a matter than Vidal makes it out to be, namely, a perfect reflection of the shabby tastes and pitiful fantasies of his countrymen.)

How does Vidal deal with Solzhenitsyn? Callowly, I should say, and callously. He refers to him more than once as "the noble engineer." After making the obligatory remarks about Solzhenitsyn's courage, he scribbles the by now crusty cliché of those who do not—or cannot—come to terms with Solzhenitsyn's work that "we must honor if not the art the author." He then goes on to dismiss Solzhenitsyn's *August 1914* in a few jokey paragraphs. Not a very impressive performance, especially when, in the same essay, he praises Mary Renault for forcing "even the dullest book-chat writer to recognize that bisexuality was once our culture's norm and that Christianity's perversion of this human fact is the aberration and not the other way round."

Not that it is surprising that Gore Vidal is dismissive of Alexander Solzhenitsyn. A figure such as Solzhenitsyn is, to put it gently, an enormous inconvenience to a writer with Vidal's politics; as great an inconvenience, in a different way, as he was to Gerald Ford and Henry Kissinger. What are those politics? It is not sufficient to say that they are conventionally left wing. They are fanatical in their conventionality, exceptional in their utter unoriginality. To get a firmer idea of what Gore Vidal's politics are, one must imagine someone who has over the past ten years read every single issue of the *Nation*, *Ramparts*, and the *New York Review of Books* and believed every word he has read. Things, in Vidal's politics, couldn't be worse—or less complicated. As sophisticated as Vidal can be in literary matters, so is he coarse in political matters. Attend to a few scraps of sentences which one can finish on one's own: "Since we are essentially a nation of hustlers. . . ."; "The United States has been a garrison state for the last thirty-two years. . . ."; we are "a nation that worships psychopaths. . . ."; "the master-criminal Lyndon

Johnson. . . ."; "the federal constitution . . . has gone on protecting the property of the worthy for two hundred years. . . ."; "The United States has always been a corrupt society. . . ."; and so on.

What Vidal has done, in the essays that comprise the section of his book he entitles "Matters of Fact," is to find books for review that result in essays which give full vent to his politics. Most of the essays are thus setups—so many milk bottles to be knocked over by Vidal's spitballs. Vidal on West Point is the usual philippic about the military-industrial complex. Vidal on a book about ITT is the standard stuff about the evils of the multinational corporations, with references down nostalgia alley all the way back to United Fruit stories. Vidal on E. Howard Hunt attempts to make a case for Lee Harvey Oswald being not a left- but a right-winger. Vidal on Robert Moses displays the stock-in-trade items about the infinite corruptibility of urban politicians.

In short, no surprises, though quite a few disappointments. Put through the meat grinder of Vidal's politics, even such appetizing subjects as the Adams family and Ulysses S. Grant are chopped up into the same dull hamburger: the first Vidal finds interested chiefly in protecting the property of what in America passes for an elite, the second was corrupted in a country that, then as now, has always been corrupt. Vidal refers to the right-wing nightmares strewn with "commie-weirdo-fag-nigger-lovers," but his own nightmares are strewn with CIA-Mafia-military-industrial-Rocke-feller-jock-heterosexuals. Crude politics makes bad literature.

STILL, VIDAL REMAINS FAMOUS for his wit. Above all else—even despite all else—it is what one reads him for. But this book forces the question, What is the nature of that wit? There is wit that is gentle, wit that is playful, wit that is wise. But Gore Vidal's wit is angry; it needs a target, some person or thing to spit on or kick over. Witty though they may be—without the wit they would be altogether unreadable—these are the essays of an angry man. One senses the vigor of grudge behind so much of what he writes. What is the source of Gore Vidal's anger?

On the face of it, he has many reasons for contentment. As a novelist, he sells well and reaches a wide audience. He has worked in Hollywood, for television, and on Broadway, and come away uncontaminated. His celebrity is substantial, the equal certainly to that of the other celebrity intellectuals of our day: Galbraith, Buckley, Capote, Mailer. Yet his anger is nonetheless real, unlike that of, say, George Bernard Shaw, who in his later years came to seem a professional maverick, a man working an act that had worked very well for him in the past. Vidal's anger is best understood if we look at the villains of his essays—Jews, academics, the middle class, and heterosexuals—and attempt to understand why he regards them as villainous.

Jews and academics are bound together in Vidal's contempt, and both, it does not seem going too far to surmise, are connected with his own discontent over his status as a novelist. As a novelist of seriousness writing for a large public, Vidal has compared himself with Saul Bellow, but he is, so far as is known, alone in making the comparison. Nobody else has done so; neither among academic nor among metropolitan critics. In "The Great World and Louis Auchincloss," Vidal refers to "the breathy commercial fictions of all Irvingses—so unlike the higher relevancies of all the Normans." Earlier he complains about Alfred Kazin's reference to Jews as "the mental elite of the power age." He is fairly open in his complaint that Jewish writers seem, as they say on the fair grounds, to have an X on the joint—the X being a monopoly, the joint being contemporary American fiction. A conspiracy is hinted at; hence the neglect of poor Louis Auchincloss. Yet, as conspiracy theories go, this one is already badly dated. The fabled renaissance in fiction by Jewish writers appears already to have petered out, and such public as exists for serious fiction has begun to look elsewhere.

A s for Vidal's hatred of the middle class, this is connected with his hatred of, if not heterosexuals, all that is implicit in heterosexuality: family, raising children, saving, looking to the future through one's children, religion, the humdrum business of life lived in the quotidian. Vidal has never made any secret of his own homosexuality—in *The City and the Pillar* (1948) he published one of the first explicit novels about homosexuality in this country—but of late he has become a propagandist for what once used to be justified as a mere preference. "The love that dare not speak its name," homosexuality used to be called; but so completely have the tables been turned that it now appears to be heterosexuals who dare not speak the name homosexuality. In the reviews of *Matters of Fact and Fiction* that I have read no one has seen fit—not in the *New York Times Book Review* or in *Harper's*—to mention that homosexuality is a strong motif running throughout the book.

It would be better literary manners not to mention sex at all— one wouldn't in the case of most heterosexual writers, with the possible exception of Norman Mailer—but it becomes impossible not to do so here, because Vidal drags (no pun intended, as he would say) it in wherever possible; to the point, even, of obsession. The respectable public (as opposed to the university) novel, he writes, "is always naturalistic, usually urban, often Jewish, and, of course, deeply, sincerely heterosexual." Part of the reason for the neglect of Louis Auchincloss is "the continuing heterosexual dictatorship that has so perfectly perverted in one way or another just about every male in the country." Remarking upon Dan Jenkins's *Semi-Tough* in his "The Ten Top Best Sellers" essay, Vidal writes:

> A peculiarity of American sexual mores is that those men who like to think of themselves as exclusively and triumphantly heterosexual are convinced that the most masculine of all activities is not tending to the sexual needs of women but watching other men play games. I have never understood this aspect of my countrymen

but I suppose there is a need for it (bonding?), just as
the Romans had a need to see people murdered.

Sometimes Vidal's obsession with homosexuality gets a bit confusing. He routs the myth that "all SS were fags," for example,
which would seem to mean that homosexuality is not itself evil.
Yet later, in a capsule standard caricature of J. Edgar Hoover—in
Vidal's view the moral equivalent of an SS man—Hoover is accused
of being homosexual. Then again he informs us that another (for
him) American SS man, Senator Joseph McCarthy, was also a
homosexual: "Just another genial pol with a drinking problem and
an eye for the boys." Whatever is going on here, it sounds unpleas-
antly like fag-baiting.

"I touch with reluctance, and despatch with impatience," wrote
Gibbon in Chapter 44 of *The Decline and Fall of the Roman Empire*,
"a more odious vice, of which modesty rejects the name, and nature
abominates the idea." In his essay on the memoirs of Tennessee
Williams, Gore Vidal writes: "I never had the slightest guilt or
anxiety about what I always took to be a normal human appetite."
On the one hand Vidal remarks upon "the homophobia which is
too much a part of the national psyche," while on the other hand
he pours on the allusions, jokes, and straight talk about homosexuality, even occasionally, as in the Tennessee Williams essay, serving it up for entertainment. When referring to the propensity for
sexual exaggeration of the young Truman Capote, for example, he
writes: "I should note that the young Capote was no less attractive
in his person then than he is today."

ONE MIGHT LEAVE ALL THIS ALONE if Vidal didn't posit the
notion that to be heterosexual is to be, somehow, stunted if
not sick. (As bad, even, as being middle class or American.) Gore
Vidal's homosexuality is of a contentious kind. He uses the word
"homosexualist" as an honorific, rather like aerialist. Unlike other
literary men who have come to terms with their homosexuality—

W. H. Auden and E. M. Forster prominent among them—Vidal, for all his talk about freedom from guilt and anxiety, has not. In a recent essay on Christopher Isherwood, not included in this collection, he lauds Isherwood—who has himself of late spoken about "why there shouldn't be the most powerful sort of love, like St. Francis's, applied to one-night stands"—for obeying what he and other homosexuals construe to be the ecological imperative of not reproducing children.

The interesting problem, of course, is to what extent Gore Vidal's politics are the result of his contentious homosexuality. Is nihilism built into a certain strain of homosexuality? Many of the Pied Pipers of the youth rebellion of the late 1960s were homosexuals. One of the disappointments of Martin Green's otherwise fascinating book, *Children of the Sun*, was the author's refusal to draw the line—or erase it completely—connecting sexual to political adventurism. Perhaps no firm connection can be made. But the question remains.

Irving Howe

The Old People's Socialist League

"A wonderful man, Irving Howe. He's done so much for Yiddish literature and for me. But he's not a youngster any more, and still, still with this socialist *meshugas*."

—ISAAC BASHEVIS SINGER, 1981

ALL THINGS CONSIDERED, the literary critic and political intellectual Irving Howe is having a good afterlife. Since his death in 1993, his reputation, at least in certain quarters, seems only to have grown greater. Every so often one reads a worshipful word about him in the *New Yorker* or the *New Republic* or the *New York Times Book Review*. In his book, *Achieving Our Country*, the philosopher Richard Rorty comes very near to apotheosizing Howe, ranking his essays with those of George Orwell and Edmund Wilson, praising "his incredible energy and his exceptional honesty," and closing with the thought that, although "Howe would have loathed being called a warrior-saint, . . . this term does help catch one of the reasons he came to play the role in many people's lives which Orwell did in his."

The documentary film *Arguing the World* chronicles the undergraduate careers of four New Yorkers—Irving Kristol, Nathan

Glazer, Daniel Bell, and Howe—and follows their political peregrinations since college days. In it, Howe seems to appear on screen more than any of the others, and to be talked about more admiringly; the last word is his; and, by virtue of the fact that he traveled the least far from his early political radicalism, he is subtly made to seem the hero of the story.

Howe is usually counted among the central figures of the group known as the New York Intellectuals: a circle of writers and critics who gathered around *Partisan Review* in the 1930s and later also around *Commentary*. Born in 1920, he was in fact a bit younger than the main figures in the group, and seems also in many ways to have been a psychologically less abstruse and more clearly driven character. Suffering no known writers' blocks, never (apparently) an analysand, he was an immensely productive writer—the author and editor of more than thirty books—as well as, starting in the mid-1950s, one of the founding editors and the main force behind the quarterly magazine *Dissent*.

Before going on to consider his career, though, I need to acknowledge a debt to Irving Howe, who encouraged me when I was a young writer. For a special issue of *Dissent* on blue-collar lives, Howe asked me in the early 1970s to write an article on the town of Cicero, outside Chicago. I was freelancing at the time, and the fee, $500, seemed to me rather grand, especially given the proletarianized look of *Dissent*. Although Howe was not an impressive editor—*Dissent*, then as now, had a fairly high unreadability quotient—he did see it as part of his job to bring along younger writers. Certainly, he attempted to do so with me. I wrote three or four more pieces for *Dissent* over the next few years, including an attack on the then-emerging movement of neo-conservatism and an introduction to the magazine's 25th anniversary issue.

I met Howe during this same period when he came to Chicago to read from *World of Our Fathers*, his big book about the immigrant Jews of New York that was then still a work in progress (it would be

IRVING HOWE

published to immense acclaim in 1976). When he arrived at my apartment, I was rather surprised at what seemed his lack of physical vanity, especially in a man one of whose weaknesses was said to be women (he married four times). To a friend who asked about Howe's appearance, I said that he looked as if his shirt were out of his pants— only it wasn't. He was tall but, after a New York youth in the socialist movement, there was nothing athletic or physically graceful about him. His tie was loose at the neck, his thin, receded hair barely combed. For a man who could command a rather elegant prose style, his physical style had about it something of the *shleppoisie*.

A kinder word, of course, would be *haimish*, or old-shoe, and Howe did have a way in conversation of making me, a youngish contributor to his magazine, feel myself his contemporary and even peer. While staying in Chicago, he was also able to convince his host, the then-chairman of the English department at Northwestern University, to offer me a teaching job. Since I had no PhD, and no teaching experience whatsoever, this must have been an interesting piece of persuasion. Thirty years later, I was still there.

When my own politics changed, Howe and I never had an official falling-out, only a falling-away. He may have thought me, in the old leftist phrase that was a favorite of his, a "sell-out"; more likely, he did not think of me at all, except perhaps as another younger writer who had slipped away. I continued to read him, mostly in the *New Republic*, sometimes in the *New York Review of Books* or the *New York Times Book Review*. I was asked to review his autobiography, *A Margin of Hope* (1982), but found it rather a joyless book and declined. By then, in any case, I had come to read Howe rather differently. I read him through a political loupe and with a slightly skeptical heart.

W HICH BRINGS ME TO a new intellectual biography by Edward Alexander entitled *Irving Howe: Socialist, Critic, Jew*. When, a few years ago, I heard that Alexander (a professor of English at the University of Washington in Seattle, and politically a conservative) was planning this book, I thought, as Igor Stravinsky is said to have remarked whenever he was presented with some new avant-gardeish musical creation, "Who needs it?" Howe was not, after all, a major figure even among his contemporaries. But now that preparations are apparently under way to make him into the American Orwell, it is good to have all the facts of his intellectual life before us. Alexander has written a solid and useful book.

Because of constraints placed upon Alexander by Howe's family—he has not been allowed, for instance, to quote from Howe's letters—*Irving Howe: Socialist, Critic, Jew* is also a relatively impersonal book. Although they knew each other (according to Alexander, Howe used to refer to him as his "favorite reactionary"), and although, from time to time, personal exchanges figure in the narrative, this is for the most part, as Alexander says, "a biography of Howe's mind": an attempt to understand the various positions, political and cultural, taken by Howe over a lengthy and contentious career.

The three terms in Alexander's title—socialist, critic, Jew—have the priorities in precisely the right order. Howe was first a socialist; then a critic; and finally a Jew, secularist division, literary branch. The three categories often fed into one another: the socialist in Howe often set the program for the literary critic, and both socialism and criticism aroused his interest in Yiddish literature, thus bringing out the Jew. But socialism was paramount.

Howe came of age in the mean teeth of the Depression, and no doubt it was the central public event of his life, conditioning and coloring all else. His father's grocery store went bankrupt in 1930, when Irving was ten, and the family, as he would report in *A Margin of Hope*, began "dropping from the lower middle class to the proletariat—the most painful of all social descents." His parents now worked in the dress trade—his mother as an operator, his father as a presser—and Howe grew up with memories of dispossessed families, all their belongings on the sidewalk.

Much more important to the young Irving Howe than the storefront *shul* in which he had his bar mitzvah was the headquarters of the Workman's Circle, where he became attracted to what was in those days known as the "movement" and would soon become, as he later called it, "my home and my passion." At fourteen, as he tells it in *A Margin of Hope*, he began attending Sunday-night meetings of the Young People's Socialist League. He would in time acknowledge that his early socialism provided something akin to a replacement for the religion he never had; once he was under its spell, "everything seemed to fall into place: ordered meaning, a world grasped through theory, a life shaped by purpose."

Howe was never a member of the Communist party; he claimed that, as a boy, he was much put off by the Communists' stringent discipline. But he did become a Trotskyist. One gathers that he never altogether lost his admiration for the figure of Leon Trotsky, who seemed to excite a great many intellectuals through his ability to wield, with stunning success, both pen and (as commander of the Red Army after the Bolshevik Revolution) sword. Howe was always an anti-Stalinist—anti-Stalinism was at the heart of Trotskyism—and he was later a strong anti-Communist. But socialism itself, backed up by an early and thoroughgoing belief in Marxism, gave him all the rope he needed to tie himself in knots.

As an undergraduate at the City College of New York, Howe studied English literature—"it struck me as the easiest major, where I could bullshit the most"—and was smitten, like so many other young men with literary flair, by the work of Edmund Wilson, whose "moral gravity moved me." He also changed his name (he had been born Irving Horenstein). He was hardly the only Jew in the "movement" to do so, the ostensible purpose being to secure a broader American audience for the views of these budding radicals. Thus, Daniel Bell was originally Daniel Bolotsky, and Philip Rahv and William Phillips, the founding editors of *Partisan Review*, were born Ivan Greenbaum and William Litvinsky.

As a young man, Howe, who had discovered in himself a gift for political oratory, must have been an intolerable prig. Irving Kristol remembers Howe from their CCNY days as "thin, gangling, intense, always a little distant, his fingers incessantly and nervously twisting a cowlick as he enunciated sharp and authoritative opinions . . . the Trotskyist leader and 'theoretician.' " Ransacking the files for his early writings, Alexander finds Howe accusing the Communist-party *Daily Worker* of the heinous sin of being "pro-American." The wartime suicide of the exiled Austrian Jewish writer Stefan Zweig is attributed by the adolescent Howe to Zweig's cowardliness as a *petit bourgeois*. An ideological opponent, Louis Fischer, is attacked as "king of the philistines," and "prince of liars."

The first large issue on which Howe, barely out of his teens, weighed in was World War II. He did so as the editor of a four-page sheet called *Labor Action*, and the line he took was that this was a war "between two great imperialist camps"—Nazi Germany on the one side, Britain and America on the other—"to decide which shall dominate the world." It was a war, in other words, "conceived and bred by world capitalism," and therefore neither side deserved the support of socialists. Although he was not alone in this view— Dwight Macdonald took it, and the philosopher Sidney Hook once told me that he had to argue Philip Rahv and William Phillips out of adopting it as the position of *Partisan Review*—one is inevitably reminded here of George Orwell's famous crack that there are certain things one has to be an intellectual to believe, since no ordinary man could be so stupid.

Howe was drafted and served in the Army in Anchorage, Alaska. But throughout the war he continued, under a pseudonym, to attack America's participation in the conflict—this, despite the fact that Hitler's systematic massacre of the Jews of Europe was becoming widely known. Anyone who did not support the so-called "third-camp" position (neither pro-Allied nor pro-Nazi) was dismissed by him as villainous at worst, a boob at best. As late as 1947, Howe felt it a mistake for the US to have entered the war; in a piece discussing the Nuremberg Trials, he claimed that the "real victims of Nazism" were the German working classes. He would later admit to the obtuseness of his views on World War II, but he remained touchy, according to Alexander, about who had the right to remind him of them.

EDWARD ALEXANDER understands the historical forces behind
Irving Howe's turn to socialism, and he recognizes, too, what
kept the socialist myth alive in Howe's mind and spirit up until the
day of his death. Socialism apart, Alexander gives his subject high
marks for acting with honor in his work as an anthologist and high
cicerone to Yiddish literature in America, for his opposition to the
student radicals and New Left intellectuals of the 1960s and 1970s,
his attacks on those who attempted to politicize the teaching of literature in universities in the early 1970s, and his later stand against
deconstructionists and other practitioners of literary theory. Alexander esteems Howe's worth as a literary critic, and he seems genuinely to have liked him as a person. He strains to treat him fairly;
and in my view, he succeeds.

But this hardly means that he forgives all the misbegotten ideas
that socialism led Howe to adopt. Politically and intellectually,
Alexander holds Howe's feet to the fire. He declines to allow, as
softer people often do, that Howe was somehow right even when
he was wrong, or was right precisely for being wrong—that his
putative idealism canceled his mistakes, from his neutrality during
the war to his on-again, off-again feelings for Israel to his willfully
blind refusal to credit the reality of the success of American democratic capitalism. Throughout, Alexander stays on Howe's case,
nailing him for errors both of commission and of omission. In this
exercise, too, I believe he treats Howe fairly.

Still, taking up Howe's political positions one by one, demonstrating how many of these positions look foolish in the light of history,
or in the light of one's own (inevitably) more sensible positions, has
its limitations. This is a method of judgment, after all, by which few
people can hope to escape whipping, history being more cunning
than the human beings who make it, and opinions—especially intellectual opinions—being as volatile as biotech stocks. A more interesting question is one that Sidney Hook put to Howe after a brutal
exchange in the 1940s, in the course of which Howe actually called

the atheist Hook a tool of the Vatican (now there's a notion to make one smile on a gray day): "I do not know whether it is your politics or your character which makes it constitutionally impossible for you to do elementary justice to people with whom you disagree."

Elementary justice is not easy to achieve with an opponent, particularly in politics. But what about in literature? Did Howe's politics also get in the way of his literary judgments?

Howe did not come to literature through advanced academic training, for he had no PhD and he was never aligned with any particular school of criticism. Beginning with his war years in Alaska, he did a vast amount of reading; he seems to have gained his education in public (as many critics do), learning as he wrote. In 1953 he was given a position at Brandeis, where Philip Rahv also taught, and he remained a university teacher—a very good one, it is said— for the rest of his days, later moving to the graduate center of the City University of New York.

As a literary and cultural critic, Howe had a genuine talent for dramatizing ideas. He was much aided in this by his penchant for heightened phrasings. In his prose, militancy is "clenched," youth is "tensed with conviction," Faulkner's characters are "chafed" by the "clamp of family," and Debsian socialism is invaded by "the *dybbuk* of sectarianism." These rhetorical flourishes, which do not always bear too close scrutiny, can give Howe's prose an impressive tension and luster.

Howe was a perceptive, even a penetrating, reader—which is all that one can ask a critic to be—but his efforts were oddly unconcentrated. He wrote often about the phenomenon of modernism in the arts, but he came too late, as a critic, to add much to the enshrinement of the great modernist writers—Joyce, Proust, Kafka, Eliot— in the canon of Western literature. His three books on individual writers (Sherwood Anderson, William Faulkner, and Thomas Hardy) are respectable but not memorable. He could, however, write the good general essay (on Edith Wharton); the stirring essay (on T. E. Lawrence); or the surprisingly well-informed essay (on the 19th-century storywriter Nikolai Leskov). And he was excellent on Yiddish literature; if I had to bet which of Howe's literary works has the best chance of surviving, my money would be on the 1953 anthology, *A Treasury of Yiddish Stories*, which he edited with Eliezer Greenberg and to which the two men supplied a lengthy and brilliant introductory essay that put the subject of Yiddish literature on the American intellectual map.

Unlike Edmund Wilson, Howe was never able to direct the literary traffic when it came to the reputations of his contemporaries. He never wrote at serious length about Norman Mailer, whose wretched essay "The White Negro" originally appeared in *Dissent*. (Howe later apologized for it.) He left Saul Bellow pretty much alone. He once advised Ralph Ellison to align himself more strongly with the protest tradition in black writing, and got absolutely scorched by Ellison in a brilliant reply. But he did resoundingly put down the early feminist writer Kate Millett, at a time when it was useful to do so. And in a 1972 essay in *Commentary* he crushed Philip Roth, who was so rattled that he composed an entire novel, *The Anatomy Lesson*, to dispatch a critic undeniably modeled on Irving Howe.

"POLITICS IN A WORK OF LITERATURE," wrote Stendhal, "is like a pistol-shot in the middle of a concert, something loud and vulgar, and yet a thing to which it is not possible to refuse one's attention." Howe quotes this famous sentence at the outset of his own book of essays on *Politics and the Novel* (1957). He has been praised by his admirers for keeping politics out of his literary criticism, and for his capacity to judge works of art in their own terms, but the truth is rather more complicated.

Not that Howe's literary criticism had an entirely polemical intent. But when it came to the crunch, he could not do what, in his essay on Leskov, he remarked that all great writers do—namely, write "in opposition to his own preconceptions." In *Politics and the Novel*, which he published while still in his thirties, Howe's politics forced him, in effect, to deny the gifts of two of the greatest writers in the history of the novel: Henry James and Joseph Conrad.

That Howe was not an all-out admirer of James is less than shocking. James is, after all, not everyone's cup of caviar, and Howe's taste generally ran to more strongly patterned, less finely textured, more conflict-laden, less subtly nuanced fiction. In *Politics and the Novel*, the text for Howe's anti-James sermon is *The Princess Casamassima* (1887), James's coruscating psychological study of the radical temperament. In considering the novel, Howe gives out little grades— this character is strong, that one wanting in credibility—but then finally dismisses it altogether, largely on the grounds that James's cultural position renders him ill-equipped for his subject. "James's conservatism," Howe writes,

> was peculiarly the conservatism of an artist who has measured all the effort and agony that has gone into the achievements of the past and is not yet ready to skimp their value in the name of the unborn and untested future.

This is hardly the only place in his criticism where Howe reveals his own preference for the ideal over the real; that "unborn and untested future" he alludes to is, of course, the possibility of Utopian socialism, while "conservatism," for a New York intellectual of that day, was a word that had the status of a profanity. But he is mistaken about James. What Howe identifies as political conservatism is really something else—a disbelief in the centrality of politics itself. In a key passage in *The Princess Casamassima*, James writes:

> The figures on the chessboard were still the passions and the jealousies and superstitions and stupidities of man, and thus positioned in regard to each other at any given moment could be of interest only to the grim fates

who played the game—who sat, through the ages, bow-backed over the table.

This is a passage that Howe neglects to quote, and little wonder: the tragic view of life it encapsulates is entirely at odds with his own, politics-ridden, mentality.

The case against Conrad is made even more vehemently in *Politics and the Novel*. Conrad wrote two of the great political novels in the English language—*The Secret Agent* (1907) and *Under Western Eyes* (1910)—and both are devastatingly anti-revolutionary. Both, that is, come out strongly for the real over the ideal. In considering these novels, Howe begins by maintaining that all of Conrad's views were formed by his father's experience in Poland, where as a fighter for Polish freedom he and Conrad's mother were seized by the Russians and subsequently died in exile, and by Conrad's own guilt not merely over his failure to continue his father's struggle but over his need, his "conservative" need, for personal order.

A good bit of critical heavy breathing, of backing-and-filling, accompanies Howe's attempt to defuse the power of Conrad's two novels. Only at chapter's end does he allow that "in our fiercely partisan age it is difficult to read books like *Under Western Eyes* and *The Secret Agent* without fiercely partisan emotions." Imagine the emotions of Howe himself—who actually brings Trotsky in at one point to refute Conrad—when he came upon the following passage from *Under Western Eyes*:

> [I]n a real revolution—not a simple dynastic change or a reform of institutions—in a real revolution the best characters do not come to the front. A violent revolution falls into the hands of narrow-minded fanatics and of tyrannical hypocrites at first. Afterwards comes the turn of all the pretentious intellectual failures of the time. Such are the chiefs and leaders. You will notice that I have left out the mere rogues. The scrupulous and

the just, the noble, humane, and devoted natures; the unselfish and the intelligent may begin a movement—but it passes away from them. They are not the leaders of a revolution. They are its victims: the victims of disgust, of disenchantment—often of remorse.

Hopes grotesquely betrayed, ideals caricatured—that is the definition of revolutionary success.

Joseph Conrad wrote that in 1910, calling every shot in the Russian Revolution that was still seven years away. You might think that he would win a point or two for political prophecy, instead, the passage, which Howe quotes in part, is answered by him with a rather pathetic retort in the form of a well-worn quotation from Orwell: "All revolutions are failures, but they are not all the same failure." (In the modern age, it turns out, they just about all are the same failure.)

GEORGE ORWELL, like Irving Howe, had a little socialism problem of his own; he, too, could not quite let go of the subject. But Orwell, who died a relatively young man in 1950, was also a more honest writer. Irving Howe could never have written *The Road to Wigan Pier* (1937), Orwell's excruciatingly truthful account of the squalor of the working class and the kookiness of those attracted to socialist remedies for its problems. Going to Spain to observe the revolution in progress and join the fight against fascism, Orwell looked the Communist devil in the eye, and when he returned home he once again told the truth in *Homage to Catalonia* (1938).

Hilton Kramer has written about Irving Howe that "whenever the mystique of radical politics in general and the myth of socialism in particular have been allowed to dominate in his work, the result is all but worthless." This is a hard judgment but, I believe, a correct one—correct as applied to Howe's literary criticism, and much more correct as applied to his writing on politics, which tends to be turgid, divorced from reality, and nearly unreadable.

Why did Howe invest so much intellectual and spiritual capital in so desiccating an idea? Socialism was, of course, the great compulsion of his youth, and it gave him both a social life and a way out of the immigrant Jewish milieu in which he was born. Socialism also provided the one political tradition in which intellectuals seemed to be able to exercise leadership and attain status. Nor is the power of displaced religious belief to be ignored. The last word in Howe's *Selected Writings, 1950–1990*, his final collection of essays, is given over to the conviction that the fall of the Soviet Union has in no way disqualified the socialist idea but that, to the contrary, once "the shadow of Stalinism recedes," socialism will emerge in its purer, uncontaminated form. Talk about waiting for the messiah.

From an early age, Howe had locked himself into a strict definition of the role of the intellectual. In his view, the intellectual was always the outsider, and intellectual life was really only valid when one lived it as a member of a minority. This minority was to be in permanent opposition, in a state of perpetual dissatisfaction with the world as it is. Only thus could one's radicalism be preserved intact.

The irony is that for Howe (as for Kazin), precisely this posture of alienation should have proved a winning ticket to the kind of worldly success he was forever claiming to deprecate. Unlike Orwell, who suffered material damage for his brave dissent from the party line on Spain, Howe never suffered at all for his radicalism. It helped land him a distinguished professorship, lectureships at Harvard and Princeton, a major commercial publisher, a MacArthur fellowship, and, now, posthumous beatification as a "warrior-saint" of our age.

Did Howe ever sense that the heavy bag of largely false ideas he had chosen to carry through life had marred much of his literary criticism and guaranteed the irrelevance of his politics? One wonders. To judge the real against an imaginary ideal and always find the real wanting; to refuse to repudiate one's youthful positions, no matter how callow, lest one be thought to have grown cynical;

to consider oneself in permanent opposition to the life of one's time; to dramatize the fear of selling out, even as the world makes a comedy of the drama by continually showering one with rewards; to live out one's days hostage to so many wrong ideas, notions, and biases—did Irving Howe ever say to himself, how do I put this bag down and take life as it and for what it is? I suppose it would be merciful to think that he never did.

Alfred Kazin

What's It All About, Alfie?

T HE AMERICAN LITERARY CRITIC Alfred Kazin was born with an undescended testicle, soon developed a stammer, and grew up, he tells us, in loneliness and shame. His immigrant parents, a taciturn father (a house painter) and an anxious yet dominating mother (a dressmaker who worked out of her kitchen), were locked in a loveless marriage. He was enthrall to psychoanalysis much of his adult life, the instruction from which did not prevent him from contracting three mis-marriages, the last costing him alimony payments, according to his biographer, of $17,000 per month. Such a man should earn our sympathy. But Alfred Kazin, about whom, owing to the publication of his *Journal*, we now know a great deal more than perhaps we ought, doesn't make sympathy easy.

Along with a vast quantity of literary criticism, Kazin wrote three volumes of autobiography: *A Walker in the City* (1951), *Starting Out in the Thirties* (1965), *New York Jew* (1978), and *Writing Was Everything* (1995), a volume of autobiographical writing on literature originally given as lectures at Harvard. Each of these books recounts a good deal about Kazin's life, but in nothing like the personal detail of *Alfred Kazin's Journal*. "Absolute frankness is the only originality," Kazin notes in this *Journal*, which he kept from high-school days until his death at the age of eighty-three in 1998. Yet what if absolute frankness ends not in originality but instead in revelations that are demeaning, even creepy?

A great many entries in *Alfred Kazin's Journal*, which comprise only a part of the 7,000-page journal deposited in the New York Public Library, are devoted to the uses of his journal or to journal-writing generally. Kazin, as he tells us, looked upon his *Journal* as his confession booth, his intellectual lubricant, his lie detector, a stay against loneliness, his lifeline, his method of ascertaining his authenticity, his soul saver. This journal, he wrote on June 27, 1955, "holds what is deepest and truest in me." He also called it his autobiography.

Journals are as various as the people who keep them. Some are mainly introspective (those of the Swiss philosopher and poet Henri Amiel are most notable in this line), others more about the great world than about their authors (Chips Channon's, Noel Coward's, and Leo Lerman's come to mind). The latter kind of journal, studded as it often is with interesting names, gives more immediate pleasure, usually of a gossipy kind. Channon, an unabashed social climber, in one of his journal entries notes that he had the Queens of two different countries at one of his parties on the same night, and became so exultant that he got drunk and didn't remember a thing about the evening.

Alfred Kazin's Journal is both introspective and, as the English say, namey, though many of the names—chiefly members of the circle known as the New York Intellectuals—have already begun to fade. (Such shocks of recognition as the names William Phillips, Lionel Abel, Josephine Herbst, Philip Rahv, and others set off today carry a very low voltage.) Along with providing brief and usually acidulous portraits of literary, intellectual, and academic figures of his day,

Kazin's journal entries recount his aspirations, his needs, and above all his unhappiness, social, domestic, and literary. "What will not be forgiven me by the reader of these diaries is my obstinate unhappiness," Kazin noted in 1968. That unhappiness is pervasive, relieved only by occasional moments of jubilation, usually owing to the entrance of a new woman in his life, and they do not last long. Kazin was a man with something very like an allergy to contentment.

Richard Cook, a professor of English at the University of Missouri at St. Louis, who edited this *Journal* and is Alfred Kazin's biographer, writes in his introduction that the book is "notable for the variety and intensity of feelings on display." The intensity is certainly there. I stopped keeping a count of how frequently in the *Journal* Kazin records weeping; music, movies, reading about Jews, Charlie Chaplin bring on tears. He also writes a fair amount about his soul. The objective here, one assumes, was to demonstrate Kazin's sensitivity, if only to Kazin himself, though he had always planned for his journal to be published.

Viewed from the middle distance, Alfred Kazin's appears a successful career. Born in 1915, he came of age in the poor Brooklyn Jewish neighborhood of Brownsville, last stop on the El. In *A Walker in the City* he chronicled his boyhood in Brownsville. While at City College of New York he did not participate in any of the political alcoves subsequently made famous by their habitués's later intellectual prominence. Bookish and in those days bashful, Kazin cultivated his literary garden. This cultivation would result in *On Native Grounds, An Interpretation of Modern American Prose Literature* (1942), a survey of American prose literature from the 1880s through the Depression that Kazin worked on sedulously over a five-year period in one of the reading rooms of the New York Public Library and that, published when he was twenty-seven, made his reputation.

In his twenties, Kazin free-lanced and was appointed literary editor of *The New Republic*, a job previously held by Edmund Wilson and Malcolm Cowley. (His undescended testicle kept him out of the service in World War II.) Over the years, he acquired a Guggenheim grant, a Rockefeller fellowship, many visiting professorships, lucrative lectures, publication in all the magazines of the day (he wrote 82 pieces for the *New York Review of Books*), travel on behalf of the US State Department, membership in the American Academy of Arts and Letters, and other prizes and plummy emoluments. None of it, though, was sufficient to remove the scowl from his face, to lighten his heart, to staunch the steady flow of grievance that is at the center of his *Journal* and apparently occupied the same position in his life.

Alfred Kazin's complaint comes down to this: he was born poor and Jewish, two strikes that he seems to have held against himself more than the world ever did. Born into the underclass, he contracted a lifetime infection of Socialism, which carried with it such symptoms as the unrelenting hope for universal justice, reverence for his own strain of radical thought, the burden of idealism, and what he took to be his unflinching integrity in the service of that idealism.

Richard Cook writes that "Kazin rarely spared himself his habits of uncompromising assessment." Yet in the end, in this assessment, he seemed always to come out with high marks. His low opinion of almost everyone else— Hannah Arendt and Edmund Wilson excepted—was matched by his high opinion of his own virtue. No one else, it seems, was quite so affected by the Holocaust, so vigilant in upholding the dream of progressive thought unmarred by ideology, so disappointed in America's squalid turn to vulgar prosperity, so sensitive generally as the author of *Alfred Kazin's Journal*. Sell-outs were everywhere, to ideology, to material success, to the security of academic life. No wonder the plaint of loneliness sounds so resoundingly through the *Journal*. No one, really, was fit company for Alfred Kazin.

Kazin was a grievance collector of Homeric proportions, always toting a knapsack filled with an *Iliad* of woes. Irving Howe, Sidney Hook, Philip Rahv, Mary McCarthy, Jacques Barzun, Norman

Podhoretz, Diana and Lionel Trilling, and so many others are found wanting, sorely so, by Kazin. He is put off by Barzun's formality and suavity, and claims to be unable to imagine him in his underwear. Alas, after the sexual revelations of the *Journal*, Kazin is rather too easily imagined in his, and the picture is less than enchanting. In *New York Jew*, Kazin speaks of women "satisfying themselves upon me as if I were a bedpost."

He doesn't like Saul Bellow: "a *kalte mensch*, too full of his being a novelist to be a human being writing . . . " He finds a "fatal particle of vulgarity" in Irving Howe, whom he also describes as "a bigger Klutz than ever. No manners, no grace, just a head like a pot belly." He refers to his students at Amherst as "young shits." He calls Philip Roth "a yenta" and a "male shrew," and scores off his fiction for its claustral quality. He attacks Mark Van Doren for his "pursy little prudence" and "when I think of Van Doren as my beau ideal at all [as he once was] I have to laugh."

At his father's funeral he calls his sister Pearl and his brother-in-law Daniel Bell "rats," and refers elsewhere to Bell's "exhibitionistic" conversation. (My friend Edward Shils, whenever either Kazin's or Bell's name came up, would happily exclaim, "Ah, the man who has the brother-in-law he deserves.") He is vicious about Cynthia Ozick and Lucy Dawidowicz. He cites Marcus Cunliffe on the New York Intellectuals as having "the subtlest understanding of everyone, but each feels that he himself is misunderstood," an observation that, though Kazin doesn't seem to notice, applies with with especial point to himself.

Lionel Trilling looms largest on his enemy list. Kazin's problem with Trilling is that he was falsely civilized, always concerned with his own reputation, too coolly detached, "no one could have been more discerning and less involved." He attacks him for his role in "deradicalizing" intellectuals. In his *Journal* Kazin accuses Trilling of blackballing him from a teaching job at Columbia. In *New York Jew*, he writes: "For Trilling I would always be 'too Jewish,' too full of my own lower-class experience." He allows that Trilling simply didn't like him, "and that nothing whatever can be done about this." Late in the *Journal* he claims that "Trilling cannot stand my vitality."

One is left free to wonder if vitality was really the problem Lionel Trilling had with Kazin. Trilling no doubt did not take to Kazin's schmaltziness. "Schmaltzy" was one of the regular charges against Kazin by various New York intellectuals, by which they meant his oily sort of sentimentality. "Sentimental idealism" Kazin himself calls it, and claims it as "my pervasive fault." He was certainly sentimental about socialism, the ideal of which he wished to keep alive no matter how dreary its effects wherever put into practice in the world. He was sentimental about immigrant Jewish culture, from which of course he fled as quickly as possible. He was sentimental, solipsistically so, above all about himself.

In his mind, as his *Journal* makes plain, Alfred Kazin lived as a character always on the periphery, alienated, the object of other people's derision. The drama always playing in his mind was that of the honorable man, a man of high principle and strong feeling, who was condemned to live out his days insufficiently appreciated, always the underdog no matter how well- established he was. He writes in the *Journal* about "my resentment of the *PR* [*Partisan Review*] group, my unending fear of their scorn." The fear was not unreal.

After seeing Kazin trail sychophantically after Edmund Wilson on the beach at Cape Cod, Saul Bellow once told me: "If Wilson wants to pretend to be Sainte-Beuve, that's one thing; but I'll be damned if I'm going to let Kazin get away with pretending to be Saint-Booboo." Bellow also told me that he was bored with Kazin's filling him in on his kinky sexual exploits. On another occasion, though not to me, Bellow said, "I would as lief look upon a piece of pastrami-stained paper as on the face of Alfred Kazin."

I met Alfred Kazin once, in Chicago, in 1978, for lunch during the time that he was a visiting professor at Notre Dame. He later recorded that the lunch was boring; I thought it excruciating, for he used the time to attack Hilton Kramer, Norman Podhoretz, and other of my friends. When I was the editor of *The American Scholar*, he sent me an essay about Henry James, whose origin must have been a talk he gave, that was so cliché-laden that I gave it, in the dry-cleaner's phrase, same-day service, returning it to him the day upon which I received it. He wrote me a letter informing me that I wrote some good things, but didn't understand my aligning myself with the "trigger-happy Reganites." I wrote back, briefly, to say that, as a literary man, he might have done better than the cliché "trigger-happy." He later wrote a piece in *The New York Review of Books* called "Saving My Soul at the Plaza" (March 31, 1983), attacking neo-conservatives and accusing me in particular of politicizing *The American Scholar*, when in fact I made it a point to keep politics as far as possible out of the magazine during the years I was its editor.

Domestic troubles are not a small item in *Alfred Kazin's Journal*. His three marriages—the first two broken off because of his philandering, the third for that with much *Sturm und Drang* added—and his troubles with his two children are sadly noted. Kazin writes of the violent arguments he and his third wife Ann Birstein had. From the way he writes about it, one might assume that the violence was verbal. But in her memoir of the marriage, *What I Saw at the Fair*, Ann Birstein writes about Kazin beating her up. Anything could bring on the beatings: what he deemed her wayward opinion of Fidel Castro (she thought him a dictator, he didn't; it cost her a broken finger); her criticism of his writing; his discontent with her lovemaking; her complaints about his not supporting her own writing—it didn't take much.

"During other arguments he would rip the sleeves out of my bathrobe..," Ann Birstein writes, "or tear at my hair, which the next day I would comb out in bunches." He would often knock her to the floor. "After these episodes, Alfred would cry, say he had never hit any other woman but me. There was a strange kind of compliment implied." So stormy was the Kazin-Birstein marriage that, when Kazin was a fellow at the Stanford Center for Behavioral Sciences, the police had to be called to their apartment several times because the screaming, dish breaking, and general tumult disturbed their neighbors. About these beatings, the "lie-detector" *Journal* offers not a word. In 1974, near suicide, Ann Birstein had to check into Bellevue. The other side of sentimentality is often brutality.

Literature takes up a fair amount of space in the *Journal*. Kazin was a good but not a great critic. His method was to attempt to get inside the mind of the writers who were the subjects of his criticism, to reveal their inner drama in the historical setting of their time. As a critical writer he had a certain flow, but was without notable powers of formulation. He claimed to live for ideas but didn't seem to have any, or at least none that seemed compelling. He writes often of his vision, but what this vision was is left murky. "Trilling," he writes in the *Journal*, "gave them [readers] a point of view, an attitude, a handy phrase . . . a leading idea. I gave them a lot of history, from every point of view? What my book [he was writing *New York Jew* at the time] needs most urgently is a basic philosophy to leave them with in the end." He neglected to supply it.

As a working critic, Kazin's primary interest was American literature. As a young man, the nineteenth-century American writers grabbed him straightaway. "I shared much of their belief in the ideal freedom and power of the self, in the political and social visions of radical democracy," he wrote in an essay written toward the end of his life called "To Be a Critic." He was more successful writing about Melville than about Emily Dickinson, about Willa Cather than about Thoreau. He often proclaimed the greatness of Emerson, without really being able to establish it through critical argument.

Among contemporary writers, Kazin vastly overrated Norman Mailer. He got off the Saul Bellow bandwagon when Bellow's political tendencies became conservative. Hannah Arendt was for him the intellectual equivalent of a goddess who could do no wrong, despite her heartless performance in *Eichmann in Jerusalem*, which he—elsewhere so publicly sensitive about the plight of Jews in the Holocaust—seems largely to have overlooked. She, he writes, "in her imperious yecke way *is* one of the *just*." Sidney Hook once told me that so many of the New York intellectuals fell for Arendt chiefly because of the impressive armory of her Germanic classical learning. "But about almost everything important," Hook added, "she was wrong."

The writers Kazin most strongly admired were William Blake and Ralph Waldo Emerson and Simone Weil and Jean-Paul Sartre, advocates of life intensely lived, but with an emphatically preacherly vein added. Kazin resembled them all in never being in doubt about his own superior rectitude. He thought himself an American Orwell, his heart always in the right place and keen to take up a position in what used to be known as "the third camp," scorning, that is, Communists and anti-Communists alike. "I have never recovered from the thirties or wanted to," he wrote in *Writing Was Everything*. "A son of the immigrant working class whose parents were tortured by poverty, I hardly needed the depression to be suspicious of moneyed power, or to see that in this society money is the first measure of all things and the only measure of many—or to learn for myself that there is no way in America of being honorably poor."

Kazin preferred to think himself a writer rather than a critic. But in his non-critical writing, without a book or author to intervene between him and the reader, his personality comes through and putrifies everything with his self-righteous sourness. Like Emerson and Thoreau, he was a blatantly self-approving writer, and the strong element of confidence about his own virtue spoils much of what he wrote apart from his criticism, including his autobiographies.

The first of these, *A Walker in the City*, which in his *Journal* he refers to as "my *Walker* poem," and "a fable of youth, sweetness, and search," today feels overwrought, over-written, straining for lyricism: "Somewhere below they were roasting coffee, handling spices—the odor was in the pillars, in the battered wooden planks of the promenade beneath my feet, in the blackness upwelling from the river." Lots of such passages occur in a book that often reads as if written by Walt Whitman bloated on fried matzos. The other two volumes of Kazin's autobiography are blighted by Kazin's need to score off enemies, left and right, real and imagined. Remove these portions about his enemies and the books go up in smoke.

One couldn't win with Alfred Kazin. The poverty of the Jews was horrible but Jewish prosperity is vulgar. Communism was a dream gone wrong, a nightmare, but anti-Communism was crude and anti-Communists usually self-serving. America was once the great hope but its craze for power drained it of its original inspiration: its behavior in Vietnam he at one point compares to that of the Germans at Auschwitz and the Russians in the Gulag. As for Israel, between "1943–1982, the 40 years that I lived entirely with the Holocaust . . . ended for me with Begin, Sharon, Shamir, and the war in Lebanon." In his *Journal* he writes: "As a state [the Jews] can only misuse, exploit, and even kill this mission" of being a chosen people destined "to teach all around them the inexpungable memory of the given source from which our lives come." He wanted a secure academic post but didn't want to be considered an academic. Late in life he buys a house in Roxbury, Connecticut, and is put off by his wealthy neighbors.

"I am unappeased and unappeasable," Kazin writes in his *Journal.* "I am dissatisfied, profoundly so, with the world," he wrote elsewhere. "But I would be dissatisfied with any world. And I'd hate to lose my dissatisfaction." He never did. In his *Journal* he notes that "I will *not* be satisfied by the mediocrity all around me." He must have thought such relentless discontent evidence of his high moral standard, a standard that lent him a certain grandeur, when it merely made him seem stiff-necked and self-congratulatory.

Toward the end of his life, Kazin wrote: "The fact is that the journals scare even me when I look them over—so much longing, so much resentment, so many names to worry about even if they don't sue me for libel: Hah Hah. . . ." He also writes: "Why, sitting on the can, do I suddenly weep?" Yes, why so much weeping, anger, envy? What's it all about, Alfie?

Kazin's *Journal* does not tell us what he finally made of his life. Surely he would have preferred a career closer to that of Edmund Wilson or, even though he consistently denigrated it, that of Lionel Trilling: a career imbued with more dignity, self-control, honor, a sense of lasting achievement. But Kazin was too anxious and too angry, too often out of control, to bring it off. He blamed his anxiety on his mother, but his anger was his own. He was a man perpetually ticked off, a walking wound in search of a saltshaker. He genuinely believed that anyone who didn't agree with him could only have the lowest possible motives for not doing so.

But agree about what, exactly? That power in and of itself is bad; that America, begun in promise, is now corrupt beyond all redemption; that Israel has forfeited its moral authority by taking steps to protect itself; that, finally, no one was as penetrating, soulful, sensitive, and virtuous as Alfred Kazin? That's a lot to have to agree with, and the publication of *Alfred Kazin's Journal* makes it impossible ever to do so.

Irving Kristol

A Genius of Temperament

As the last of the New York Intellectuals depart the planet, it becomes apparent that Irving Kristol, who published less than most of them, had a wider and deeper influence on his time than all of them. Just how and why is not all that clear, but it is so. Nor is it clear how best to describe Irving. He wasn't a writer exactly, or at least not primarily; neither was he chiefly an editor, though he in fact edited some of the best intellectual magazines of his day. He wrote political journalism, but to call him a political journalist is severely to limit him. That baggy-pants term public intellectual doesn't do the job, either. He was over his lifetime associated with various institutions—magazines, universities, think tanks—but he always seemed somehow slightly outside of, somehow larger than, all of them.

Irving was the ultimate free-lance. If my father were alive, he would say of Irving Kristol that he worked out of his car, with the irony added that Irving, who grew up in New York to immigrant parents, never learned to drive. Sui generis was what Irving was—an amazing figure, whose like we shall probably not see again for the simple reason that no one quite like him existed before.

He wrote with clarity and force, subtlety and persuasiveness, but, unlike a true writer, didn't feel the need to do it all the time. He was a splendid speaker, non-oratorical, casual, off-the-cuff division: witty, smart, commonsensical, always with a point to make, one that one hadn't considered before. I recall once hearing Irving introduced by Christopher DeMuth in a room that had a large movie screen behind the speaker's desk. "I see," said Christopher, "that Irving has brought his usual full panoply of audio-visual aids." "Yes," replied Irving, "a cigarette," which he took out of his pocket and tapped on the desk before beginning to speak.

Irving's reigning intellectual note was that of skepticism. As an intellectual, he lived by ideas, but at the same time he greatly distrusted them. All ideas for him, like saints for George Orwell, were guilty until proven innocent. "Create a concept and reality leaves the room," Ortega y Gasset wrote, and my guess is that Irving would have seconded the motion. In the realm of ideas, he preferred those that existed in the world as it is as against those that had to be imposed by elaborate argument or government fiat.

At the same time, he liked to play with ideas. I remember a Chinese dinner with him at which he tried out the idea that Modernism in the arts was the devil's work. He meant the actual capital-D Devil. Was he serious? I'm not certain even now, but the discussion, in which Irving argued that Modernist art undermined tradition and as such human confidence in institutions, was provocative in the best sense, causing a true believer (that would be me) to defend Modernism by arguing that the best of it was based precisely on tradition.

Irving himself did not provoke. I never saw him angry. Polemical though he could be in his political journalism, I never heard him put down political or intellectual enemies in conversation. If I could have any of his gifts, it would be his extraordinary ability not to take things personally. Accusations, insults, obloquy, all seemed to bounce off him. He had a genius of temperament.

He also seemed to be without vanity. I never heard him claim credit for any of the things that obituarists are now claiming for him: helping to elect Ronald Reagan, launching neoconservatism, discovering youthful talent, and the rest of it. I never heard him quote himself, or remind other people of things he had written, or make any claims about himself whatsoever. I once told him that I thought *Encounter*, which he edited with Stephen Spender in London, and on which, I am certain, he did the lion's share of the work, was the best intellectual journal of my lifetime, but my praise appeared only to embarrass him. He didn't seem to wish to talk much about it.

Irving's specialty was the insertion of common sense into places where one wasn't accustomed to find it. He advised the young not to bring along a novel when being interviewed for a job, because, however mistakenly, it creates the impression of dreaminess. When Michael Joyce became the head of the Olin Foundation, with responsibility for doling out large sums of money, Irving, while congratulating him, told him that in his new job he could promise him two things: First, he would never eat another bad lunch; and, second, no one would ever speak truthfully to him again. I once gave a lecture on friendship in which I made the argument that we mustn't expect our friends to share our opinions, but look instead for something beyond mere opinion to that more important entity, point of view. Irving, who was in the audience, told me afterwards that I had a good point, and he agreed with it, "except of course for Israel and Palestine."

The older one gets as a writer the fewer people are around whose approval means much. Irving was one of those remaining people for me. When I heard that he took pleasure in my short stories, I was genuinely delighted. He once introduced me at a talk I gave at the American Enterprise Institute, saying that I was in the tradition of the cosmopolitan wits. I was so pleased by this that before beginning my talk I couldn't refrain from saying that being introduced in this way by Irving I felt as if I were Andy Williams introduced by Frank Sinatra saying this guy can really sing, or Rodney Dangerfield introduced by Charlie Chaplin saying this guy has some wonderful moves.

Irving was an extraordinarily selfless husband—a feminist in action if decidedly not in ideology. By this I mean that in Irving's biography, in the early 1940s, there is a lacuna, during which he took time away from his own then youthful career so that his wife Bea (who is Gertrude Himmelfarb, the historian of Victorian intellectual culture) could do her graduate studies at the University of Chicago and later research for her doctorate in London. How many men, of whatever political views, would have done that 60 years ago?

Irving and Bea were the Nick and Nora Charles of American intellectual life. They were always on the case together. They had a marriage in which the question of equality seemed simply never to have arisen. Congruent in their opinions, perfectly joined in what they valued, they were as united as any couple I have ever known.

One of my fondest memories is of a panel at Harvard on which sat Irving, Michael Walzer, Martin Peretz, and Norman Podhoretz. I don't recall the subject, but only that Irving, without being the least pushy about it, dominated, lighting up the room with his easy wit and charming good sense. I looked over at Bea, who was sitting a few rows in front of me and to my left, and could see how utterly enthralled she was by her husband's brilliance. After more than 50 years of life together, she still had a crush on him. I didn't have the least difficulty understanding why.

Arthur M. Schlesinger, Jr.

The Man on Whom
Everything Was Lost

"Stravinsky had a good deal of drink during dinner, and after-wards, in a somewhat blatant way, Arthur Schlesinger said to him, 'Well, Mr. Stravinsky, how does it feel to be in the White House?' Stravinsky threw out his hands and announced, 'It—feels—dronk!' [President] Kennedy said to Arthur, 'Go to your kennel.'"

—EDMUND WILSON, *The Sixties*

OTHERS HAVE OFFERED A KINDER, gentler view of Arthur M. Schlesinger, Jr. than the one provided by Edmund Wilson in his diaries. "He was a great historian and an incomparable witness," said Paul LeClerc, president of the New York Public Library, in announcing the library's acquisition of Schlesinger's voluminous personal papers. LeClerc went on to compare Schlesinger, who died in 2007 at the age of eighty-nine, with Voltaire—to the latter's detriment. Voltaire, after all, may have been "the historian of France, but he didn't get in the inner circle the way Schlesinger did."

The recent publication of Schlesinger's diaries is a useful reality check on such claims. The book also provides an account of a career in American liberalism that is, in microcosm, a partial account of the career of the liberal temperament itself over the past half-century.

A CHARMED LIFE, ARTHUR SCHLESINGER'S, or so it might seem from the middle distance. He was the son of the Harvard historian Arthur M. Schlesinger, Sr. (1888–1965), a scholar noted for polling other historians on who were the great Presidents and for setting out a cyclical view in which conservative and liberal waves altered in American politics. Arthur, Jr., who was born in 1917, was the very model of the good student: in his memoir of his early years, *A Life in the Twentieth Century* (2000), he mentions getting only two Bs in his four years at Harvard. His undergraduate thesis, a study of the Transcendentalist figure Orestes Brownson, was published by Little, Brown when he was twenty-one, to acclaim from Henry Steele Commager and Charles Beard.

After college and a year abroad on a Henry fellowship at Cambridge, Schlesinger returned to Harvard as a junior member of the school's elite Society of Fellows, an institution set up to combat the tendency toward the too-narrow specialization in academic life brought on by the rising popularity of the PhD While a junior fellow, Schlesinger worked on *The Age of Jackson* (1945), published when he was twenty-eight. This book won a Pulitzer Prize and gained him an early seat at the high table of American historians. Offers of teaching jobs followed from Yale, Johns Hopkins, Chicago, Minnesota, and Harvard. A man who always carried a well-lubricated status detector, he settled in at Harvard.

Early in his faculty days, Schlesinger set to work on a multi-volume biography of Franklin Delano Roosevelt, of which over the years he completed three volumes. His plan was to emulate the method of James Parton's biography of Andrew Jackson, a work built on interviews with many of the people still alive who had served in, or opposed, Jackson's administration. The ultimate Partonian method would be available to Schlesinger when he came to write his books about John F. Kennedy (*A Thousand Days: John F. Kennedy in the White House,* 1965) and Robert F. Kennedy (*Robert Kennedy and His Times,* 1978), two men whose political ambitions he himself served faithfully.

Although he had grown up in an academic household and had mastered the moves of the serious scholar, Schlesinger never felt entirely comfortable as an academic. In his *Journals* he reports that he was a good enough teacher, but that his heart was always elsewhere. The great world beckoned, and though through most of his adult life he would enjoy the security of tenure and the status of an academic eminence, the great world is what, for better and worse, he attained.

Schlesinger had an early taste of that world in 1945–1946 when, with the offer from Harvard in his pocket, he took a year off to live as a freelance. With his wife and infant twins he moved to Chevy Chase, Maryland, just outside Washington. Through connections made in the OSS and OWI during the war, he was soon invited to dinners with members of the circle around the columnist Joseph Alsop. They included Philip and Katharine Graham of the *Washington Post*, Felix Frankfurter (a friend of his parents), James Byrnes, Averell Harriman, James Forrestal, Clark Clifford, Chip Bohlen—in short, the Democratic or, really, the old New Deal establishment. At Alsop's he also met the important journalists James Reston and Walter Lippmann, and a young congressman named John Fitzgerald Kennedy.

During his freelance year, Schlesinger wrote articles for *Fortune*, which at the time also employed John Kenneth Galbraith, John Hersey, Dwight Macdonald, Theodore H. White, and other liberals and left-wing anti-Communists. ("For some goddamn reason," remarked Henry Luce, *Fortune*'s publisher, "Republicans can't write.") He also wrote for *Look*, *Life*, the *Saturday Evening Post*, and the highbrow *Partisan Review*. Perhaps his most famous bit of journalism from that year was a *Fortune* article on the Supreme Court, drawing a distinction (taken from a professor at Harvard

Law School named Reed Powell) between judicial restraint and judicial activism. During this year, too, he did a bit of minor speechwriting for President Harry Truman, setting a pattern for the future when he would be frequently called upon to draft or redraft speeches for major figures in the Democratic Party, some-times for two opposing candidates in the same campaign.

SCHLESINGER FIRST BECAME HEAVILY INVOLVED in politics in connection with the 1952 presidential campaign of Adlai Stevenson. He was among a goodly number of academics excited by Stevenson, then the governor of Illinois and a man of great personal charm. Stevenson, they felt, held out the promise of raising the quality of Democratic-party politics, taking it out of the hands of ward-heelers and making it more idealistic, civilized, serious. "Madly for Adlai" was the Stevenson campaign slogan, and Schlesinger was as madly for him as anyone.

"An original personality in our public life," Schlesinger calls Stevenson in one of his early journal entries—"the start of something new." The start and, one has to add, also the finish. Attractive as he was, Stevenson seemed to specialize in disappointing; he had the quality, fatal to any serious politician, of being unable to admit, perhaps even to himself, that he wanted power. In 1960, after two defeats in presidential elections against the very popular Dwight Eisenhower, Stevenson, hoping to be nominated for a third run, dallied, dithered, awaited a draft, and finally lost the nomination that might otherwise have been his.

Arthur Schlesinger's *Journals* begin with his devotion to Adlai Stevenson. As both a historian and a political activist, Schlesinger was a man in need of heroes. He viewed Andrew Jackson as chiefly thus. Franklin Delano Roosevelt was an even larger hero to him: "I remain to this day," he would later write, "a New Dealer, unreconstructed and unrepentant." And Schlesinger preferred his heroes neat; no warts allowed. In the *Journals* he does not want to believe the substantial evidence suggesting that FDR failed to do everything he could have done to save the European Jews from Hitler. Burnished was how he liked his heroes, and in his own writing about them he applied the sheen.

No hero would compare for Schlesinger to John F. Kennedy, his infatuation with whom finally gave such meaning as it had to his life. As the *Journals* make unmistakably clear, this infatuation— adoration is a more precise word—extended to the vast Kennedy family. First Jack, then Bobby, ultimately the entire clan— Schlesinger seems never to have met a Kennedy he did not adore. The result, as even he seems vaguely to grasp, would be the ruin of his reputation as a serious historian. A 1993 journal entry notes that the writer Joe McGinnis had announced on television—"lightly, I assume"—that "he would like to do a biography of me to show how an eminent historian had lost his integrity in order to curry favor with the Kennedys." This indeed has become the standard view of Arthur Schlesinger, and nothing in his *Journals* disproves it.

When Schlesinger abandoned Stevenson at the 1960 Democratic convention to jump to the side of John F. Kennedy, he recounts that he "felt sick about it; and still feel guilty and sad." He also had his hesitations. "I am quite sure now that Kennedy has most of FDR's lesser qualities," he writes while attending the nominating convention. "Whether he has FDR's greater qualities is the problem for the future." But once on the Kennedy bus, Schlesinger never got off, and never again would he compare John F. Kennedy unfavorably with anyone. If JFK did not in fact come anywhere close to having "FDR's greater qualities," Schlesinger, in writing about him after his death, would award them to him with oak-leaf clusters.

JOHN KENNEDY was four months younger than Schlesinger, and two classes behind him at Harvard. (Ever the good student, Schlesinger had entered college early.) Part of the attraction felt by Schlesinger must have been that of the bookish boy for the good athlete, of the man with thick glasses and a slight lisp for the man who always got the girl, of the middle-class man for the man who goes through life without ever having to consult his wallet.

Arthur Schlesinger took the Kennedys at their own high self-valuation—which is to say, as American aristocrats. On his first visit to the family compound in Hyannisport in August 1960, he notes that what he found there reminded him of what he had found in visiting Adlai Stevenson:

> the same spacious, tranquil country house; the same upper-class ease of manners; the same sense of children and dogs about; the same humor; the frank conversation about a wide variety of subjects; the same quick transition from the serious to the frivolous. . . . I was able to talk freely with Jack most of the time. He talked about everything without constraint.

What Schlesinger did not seem to notice was that he was being given the full-court press of seduction. A past master at the art, Kennedy would turn his considerable charms on other Harvard figures: Galbraith, Daniel P. Moynihan, McGeorge Bundy. Along with Theodore Sorensen, his chief speechwriter, and Richard Goodwin, these were the men who gave us—and some of whom continue to give us—the fantasy of the brief Kennedy years as a place of mythical brilliance: Camelot, in the inflated term first applied by Theodore H. White. In an otherwise perfectly mediocre presidency, the one savvy thing John F. Kennedy did, at least for his own reputation, was to bring these Cambridge intellectuals on board. After his death, a number of them would dedicate their lives—and none more thoroughly than Schlesinger—to portraying him as a great man and his administration as, in the cant phrase, a defining moment in American history.

John Kennedy clearly found Schlesinger's connections useful. More than once he would call upon him to explain his positions to such influential journalists as Lippmann and Reston. But otherwise he did not make much use of Schlesinger during the 1960 election campaign. "Jack," writes Schlesinger in his journal, "obviously did not much need the kind of thing I was good at," though he does not say what exactly that was. After the election there was brief talk of Schlesinger's being appointed National Security Adviser, a job that went instead to Bundy. Having declined an ambassadorship and then a position as Assistant Secretary of State for Cultural Affairs, he eventually signed on as Special Assistant to the President, with an office in the East Wing.

At the White House, Schlesinger proved to be an odd-jobs man: sent off with Bundy to tamp down troubles in Latin America, contributing to presidential speeches, sitting in on Oval Office meetings. But his larger assignment seems to have been the self-appointed one of attempting to keep the President on the liberal track—at which he was far from successful—and of explaining to liberals that Kennedy was not as disappointing to their hopes as he seemed, especially after he had made a number of rather conservative cabinet appointments, insisted on moving slowly on civil rights, and continued to express traditionally hawkish views on the cold war.

No evidence exists that Arthur Schlesinger had much influence on the Kennedy administration. He stopped nothing, changed nothing. In domestic policy, he was somewhat handcuffed, owing in part to a piece he had written for a symposium in *Partisan Review* on the future of socialism, for which he held out hopes. In foreign policy he tried to persuade Kennedy not to resume nuclear testing, but the President "was not interested in hearing more liberal guff on this matter." His connection with the Cuban Missile Crisis he describes as "peripheral." He blames Dean Rusk, Kennedy's Secretary of State, for most of the administration's foreign-policy failures, and the CIA for the rest. The President, however, is never wrong, not really, not finally. After the disastrous Bay of Pigs adventure, Schlesinger notes in his *Journals*: "Beneath his total control, he saw from the moment things began to go wrong the whole proportions of the catastrophe. He is wholly honest with himself, I think."

Arthur Schlesinger must have believed he was signing on as intellectual *consigliere* to Kennedy. If so, he can only have been disappointed. "I have the feeling," Schlesinger writes in his *Journals*, "that the President somewhat discounts my views, primarily because he regards me as a claiming agency for standardized liberalism, partly also because he considers me to be, after all, an intellectual and insufficiently practical and realistic." But when the Kennedy political saga ended that afternoon in Dallas, the failed *consigliere* straightaway took up his lifetime post as the President's most ardent panegyrist. "It will be a long time," he writes in his journal, "before this nation is as nobly led as it has been in these last three years." Before the coffin is closed, he gazes in grief upon "my beloved President, my beloved friend."

Schlesinger was persuaded to stay on at the White House for a bit by Lyndon Johnson, a man for whom he had no great regard— he felt Johnson to be a man of low taste—and would have even less once Johnson had expanded the Vietnam war. When he learned that he had been replaced as White House intellectual by Eric Goldman, a historian from Princeton, he resigned.

IN 1968, ROUSED AT LAST from his depression over Kennedy's death and Johnson's escalation of the war in Vietnam, Schlesinger got on the Bobby Kennedy bus. In his usual uncritical way he thought Bobby equipped with perfect political instincts, a man always acting "essentially out of conscience." He could not understand how anyone would fail to recognize Bobby's genius and purity; in the *Journals* he is startled to discover that he himself is despised by the New York intellectual crowd—Robert Lowell and Elizabeth Hardwick, Alfred Kazin, Jason and Barbara Epstein—for preferring Bobby to Eugene McCarthy. But the June 6, 1968, assassination of Bobby Kennedy in Los Angeles put an end to Schlesinger's dream of returning to the White House.

Enter, next, Ted Kennedy—to, as a screenwriter might put it, "strains of 'Bridge over Troubled Waters' playing faintly in the background." The bridge, of course, was the one at Chappaquiddick, and it put paid to any presidential aspirations entertained by the then-junior Senator from Massachusetts. The temper of the times had also changed: never again would the press be so accommodating to the foibles of politicians as it had been to John Kennedy's: ignoring his illnesses, his sexual athleticism, even his golfing. Yet Schlesinger in the *Journals* remains hopeful throughout that Ted Kennedy will make a run for it; in 1979, he writes that "I now begin to feel that Ted Kennedy may be planning to run after all" (as indeed he very briefly did), and as late as 1984 his hopes were still alive. His waiting for Teddy left Schlesinger rather in the position of the poor village idiot paid by his *shtetl* to sit at the outskirts of town awaiting the arrival of the messiah.

Schlesinger's views of presidential candidates were in general, and with one exception, entirely predictable: he was always for the candidate he judged the most liberal—a term whose definition shifted over time. The exception was Jimmy Carter, whom he and a great many other liberals could not stand. "He seems a mean little man," Schlesinger writes in his *Journals*, by which he may merely have been telegraphing his displeasure at being entirely excluded from the action. In the 1976 election, between Carter and Gerald Ford, he went for John Anderson, the Independent.

By this time, Schlesinger was motivated largely by nostalgia for the past and for "the really quite active role I had in national politics in the 1950s." He was also feeling more than a touch sorry for himself: "I have been totally out of things since RFK died, and never more so than this year [1976]. I am frank to say that I miss it." Not long afterward, having been awarded an Albert Schweitzer professorship at the City University of New York, he moved into a townhouse on East 64th Street with his second wife and their two children. Richard Nixon, who bought the house aligned with his on East 65th Street, became his very unwelcome back-fence neighbor.

SOCIALLY, SCHLESINGER FLOURISHED IN NEW YORK, becoming a fixture at the Century Club, a friend of Lauren Bacall and Leonard Bernstein, invited to parties and dinners at the homes of Bianca Jagger, Diana Vreeland, and Brooke Astor. In his brightly striped shirts and large bowties, he was the very model of the social butterfly.

He never got back to his FDR biography. Instead, he contributed op-eds, appeared on *The Charlie Rose Show*, *Today*, and other programs, wrote reviews, defended the Kennedys against what he took to be the malicious lies of critical biographers, and was often called on, not so much for the truth—it had long been recognized that he hadn't a scintilla of impartiality—as for the liberal position on issues and questions of the day. The columnist David Broder described him as "James Carville in cap and gown."

Over the years, as Jimmy Carter was followed by two terms of the "trigger-happy" Ronald Reagan and one of George H. W. Bush, Schlesinger, in his alienation, moved further and further to the Left. True, he was put off by the hippie version of the New Left. He disdained the cultural influence of Andy Warhol, rightly characterized Tony Kushner's play *Angels in America* as "a pile of pretentious crap," and published a book, *The Disuniting of America*, attacking the effects of multiculturalism in education. Yet having once been a strong anti-Communist, he now turned against the anti-Communists, and scorned such old allies as Sidney Hook and Hubert Humphrey. He declined to see that the Democratic party, ever since being taken over in 1972 by the forces of McGovernism—the coalition of victimhoods—had been moving steadily leftward, bringing its most radical elements into the center of the action and altering its character permanently. Eugene McCarthy called George McGovern "the man who destroyed American liberalism." That was not the way Schlesinger viewed it.

Captured with present-tense fidelity, his *Journals* provide the sad portrait of the liberal New Dealer in his old age: a man who believes that America has become an international bully, and who cannot imagine a greater evil in the world than the figure of Richard Nixon; who assumes that business is inherently vile, capitalism utterly corrupt, and government essentially benevolent; whose political judgments are formed chiefly on the basis of taste (which is to say, on snobbery); and who, filled with a stirring sense of his own virtue, proclaims his concern for the people, for justice, and for enlightenment without feeling the least need to sacrifice on behalf of any of these things.

Not once in these pages does Schlesinger have anything good to say about business or businessmen, and his opinion of capitalism is best expressed by the term "unbridled" that usually appears before it. Into his seventies and eighties, he is convinced that nothing done by private enterprise cannot be done as well or better or more fairly by government. "I have a good feeling about Clinton," he writes: "essentially, I think, he believes in government, which Carter did not."

Like the late-model liberal that he became, Schlesinger continued to insist on his love for the people, and to be always concerned with the human face of suffering. Somewhat contradictorily, he also refers to his "disrespect for organized religion." Although he records the influence on him of the thought of Reinhold Niebuhr—a belief in original sin that does not excuse one from fighting to eliminate evil—nowhere in the *Journals* or in his memoir *A Life in the Twentieth Century* do the multiple mysteries of human existence, to which religion addresses itself, touch or interest or in the least perplex him. As it happens, Schlesinger's grandfather was a Jew from East Prussia who, after emigrating to the town of Xenia, Ohio, married a Catholic woman; the couple split their religious difference by becoming Protestants.

Such judgments make all the more arresting a passage in the *Journals* in which, after expressing his disappointment at Bill Clinton's embrace of the sweeping welfare-reform policy backed by the Republican party, Schlesinger writes:

> In the meantime, poor people will be hurt. Maybe some of them will become angry. The rich in this country seem to think that they can oppress the poor indefinitely, not recognizing that welfare is one price society pays for social peace.

This, for the kind of liberal Schlesinger became, is evidently what being "for" the poor had come to mean—not enabling them to help themselves and better their lot but, in the manner of the older welfare programs, keeping them in their place so as to prevent them from storming the barricades.

Arthur Schlesinger will probably go down in history as an unregenerate publicist for a line of progressive ideas that by the late 20th century would lose its hold on the imagination of many Americans. The reason for this political decline was one that he himself, as a historian pondering the career of the British left-wing political scientist Harold Laski, had once recognized: Laski's "besetting sin," Schlesinger wrote, was "the substitution of rhetoric for thought."

The *Journals* perfectly reflect this fateful substitution, along the way providing insight into how liberalism, a political doctrine that once seemed so honorable and generous, came to seem so flaccid and empty. They also reflect something about their author that does not seem entirely unrelated.

Schlesinger is forever ascribing the views and actions of people he disagrees with to their presumed moral or psychological deficiencies. Lyndon Johnson escalated the war in Vietnam as a cover for "his personal cowardice." Averell Harriman went along because his weakness was "the desire to be near power." Ralph Ellison supported the war because he was frustrated by his inability to complete a second novel. Hubert Humphrey's problem with our Vietnam policy was his "lack of a sense of the concrete human dimension."

To gauge by the *Journals*, supplemented by his memoir *A Life in the Twentieth Century*, obliviousness to human character was Arthur Schlesinger's trademark. Although weighing in at 928 pages, and admittedly concentrating on politics, the *Journals* devote an infinitesimal amount of attention to self-examination. His insight into others rarely rises above the banal.

"It never occurred to me that Joe [Alsop] was homosexual," Schlesinger writes in his memoir. He seems no more perceptive about Sumner Welles, a WASP *extraordinaire* whose homosexuality also eluded him. Edmund Wilson underscores this imperceptiveness time and again in his own journal, where he writes of Schlesinger's replying to some point about men and women "with his usual naiveté," and of his "innocence about the history of sex." So pathetically naïve was he on the subject of Jacqueline Kennedy, drawn as a great lady throughout the *Journals*, that the news of her marriage to Aristotle Onassis came as a great shock to him. According to Wilson, he said that the event had "profoundly shaken his faith in his ability to judge character."

More than once Schlesinger remarks that politics is the "best of all spectator sports," and from his office in the East Wing he had one of the finest seats in the house from which to view it. Yet the *Journals* do not add much to the fund of inside White House gossip during the Kennedy years. He has nothing of interest to say of JFK's many illnesses, which the President was able to keep hidden from the public. His accounts of New Frontier partying—Teddy Kennedy jumping into swimming pools and all that—are tepid stuff. When Marilyn Monroe dies, all he has to report of their one encounter is the air "of terrible unreality about her." No talk herein about the 35th President of the United States' dealings upstairs at the White House with Marlene Dietrich, Judith Exner, Angie Dickinson, and others.

Schlesinger's hero worship was such that once, when the President telephoned him in his East Wing office, he put on his suit jacket to take the call. On another occasion, he fawningly asked JFK why he thought "the Kennedys turned out so well [as a family] and the Churchills and the Roosevelts so badly." The President allowed that the credit went to his father.

Later in the *Journals*, Schlesinger notes that he regards Richard Nixon "as the greatest shit in 20th-century American politics." Reading this sentence, one cannot help thinking back to Joseph Kennedy, patriarch of America's most famously dysfunctional family and surely, given the history of his political sympathies, a prime contender for the title Schlesinger reflexively confers on Nixon. But then, in youth as in age, Arthur Schlesinger, our American Voltaire, turns out to have been a man on whom everything was lost.

A. J. Liebling

Death by Fork

"Thirty years later I had a prolonged return match with Côte Rôtie, when I discovered it on the wine card of Prunier's in London. I approached it with foreboding, as you return to a favorite author whom you haven't read for a long time, hoping that he will be as good as you remember."

—A. J. LIEBLING, "Just Enough Money"

SINCE HIS DEATH at the age of fifty-nine in 1963, the *New Yorker* writer A. J. Liebling has had a good posthumous run. His books have been in and out of print and then back in. He is often anthologized. His name pops up with some regularity, in the way that H. L. Mencken's used to do. Ah, people say, wistfully, if only A. J. Liebling were alive to write about this or that event or personality!

Most frequently, they say this in connection with some piece of scandalous behavior on the part of the press—for Liebling was one of the first journalists to make the behavior of newspapers a part of his regular beat. But it was only a part. Francophile, gourmand, boxing aficionado, *flâneur* on an expense account, Liebling had the splendid luck to be able to write about anything that interested him for a good wage and for the large audience the *New Yorker* provided in what are generally considered to have been its glory days.

There were four hardy perennials in the magazine's garden in those days. Liebling was one, and E. B. White, James Thurber, and Joseph Mitchell were the other three. (I make an exception of Edmund Wilson, who wrote regularly for the magazine but was never, strictly speaking, a *New Yorker* writer.) None of them has worn all that well. Aside from a couple of essays and his two popular children's books, *Stuart Little* and *Charlotte's Web*, White's writing seems thin, overly delicate, self-approvingly sensitive. A few years ago, the Library of America devoted a volume to Thurber; reading through it, I found him, at best, only faintly amusing. As for Joseph Mitchell, who suffered a writer's block of some 30 years' duration, his career underwent a revival not long before his death with the appearance in 1992 of a retrospective collection, *Up in the Old Hotel and Other Stories*; admirable though much of the writing seemed as reportage, it also seemed closer to history, or to historical curiosity, than to literature.

Which leaves A. J. Liebling. A new collection of his writing, *Just Enough Liebling*, has just come out, with an introduction by David Remnick, the current editor of the *New Yorker*. The book offers ample portions of journalism in his various bailiwicks: as World War II correspondent, boxing writer, gastronome, press critic, and chronicler of colorful urban characters. How has he held up?

O F THE FOUR REGULAR *NEW YORKER* CONTRIBUTORS, Liebling was the one whom I read with the greatest pleasure in my early twenties. Thurber and E. B. White, after all, wrote chiefly about small-town America, and Joseph Mitchell, whom I eventually came to know a little and like a lot, was a Southerner writing about the wonders of New York as essentially a refined and sympathetic tourist. Only Liebling seemed intensely urban and, to my mind, elegantly urbane.

He also happened to be the only Jew among them—or so one assumed from both his name and his sensibility, which was, in a phrase,

worldly-ironic. His beat, too, was partly "Jewish": New York book-
ies, promoters, people around the fight game, hustlers, and characters like Morty Ormont (formerly Goldberg), the manager of the
Jollity Building on Broadway, the *tummler* Hymie Katz, and the
gang at Izzy Vereshevsky's I. & Y. Cigar Store.

Apart from some pieces he wrote about the Middle East late in
his career, Liebling never mentioned his Jewishness. In *Wayward
Reporter: The Life of A. J. Liebling* (1980), Raymond Sokolov makes
the case that he was uneasy about it. His father, an immigrant from
Austria, had come to America with nothing as a boy and done well.
His mother was of a moderately wealthy Jewish family in San Francisco. In most ways, his was a privileged youth: German govern-
esses were on the premises for him and his younger sister, and there
was even a butler at their Long Island home.

Liebling would claim his parents had no social aspirations,
but even his first name, Abbott, a pretentious Americanization
of Abraham, bothered him; as early as he could, he insisted that
friends call him Joe. On more than one occasion, he went out of his
way not so much to put down as to cast aside his Jewishness. Part of
the impression he wished to give was that of a citizen of the world:
a man beyond mere religion or even ethnic identity.

One way in which Liebling was not privileged was in his physique. Near-sighted, a fat boy with dainty hands and disproportionately small feet, ill-coordinated, two years ahead of himself in
school, he came to admire the Irish kids in the neighborhood who
were better athletes, tougher, and generally more at ease than he.
He was one of those little boys who become absorbed with military history because they know that they are unlikely to create any
on their own.

As a schoolboy writer, Liebling must also have known that his
was to be a spectatorial life, a life spent leaning against the wall
watching other people dance and then running home to record
his impressions. But if one was condemned to live life at a second

remove, journalism offered the best ringside seat. H. L. Mencken, with whom Liebling is often compared, remarks in one of his auto-biographical volumes that when he finished high school he had the choice of going to college, which would mean listening to the prattlings of boring German professors and on Saturdays sitting in the football stands wearing a raccoon coat, or of getting a job on a newspaper, which would mean flying off to fires, attending executions, and going along on raids of bordellos.

No real choice here, as Mencken saw it, and he took a pass on college. Liebling himself, although he went to Dartmouth at sixteen, soon cut loose to enter the larger world of metropolitan journalism. He worked first in Providence, then in New York, and eventually pitched up at the *New Yorker*, where he found a permanent home.

R IGHT OUT OF THE CHUTE as a journalist, Liebling set himself up as a man of the world. Not yet truly worldly, he gave a fine impression of it even when young, and would keep it up all his life in whatever he wrote. If cynicism, as he would later write, "is often the shamefaced product of inexperience," worldliness is the product of more than one walk around the block; and he managed to get around that block quite a few times.

Three things he admired above all else: courage, craft, and con. He honored gallant soldiers, hardworking boxers who knew their craft, and con men in possession of panache. He wrote about soldiers in his dispatches from Europe during World War II, a period he would later recall in his memoir, *Normandy Revisited.* About boxers he wrote mostly in the 1950s, which is when the sport was in the midst of a great era in every weight division. I never thought a championship fight was quite over until I read Liebling's account of it in the *New Yorker* a week or so later. Although he claimed that the English essayist William Hazlitt was a dilettante when it came to boxing, he took Hazlitt's famous essay, "The Fight," for his model of how to proceed, writing about preparations for the fight, getting to the fight, the fight itself, and the aftermath of the fight.

Liebling's writing on boxing tended to shade into his pieces on New York low-lifes: men who could turn a quick buck through ingenuity and without undue perspiration. Preeminent among them was an old racing writer for the *New York Evening Journal* named J. S. A. Macdonald, who also called himself Colonel John R. Stingo. Liebling published a number of pieces on the Colonel, brought together as a fake as-told-to book titled *The Honest Rainmaker* (fake in the sense that Liebling probably supplied lots of what movie credits used to refer to as "additional dialogue").

In an early chapter of his last book, *The Earl of Louisiana*, Liebling reported on a tour he had taken of the Council Chamber of the city of New Orleans, his guide announcing that "each session of the Council is opened with a prayer by a minister of one of the three great faiths, Catholic, Protestant, and Hebrew. They take it in rotation." To which Liebling adds, rounding out the paragraph, "I touched my breast, to make sure my wallet was still with me."

Always on the *qui vive* for scam artists, he was also inordinately fond of them. His own great scam, or so he allowed his readers to think, was journalism itself. He could make the writing of a *New Yorker* piece sound more like a night on the town than the kind of effort that craft of the sort he commanded requires. The picture he would draw of himself, a fat man stopping for a snack of pork chops and bourbon in a Harlem restaurant before taking off for a championship fight at the Garden, all expenses paid, was itself pleasing to contemplate. Whatever his subject, he caused his readers to believe that life was a great amusement, a sweet adventure, and even if they could not participate in it directly, in him they had the best possible cicerone, the man in possession of the real lowdown, the true gen, on all the proceedings.

Of Liebling's various subjects, food, mostly the food he had eaten in Paris as a young man, was the one with obsessional standing. It pops up almost everywhere; he mined it for metaphors; and, no mere theoretician, he consumed it in sufficient quantities that, bald and round-pated and wearing round wireless glasses as he did, he came to resemble nothing so much as an octopus without the advantage of tentacles.

Unfortunately, Liebling proved unable to follow the sensible regimen of his idol Colonel Stingo, who proclaimed: "I have three rules of keeping in condition. I will not let guileful women move in on me, I decline all responsibility, and I shun exactious luxuries, lest I become their slave." Liebling had three marriages, two of them disasters and the third, to the writer Jean Stafford, itself no *déjeuner sur l'herbe*. Despite his impressive literary productivity, his high living kept him always in debt. Food and drink gave him the gout as well as the systemic kidney and heart troubles that eventually killed him. Luxuries hardly get more exactious than that.

I F COLONEL STINGO WAS, in Liebling's description, "the best curve-ball writer since Anatomy Burton and Sir Thomas Browne," Liebling himself threw lots of knuckleballs. You could never know where many of his sentences were going, though they invariably managed to wind up smack in the catcher's mitt for a clean strike. In writing about the European theater in World War II, his prose was plain but efficient, with occasional ironic touches. But the older he got, the lower his subjects became, the more rococo grew his prose. As a stylist, he belonged to the category of deliberate overwriters for comic effect. Other famous practitioners in this line include Mencken, Westbrook Pegler, and Murray Kempton, who, when the mood struck him, could write about Jimmy Hoffa in the cadences of Lord Macaulay.

A characteristic Liebling sentence is stoked with an unexpected allusion snugly woven into complex syntax, usually topped off with a striking image. Here he is on a secondary corner man at Wiley's Gym in New York:

His thin black hair was carefully marcelled along the top of his narrow skull, a long gold watch chain dangled from his fob pocket, and he exuded an air of elegance, precision, and authority, like a withered but still peppery mahout in charge of a string of not quite bright elephants.

A 19th-century boxing writer named Pierce Egan is said to have given Liebling his clue to the device of applying high reference to low subject. But no one could have taught him his gift for metaphor and simile, which, as Aristotle instructs in the *Rhetoric*, is god-given. He could do the quick, sharp simile: "Southern political personalities, like sweet corn, travel badly." He could do the complex simile: "The moon slipped into a cloud abruptly, like a watch going into a fat man's vest pocket, and didn't come out again." And he could do the elaborately extended metaphor, as when he strung a 4,000-word essay about Stillman's Gym out of its jokey metaphoric title, "The University of Eighth Avenue."

His style gave Liebling a nice comic distance from his subject, allowing him to view the world as if he were an anthropologist from another planet, or perhaps an ironist from an earlier century. In this capacity he wrote an exceptionally large number of amusing sentences, and no one was more amused by them than he. At the office of the *New Yorker*, he could be heard laughing out loud in the act of composition. His own assessment of his talent was that he "could write better than anyone who could write faster, and faster than anyone who could write better."

Not all the similes came off. "Newspapers can be more fun than a quiet girl," for example, isn't even on the dartboard. And sometimes the whole bit could seem gratuitous and overworked, as when he brought in Henry James while commenting on a boxer who had strangled a monkey; reading such stuff today, you can almost hear the shriek of a whistle, the spray of ice, the referee calling a penalty for high *schticking*.

Liebling's attitude toward his subjects was another matter. The *New Yorker* had three writers on the low-life beat: Liebling, Joseph Mitchell, and the now nearly forgotten John McNulty. Mitchell entered into the low-life scene with genuine sympathy. McNulty did not have to enter into it, having come out of that life himself as the child of working-class Irish parents; if he reported the elevator man in his building playing the ponies every day, he did so without condescension, for he was playing them, too.

Liebling's view of the low-life scene gives a clue to his limitations. It was almost consistently condescending; in the end, his was a form of highly amusing slumming on behalf of middle-class readers. He played the bad grammar and mispronunciations of the trainer Whitey Bimstein for laughs; he regarded anyone not from New York or France as a yokel; and he never really moved beyond treating his subjects as other than colorful characters. "I never married," the boxing manager Charlie Goldman says, "I always live a la cart." Raymond Sokolov thinks "this bending down of Liebling's to his material" not snobbish but rather "a trick of perspective that did not diminish Liebling's subject but did serve to enlarge and exalt Liebling." This, however, is precisely how snobbery works.

Much of Liebling's writing seems dated now, as dated as Joseph Mitchell's and for some of the same reasons. Something grim has happened to the culture. Today we no longer have "characters" but only "cases." The interesting drunks in McSorley's saloon, written about so sympathetically by Mitchell, have been reduced in our understanding to alcoholics suffering from a genetic disease; the outlandish Joe Gould, who confided in Mitchell that he was writing a history of the world, strikes us today as little more than a pathetic homeless man edging into psychosis.

Most dated among all of Liebling's writings are the ones for which he is currently most honored: his essays on the press. In his time, he was considered heroic for taking on his own medium of journalism, but neither the press he was critical of nor the issues he thought central really exist any longer. He regarded nothing as more dangerous than a one-paper town, and looked upon the swallowing up of one newspaper by another—as happened in the early 1960s in New Orleans and elsewhere—a disaster for democratic discourse. He felt newspaper ownership was largely in the hands of Republican fat cats who tyrannized over their reporters, forcing them to write both news and editorials the way they, the owners, wanted. "Freedom of the press," he wrote in what has become his best-known aphorism, "belongs to them who own one." Today one can only say: tell that to the publishers of the *New York Times* and the *Washington Post*, who, far from tyrannizing over their staffs, seem to have acquired their inadequate education and ideas from reading their own employees.

Liebling's other criticisms seem similarly irrelevant today. A one-paper town is now a smaller problem than the fact that fewer and fewer people read newspapers at all. Journalism is less and less about scouting stories than about cultivating leaks—Pulitzer prizes in our time go to those with the best undisclosed sources. The editorial page has increasingly given way to the op-ed mentality, in which an editor finds people who could not possibly agree on anything and turns them loose in the hope that something mystically known as "dialogue" will ensue. Then there is what appears to be the lessening of the national attention span, first understood by *USA Today*, whose editors picked up on the hard truth that people do not want more but briefer news, and most of it, thank you very much, about sports and celebrities.

Next to these and other matters, Liebling's complaints about unfair coverage of labor disputes or journalists faking things when they lack real information—an example included in *Just Enough A. J. Liebling* is the reporting on Stalin's illness and death when no one could be quite sure of either— now seem quaint and not especially readable.

ORLDLINESS, ALAS, PALES and very quickly stales. It is a
fine thing to know the score; but the problem is, the score
is always changing. Charm, too, can wear thin if there is not much
else behind it, and it is difficult to say what else but charm there
was behind Liebling's writing. Is it sufficient that he was indeed
vigilant in his refusal not to let anyone, in the phrase of E. E. Cum-
mings, pull the wool over his toes? In the end we want to know
what a writer thinks of life.

The writer to whom Liebling is most frequently compared is H. L.
Mencken. The comparison much favors Mencken. He, too, prided
himself on being worldly and unconnable, but he was deeper, more
thoughtful, and more learned than Liebling, whose own reading
and general culture were thin. Although Liebling rarely missed a
chance to mock "the boys from the quarterlies" or take a shot at
people who got a charge out of using the word "dichotomy," Menck-
en's attacks on intellectual quackery were wider-ranging and more
penetrating because they had philosophical backing. In an essay in
one of his *Prejudices* volumes, Mencken wrote:

> No one knows Who created the visible universe. And it
> is infinitely improbable that anything properly describ-
> able as evidence on the point will ever be discovered.
> No one knows what motives or intentions, if any, lie be-
> hind what we call natural laws. No one knows why man
> has his present form. No one knows why sin or suffer-
> ing were sent into this world—that is, why the fashion-
> ing of man was so badly botched.

It is difficult to imagine Liebling writing such a passage, or having
such thoughts about such things, even inchoately.

What *did* Liebling think? Politically he was a liberal, in the old-
fashioned and honorable sense of being on the side of the underdog. He was generally for fairness, though he was not always fair
himself, to put it mildly. To his credit, his political sentiments

did not extend to sharing a taste for the strong anti-Americanism espoused by a writer like Graham Greene. (One of the last pieces he wrote for the *New Yorker* was an attack on Greene's *The Quiet American*.) Yet nothing like a vision or view of the world emerges from his voluminous journalism.

In his biography of Whittaker Chambers, Sam Tanenhaus reports that Liebling not only repeated stories about Chambers's paranoia but at one point became a "clandestine operative for Alger Hiss," tricking the Columbia literary scholar Mark Van Doren into "handing over his Chambers correspondence and then deliver[ing] the letters to Hiss's attorney Harold Rosenwald." With what Tanenhaus calls "remarkable audacity," Liebling then "continued to report on the case in his 'Wayward Press' columns [in the *New Yorker*] even as he tweaked the nation's dailies for their biased coverage."

When John Lardner, his colleague at the *New Yorker*, died, Liebling was assigned the obituary. Lardner "was a funny writer," he wrote, "and, though he would never have admitted it, an artist." I suspect Liebling, if so accused, would have been pleased to admit it. Sokolov's case for Liebling's artistry is that he "possessed a first-rate literary sensibility and worked intricately in genres the world dismisses as second-rate." I prefer the assessment of the *New Yorker*'s cover artist Saul Steinberg: "He was out of an 18th-century world of elegance based on artificiality, and he had prepared a sort of personality for himself."

In its day, that personality not only charmed but suggested inner depths that, sadly, were not really there. In that sense, *Just Enough A. J. Liebling*, the title of this newest collection, is peculiarly apt. Rather than enticing us to read on, it suggests satiety: we've had just enough. About a writer I once admired, even adored, I derive no pleasure in saying this.

John Frederick Nims

The Kareem in My Ca-*Va*-Fee

I DO NOT SEEK THE COMPANY of poets, nor would I wish either of my two granddaughters to marry one. I have long admired poetry, which, practiced at its highest power, represents literature in its most enticing, its most elegant, its most elevated form. Yet poets all too often stand in relation to poetry as Christians do to Christianity: far short, alas, of the ideal.

In my experience of them, poets tend to be self-absorbed, and quite as career-minded as most successful businessmen, lawyers, or politicians I have known. The subject of the poet, in writing and (worse) conversation, is too often himself. A poet sees a famous painting, a tree lose its leaves, visits Prague, or watches his mother die (as most tend eventually to do), and feels that, because it was him this happened to, he should cobble some words together so that the rest of us know what a sensitive dog he is. I don't, as the kids say, think so.

One of the few exceptions in my experience was John Frederick Nims, who was least like a poet in his modesty, sociability, and self-deprecatory good humor as it was possible to be. I don't believe he once mentioned his own writing, let alone bragged about his not inconsiderable achievements, in my presence.

John and I lived in the same city, Chicago, and I first met him at a New Year's Eve party at the Lake Shore Drive apartment of a celebrity-hunting attorney named Samuel Friefeld. Upon meeting I told him how indebted I and all the devotees of *Poetry* were for his salvaging work when he took up the editorship of a then badly flailing magazine. But before we could mount much of a conversation my attention was distracted by—get ready for a heavy name-drop here—my being introduced to Myrna Loy, who was also at the party and who turned out to be quite as winning as the actress who was married to William Powell in the *Thin Man* movies.

I next met John at a dinner party in Hyde Park. This was in the seventies, the years of ambitious cookery, and our hostess served ramekin-sized dishes of sorbet to her guests between courses. Eating my sorbet, I happened to mention that so minuscule a portion presented no fear of an ice-cream headache. John said that he had never heard of such a thing as an ice-cream headache. I expressed amazement that he had not, mentioning that James Jones had even published a book called *The Ice-Cream Headache and Other Stories.*

A few hours later, when the party was breaking up, I asked John if he and his wife Bonnie needed a ride back to the north side. "No," he said, "we drove. And besides, I can't leave just yet. I seem to have this terrible carrot-cake headache." I knew then that I wanted to know this man a lot better.

In subsequent years I did come to know John better. Bonnie Nims sometimes referred to her husband as Nimsy, but I thought of him as Whimsy, or John Frederick Whims. For his humor ran almost exclusively to the whimsical, featuring puns, plays on words in various languages, sweet absurdities. Even though he had strong opinions, there was nothing of the put-down artist about John. And even when one was (ever so slightly) put down by him, it left no scar. I once told him that I had just completed an essay on Cavafy, whose name I blithely mispronounced, wrongly putting accents on the first and final syllables. "You know, Joe," John said gently, "I believe the name is pronounced Ca-*Va*-fee, accent on the second syllable. The mnemonic device is, 'He's the kareem in my ca-*Va*-fee.'"

I had dinner at the Nims's grand apartment at 3920 North Lake Shore Drive perhaps half a dozen times. On these evenings John always played the cordial host, taking drink orders, drawing out his guests, never needing the limelight for himself. Dinners were served in a dining room that contained John's very impressive collection of perhaps two thousand volumes of modern verse. From the kitchen, one could see Wrigley Field. John was a sports fan, especially keen on the Bears. One often had the feeling that he would rather talk about the Bears, or visual art, or the comedy of the human condition, or just about anything other than poetry.

Yet, if one drew him out, one quickly grasped John's regard for the great Modern poets: for the generation of Eliot, Stevens, and Frost. Poetry was, after all, John's calling, that to which he had devoted his life. He also had lots of amusing gossip about poets, and seemed to have met them all. He was funny about their pretensions and their ghastly behavior. He was old enough to have witnessed, firsthand, the horrors wrought by those maniacal *poètes-monstres* Robert Lowell, James Dickey, and Dylan Thomas. (Who was it that likened being kissed by Thomas in the back of a cab to being embraced by an intoxicated octopus?) And he could be slyly comical about those poets whose ambition greatly exceeded their talent.

I used to speculate on John's age—this was before Google came into being and put all such questions quickly to rest—which was not easily determined by either his physique or his conversation. For one thing, he had kept most of his hair, which had stayed dark. He moved well; no prostate shuffle for him. For another, he seemed never to say things that dated him, unlike people, say, who drop the name of Myrna Loy. I assumed that he was perhaps ten years older than I. When he died I learned that he was in fact twenty years older: *John Frederick Nims, Poet, 85, Dies*, ran the *New York Times* obituary headline, or so I seem to recall.

The next time we met after John's death, I asked Bonnie Nims how John was able to remain so splendidly ageless. "He had a secret method," she said. "He never talked about the past." And it was so. John, in his conversation, if not in the inner recesses of his mind, stayed full-time in the present tense. This prevented him from ever becoming either a snob or a crank. He was a terrific guy, John, so much fun to be with that I never for a moment thought of holding his being a poet against him.

Susan Sontag
A Very Public Intellectual

S USAN SONTAG, as P. R. Leavis said of the Sitwells, belongs less to the history of literature than to that of publicity. Anyone with the least intellectual pretension seemed to have heard of, if not actually read, her. Outside of the movies and politics, Sontag must have been one of the most photographed women of the second half of the past century. Tall and striking, with thickish black hair later showing a signature white streak at the front, she was the beautiful young woman every male graduate student regretted not having had a tumble with, a fantasy that would have been difficult to arrange since she was, with only an occasional lapse, a lesbian.

A single essay, "Notes on 'Camp,' " published in *Partison Review* in 1964, launched Susan Sontag's career, at the age of 31, and put her instantly on the Big Board of literary reputations. People speak of ideas whose time has not yet come; hers was a talent for promoting ideas that arrived precisely on time. "Notes on 'Camp,' " along with a companion essay called "Against Interpretation," vaunted style over content: "The idea of content," Ms. Sontag wrote, "is today merely a hindrance, a subtle or not so subtle philistinism." She also held interpretation to be "the enemy of art." She argued that Camp, a style marked by extravagance, epicene in character, expressed a new sensibility that would "dethrone the serious." In its place she would put, with nearly equal standing, such cultural items as comic books, wretched movies, pornography watched ironically, and other trivia.

These essays arrived as the 1960s were about to come to their tumultuous fruition and provided an aesthetic justification for a retreat from the moral judgment of artistic works and an opening to hedonism, at least in aesthetic matters. "In place of a hermeneutics," Sontag's "Against Interpretation" ended, "we need an erotics of art." She also argued that the old division between highbrow and lowbrow culture was a waste not so much of time as of the prospects for enjoyment. Toward this end she lauded the movies—"cinema is the active, the most exciting, the most important of all the art forms right now"—as well as science fiction and popular music.

These cultural pronunciamentos, authoritative and richly allusive, were delivered in a mandarin manner. They read as if they were a translation, probably, if one had to guess, from the French. They would have been more impressive, of course, if their author were herself a first-class artist. This, Lord knows, Susan Sontag strained to be. She wrote experimental fiction that never came off; later in her career she wrote more traditional fiction, but it, too, arrived dead on the page.

The problem is that Sontag wasn't sufficiently interested in real-life details, the lifeblood of fiction, but only in ideas. She also wrote and directed films, which were not well reviewed: I have not seen these myself, but there is time enough to do so, for I have long assumed that they are playing as a permanent double feature in the only movie theater in hell.

"Intelligence," Sontag wrote, "is really a kind of taste: taste in ideas." In her thrall to ideas she resembles the pure type of the intellectual. The difficulty, though, was in the quality of so many of her ideas, most of which cannot be too soon forgot. Her worst offenses in this line were in politics, where her specialty was extravagant utterance.

During the Vietnam War, Sontag went off to Hanoi as one of those people Lenin called "useful idiots"—that is, people who could be expected to defend Communism without any interest in investigating the brutality behind it. There she found the North Vietnamese people noble and gentle, if a touch boring and puritanical for her tastes. Doubtless that trip led to her most famous foolish remark, when she said that "the white race is the cancer of human history," later revising this judgment by noting that it was a slander on cancer. Hers was the standard leftist view on Israel, which was—natch—that it is a racist and imperialist country. All her political views were left-wing commonplace, noteworthy only because of her extreme statement of them.

Some might think Sontag's renunciation of communism an exception to this record of nearly perfect political foolishness. In a 1982 speech at New York's Town Hall, she announced that communism was no more than "fascism with a human face." The remark drove *bien-pensants* up the (still standing Berlin) wall. Others who had fallen for the dream of communism had got off the train as long as 50 years earlier. And whatever can Sontag have meant by "a human face" to describe a monstrous system of government that in Russia, Eastern Europe, China, and Cambodia slaughtered scores of millions of people?

Rounding her political career off nicely, when the Twin Towers were destroyed and nearly 3,000 people murdered, Sontag, in *The New Yorker*, wrote that the attack was "on the world's self-proclaimed superpower, undertaken as a consequence of specific American alliances and actions"—and so America, in other words, had it coming. Intellectuals have devised many stupid ideas, and Susan Sontag seems, at one time or another, to have believed them all.

Sontag was an aesthete and held that "the wisdom that becomes available over a deep, lifelong engagement with the aesthetic cannot, I venture to say, be duplicated by any other kind of seriousness." Some might argue, though, that she gave aestheticism a bad name and that her kind of aesthetics fed nicely into her political foolishness. Apropos of Sontag, Hilton Kramer remarked: "Aestheticism is not, after all, primarily a philosophy of art. It is a philosophy of life." This woman who eschewed morality and judgment in art never had the least doubt about her own moral superiority and the righteousness of her views.

In literature Ms. Sontag's taste in ideas ran to the dark, the oblique, and the violent. As Camille Paglia put it, she "made fetishes of depressive European writers." One is reminded here of the Romanian writer E. M. Cioran, who, when young, felt a special partiality to writers who had committed suicide. Antonin Artaud, Roland Barthes, Samuel Beckett, Walter Benjamin, Elias Canetti, and Cioran himself were among the writers about whom Sontag wrote most enthusiastically.

Enthusiastically but not convincingly. Walter Benjamin, one of her enthusiasms, must surely be among the 20th century's most overrated writers. Paris, Berlin, Moscow, Karl Kraus—Benjamin could render the juiciest of subjects arid. In her essay on Elias Canetti, Sontag notes his admiration for the novelist Hermann Broch and "those great patient novels *The Death of Virgil* and *The Sleepwalkers*." Anyone who has read Broch's books will know that the burden of patience chiefly falls on the reader, for Broch's heavily longueur-laden novels are proof yet again of Santayana's discovery that the Germans are utterly devoid of the emotion of boredom.

In the end, Susan Sontag may have been most notable as a photographic subject and for the querulous interview, of which she gave a bookful (see *Conversations with Susan Sontag*). She was photographed by the best in the business, in poses sexy, earnest, sultry, brainy, and sublimely detached. She did the siren in a thousand faces.

Her last partner, Annie Leibovitz, is, appropriately, best known as a celebrity photographer. Sontag's obituary in the *New York Times* was accompanied by no fewer than four photographs—an instance of intellectual cheesecake.

If Susan Sontag had been a less striking woman when younger, her ideas would not have had the reach that they did. Something similar could be said about Mary McCarthy, another attractive writer, who claimed that Sontag was "the imitation me." Today, more than six years after Sontag's death, not her writing—as a prose stylist she gave no pleasure—but only the phenomenon of Susan Sontag is of interest.

This interest is nicely fed by *Sempre Susan*, a brief memoir by the novelist Sigrid Nunez, who, at the age of 25, became Susan Sontag's secretary and her son David Rieff's lover. The year was 1976. Sontag was then 42. Such was Sontag's fame that she was in the condition of Herbert von Karajan, who, when asked by a Parisian cab driver where he wished to go, replied: "It doesn't matter. They want me everywhere." Ms. Nunez, in fact, was hired to help with Sontag's overflowing correspondence.

Sempre Susan records their relationship over the next three decades and displays Susan Sontag in all her neediness and vulnerability—she suffered three bouts of cancer, dying from the third, leukemia—but even more emphatically in all her distance from reality. Her domestic style was bohemian, with the temperament of a diva added. She claimed not to be egocentric, but self-centered she certainly was. Her thoughts all seemed to be about herself.

Ms. Nunez fills us in on Susan Sontag's love affairs, mostly with women but also with Joseph Brodsky, who let her down, hard. Yet how could she refuse a great Russian writer, a future Nobel Prize winner, even if he felt that poetry, which he wrote, was the air force and prose, which she wrote, was the infantry?

This little memoir is perhaps most interesting on Susan Sontag's relationship with her son. Disliking her own childhood, she determined that her son would take a pass on his, and she treated him, from an early age, as if he were grown-up. She left him for long stretches with other people when he was young, while she traveled abroad. She appears to have regarded him more as a younger brother than a son. An Israeli writer named Yoram Kaniuk, who knew them well, claimed that "she was not a mother, and he was not a son."

Sigrid Nunez and David soon became a couple, in an arrangement brought about by Sontag: "He was shy," Ms. Nunez writes. "She was not." When Sontag learned that Ms. Nunez was not using any birth-control pills, she worried that the two might have a child, which, she felt, would be a terrible drag on her son's career. Her advice to the couple was to desist from fornication and instead practice—I revert to the French to protect the innocent—*soix-ante-neuf.* Ms. Nunez doesn't mention either her own or David's reaction to this maternal advice, but let us rest assured that neither replied, "Golly, Mom, thanks."

Although Sigrid Nunez appreciates Susan Sontag's curiosity, wide reading, courage in the face of bad health, and independence, her unreality, her deep and abiding unreality, is the final impression that *Sempre Susan* leaves on the reader. Sontag didn't mind whose feelings she hurt. Her trips to give talks at universities are strewn with stories of her disregard of her audience and astonishing impudence. No one was allowed to get in the way of her desires or disrupt her sense of her own high seriousness.

At the end of *Sempre Susan*, Ms. Nunez presents a woman who is filled with regrets, not about her treatment of others but about her own achievement. Still confident of her "worthy contribution to culture and society," she nonetheless wishes that she had been "more artist and less critic, more author and less activist. . . . No, she was not happy with her life's work. . . . True greatness had eluded her." Deluded to the end, Susan Sontag had no notion that not literature but self-promotion was her true métier.

Englishmen

Max Beerbohm

The World's Greatest Minor Writer

L OVERS—NO LESSER WORD WILL DO—of the prose, caricatures, and mind of Max Beerbohm constitute a cult. Membership in the cult requires a strong penchant for irony, a
skeptical turn of mind, and a sharp taste for comic incongruity.
Like all impressive cults, the Beerbohm cult is small, very small,
and always in danger of guttering out—but never, I'm happy to
report, quite doing so.

When Max Beerbohm died, in his eighty-fourth year, he was
buried in St. Paul's Cathedral, along with a very select company
of roughly three hundred other English heroes of war, politics,
and culture. His family's house in Kensington, at 57 Palace Gardens Terrace, has long borne one of those periwinkle blue plaques
noting that an important figure had resided there. In his lifetime,
he was knighted, praised by everyone whose praise mattered (T. S.
Eliot, Virginia Woolf, Evelyn Waugh, E. M. Forster, Edmund Wilson, and W. H. Auden, among others, weighed in), and was widely
respected if not revered by people of literary sensibility.

Still, he was always what Arnold Bennett called a "small-public" writer. Beerbohm, even when alive, thought he had a readership of no more than fifteen hundred in England and another thousand in America. He had no delusions about the breadth of his appeal. His "gifts were small," he felt, and he told his first biographer, a man named Bohun Lynch, that he "used them very well and discreetly, never straining them; and the result is that I've made a charming little reputation."

But reputations for charm do not usually long survive the lives of those who exhibit them, however well and discreetly. Something more than charm has kept the small if scarcely gem-like Beerbohmian flame alive. I am myself, as you will perhaps by now have gathered, a member of the Beerbohm cult. Ten or so feet behind my back, three of his caricatures (of Byron, Matthew Arnold, and Dante) hang above a bookcase. A picture of Max Beerbohm is on a wall roughly six feet from where I am now writing about him. The photograph shows an elderly man—born in 1872, he lived until 1956—sitting on a cane chair on the terrace of his small villa in Rapallo. Ever the dandy, he is wearing a boater at a jaunty angle, a light-colored and slightly rumpled suit, a white waistcoat, and dark tie with a collar pin. His left leg is crossed over his right. His head and hands seem rather large for his body. His hooded eyes peer out of deep sockets, his thick white mustache does not droop. His countenance, slightly dour like that of so many great comedians, is that of a man on whom, right up to the end of life, not much has been lost.

I first began reading Max Beerbohm the year before his death. Of all the comic reputations of that day—S. J. Perelman, James Thurber, Frank Sullivan—his is the only one, nearly fifty years later, whose comedy holds up for me. The combination of common sense and whimsy that were his special literary blend continues to work its magic. All is presented in a calm and unfaltering style of what I think of as formal intimacy; if he ever wrote a flawed sentence, I have not come across it. "To be outmoded is to be a classic," he once said of himself, "if one has written well." His economy of formulation touched on genius. Asked by the playwright S. N. Behrman what he thought of Freudianism, he replied: "A tense and peculiar family, the Oedipuses, were they not?" Ten perfectly aimed words and—poof!—a large and highly fallacious school of thought crumples to dust.

I have been referring to him as Beerbohm or Max Beerbohm, but members of the cult tend to refer to him as "Max" merely, which is how he signed his caricatures. The cult itself sometimes goes by the name "Maximilians." George Bernard Shaw, when turning over the job of drama critic on the English *Saturday Review*, said he was making way for "the incomparable Max." (Tired of the sobriquet, Beerbohm more than once implored, "Compare me, compare me.") Something of the intimacy of his style seems to make calling him "Max" rather less objectionable than, say, calling Shakespeare "William," or Joyce "Jim." Yet I find I cannot quite bring myself to do it.

In his two books on Beerbohm, N. John Hall calls him Max, but I should say that Hall has earned the right to do so, having served him so sedulously. Five years ago, Hall published a beautiful and impeccably edited collection entitled *Max Beerbohm Caricatures*, to which he supplied a fine and splendidly informative accompanying text. In that work, Professor Hall (tempted though I am, I shall refrain from calling him "N.") displayed a wide knowledge of Beerbohm and his milieu and a depth of sympathy for the large comic enterprise that are his caricatures. He produced a book in every way worthy of its subject: modest, elegant, charming, and useful—a keeper, as fishermen like to say.

Now Hall is back with a prose work that he has chosen to call *Max Beerbohm: A Kind of a Life*. As it happens, *A Kind of a Life* turns out to be "A Sort of a Biography"—a rare and unusual sort. There have been other Beerbohm biographies, the most complete of which is that written by the English man of letters David Cecil;

and there have been various studies, none of them silly or obtuse: To be drawn to Beerbohm as a subject almost automatically insures one against pomposity, humorlessness, or academic pretentiousness. Yet for all that has been written about Max Beerbohm, no one has come close to capturing the extraordinary personality behind his small but remarkable creations both in prose and with pencil. Professor Hall comes near to suggesting that there is nothing really that needs to be captured.

Biography, ideally, operates at three depths: The biographer shows how a man appears to his public, how he appears to his friends and family, and how he appears to himself. Hall's biography touches on all three, none in smothering detail, though he is stronger on the first two than the third. His book is not meant to be exhaustive or in any way definitive, and in some ways it is all the more pleasing for its modesty of intentions. "I shall keep this book relatively short," he writes, "and I shall not attempt to ferret out the inner man. The 'inner man of Max Beerbohm' sounds oxymoronic. He was very self-aware, but he was not given to introspection or soul-searching. If he did look deeply into himself—and I don't believe he did so very often—he did not tell us about it."

What this leaves Hall in his biography is a review of Max Beerbohm's career, an appreciative yet critical sorting out of his various works, and a consideration of the main unresolved questions about his remarkably quiet life. Drawing on other biographies, his book is a *vade mecum* of Beerbohmian information. Our biographer is immensely companionable, admitting his ignorance when it arises and deciding that many things really are not worth going into. He will provide an interpretation for, or offer a possible motive behind, a work and then blithely add, "I may be wrong," or "But these are merely biographer's fancies." For those of us who do not quite believe in biographical truth, but are much more impressed by (in W. H. Auden's phrase) "the baffle of being," such casualness, far from seeming quirky, is instead rather refreshing and even admirable.

When critical, Hall often levels his criticisms in an amusingly oblique way that his subject would probably have much approved. Of the small number of fairy tales Beerbohm wrote, Hall suggests: "These three stories may be easily avoided by even the most devoted of Maximilians, if only they will try." The ironic tone of that sentence is reminiscent of Beerbohm himself once writing that, apropos of the need for historical background to write about the year 1880, "to give an accurate account of that period would need a far less brilliant pen than mine."

Hall's judgments of Beerbohm's works are sound. I know this is so because they agree with my own—always of course, the best evidence for high intelligence in others. He thinks Beerbohm's single famous work, *Zuleika Dobson*—the novel about a beauty whose arrival at Oxford causes the death by suicide of all the university's undergraduates—rather overdone and therefore tending toward the monotonous, though even so he includes it among Beerbohm's best work. He thinks the early essays, written in the (Oscar) Wildean manner, more than a touch precious, and he believes the volumes of drama criticism suffer from having been written chiefly about second- and third-rate playwrights. He recognizes that Beerbohm tended to underrate Shaw—he had a real antipathy to geniuses, whom he thought "generally asinine"—and to overrate Lytton Strachey. The best of Beerbohm, Hall holds, includes Beerbohm's book of parodies, *A Christmas Garland*; his perfectly polished final collection of essays, *And Even Now*; and his book of short stories got up to read as if they were memoirs, *Seven Men and Two Others*.

Hall expends rather less space on Beerbohm's caricatures, having already devoted a lengthy book to the subject. He provides an excellent account of his subject's brief but brilliant performances over the BBC. But he reminds us that Beerbohm always found drawing easier than writing; and we know that, after he ceased to write for publication in his late thirties with his permanent move to Italy, he devoted himself almost wholly to the delicate and (in his hands) often devastating art of caricature. On this subject, in an early book on Beerbohm, John Felstiner, the biographer of Paul Celan (to have written books on Max Beerbohm and Paul Celan: talk about the comedy of incongruity) rightly says that "generally Beerbohm's caricatures tend to ridicule, while his judgments in writing are less direct—the rough distinction is between satire and irony." Felstiner goes on to say that his innovation as a caricaturist was in bringing "the dynamics of parody into caricature," and it is quite true that the captions to Beerbohm's drawings are often quite as brilliant as the draftsmanship.

Max Beerbohm tended to worry about the cruelty of his caricatures and claimed not to be able to explain it, since only in rare cases—Shaw, Kipling, a now-forgotten novelist named Hall Caine—did he feel a murderous impulse behind his work in this line. (He almost never drew women.) My own feeling is that, as with so many genuine artists, he had great powers of detachment: "I have a power of getting out of myself," he wrote. "This is a very useful power." Writing about Aubrey Beardsley, he noted the aloofness of many artists, which allows them to see "so much" and "the power to see things, unerringly, as they are." His own detachment allowed him a serene objectivity that easily spotted the pretensions and comic self-presentations of others. He was, in the phrase of Henry James, whom he much admired, "infinitely addicted to 'noticing.'" The result, issuing from the end of his pencil, was laughter, usually, in the nature of the case, at the subject's expense. Much as I would have loved to have known Max Beerbohm, I'm not sure that personal acquaintance with him would have been worth the pain of gazing upon his drawing of me.

Some years ago, before his late-life turn to Christianity, Malcolm Muggeridge, then still an exquisite troublemaker, wrote in the pages of the *New York Review of Books* that Max Beerbohm "was in panic flight through most of his life from two things—

his Jewishness and his homosexuality." Always audacious and often utterly wrong, the old Mugger this time out missed on both counts.

On the first count, David Cecil writes that of the Beerbohm family "it has often been suggested that they were Jewish . . . ; and the notion gains color in Max's case from his brains, taste for bravura, and his propensity to fall in love with Jewesses." (He finally married one, an American actress named Florence Kahn.) Although Beerbohm claimed he rather wished he had Jewish blood, in fact the Beerbohm family was part Dutch, German, and English in origin. Asked by Shaw if he had any Jewish ancestors, Beerbohm replied: "That my talent is rather like Jewish talent I admit readily. . . . But, being in fact a Gentile, I am, in a small way, rather remarkable, and wish to remain so."

"Jewish talent"—of what might it consist? I think for Max Beerbohm it had to do with his aloofness, his not-quite-fully belonging to any groups or coteries, and with his ironic approach to life. ("I wish, Ladies and Gentlemen," he said in one of his famous BBC broadcasts during World War II, "I could cure myself of the habit of speaking ironically. I should so like to express myself in a straightforward manner.") A woman friend said he "combined an accurate appreciation of worldly values with an ultimate indifference to them." Very Jewish, this, or at least a quality that often shows up in Jews. Finally, there was his essentially comic approach to life. Believing that "only the insane take themselves quite seriously," Beerbohm was primarily and always an ironist, a comedian, an amused observer standing on the sidelines with a smile and a glass of wine in his hand. G. K. Chesterton said of him that "he does not indulge in the base idolatry of believing in himself." Rather Jewish, much of this, too.

As for Muggeridge's second count, that Max Beerbohm was attempting to hide his homosexuality, here the evidence appears to be purely guilt by association. As a young man, he was on the periphery of the Oscar Wilde circle. (Wilde had a high opinion of

Beerbohm, but it was not always returned—"he was never a real
person in contact with realities," Beerbohm wrote—and some of
his most brutal caricatures are of poor Wilde run to bestial fat.)
Beerbohm's best friend, Reggie Turner (a novelist remembered
now only for his quip that his rarest books were his second editions), was also homosexual. David Cecil writes that, "though he
showed no moral disapproval of homosexuality, [Beerbohm] was
not disposed to it himself; on the contrary he looked upon it as a
great misfortune to be avoided if possible." Cecil quotes a letter
from Beerbohm to Oscar Wilde's friend Robert Ross in which he
asks Ross to keep Reggie Turner from the clutches of the creepy
Lord Alfred Douglas: "I really think Reg is at a rather crucial point
of his career—and should hate to see him fall an entire victim to
the love that dare not tell its name."

David Cecil thought that Max Beerbohm was a man of "low
vitality," and he was too much the gentleman to place the adjective
"sexual" before the noun. The publisher Rupert Hart-Davis, an editor of Beerbohm's letters and a cataloger of his caricatures, thought
him asexual and his marriage to Florence Kahn a *mariage blanc*.
Refereeing the dispute in *Max Beerbohm: A Kind of a Life*, N. John
Hall says, at one point, that Beerbohm's private life doesn't matter—but then, later in the book, sides with Hart-Davis in thinking
him asexual despite his marriage. A case cannot be made for Max
Beerbohm as a notorious heterosexual, but I would like to weigh in
with the fact that, in his essay "Laughter," he wrote that "only the
emotion of love takes higher rank than the emotion of laughter."
The sadness, of course, is that a case of any sort need be made at all.

Max Beerbohm was the world's greatest minor writer, with the
full oxymoronic quality behind that epithet entirely intended. He
claimed to be without either envy or ambition, wanting only "to
make good use of such little talents as I had, to lead a pleasant life,
to do no harm, to pass muster." His tact was consummate; and one
has never grown less tired of a man who wrote so much in the first

person, for he knew the difference, as he once told his wife, between "offering himself humbly for the inspection of others" and pushing himself forward through egotism. He felt that a goodly portion of such success as he enjoyed was owing to his not having "tired people."

Asked to give the 1941 Clark Lectures at Trinity College, Cambridge, Beerbohm responded, "I have views on a number of subjects, but no coordinated body of views on any single subject. I have been rather a lightweight; and mature years have done nothing to remedy this."

I don't think he really believed it. What he believed was that "many charming talents have been spoiled by the instilled desire to do 'important' work! Some people are born to lift heavy weights. Some are born to juggle with golden balls."

He added that the latter were very much in the minority in England then, and, of course, now. But when haven't they been? The golden jugglers are the ones with wit, the ability to pierce pretension, and the calm detachment to mock large ideas and salvationist schemes. They eschew anger and love small perfections. They go in for handsome gestures (Beerbohm refused to accept a fee for speaking about his recently dead friend Desmond MacCarthy over the BBC), have wide sympathies, and understand that a complex point of view is worth more than any number of opinions.

Nothing lightweight about any of this—quite the reverse, I'd say. Had he met Isaac Newton, Beerbohm remarked, "I would have taught him the Law of Levity." It's a powerfully useful and important law, one that Max Beerbohm helped write and that must never, not ever, be allowed to go off the books.

George Eliot
Eminent Victorian

THROUGH PORTRAITS OF A FEW carefully chosen Victorian figures, and with the aid of a deft prose style, acidic with irony, Lytton Strachey, in *Eminent Victorians*, set out to squelch the Victorians. He mocked Victorian earnestness, debased Victorian energy, and lacerated what he took to be the essential hypocrisy of the Victorians and their pretense to an elevated spirit leading on to good works. The immediate effect, lasting for decades afterwards, was devastating.

Strachey was a central figure in the group of writers and intellectuals known as Bloomsbury, and his attack is understandable. We know, as the cant phrase has it, where he was coming from. The Bloomsbury Group—a name that today sounds suspiciously like a dubious hedge fund—stood opposed to everything the Victorians stood for: earnestness, probity, the struggle with fundamental social, political, and moral problems and issues. The Victorians came at things straight on; the Bloomsbury writers—Virginia Woolf, E. M. Forster, Clive Bell, Strachey, et alia—preferred irony and obliquity.

The Victorians had a comprehensive and confident view of human nature; the Bloomsbury writers could only assert, as Woolf contended, that human nature had changed in 1910, though she neglected to say precisely from what to what. The Victorians asserted the need for soundness of thought, high principles, and life considered in the long run; John Maynard Keynes, Bloomsbury's economist, said that in the long run we are all dead, which eased the way for his fellow Bloomsburyites rather joylessly to philander, bugger, and stress personal relations over national destinies. For a long spell, it appeared that Bloomsbury had won, making the Victorians seem little more than a roster of prudish neurotics dedicated to nothing grander than sexual repression.

No longer, for today the Victorians have regained their rightful stature, and this owing in great part to the work of the intellectual historian Gertrude Himmelfarb. She is the anti-Lytton Strachey; her work over a long career—her first book, *Lord Acton: A Study of Conscience and Politics*, was published in 1952—has wiped the irony from the Strachey title, and reminded us how genuinely eminent the Victorians were. Darwin, Macaulay, Mill, Dickens, Carlyle, the Brontës, Matthew Arnold, Thackeray, Ruskin, Newman, Trollope, Acton, Tennyson, Browning, Bagehot, Disraeli, Gladstone, the cavalcade of Victorian genius is greater than that of any other period in any other nation in the history of the world. In her several book-length studies of the Victorians and their milieu, Gertrude Himmelfarb has elegantly and incisively set out the nature of the Victorians' achievement, honoring the complexity of their lives and works, reminding us that giants once walked the earth without unduly emphasizing that pygmies—sorry to report that they would be us—do now.

Of all the great Victorians, perhaps none was more complex, unpredictable, and finally astonishing than Mary Ann Evans, better known as George Eliot. When the 26-year-old Henry James visited her in 1869, he wrote to his father that "she is magnificently

GEORGE ELIOT (*Mary Ann Evans*)

ugly—deliciously hideous." He added that "in this vast ugliness [which James describes] resides a most powerful beauty which, in a very few minutes steals forth and charms the mind, so that you end, as I ended, in falling in love with her." James wrote of the "great feminine dignity and character in those massively plain features," and concluded by saying that "altogether she has a larger circumference than any woman I have ever seen."

By circumference I take James to mean breadth of understanding, largeness of spirit, depth of sympathy—the qualities possessed by only the greatest of novelists. That George Eliot is among the small company of the world's great novelists is without doubt. She is a central figure in F. R. Leavis's *The Great Tradition.* Her place at the very top rank in Anglophone literature is secure. I'm not sure of her reputation among the French, Italians, or Germans, though some have suggested that *Daniel Deronda* (1876), her last and most complex novel, may be the best German novel ever written in English.

The intellectual background, composition, and critical reception of *Daniel Deronda* is the subject of Gertrude Himmelfarb's *The Jewish Odyssey of George Eliot.* The book is replete with the serious scholarship, intellectual penetration, and good sense that readers have come to expect from Himmelfarb. Her deeper subject is how George Eliot, the daughter of a churchgoing country estate manager in Warwickshire, came to her understanding of the Jews, their condition in the 19th century, their aspirations, their fate in a world historically hostile to them. Among her other remarkable qualities and accomplishments, George Eliot turns out to be among the earliest and most sophisticated of Zionists.

66 "ELIOT WAS THE RARE NOVELIST," Himmelfarb writes, "who was also a genuine intellectual, whose most serious ideas found dramatic expression in her novels." Henry James took this point a bit further, putting a critical twist to it, when he averred that "the fault of most of her work is the absence of spontaneity, the excess of reflection; and by her action in 1854 (which seemed superficially to be of the sort that is usually termed reckless), she committed herself to being nothing if not reflective, to cultivation of a kind of compensatory earnestness."

The "action in 1854" was Mary Ann Evans's union with George Henry Lewes, an intellectual journalist then at work on his *Life of*

Goethe. She had met Lewes three years earlier. Owing to legal complication that made him unable to obtain a divorce from his wife, Lewes and Mary Ann Evans went off together to Germany, where she mastered German. Theirs was the closest of relationships, dear and deep, a mating of souls and intellects, heightened by each helping the other in every way possible. Nor had it anything of the air of bohemianism about it, the least tincture of acting in defiance against the norms of society. Instead, their union was the act of two people who adored each other but discovered all conventional means of connection closed off to them. Once united, they never thought of each other as other than husband and wife. She dedicated *The Mill on the Floss* "to my beloved husband, George Henry Lewes."

[margin handwriting: bohemianism]

Lewes it was who encouraged George Eliot (as she later became) to write fiction. Hitherto she had restricted herself to criticism, reviewing chiefly for the *Westminster Review*, of which she was an assistant editor, and doing translations of Feuerbach, Spinoza, and other erudite works. She began writing fiction at the age of 37, and published her first full novel, *Adam Bede* (1859), at 40. From there she went, as the Victorians had it, from strength to strength: writing, to mention her best-known novels, *The Mill on the Floss* (1860), *Silas Marner* (1861), *Romola* (1863), *Felix Holt, The Radical* (1866), *Middlemarch* (1871), and *Daniel Deronda* (1876). Lewes supported her in every way—Henry James calls him "the administrator of her success"—a support that ended only with his death in 1878. George Eliot died two years later.

Henry James remarked that the unconventionality of George Eliot's union with G. H. Lewes kept her from moving freely in the society of her time, and thus restricted her opportunities for social observation. He also suggests that Lewes may have turned her interests more in the direction of science and philosophy than was salubrious for the novelist in her. James did allow that she had an "overflow of perception," and after all it was James himself who wrote on the nature of genius in art, in *The Tragic Muse*, that *genius* "genius is only the art of getting your experience fast, of stealing it as it were."

Certainly this was true of George Eliot; being a person on whom little was lost, she acquired a great deal from what experience was available to her. But she also, as Himmelfarb notes, gained a vast amount from her reading, which was extensive, serious, and as far as possible from desultory. Himmelfarb cites the wide range of writers George Eliot mentions having read in her letters, and when she comes to consider her preparation for writing *Daniel Deronda*, her novel with Jewish characters at its center, provides more detailed information:

> Eliot's notebooks for this period contained excerpts from the Bible and Prophets, the Mishnah and Talmud, Maimonides, medieval rabbis and Kabbalistic works, as well as contemporary German scholars (Moses Mendelssohn, Heinrich Graetz, Moritz Steinschneider, Leopold Zunz, Abraham Geiger, Abraham Berliner, Emmanuel Deutsch), French scholars (Ernest Renan, Jassuda Bedarride, Georges Depping, Salomon Munk), English scholars (Henry Milman, Christian David Ginsburg, Abraham Benisch, David de Solar, Hyam Isaacs), and scores of others.

Himmelfarb remarks on George Eliot's restrained use of all she had learned before creating the intensely Jewish characters in *Daniel Deronda*. Like the true artist she was, she obtained all she needed to know, and deployed her knowledge with precision and artistic tact.

The controversy about *Daniel Deronda* is over just how good a novel it is. Gertrude Himmelfarb thinks it a great novel, among the very greatest. The wide variety of its characters, its high level of penetrating observations, the intricacy of its plot, its delicate but devastating satire, the powerful emotions it evokes, all are of the stuff of a masterpiece. Yet some powerful critics, F. R. Leavis most notable among them, thought *Daniel Deronda* a great half-novel, feeling that the other half—specifically, the parts of the novel featuring its Jewish characters—a distraction that would have been better expunged.

Leavis rated George Eliot among the world's great novelists. He claimed she was not as great as Tolstoy, but "she *is* great, and great in the same way," for "her best work has a Tolstoyan depth and reality." He found, moreover, some of this best work in *Daniel Deronda*. He makes the persuasive point that Henry James is unlikely to have written *The Portrait of a Lady*, without the richer models—richer, that is, than Isabel Archer and Gilbert Osmond— of the characters Gwendolen Harleth and Henleigh Grandcourt from *Daniel Deronda* to draw upon.

But in Leavis's view the novel's Jewish characters—the eponymous hero; Mirah, the young woman he rescues from suicide and later marries; and Mirah's prophetic brother Mordecai, who sees in Daniel a successor who will lead the Jewish people to their historical destiny in the Zion of Palestine—are too ideal, too flat, too cardboard-like in their creation. Leavis's notion was to lop them off, and change the novel's title to *Gwendolen Harleth*, after the chief female character in the novel, the story of whose wretched marriage to the cold-blooded aristocrat Grandcourt runs alongside those of the novel's Jewish characters.

Two plots run concurrently in *Daniel Deronda*. One is the story of Gwendolen Harleth, a great natural beauty, self-absorbed to the highest power, born to a widowed mother without means, who uses the beguilements of her radiant charm to contract a disastrous marriage to a domineering, cold-blooded aristocrat. The other is the story of Daniel Deronda, whose true parentage and Jewish origins are revealed to him late in the novel, a revelation that comes as a gift to a man who has, as another character says of him, "a passion for people who have been pelted." The two plots are elaborately

interlaced, with Deronda, raised by the baronet Sir Hugh Malin-
ger, who is the uncle to Grandcourt, bridging the novel's two
worlds, Jewish *déclassé*, and English gentry.

Gertrude Himmelfarb argues against F. R. Leavis's notion of
decapitating the Jewish portions of the novel, and rightly so, for
Daniel Deronda would be much diminished without the Jewish
element. Deronda's sense of mission as a Jew gives his life a purpose, and the novel itself a meaning, well beyond the story of a
mere abortive romance between Gwendolen and Daniel. "The idea
that I am possessed with," Deronda tells Gwendolen at their final
meeting, "is that of restoring a political existence to my people,
making them a nation again, giving them a national center such
as the English have, though they are scattered over the face of the
globe." From this sense of mission Deronda derives his stature.
"But were not men of ardent zeal and far-seeking hope everywhere
exceptional," writes Eliot.

If *Daniel Deronda* has a weakness, it is in George Eliot's lapsing
into philo-Semitism. One of the most difficult tests confronting a
novelist is the creation of characters who are at once thoroughly
good and yet still believable—think of those mawkish young
women in Dickens, Little Nell in *The Old Curiosity Shop*, Agnes
Wickfield in *David Copperfield*, and the rest. George Eliot does
not always pass this test. She tends to idealize her three principal
Jewish characters. Daniel Deronda, for example, whose altruism
borders on beyond the believable, often sounds sententious, if not
priggish. Still, the cast of the novel's Jewish characters, from the
family of the pawnshop-owning Ezra Cohen to the musician Kles-
mer (said to be loosely modeled on Franz Liszt) to Deronda's long-
lost actress/singer mother, to Mirah's thieving father Lapidoth
with his gambling addiction, far from being idealized, are so rich
in their variety and various in their richness as to qualify Eliot as a
connoisseur of Jewish types. This is all the more extraordinary since
her personal acquaintance with Jews was scarcely wide. Emmanuel

Deutsch, an assistant in the library at the British Museum, whom Himmelfarb describes in two concise pages, was one Jew whom she did know moderately well and whose Jewish scholarship made a strong impress on her.

Because it is outside her line of inquiry, Gertrude Himmelfarb does not mention the strong strain of feminism running through *Daniel Deronda* (though she does mention that George Eliot was not in favor of female suffrage). How could it be otherwise in a woman who felt she needed to masculinize her name, lest her fiction be passed by as the jottings of merely another trivial woman novelist? George Eliot's feminism is of a superior kind. Gwendolen Harleth's financial problems in the novel, which propel her into her wretched marriage, would not have confronted a man, whose fate would be more firmly lodged in his own hands, and would not have needed to turn to marriage for their solution. And Deronda's mother, when she tells her son that she abandoned him and her Judaism for a career in the theater, is surely partially speaking for George Eliot when she says to her son: "You are not a woman. You may try—but you can never imagine what it is to have a man's force of genius in you, and yet to suffer the slavery of being a girl."

As for George Eliot's penchant for abstraction, complained about by James and others, it takes the form of generalization, commenting, as if from the sidelines, on the action going on in the novel. So Eliot writes that, apropos of Gwendolen's detestation of her husband: "The intensest form of hatred is that rooted in fear, which compels to silence and drives vehemence into a constructive vindictiveness, an imaginary annihilation of the detested object, something like the rites of vengeance with which the persecuted have made a dark vent for their rage, and soothed their suffering into dumbness." Then, neatly gliding back into her narrative, she continues, "Such hidden rites went on in the secrecy of Gwendolen's mind."

Ruminations of this sort—on temperament, on the nature of thinking, on second-sight, on gambling, on a vast deal more weave in and out of the narrative proper. One of the modern fiction workshop laws is that a writer should always show and never tell; George Eliot did both and with sufficient success to wipe the law off the books. Tell all you want, the new law should read, so long as you remember to do it brilliantly.

THE LARGER QUESTION LOOMING over *Daniel Deronda* is how did George Eliot come to have her profound imaginative sympathy for the Jews. One might think her being a literary artist—a human type supposedly specializing in both imagination and sympathy—would suffice as the answer. But the fact is, if one runs through the names of the great playwrights, poets, and novelists writing in English, beginning with Shakespeare and far from ending with Ernest Hemingway and F. Scott Fitzgerald, one discovers that almost all of them saved a cold place in their hearts for the Jews. The great writers of the Western world have much more often than not joined the brutes, thugs, and tyrants in going along with commonplace prejudice against the Jews.

George Eliot is distinguished in not being among them. Himmelfarb traces out Eliot's views about Jews, from her early, vaguely contemptuous view to her profound understanding of the significance behind Jewish history and religion. Writing about the Jews as she did, Himmelfarb claims, required "audacity" on Eliot's part. And she did not fall into the platitudes of Jewish-Christian Brotherhood Week. In *Daniel Deronda* she didn't write a novel to show that the Jews were a civilized, progressive people, eager for assimilation into ever more enlightened European societies. "Her Jewish question," Himmelfarb writes, "was not the relation of the Jews to the Gentile world, but the relation of the Jews to themselves, to their own people and their own world, the beliefs and traditions that were their history and their legacy."

George Eliot's prescience here, as exhibited in *Daniel Deronda* and elsewhere, is little short of astonishing. She understood the prejudice against the Jews of her day, which is not very different than it is in our own. In an essay titled "The Modern Hep! Hep! Hep!" she characterized this prejudice thus: "A people with oriental sunlight in their blood, yet capable of being everywhere acclimatized, [the Jews] have a force and toughness which enables them to carry off the best prizes; and their wealth is likely to put half the seats in Parliament at their disposal." She understood the mission of every Jew, who

> should be conscious that he is one of a multitude possessing common objects of piety in the immortal achievements and immortal sorrows of ancestors who have transmitted to them a physical and mental type strong enough, eminent enough in faculties, pregnant enough with peculiar promise, to constitute a new beneficent individuality among nations, and, by confuting the traditions of scorn, nobly avenge the wrongs done to their Fathers.

She also understood the necessity of a Jewish nation as a rallying point and political means for the carrying of this mission to completion. In *Daniel Deronda* she puts this vision in the words of Mordecai, the poor Jewish tutor, living on charity, who at the novel's end becomes Daniel Deronda's brother-in-law:

> In the multitudes of the ignorant on three continents who observe our rites and make the confession of the divine Unity, the soul of Judaism is not dead. Revive the organized center: let the unity of Israel which has made the growth and form of its religion be an outward reality. Looking towards a land and a polity, our dispersed people in all the ends of the earth may share the dignity of a national life which has a voice among the peoples of the East and the West—which will plant the wisdom and skill of our race so that it may be, as of old, a medium of transmission and understanding.

The role of the Jews, as George Eliot understood it, and as Himmelfarb underscores, was a combination of separation and communication. They were to remain, through their religion and sense of peoplehood, separate, but always a people with much to communicate to the rest of the world. In a brilliant passage toward the end of *The Jewish Odyssey of George Eliot*, Himmelfarb writes that *Daniel Deronda*, published well before the Holocaust and the founding of Israel, before the Dreyfus Affair and the pogroms in Eastern Europe, "reminds us that Israel is not merely a refuge for desperate people, that the history of Judaism is more than the bitter annals of persecution and catastrophe, and that Jews are not only, certainly not essentially, victims, survivors, martyrs, or even an abused or disaffected people." George Eliot's great prescient point is that, as Himmelfarb notes, it was not anti-Semitism but "Judaism, the religion and the people, that created the Jew. And it was Judaism that created the Jewish state, the culmination of a proud and enduring faith that defined the Jewish 'nation,' uniting Jews even as they were, and as they remain, physically dispersed."

That George Eliot, who was herself neither Jewish nor ever thought of becoming Jewish, understood so well and sympathized so completely with Jewish aspirations, that she grasped the Jews' true historical destiny, that in many ways she came to know the Jews better than they knew themselves, is a tribute to a great writer. Gertrude Himmelfarb's splendid book, lucidly setting out George Eliot's accomplishment in this richest of her novels, reminds us that the powers of imagination and sympathy, in the hands of a true artist, are limitless.

Maurice Bowra

The Oxford Man

THE IMMORAL FRONT, which may have escaped your notice, was led by a short stocky man, an Oxford don named Maurice Bowra, and was in business from the early twenties until 1971, when its leader died at the age 72.

A classicist by training, an iconoclast by temperament, Bowra was a disciple-maker by instinct. He cultivated the young, even when quite young himself, cultivated them toward the end not of supporting any specific line or precise doctrine but of standing opposed to all that was stuffy, dreary, or closed one off to harmless pleasure and widening experience. Better to be immoral, the unwritten motto of the Immoral Front might read, if conventional morality ended in deadening the spirit. The Immoral Front, as Noel Annan noted, "embraced all those of whom the smug Establishment of the age of Baldwin disapproved—Jews, homosexuals, people whose odd views, or ways of life, or contempt for stuffiness made disreputable."

"He was the most celebrated Oxford character since Jowett, whom he surpassed in scholarship and warmth of character," Hugh

Lloyd Jones wrote of Maurice Bowra. "Using the word in its time-honored sense," wrote Annan, "he was beyond doubt or challenge the greatest don of his generation." Lest one be lulled by the eulogistic note, consider, please, the other side, a piece in the London *Observer* that noted of Bowra that "he seemed to convey to bright young men the dazzling possibility that malice might be a form of courage and gossip a form of art." No one who knew him could be neutral about Maurice Bowra. But, then, Bowra himself did not view the world neutrally either, seeing it instead as implacably divided between friends and enemies.

Oxford during Maurice Bowra's years was a Versailles for intellectuals; picking up on this notion, Elizabeth Longford called Bowra "Voltaire and the Sun King rolled into one." The university was filled with complex intramural machinations, refined back-stabbing, played out by a cast of extraordinary characters. "I really ought to keep Oxford memoirs," Isaiah Berlin wrote to a friend, "so many funny things happen between my colleagues, such cold persecutions, such peculiarly grotesque views of one another."

Born in 1898, son of a father who spent his professional life as a high-level customs official in China during the age of British empire, Bowra was just old enough to fight in World War I. (When greeting E. R. Dodds, a contemporary who was a conscientious objector and whose candidacy won out over his for the Regius Professorship of Greek, Bowra is supposed to have said, "So what did you do during the war, Doddy?") He visited Russia before the Revolution and, along with an English public schoolboy's impressive knowledge of Greek and Latin, soon acquired reading knowledge of Russian and of all the major European languages. The most English of Englishmen, he nonetheless had a cosmopolitan spirit, and claimed to feel more at ease in Asia and the Middle East than in England.

Bowra early came by a distaste for authority and a pleasure in breaking rules. If he had a politics—he accorded politics generally a low rank in the scale of human importance—he was perhaps a libertarian of the left. Without indulging in snobbery, he was nonetheless a thorough elitist, a boy and then a man who hated the establishment, any establishment, and hated it, so to say, as such. This lent a nice contradiction to his career, for he was keen for official praise and recognition, delighted in all the honorary degrees, the Oxford Professorship of Poetry, and other offices and prizes that came his way, including a knighthood over which, in the best Oxonian spirit of sniping, some of his friends mocked him. John Sparrow, himself later warden of All Souls College, proposed, according to Isaiah Berlin, to write congratulating Bowra "on his baronetcy (due to faulty intelligence), explaining how much more distinguished this was than a paltry knighthood, which nowadays went to every Tom, Dick, and Harry."

The sexual preference for every Englishman of Bowra's generation has to be stipulated, and his own was homosexuality, at least during the years of his early manhood. He was later infatuated by many women, proposed marriage thrice, and was once even formally engaged. When someone noted of his courting Sir Thomas Beecham's niece that she was reputed to be a lesbian, he riposted that "buggers can't be choosers."

"Almost certainly Bowra was not exclusively homosexual," writes Leslie Mitchell, his biographer, who adds that "to worry too much about Maurice's sexuality was somehow to miss the point. He was to be considered as sage, jester, or ringmaster, but not as lover." Late in life, Bowra himself, according to Mitchell, "dismissed 'buggery' as being merely useful for filling in that awkward time between tea and cocktails."

For a man with the reputation of an intellectual bully, Bowra was, as perhaps many bullies are, vulnerable and insecure. He felt himself vulnerable about his homosexuality—fearful that it might be used against him, even in less than notoriously heterosexual Oxford society, and undermine his authority. And he felt a strong element of intellectual insecurity, bestowed upon him as an undergraduate, the gift of a fiercely pedantic tutor at New College named H. W. B. Joseph, whom he had for the Greats (or historical and philosophical) portion of his degree in classics. Joseph did his best weekly to humiliate him and convince him that his wasn't a first-class mind. As Leslie Mitchell writes, "Much decorated and applauded [later in life] though he was, Bowra was never completely convinced of his credentials as a scholar. Joseph remained a demonic presence throughout his life."

Writing Maurice Bowra's biography, the first on its subject, cannot have been an easy chore. The power of an Oxford don is finally, whatever its charm, narrowly circumscribed. To make things more difficult, Bowra was a notable conversationalist—the philosopher A. J. Ayer claimed Bowra, Isaiah Berlin, and Cyril Connolly were the three great conversationalists of his day—shooting off *mots*, puns, *aperçus*, and lacerating put-downs at rapid fire, and glittering conversation, like beauty and goodness, is neither easily nor persuasively captured on the page. A man of prodigious vitality, an unrelenting tornado of energy, the chief presence and centerpiece in any room he entered, Bowra dominated by force of his wit and intelligence.

"His influence stemmed from his being the cleverest and funniest man one had ever met," Mitchell, who knew Bowra when himself an undergraduate, reports. No one parted company with him without taking away a memorable riposte, deliciously oblique irony, or thumping takedown. Mitchell has collected many of these, and sets them out to good effect in his lucid and nicely measured biography.

Bowra was not a dreary, or even a dull, writer; yet, because not so dazzling a writer as a talker, he tended to be, for those who knew his talk, either through personal experience or legend, a disappointing one. Attempting to account for this, Mitchell suggests that some of this may have been owing to his deliberate decision to keep his personality out of his writing, especially his scholarly writing about the ancient Greeks. Cyril Connolly nicely captures the temper of Bowra's mind as exhibited in his prose: "He has the quality which certain judges possess of cutting through the nonsense and assessing human worth; he is anti-fusser, an anti-bunker rather than a debunker, who wears his humanism like a bullet-proof vest." Far from unproductive, he turned out some 30-odd volumes of criticism and translation.

Mitchell reports that Bowra's family knew nothing of his academic distinction, and people who knew Bowra for decades were unaware that he had brothers and sisters. This speaks to how thoroughly anchored in Oxford his life was. He went to Oxford from Cheltenham, a public school meant to train boys for a military career, in which he had no interest. He began at New College, where he earned a first-class degree, whence he was appointed a tutor, then dean, and finally warden of Wadham College, a post he held for 32 years, between 1938 and 1970, so that, as Mitchell notes, "Wadham and Bowra's name became synonymous."

The differences setting off one Oxford (and Cambridge) college from another are neatly set out by Mitchell's mention of the game of the time in which they were compared to European federated republics. Thus, New College was England; Christ Church was France; Balliol, America; Jesus College was Yugoslavia; Exeter, Romania; Corpus Christi, Denmark. What country Wadham was properly compared to isn't specified, though Bowra greatly raised its prominence. Stuart Hampshire claimed he wanted to make it into "Czechoslovakia, small but enlightened and respected," which he seems to have done through careful appointment of fellows and selection of undergraduates and, most of all, through the force of his own powerful personality.

As an Oxford don, Bowra thought himself in the tradition of Gilbert Murray: someone who did intensive scholarship yet wrote for intelligent general readers, keeping the tradition of Greek culture alive while disseminating it as widely as possible. He translated Pindar, wrote an important book on Homer, and, though his work in Greek scholarship came to be thought old-fashioned, he was not in the least reluctant to continue working in this vein throughout his life: first, because he believed the ancient Greeks still supplied the best model available of the good life, and second, as Leslie Mitchell writes, because "his Greek studies were so intimately entwined in aspects of his personality that they could not be easily readjusted."

If Bowra may be said to have been a proselytizer, it was on behalf of the Greek ideal and of the centrality in life, to the cultivated classes, of the elevation that great poetry made to the enhancement of life. When young, Bowra wished to write serious poetry himself; but recognized it wasn't in him to do so. His taste in contemporary poetry was less than infallible; among the poets he admired and promoted were Yeats and Edith Sitwell, Dylan Thomas and Sidney Keyes. He wrote well on Dante, Milton, Pushkin, and others, and thought himself a servant to poetry. But most assuredly, to no one or anything else.

Cultivating the young was for Bowra both a way of exerting his influence and a way of alleviating his loneliness. Apart from mornings working at his desk, he seems seldom to have been alone. Once, on a rare occasion when he went off on holiday by himself, he reported: "I found myself—a horrible discovery. I have been trying ever since to lose myself." He was a thoroughly social being, lonely as only a deeply gregarious bachelor can be, a man, by nature, of the group, the clique, the coterie. He held, as his friend the medieval historian Ernst Kantorowicz put it, that "happiness is not to be found in power nor in money, but in good food and truth and wine."

THE ROSTER OF BOWRISTAS, as Bowra's young acolytes were known, is impressive, and includes: C. Day-Lewis, Kenneth Clark, A. J. Ayer, John Betjeman, Noel Annan, Stuart Hampshire, Isaiah Berlin, Anthony Powell, Henry Yorke (the novelist Henry

Green), Cyril Connolly, John Sparrow, and Hugh Gaitskell, who disappointed Bowra by wasting his life in politics and becoming leader of the British Labour party. To be a Bowrista was to be taken up as a friend to Bowra, who always remained first among equals.

The reward was, from most accounts, to feel a sense of liberation. Under his spell, life seemed filled with promise, charm, comedy. Bowra taught the chosen undergraduates, as Mitchell puts it, "that life could be about what was possible, rather than what was allowed." Yet if one lingered too long under Bowra's influence, the result could be an uncomfortable domination. "I think," Anthony Powell wrote, "for young men who wanted to develop along lines of their own—it was best to know Bowra, then get away; if necessary return to him in due course to appreciate the many things he had to offer."

To be among the chosen was to be invited to attend Bowra's dinners, at which splendid food accompanied radiant talk, much of it expressed in Bowra's own pointed language of derogation. Up for slaying were smugness and pomposity; so too the confidence of scientists in their superiority and the self-importance of politicians, whose posturings Bowra enjoyed seeing crushed by scandal.

Among the Bowristas, one could be cruel only if also witty. Of an Oxford character known for his false geniality, Bowra remarked that at their last meeting the man gave him "the warm shoulder." Of a mediocre figure rising in the world, he remarked: "You cannot keep a second-rate man down." He once allowed that the suicide rate of undergraduates was "higher than it ought to be." The term *homintern*, denoting the assumed cabal of homosexuals, a play on the Communist Third International, was his invention. "You don't get the best value out of your selfishness," he once remarked, "if you're selfish all the time." Bowra could in fact be extraordinarily generous to friends.

The devastating yet understated put-down has long been a specialty of the house at Oxford and at Cambridge. If not started by Maurice Bowra, it was given a great boost by him. Although I attended neither school, I experienced it in ample measure through the conversation of my friend Edward Shils, who was a fellow of King's College and Peterhouse at Cambridge and was a talker, I believe, the equal of Bowra in his powers of subtle derogation. Of Isaiah Berlin, for example, Edward would say, "He is a charming man and has doubtless given great pleasure to his friends." Uncoded, this meant that Berlin's writing was shallow and he was utterly without intellectual courage. (Edward also told me that behind Berlin's unwillingness to speak out against the student uprising of the 1960s was his fear of the disapproval of Maurice Bowra and Stuart Hampshire.)

When I introduced Edward to the bounderish English journalist Henry Fairlie, he said: "Mr. Fairlie, you wrote some brilliant things in the 1950s [the year was then 1978], but now I understand you have become a socialist. Justify yourself please." Fairlie answered that he had turned to socialism after hearing Michael Harrington lecture in Chicago, to which Edward, without missing a stroke, replied: "Michael Harrington in Chicago—surely a case of worst comes to worst."

To be thought a disappointment to Bowra was, among the Bowristas, a serious blow. "I have known what it is to be hated by Maurice," wrote Cyril Connolly, "and I have spent several years in the wilderness; it was a devastating experience. One would wake up in the middle of the night and seem to hear that inexorable luncheon-party voice roar over one like a bulldozer."

John Sparrow, warden of All Souls and, like Connolly, a well-known under-producer, was another Bowrista who disappointed Bowra. When Sparrow published his once-famous essay on what Lady Chatterly and the gamekeeper were really doing in the sack, Bowra wrote to him:

> Well done. It is good to see the old cause of dirt so well
> defended, and I admire you very much for your skillful
> argument and even more having been able to read and

remember the book, which must have been a grueling experience for you. I comfort myself with the thought that now I need never read it.

Sparrow, with whom I had spent some time, began a dinner we had together by asking me whether it was true that Americans believed that all men were created equal. I averred that one of our key documents did so state. "Well," he said, "I suppose they had better believe it, for there's no actual evidence for it." On another occasion, after a dinner in his honor at the University of Chicago, Edward Shils and I repaired to Sparrow's room at the Quadrangle Club, where he, in dinner clothes, clutching a bouquet of roses, perhaps one-and-a-half-to-two-sheets to the wind, began to attack dogs. He attacked them for their subservience, for their sucking-up propensities, for their uncritical adoration of their masters; so much less interesting were they than cats.

"Mr. Sparrow," I said to him, "I have to confess to you that I own a dog. He is a small dog, to be sure, but I love him "

"I see," he replied. "Very well, then, keep him. But when he dies, pray do not replace him."

Englishmen, as has been said, are divisible into two groups: boys and old boys.

Slight though Bowra's renown is today, it lives on, or so many people believe, in his being the model for Mr. Samgrass, the snobbish Oxford don who cultivates the wealthy Marchmains in Evelyn Waugh's *Brideshead Revisited*. Bowra spotted this, and pretended to enjoy it. Waugh was a borderline Bowrista, but relations between the two powerful personalities were never easy. Bowra thought that Waugh's best writing was inspired by hatred, and when Bowra was knighted, Waugh, no slouch at derogation himself, wrote to Nancy Mitford: "It is really very odd as he had done nothing to deserve it except be head of the worst college at Oxford and publish a few books no one has ever read."

Leslie Mitchell finds the character of Mr. Samgrass, however interesting in himself, well off the mark of its life model. He notes that Bowra's snobbery was not social but entirely intellectual: "He preferred clever people to stupid people. The only entry qualification into his court was intelligence." One is reminded here of Bowra's own hierarchical order for admitting undergraduates to Wadham: "Clever boys, interesting boys, pretty boys—no shits."

On the snobbery front, Bowra did not find Bloomsbury at all appealing, and of Virginia Woolf remarked that "I find her a bore, dislike her imagery, suspect her psychology." As for Bloomsbury generally, he found it pretentious in the extreme, "with its ridiculous little philosophy about beautiful states of mind." The Garsington of Lady Ottoline Morrell, whom he described as "a baroque flamingo," was more to his liking. He was also a regular guest at Margot Asquith's literary salon, where a combination of political and literary figures was on offer, and which gave him a cachet, upon his return to Oxford, as a man of the great world outside the university.

No doubt Bowra would have preferred to be more worldly still, but, with the outbreak of World War II, no one offered him interesting work—nothing diplomatic in America, nothing at Bletchley breaking codes, nothing doing spy work. He had to settle for being a member of the Home Guard. He felt wounded and left behind. Only later were his spirits revived, when he was made vice chancellor of Oxford and, later, president of the British Academy. He turned out to be an effective if always impatient administrator, setting records for the briefness of his meetings.

"Bowra had," Mitchell writes, "the confidence of a man who had belief." Belief, firmly held, gives one a point of view, and combined with the right temperament, a sense of humor. Bowra believed that the university was a sacrosanct institution, with barbarians always hovering just outside the gates. In the matter of honorary degrees, he felt, as Mitchell writes, that "whom the University chose to honor was a public statement of its own purpose." (Northwestern

University, where I taught for many years, has in recent years awarded honorary degrees to Robert Redford, Julia Louis-Dreyfus, Studs Terkel, and Stephen Colbert, which is certainly a fine statement of its own purpose.) As for appointments, he deemed it important that people who valued what he, Bowra, did be in place to carry through those things that most deserved to live on.

What Maurice Bowra valued was literary culture, anchored in ancient Greece. The literary point of view was what he admired above all; the quality of any nation, he felt, was to be found in the quality of its literature. He was properly suspicious of social science, and less than enthusiastic about science itself. No Bowristas were scientists. Organized religion, always a target for his humor, he called "marvelous rot," but claimed that without it "the boys will believe, alas, in science, and think it will cure all their ills, poor poops."

A one-culture man, he said, "I wish I knew why we had to keep up with technological developments, and suspect that much of it is bogus." Loathing bureaucracy, he feared the interference of government in university affairs. And while himself democratic in spirit, and welcoming to the grammar school boys who now had a chance at an Oxbridge education, he didn't believe that democracy otherwise had anything to do with education.

From all this one can see that Maurice Bowra was doomed to become a back number in his lifetime. When he wrote his memoirs, called *Memories*, he ended them in 1939. He did so because he understood that World War II and its aftermath would soon put paid to the Oxford he loved, and marked "the end of an era for the world and for me." He claimed not to understand the students of the 1960s, and found the entire time, in Leslie Mitchell's words, "often baffling and upsetting." Television, on which he refused to appear, appalled him: "All television corrupts," he said, "and absolute television corrupts absolutely." Evelyn Waugh knew the game was up for Bowra when he discovered that students at Wadham began referring to their warden as "Old Tragic."

Bowra was permitted to serve two years past the normal mandatory retirement age as warden of Wadham, and after his retirement was given rooms in the college. He was succeeded in the wardenship by a Bowrista, the philosopher Stuart Hampshire, which must have eased the blow of retirement somewhat.

Santayana says that, as we approach death, the world itself begins to look dark to us because we cannot imagine it being much good without us in it. Some of this darkness crept into Bowra's conversation. The decline of classical education dismayed and depressed him; the fading of the importance of literature, now everywhere surpassed by government financing of science in universities, was connected to this. Add on the diminutions that that relentless spectre, age, bring to the party. Like so many great talkers, Bowra became hard of hearing; eyesight and memory were dimming.

"I am going deaf and blind, and losing my memory," he wrote to Noel Annan. "It is time I became a bishop." He began to give out his address as Reduced Circumstances, Oxford. He died, of a heart attack, as he had hoped, in 1971.

Anyone of the least imagination who has visited Oxford, but never went there when young, cannot but feel a strong yearning for a world one has never known. But it is not contemporary Oxford for which one yearns, but the Oxford of the years between the wars and shortly thereafter. This was the Oxford of high intellectual style and gaiety, of dash and slashing wit, of oddballs and eccentrics, of brilliance and the love of serious learning—the Oxford, in short, of Maurice Bowra.

T. S. Eliot

The Demise of the
Literary Culture

N O ONE WRITING in the English language is likely to
establish a reigning authority over poetry and criticism
and literature in general as T. S. Eliot did between the
early 1930s and his death in 1965 at the age of 77. Understatedly
spectacular is the way Eliot's career strikes one today, at time when,
it is fair to say, poetry, even to bookish people, is of negligible interest and literary criticism chiefly a means to pursue academic tenure. Literary culture itself, if the sad truth be known, seems to be
slowly but decisively shutting down.

The fame Eliot achieved in his lifetime is unfathomable for a
poet, or indeed any American or English writer, in our day. In 1956,
Eliot lectured on "The Function of Criticism" in a gymnasium at
the University of Minnesota to a crowd estimated at 15,000 people.
"I do not believe," he remarked afterward, "there are fifteen thou-
sand people in the entire world who are interested in criticism."
Eight years earlier, in 1948, he won the Nobel Prize in literature.
In later years, when he went into the hospital, which he did with

some frequency, suffering from bronchitis and heart troubles, news of his illnesses appeared in the press or over the radio both in England and America; and so too did news of his second marriage, in 1957, at the age of 69, to his secretary, a Miss Valerie Fletcher, 38 years younger than he. He lectured often and everywhere, so much so that Lyndall Gordon, his most penetrating biographer, wrote that his "face acquired a sort of exposed reticence from the habit of looking down from a lectern into rows upon rows of eyes." Eliot was the equivalent in literature of Albert Einstein in science in that everyone seemed to know that these men were immensely significant without quite knowing for what.

An immitigable highbrow, Eliot was concerned about the slackening of high culture and the diminishing quality of education—concerns that have proved prophetic. The poetry on which his reputation as a leading figure of the modernist avant-garde was based was not easily comprehended. "Poets, in our civilization, as it exists at present, must be difficult," he wrote, but he also wrote that "genuine poetry can communicate before it is understood," which seems to have been the case with his. His criticism, much of which began as lectures, always came from on high. This was not a man who wrote or spoke down to his audience, ever. Which makes all the more curious his widespread fame.

Far from its being accidental, Eliot's fame was planned for, carefully cultivated, and nurtured once it arrived. From the first volume of Eliot's letters, newly revised and recently released in Great Britain,* we learn that, in 1919, when he was 31, he wrote to J. H. Woods, his philosophy teacher at Harvard: "There are only two ways in which a writer can become important—to write a great deal, and have his writings appear everywhere, or to write very little." He chose the latter: to write very little but always to dazzle.

---

* The revised edition is *The Letters of T. S. Eliot, Volume 1: 1898–1922*, along with *The Letters of T. S. Eliot, Volume 2: 1923–1925*. Both are edited by Valerie Eliot and Hugh Haughton and have been published in London by Faber and Faber.

T. S. ELIOT

"My reputation in London is built upon a small volume of verse, and is kept up by printing two or three more poems in a year," he wrote. "The only thing that matters is that these should be perfect in their kind, so that each should be an event."

Eliot worked at Lloyd's Bank between 1917 and 1925 as the head of a small department stationed in the basement and assigned the translation of foreign documents and overseeing the analysis of the economic behavior of foreign governments. When friends formed a foundation of sorts to bail him out of what was thought drudgery taking him from his creative work, or when he was offered a sub-editorship on the *Athenaeum* magazine, he eschewed both, preferring to remain at the bank. He felt that, as he put it, he could "influence London opinion and English literature in a better way" by remaining slightly outside of things. The bank, moreover, with its distance from the standard literary life, lent him, as he noted, "aura." He wrote to his mother in 1919: "I really think that I have far more *influence* on English letters than any other American has ever had unless it be Henry James. I know a great many people, but there are many more who would like to know me, and [working in the bank] I can also remain isolated and detached." Those are the words of a man carefully but decidedly on the make.

THOMAS STEARNS ELIOT was born in St. Louis in 1888, the son of a successful manufacturer of bricks and the scion of many illustrious Eliots of Boston and Cambridge, Massachusetts. His grandfather founded Washington University in St. Louis; Charles William Eliot, a cousin, was president of Harvard when Eliot was an undergraduate there. The Eliot family was centered (anchored might be more precise) in New England, where it spent its summers, and Tom later came to think himself a New Englander, though not so thoroughly as he would one day consider himself English.

Part of what makes Eliot's literary career so impressive is that he achieved all he did, in effect, in nationality drag. He willed himself into an Englishman, which technically he became only in the year 1927, when he acquired British citizenship. After attending one of Eliot's readings in New York in 1933, the critic Edmund Wilson wrote to the novelist John Dos Passos: "He is an actor and really put on a better show than Shaw. . . . He gives you the creeps a little at first because he is such a completely artificial, or, rather, self-invented character . . . but he has done such a perfect job with himself that you end up admiring him."

Eliot wrote of Henry James, in subtle ways his literary model, that "it is the final perfection, the consummation of an American to become, not an Englishman, but a European—something which no born European, no person of any European nationality, can become." James had become, as Eliot also put it, a European but of no known country, while Eliot, with his bowler hat and rolled umbrella and what Virginia Woolf called "his four-piece suits," turned himself into something resembling the caricature of an Englishman.

This most politically conservative of writers made two radical decisions when young that drastically changed the course of his life. On a traveling fellowship to Europe from the Harvard philosophy department, where he was completing work on a doctorate on the Idealist thinker F. H. Bradley, Eliot determined no longer to live in America or as an American but instead to settle in England. And not long after, in 1914, he married an attractive young woman named Vivien Haigh-Wood, who, most inconveniently, happened to be insane.

Both decisions were made against the wishes of his strong-minded parents. Ezra Pound offered to write a letter to Eliot's father explaining the importance of his remaining in England. Eliot had met Pound in 1914; Pound was only three years older than Eliot but had already made himself the impresario of the literary avant-garde and was a generous promoter of other people's talents. When he read Eliot's early poetry, he knew he had come upon a talent worth promoting. He arranged to have Harriet Monroe at *Poetry* magazine publish "The Love Song of J. Alfred Prufrock"; he placed other early Eliot poems in Wyndham Lewis's *Blast* and Alfred Kreymborg's *Others*. Propelled by Pound's powerful promotional engine, T. S. Eliot's career as a poet was off with a great whoosh.

In his letter to Eliot's father, Pound insisted that London was the place, certainly a much better place than anywhere in America, for his son to make his reputation as a poet. He was correct about that, even if the senior Eliot hadn't the least interest in Tom's becoming one. The prestige of the avant-garde was much less in America in those years than it was in England and on the Continent. In literature, America meant provincialism; London, the great world.

Some surmise that Eliot married Vivien Haigh-Wood because, having had sex with her, he felt a strong sense of obligation. Others that it was his way of putting his foot in the river of life, for Eliot's first published poem, "The Love Song of J. Alfred Prufrock," and much else he wrote in his early years, is about the buried life, or the fear of living—"Shall I part my hair behind? Do I dare to eat a peach?"—another way in which he resembled Henry James.

In "Stuff," one of the American writer Mary Gaitskill's short stories, a character says, "Isn't Eliot that turd who made his wife think she was crazy?" Nearly the reverse was the case: the marriage came close to driving Eliot, a man with a highly delicate nervous organization, mad himself. Vivien claimed that her husband never fully opened up to her, never gave her the affectionate attention she required. This may be partially true—in the emotional realm, Eliot was far from effulgent—but in all likelihood no one else could have done so either. Eliot cannot be accused of being undutiful to her. Most of his earnings went into paying the bills for the quackish physicians then interested in mental illness or for moving his wife into and out of the countryside in hopes of reviving her health. Virginia Woolf described Vivien as "a bag of ferrets" around Eliot's neck. In a letter to the American critic Paul Elmer More, Eliot described his marriage as resembling a bad Dostoyevsky novel. In 1938, Vivien Eliot was committed to a mental asylum, where she died nine years later, at the age of 58.

The marriage was the signature event of Eliot's life. His failure even mildly to assuage his wife's condition and then his separating himself from her after 13 years of a hellish life together left him in despair and on the brink of emotional collapse. The separation also left him with a relentlessly throbbing bad conscience and was a key factor in his conversion to High Anglicanism. He had grown up in St. Louis under the extreme liberal wing of Unitarianism, but his family's earlier religious tradition was Calvinist. And Calvinist, the Puritanical division, T. S. Eliot always seemed. Calvinist guilt, if Eliot's be an example, makes quotidian Jewish guilt seem like puff pastry.

Eliot's conversion was an event that gave order and meaning to his life and coherence to his thought. Peter Ackroyd, another of Eliot's biographers, writes: "He explained that Christianity reconciled him to human existence, which otherwise seemed empty and distasteful." Eliot never attempted to win other converts and, as Ackroyd again notes, "rarely asserted the positive merits of his faith, but characteristically exposed the flaws and follies in other competing ideologies."

Eliot would go on to have two further extended relationships— it is far from clear if either was sexual—one with an American of his Boston family's social set named Emily Hale, the other with an Englishwoman named Mary Trevelyan. Each woman mistakenly assumed Eliot would marry her. In his second, late-life marriage to Valerie Fletcher, Eliot found what perhaps he required all along in a wife: uncritical adoration, unflagging loyalty, and protection of his reputation even after death.

The second Mrs. Eliot has certainly been a most sedulous care-taker of her husband's posthumous career, allowing no official biography and overseeing the printing of his letters, of which she has functioned as co-editor, with all deliberate want of speed. *The Letters of T. S. Eliot* are now up to only 1925 and end before Eliot's career as a great man was fully established. (At this rate of publi-cation, there is an excellent chance that no one reading this essay will live long enough to see the entire collection of Eliot's letters in print.) The first volume chronicled Eliot's youth and Harvard years, his decamping to England and early years there. This second volume has chiefly to do with his struggles with his wife's mental illness and his editorship of the *Criterion*, the intellectual maga-zine he founded in 1922.

Eliot worked on the *Criterion* at night, after his full day at the bank, most of the time with no secretarial help and without salary. (Vivien, it must be said, aided him on the magazine during her sane stretches.) The journal never had a circulation of more than 1,000. Yet it had the highest repute and even today is part of the mythos of literary modernism. The *Criterion* was highbrow but not all that avant-garde. Conservative in its tendency, Eliot never allowed it to be hostage to any party. "My belief is that," Eliot wrote to a contributor, "if one has principles at all, they will have their consequences in both literature and politics, they will apply to both." He would later describe his own positions as "Anglo-Catholic in religion, classicist in literature, and royalist in politics."

"The *Criterion*," as he wrote to various writers he solicited for contributions to the magazine, "does not aim at a very large circulation, but aims solely at publishing the highest class of work. While a contribution to this paper does not reach a very large audience, it probably receives more intelligent attention than any other review and the audience is not limited to Great Britain." His aim for the journal was international, and he hired translators to provide summaries of important articles in French, German, Spanish, Italian, and Dutch intellectual journals. Most of the great figures of the day wrote for him: James Joyce, D. H. Lawrence, Yeats, Ortega y Gasset, E. R. Curtius, Paul Valéry, and others.

Fees for writing for the *Criterion*, while not derisory, were less than grand: £10 for articles of 5,000 words, though he doubled that fee for four special contributors: Yeats, Virginia Woolf, Pound, and Wyndham Lewis. The greater incentive was appearing in good company before an elite audience. "A review is not measured by the number of stars and scoops that it gets," Eliot wrote to Ford Madox Ford, when the latter was about to begin his own magazine, the *Transatlantic Review.* "Good literature is produced by a few queer people in odd corners; the use of a review is not to force talent, but to create a favorable atmosphere" in which it might thrive.

Editing the *Criterion* greatly enhanced Eliot's reputation, making him a significant force in the formation of the literary taste and intellectual culture of his day. "If the review can satisfy a small international elite," he wrote, "I shall be compensated for the work involved." He was also publishing a fair amount of his own criticism, though, during this time, no poetry at all.

Of his criticism, Eliot wrote to F. S. Flint, a regular contributor to the *Criterion*, that "I am myself very poorly educated and have a smattering of a great variety of subjects." He certainly did not present himself that way in print, where he gave off fumes of great erudition, was never less than magisterial in confidence, and seemed to speak for literature itself. His prose style had a built-in gravity; every word measured, precise, every phrase carefully formulated, tossing off aphorisms, significance shimmering in everything he wrote, even when it wasn't quite there. (He had the critical style Lionel Trilling ardently desired but could not always bring off.)

Authority, the sine qua non for any serious critic, Eliot had from the outset. By his early 30s, he had mastered the ex cathedra tone; in later years, he would in fact be known as the Pope of Russell Square, the location of the publishing firm of Faber & Faber, where he became a director and worked as an editor after Geoffrey Faber, the firm's founder, had agreed to take over publication of the *Criterion*.

As a critic, Eliot was splendid on particular writers or works. Who else but he could have questioned the artistic quality of *Hamlet*: "[M]ore people have thought *Hamlet* a work of art because they found it interesting, than have found it interesting because it is a work of art"? Who else could have lowered the position in the canon of Milton (a matter on which he later revised himself) and raised that of Dryden: "Much of Dryden's unique merit consists in his ability to make the small into the great, the prosaic into the poetic, the trivial into the magnificent"? He brought the so-called Metaphysical Poets—John Donne, George Herbert, Richard Crashaw, and others—from a peripheral to a central place in English studies, arguing that they were the last English poets not to suffer from "the dissociation of sensibility" between feeling and intellect.

"The dissociation of sensibility" is a reminder that Eliot, as he himself noted, launched "a few notorious phrases which have had a truly embarrassing success in the world." Among these were "objective correlative" and "the auditory imagination." Then there are all those sentences of his that, once read, are never forgotten:

"He had a mind so fine no idea can violate it" (this of Henry James).

"The more perfect the artist the more completely separate in him will be the man who suffers and the mind which creates."

"The progress of an artist is a continual self-sacrifice, a continual extinction of personality."

"Poetry is not a turning loose of emotion but an escape from emotion; it is not the expression of personality, but an escape from personality. But, of course, only those who have personality and emotions know what it means to want to escape from these things."

"Immature poets imitate; mature poets steal; bad poets deface what they take, and good poets make it into something better, or at least something different."

Eliot claimed that the best method for being a critic was to be very intelligent, and no critic in the modern era was more intelligent than he. "English criticism," he wrote, "is inclined to argue or persuade rather than to state." He had no problem making straightforward statements, and when he did so it was with a higher truth quotient than any other critic of his day or ours.

In his general essays—"Tradition and Individual Talent," "The Function of Criticism," "Religion and Literature," and others— Eliot wrote with a range and an amplitude of interest not seen in literary criticism since Matthew Arnold in the previous century or Samuel Johnson nearly two centuries earlier. This breadth, in which he spoke not for literature alone but also for the larger social context in which literature was created, made Eliot seem, somehow, grander, more significant than such estimable American critics as Wilson and Trilling. Through the power of his prose style, Eliot was able to convey, even when writing about the most narrowly literary subjects, that something greater than mere literature was at stake.

Wallace Stevens's poetry is more beautiful, and Robert Frost's often more powerful, than Eliot's, but the latter's, once read, refuses to leave the mind. How much does memorability matter in literature? A vast deal, I suspect, and in poetry above all. And here, in the realm of the memorable, Eliot has left a greater literary residue than any other poet of the 20th century. A sampler follows:

> "Let us go then, you and I
> When the evening is spread out against the sky
> Like a patient etherised upon a table; ... "

> "I grow old ... I grow old ...
> I shall wear the bottoms of my trousers rolled."

> "In the room the women come and go
> Talking of Michaelangelo."

> "I have measured out my life with coffee spoons;
> I know the voices dying with a dying fall
> Beneath the music from a farther room.
> So how should I presume."

> "Here I am, an old man in a dry month
> Being read to by a boy, waiting for rain."

> "Apeneck Sweeney spreads his knees
> Letting his arms hang down to laugh,
> The zebra stripes along his jaw
> Swelling to maculate giraffe."

> "April is the cruellest month ... "

> "These fragments I have shored against my ruin."

> "Time present and time past
> Are both perhaps present in time future
> And time future contained in time past ... "

"Humankind cannot bear too much reality."

"This is the way the world ends
Not with a bang but a whimper."

In 1922, the year the *Criterion* began publication, Eliot published *The Waste Land*, the lengthy work that established his reputation as a major poet. "It happens now and then," Eliot wrote in his essay on Tennyson, "that a poet by some strange accident expresses the mood of his generation, at the same time that he is expressing a mood of his own which is quite remote from that of his generation," which is as good a gloss as any on *The Waste Land*. Along with Stravinsky's *Le Sacre du Printemps*, Joyce's *Ulysses*, and the paintings of Picasso and Matisse, *The Waste Land* was from its inception, and has remained in our time, one of the landmark works of modernism. Lyndall Gordon calls it "the poem of the century."

That he was indisputably a major artist lent Eliot enormous weight as a critic, and as a moral instructor. No other artist of his rank wrote so much criticism. The two in harness, artist and critic, proved a powerful combination. Eliot's own view was that the artist was likely to be the best critic, for "his criticism will be criticism, and not the satisfaction of a suppressed creative wish—which, in most other persons, is apt to interfere fatally." This may or may not be so, but in Eliot's case, his being the toweringly important artist he was made him, for a time, unassailable.

So much so that most people were willing to overlook that Eliot's extra-literary views were deeply conservative and that he might have had, not to put too fine a point on it, a Jew problem.

The character in Mary Gaitskill's story might as easily have said: "Isn't Eliot that turd who took out after the Jews?" Whether he did or not, whether Eliot was an anti-Semite or not, has been a subject of much controversy on which full-blown books have been written: *T. S. Eliot, Anti-Semitism, and Literary Form* by Anthony Julius arguing the case for Eliot's being an anti-Semite, and *T. S.*

Eliot and Prejudice by Christopher Ricks arguing the case against, with many others joining in on both sides of the issue.

The evidence against Eliot is not new; it is all in print. The new letters, it must be said, do not add much. There is a single letter to John Quinn, the art and manuscript collector, one of the young Eliot's benefactors and himself a genuine bigot, in which Eliot refers to being "sick of dealing with Jew publishers who will not carry out their part of the contract unless they are forced to." Less unpleasant is a reference to "a young Balliol man of my acquaintance, a clever Jew from Alexandria named Jean de Menasce."

The most damaging evidence remains where it has always been, in the poems. In "Gerontion," there is "the Jew [who] squats on the window sill, the owner,/Spawned in some estaminet of Antwerp/ Blistered in Brussels, patched and peeled in London."

In "Sweeney Among the Nightingales," "Rachel *née* Rabinovitch/Tears at the grapes with murderous paws."

In "Burbank with a Baedeker: Bleistein with a Cigar" we have the wretched Bleistein: "Chicago Semite Viennese./A lustreless protrusive eye/ Stares from the protozoic slime/At a perspective of Canaletto"; and, worse, "On the Rialto once./The rats are underneath the piles./The Jew is underneath the lot./Money in furs."

In *After Strange Gods*, a book made from lectures given at the University of Virginia, Eliot, in limning his ideal society, argues that its population should be homogeneous, with "a unity of religious background; and reasons of race and religion combine to make any large number of freethinking Jews undesirable."

Anthony Julius, an English attorney with literary training, takes up these and all other bits of anti-Jewish evidence he can find against Eliot. His case is not merely adversarial but prosecutorial, expertly handled, let it be said, and very thoroughly documented (56 pages of footnotes to 217 pages of text). Forensic in style, polemical in tone, the book is a prime example of what Milan Kundera has called criminography, a work setting out to convict a writer of intellectual or ideological crimes. As Eliot wrote apropos of Pascal's *Letters to a Provincial*, the philosopher's Jansenist case against the Jesuits, Julius's arguments have in common with all superior polemics that "they persuade, they seduce, they are unfair."

Eliot never believed himself an anti-Semite and actually loathed being thought one, claiming, interestingly, that, for a Christian, anti-Semitism "is a sin." Yet he never came forth publicly to announce his regret for the anti-Semitic references in his work; how easily, after all, he might have made it an Armenian who owned the building in which the man telling his tale in "Gerontion" lived, or had a fellow named Simpson instead of Bleistein with a cigar, and had Rachel *née* Seton-Watson tearing at those grapes, and worried about "freethinking intellectuals" rather than Jews corrupting his ideal society. He never, it should be said, allowed *After Strange Gods* to be reprinted.

Perhaps Eliot is best indicted by his own poetic theory, specifically, by his notion of "the objective correlative." He believed that the art of poetry was in capturing emotions and feelings that were beyond standard intellectual formulation or even of language itself. The problem with *Hamlet*, for example, is that the character Hamlet's "bafflement at the absence of the objective equivalent to his feelings is a prolongation of the bafflement of his creator in the face of his artistic problem." Eliot apparently had no such problem when he wished to express his loathing for the decay of society, the loss of all social decorum, and the horror of sexual depravity: he found his objective correlative in the Jews.

Among writers, great writers, Eliot scarcely stands alone in making use of the always ready-to-hand convenience of the Jew as a symbol. One could put together a hideous anthology of anti-Semitic passages from great English writers—Anthony Julius has, in effect, done just that in his newest book, *Trials of the Diaspora*. No further sermonettes are required on the subject of anti-Semitism, but it seems doubly deplorable to find it in imaginative writers (poets, novelists, playwrights), for anti-Semitism is, among other things, a grave failure of imagination—an inability to concede simple humanity to a people because of their religious or social origins—and a failed imagination is for writers the most heinous failure of all.

But might it be allowed that one can write or say anti-Semitic things without being an anti-Semite? Eliot is guilty of the former, but does not, I think, stand guilty of the latter. There is no record of anything on his part resembling anti-Semitic actions. He had good friends who were Jews. Not that this excuses him, but everything anti-Semitic he wrote was composed before the Holocaust. He obviously wasn't Jew-crazy, like his difficult friend Ezra Pound, who could blame the Jews for bad weather. Eliot made a wretched mistake in the references to Jews in his poetry, and one would like to think that, as a devout Christian, it added to the burden of his guilt.

Julius ends his book on Eliot with a scene set in 1950 in a hall in London in which Emanuel Litvinoff, an Eastern European Jew who survived Treblinka, read "I Am the Lizard," a poem dedicated to Eliot. Its most powerful passage reads:

> I am not one accepted in your parish.
> Bleistein is my relative and I share
> the protozoic slime of Shylock, a page in Sturmer,
> and, underneath the cities,
> a billet somewhat lower than the rats.
> Blood in the sewers. Pieces of our flesh
> float with the ordure on the Vistula.
> You had a sermon but it was not this.

According to an account by the English-Jewish poet Dannie Abse, who was in the audience, Eliot's friend Stephen Spender (born of a Jewish mother) rose up to shout, "Tom's not anti-Semitic in the least." Abse heard Eliot, sitting in the row behind him, his head down, mutter, "It's a good poem, it's a very good poem."

Is T. S. Eliot today a figure merely of historical interest: an avant-garde poet in an age now bereft of either a convincing avant-garde or a genuine interest in poetry; a critic with no further discriminations to make, nothing more to teach, and no real literary community to attend to his pronouncements?

Eliot's best poems still work their magic, his powers of manipulating language to reveal unspeakable truths still resonate and register. His pitch-perfect phrasings stay in the mind the way litanies learned in childhood do. An unsolved mystery is why no poetry written since the time of Eliot, Yeats, Stevens, Frost, or possibly Auden has anything like the same memorability as theirs, and among them no one's poetry, as I have suggested, is more memorable than T. S. Eliot's.

In his criticism, Eliot wrote much that was prophetic of the age in which we now live. As early as the 1920s, he remarked "on the vague jargon of our time, when we have a vocabulary for everything and exact ideas about nothing." He foresaw the rise of "the half-formed science [of] psychology, [which] conceals from both writer and reader the utter meaninglessness of a statement." He anticipated the loss of authority of universities in the intellectual life of England and America: "They have too long lost any common fundamental assumption as to what education is *for*, and they are too big. It might be hoped that they would eventually follow, or else be relegated to preservation as curious architectural remains; but they cannot be expected to lead."

In my opening paragraph, I spoke of literary culture shutting down. The standard explanations for this are the distractions of the Internet, poor rudimentary education, the vanquishing of seriousness in university literature departments owing to the intellectually shallow enticements of modish subjects, and the allure of the pervasive entertainments of popular culture. Although none of these things help, literary culture is, I believe, shutting down chiefly because literature itself has become unimportant: what is being created in contemporary novels, poems, and plays no longer speaks to the heart or mind.

Eliot spoke to this point, too. He did so most incisively in his essay "Religion and Literature." There Eliot reminds us that the "greatness of literature cannot be determined solely by literary standards." Ethical, theological, and moral standards must contribute to such determinations. Criticism can only be effective where there is agreement on these other standards, and in his day, he claimed, "there is no common agreement." If an arguable proposition about Eliot's day, it is unarguable in our own.

Eliot held that "moral judgments of literary works are made only according to the moral code accepted by each generation." Obviously the code changes from generation to generation. Some take this regular change as equivalent to progress, as over the generations we jollily make our way to perfectibility. For Eliot, such regular change "is only evidence of what insubstantial foundations people's moral judgments have." He also believed that "those who read at all, read so many more books by living authors than books by dead authors; there was never a time so completely parochial, so shut off from the past."

Writers, in his view, tend to be not much better than general readers: "The majority of novelists are persons drifting in the stream, only a little faster. They have some sensitiveness, but little intellect." He doesn't speak of poets, but, considering the vast quantity of them being turned out by contemporary MFA programs, he could scarcely have thought the poets of our time as other than in an equally irrelevant stream of their own.

For Eliot, literature was a moral enterprise, but moral in a way that purely secular moralists—the moralists of economics, of social science, of contemporary politics—cannot hope to grasp. He wasn't accusing modern writers of immorality, or even amorality, but of ignorance "of our most fundamental and important beliefs; and that in consequence [contemporary literature's] tendency is to encourage its readers to get what they can out of life while it lasts, to miss no 'experience' that presents itself, and to sacrifice themselves, if they make any sacrifice at all, only for the sake of tangible benefits to others in this world either now or in the future." Not, any of this, good enough.

Rereading Eliot, his poetry and his criticism, a half-century after first reading him as a college student, I am no less, in fact even more, impressed with his high intelligence, his subtlety, the depth of his penetration. His was the literary mind par excellence, and it makes the scientific, the social scientific, even the contemporary philosophical mind seem inadequate, if not paltry.

If the literary culture that T. S. Eliot, at his best, represented is over and done, a thing of the past never to be recovered, the loss is of a seriousness beyond reckoning.

Cyril Connolly

Nothing Succeeds Like Failure

W HEN MAURICE BOWRA, then a young don and not
yet Warden of Wadham College, Oxford, used to
introduce Cyril Connolly, a man six years his junior,
he would say, "This is Connolly. Coming man." After which he
paused, then added, "Hasn't come yet." Nor would Cyril Connolly
come—not quite, never ever, really, at least not by his own lights.
To be promising when young can be a terrible thing, for one's
promise all too often turns out to be a pledge on which one isn't
able to deliver. "Promise is guilt," Connolly would write in his thirties, "promise is the capacity for letting people down."

When young, Cyril Connolly had that easy brilliance that
prods predictions of great things ahead. But he had a taste—a propensity?, an aptitude?—for failure that never left him. He first
indulged it seriously by taking a third-class degree—easily enough
done when one chooses not to prepare for examinations—which
finished off any hopes he might have had for a university career. He
nicely kept the pressure off himself by doing near the absolute minimum after coming down from Oxford. He took a job tutoring a

spoiled child in Jamaica, which entailed two hours of work at midday, with the rest of the time devoted to tennis, bridge, and tropical drinks. He hired on as secretary to the fifty-nine-year-old Logan Pearsall Smith, a wealthy man of letters, a transplanted American, brother-in-law to Bertrand Russell and to Bernard Berenson. The job called for supplying Pearsall Smith with a one-man audience for his aesthetic and anti-American views and acquiring the older man's taste for good living, for which Connolly himself already had a powerful affinity if not the wherewithal to pay for on his own. From Pearsall Smith he also obtained the view that a superior work of art was of greater value than anything else in the world, including people, perhaps the only thing that truly mattered.

Through Pearsall Smith Connolly met Desmond MacCarthy, another man of promise who, true to the breed, failed to deliver. Both Pearsall Smith and MacCarthy bought into Connolly's promise. Pearsall Smith wrote to him: "You seem to be the one person who can express the modern sensibility—the ways of feeling of your generation—and when you have a book to publish you will have a delightful success." (Never, as we nowadays say, happened.) MacCarthy told him that "you have the intellectual daring necessary as well as the indispensable power of perception. I believe in you, and I don't readily believe in people's gifts."

MacCarthy was able to obtain a job for Connolly on *The New Statesman*, initially as a proofreader and writer of brief, unsigned reviews, later as the contributor of a biweekly literary article or review. Connolly later performed the same service for *The Times* of London, which he continued at until end of his days. The problem was that Connolly didn't really believe regular reviewing was a job worth doing. "I review novels to make money," he wrote in his journal, "because it is easier for a sluggard to write an article a fortnight than a book a year, because the writer is soothed by the opiate of action, the crank by posing as a good journalist, and having an airhole. I dislike it. I do it and I am always resolving to give it up."

In fact, Cyril Connolly was a superior reviewer. In the afterword to his book *The Rise and Fall of the Man of Letters*, John Gross writes of Connolly that, "within his limits, how much imagination and wit he brought to his task! A Connolly review (except perhaps towards the end) was always liable to contain a provocation, a suggestive parallel, a phrase that stayed with you, an incitement to read and find out for yourself."

For Cyril Connolly, this was nowhere near good enough. Men of letters, in most circles an honorific term, were in his view nothing more than those "trained from their birth to festoon the world with verbiage, to delay, to decorate, to scheme and windify over the reputations which they exist to celebrate, these armchair adventurers, with their arch humor, their quaint, apologetic egoism, their eminence socially and academically, each in his own right a gentleman and a gasbag. . . ."

WHAT CYRIL CONNOLLY ardently wished to be was a highbrow novelist in the grand modernist tradition. He seemed always to be starting a novel, which invariably fizzled, with one exception, a very slender, altogether negligible, now quite properly forgotten little book called *The Rock Pool.* Perhaps, as John Gross suggests, he suffered from "an unduly Flaubertian ideal of what literature ought to be." More likely, he hadn't the necessary combination of talent and patience, nor the dramatic sense to sustain a complex plot, required by a good novelist. David Pryce-Jones, whose *Cyril Connolly, Memoir and Journal,* is the best book written about Connolly—I have made copious use of it herein—notes that "exploration of his ego and all its works interested [Connolly] far more" than "the invention of a plot." He had, in other words, too vast a quantity of self-regard to get out of his own skin to write about other people. Connolly's was the temperament and spirit of the romantic, melancholy division, and there are no great romantic novelists.

What Connolly did instead was write about his inability to write, or at least to do the kind of writing he would himself have liked to have done. This literary threnody became so well established over the years that Edmund Wilson, a man to whom literary costiveness was as alien as sexual temperance, wrote the following ditty:

> Cyril Connolly
> Behaves rather fonnily:
> Whether folks are at peace or fighting,
> He complains that it keeps him from writing.

Connolly's *Enemies of Promise* postulates that a successful book is one that will last for ten years. Originally published in 1938, the book reappeared, seventy years later, under the imprint of its third publisher. Connolly also wrote, in the first sentence of *The Unquiet Grave*, his miscellany of the aphorisms and *aperçus* that shaped and represented his own thinking, "the more books we read the clearer it becomes that the true function of a writer is to produce a masterpiece and no other task is of any consequence."

If *Enemies of Promise* appears to have passed the ten-year test—or so its republishers appear to believe—it is very far from the masterpiece that was the name of Connolly's desire. The subtext, or hidden theme, of the book, as David Pryce-Jones remarks, is "the loss of willpower and failure of nerve among the English" of its author's time and social class. In Connolly's case, that class was the impoverished upper class. His family was Anglo-Irish, down on its luck. He was the only child born to a military father, much indulged by his paternal grandmother. In one of the autobiographical chapters of *Enemies of Promise*, Connolly tells of being torn as a child in a toy shop over wanting two different toys, and of his grandmother eliminating the conflict by buying him both. The rest of his life, the import behind this story is, he wanted both toys—wanted all the toys, really. His crowded toy box would include wives, travel, exquisite food, lots of drink—it was Connolly who wrote that "imprisoned within every fat man a thin man is wildly signaling to be let out"—exotic animals, much party-going. The only toy he failed to acquire was the one he claimed to want most ardently of all: the magnificent novel he never found the time, or marshaled the will, to write.

*E*NEMIES OF PROMISE can be read as an explanation of why the cards were stacked against Connolly writing that novel. The first third of the book is, ostensibly, an examination of prose style. In it he describes and provides examples of what he takes to be the two reigning styles of the day—a period running from roughly the turn of the twentieth century to the late 1930s—the mandarin and the vernacular. Notable among the mandarins were Henry James, Lytton Strachey, Virginia Woolf, Aldous Huxley, James Joyce, Ronald Firbank, the Sitwells, Paul Valéry. With their lengthy sentences, their unstinting emphasis on elevated language, their vaunting of the powers of the imagination, the mandarin writers offered, after the disillusion of World War I, "a religion of beauty, a cult of words, of meanings understood only by the initiated at a time when people were craving such initiations."

Not all that many people felt this craving, let it be added. "A great writer," Connolly notes, "creates a world of his own and his readers are proud to live in it." The mandarins wrote under the assumption that their readers were their equals, though they didn't much care if they weren't. Connolly quotes Logan Pearsall Smith remarking that "unsaleability seems to be the hallmark, in modern times, of quality in writing." Connolly himself later wrote: "Better to write for yourself and have no public, than to write for the public and have no self."

The vernacular style, exemplified by such writers as Somerset Maugham, Ernest Hemingway, E. M. Forster, D. H. Lawrence, and George Orwell, is by design less determinedly elegant than the mandarin. While the mandarin style is intentionally as far from spoken language as possible, the vernacular, like "the best journalism is the conversation of a great talker," including "nothing that cannot be said."

Each style, the mandarin and the vernacular, has its weakness: the mandarins tend toward perfection, "the art-for-art-sakers, finding or believing life to be intolerable except for art's perfection, by the very violence of their homage can render art imperfect." The weakness of the vernacular style is in its uniformity. "The penalty of writing for the masses" is that "as the writer goes out to meet them half-way he is joined by other writers going out to meet them half-way and they merge into the same creature—the talkie journalist, the advertising, lecturing, popular novelist." Here, by way of demonstration, Connolly composed a paragraph in which he included sentences from Orwell, Hemingway, and Isherwood, to show that, stylistically, there wasn't much to choose among them.

The great hope, obviously, was to combine the best of the mandarin with the best of the vernacular styles. This new style would take from the mandarin, in Connolly's formulation, "art and patience, the striving for perfection, the horror of clichés, the creative delight in the material, in the possibilities of the long sentence and the splendor and subtlety of the composed phrase." From the vernacular it would take "the poetical impact of Forster's diction, the lucidity of Maugham, the smooth cutting edge of Isherwood, the indignation of Lawrence, the honesty of Orwell," and, above all, the careful pruning of the element of the excessive and the discipline of careful construction and execution of plot.

Sounds sensible, even straightforward enough, until Connolly, in the second third of his book, sets out the manifold obstacles in the path of the writer of his time, which makes this and nearly all other attempts at writing seem all but impossible. These obstacles are the veritable enemies of promise. First among them Connolly felt is that the day had long since past— it ended toward the end of the seventeenth and the beginning of the eighteenth century—when it was impossible to write badly, for until then "to write naturally was to write well." Connolly holds

Joseph Addison, in his attempt to make writing popular, partly to blame here for inflating language, bringing affectation into prose style, divesting words of their precision and clogging their meanings with irony and whimsy. Add to this that not only can a writer no longer count on a ready audience, but also he "can have no confidence in posterity"; he can't even depend on the culture itself surviving. When Connolly asked, "Is this age really more unfavorable to writing than any other?," it is evident that he thought it indubitably was, for the writer is faced with heavier financial burdens than ever before, burdens that have set further traps to subvert his grand aspirations.

Connolly warms to his subject when he gets down to cases, or particulars, which is to say to "the parasites on genius . . . the blights from which no writer is immune." In recounting these blights, one assumes that Connolly was talking about traps he stepped into in his own career. Among them is veering off into journalism, with its pleasures of "being paid and praised on the nail." Connolly writes: "Myself a lazy, irresolute person, overvain and overmodest, unsure in my judgments and unable to finish what I have begun, I have profited from journalism." The art of self-debasement was a Connolly specialty.

Then there is politics, which, when Connolly was writing his book in the late 1930s, with the smell of the civil war in Spain still in the nostrils, Hitler and Stalin on the march, was unavoidable. Politics during such periods was not merely a distraction to writers but threatened to become a full-time job. Connolly was himself engaged but not engorged by politics. He was without keen political insight; his own politics were standard left-wing loopy, nobody-could-be-so-stupid-as-an-intellectual stuff, so that he could write "capitalism is expelling the artist as Spain expelled the Jews" or suggest that "success is most poisonous in America."

Sloth, another of the enemies of promise, was closer to Connolly's temperament. "Sloth in writers," he noted, "is always a symptom of an acute inner conflict." The enemy he called Escapism had to have also been high on his list; it included drinking (also drugs and religion, two further enemies), and incontinent conversation. The latter is likely to have been most attractive to Connolly, himself a schmoozer of a high power, who writes that "most good talkers, when they have run down, are miserable; they know that they have betrayed themselves, that they have taken material which should have a life of its own, to dispense it in noises in the air." This sentence has more than a mere whiff of the autobiographical about it, with the sound of ice cubes tinkling in the glass behind it.

Sex and marriage were two more of Connolly's enemies. "As far as one can infer from observation," he writes, "it is a mistake for writers to marry young, especially for them to have children young; early marriage and paternity are a remedy for loneliness and unhappiness that set up a counter irritant." Children, he claims, "dissipate the longing for immortality which is the compensation of the writer's life." (Not in the case of Leo Tolstoy, who had even more children than he wrote novels.) Yet, Connolly adds, "There is no more somber enemy of good art than the pram in the hall." All this is nonsense, of course, and on the subject of writers and marriage, I should say that for the writer, as for nearly everyone else, marrying or remaining single, neither, clearly, is a solution.

ONE DOESN'T HAVE TO READ too far into *Enemies of Promise* to recognize that Connolly prefers his writers to be unhappy, for he speaks of "the necessary unhappiness without which writers perish." (Maurice Ravel, taking on the myth of the suffering artist, said that he got more artistic benefit out of fifteen minutes of pleasure than out of three months of suffering.) Connolly takes things a step further to prescribe that a writer's health should not be too good: "rude health, as the name implies, is averse to culture and demands either physical relief or direct action for its bursting energy." From all of this it would seem naturally to follow that the contemporary artist must bear a wound, "which we [artists]," as Connolly claims, quoting Gide, "must never allow to heal but which must always remain painful and bleeding, the gash made by contact with hideous reality." Oppressed by financial burdens, unhappy, in poor health, psychologically wounded—one wonders how any writing by anyone got done at all.

In the final third of *Enemies of Promise*, Connolly describes his childhood and schooling. He was sent to St. Cyprian's, the same school that George Orwell so memorably devastated in his essay "Such, Such Were the Joys." Connolly holds that, when he was not even seven years old, his character had already begun to deteriorate. Schooling did not rebuild it, though at St. Cyprian's he learned about literature from Orwell and about art from Cecil Beaton, another friend acquired there. At St. Cyprian's he "occupied the position [he] was so often to maintain in after life, that of the intellectual who is never given the job because he is 'brilliant but unsound.' " There, too, he began to cultivate the art of pleasing people.

At Eton, which he entered as a Colleger—that is, on scholarship—he discovered that popularity depended on "a mixture of enthusiasm with moral cowardice and social sense," all of which he readily enough applied. He also learned that "intelligence was a deformity which must be concealed," which he was also only too willing to do. As a result, he succeeded, being elected to Pop, as the school's elite intramural club was called. He later won a scholarship to Balliol College, Oxford. If this scholarship appears to confute his claims to supine and sublime slothfulness, he writes, apropos of studying for examinations, that "like many lazy people, once I started working, I could not stop; perhaps that is why we avoid it."

In fact, Connolly emerged from Eton with impressive erudition and highbrow aspirations. Included among his generation at Oxford were Harold Acton, Robert Byron, Anthony Powell, and Henry Green. He emerged from there, as he says, wishing to be a poet but "well-grounded enough to become a critic and drifted into it [criticism] through unemployability."

I**n the end,** *Enemies of Promise* is an ingenious *apologia pro vita sua* for Cyril Connolly's inability to write his masterpiece. Among the many reasons he adduces for this failure are his parentage, his upbringing, his schooling, his temperament, the era in which he came into maturity, the economy, the conditions of English culture, everything, really, but the weather. The old boy, one begins to think, never had a chance.

"Talent is something which grows and does not ripen except in the right kind of soil and climate," Connolly writes. "It can be neglected or cultivated and will flower or die down. To suppose that artists will muddle through without encouragement and without money because in the past there had been exceptions is to assume that salmon will find their way to the top of a river to spawn in spite of barrages and pollution. 'If it's in you it's bound to come out' is a wish fulfillment. More often it stays in and goes bad."

The sad truth is that Cyril Connolly's petering out seems to have been innate. It wasn't in him to be the kind of writer he wanted to be. His were the skills of the *littérateur*, not of the artist; he was in possession of a lush vocabulary, he had wide learning, and imitative power that he put to good use in his parodies and burlesques. But he was without the depth or the drive required to produce major imaginative art.

He had a good run in the 1940s as the founder and editor of *Horizon*, which was published from the beginning of 1940 to the end of 1949 and was one of the best intellectual journals of the past century—no small accomplishment and a tribute to his high literary taste.

Connolly was not a man without ideas, though he hadn't the stamina to work them out. In his journal, for example, he writes brilliantly, if all too glancingly, about the shortcomings of Virginia

Woolf: "She is not really a novelist—she does not care for human beings . . . "; "her critical essays are full of clichés . . ."; "She grows intoxicated on her own language and suggestion of tipsiness quickly cloys. . . . " How fine it would have been to have had a lengthy attack on Virginia Woolf from Connolly forty or fifty years ago—and how many dreary subsequent books extolling her genius, had that essay been written, we should have been spared! But, alas, he was a short-distance runner who had no wish to be lonely.

Cyril Connolly published *Enemies of Promise* when he was thirty-four. He had thirty-seven more years to slog through, writing his reviews, sending them off from Spain, the south of France, and other gentle climes where he indulged his sybaritic tastes. "It was almost as if," David Pryce-Jones writes, "he were under an obligation to spoil near-ideal conditions by ingenious contrivances for wasting time and resources." He grew fat, which he viewed as "the outward symbol of moral and mental fat and that is why I dislike it." A hedonist with a bad conscience, he appears to have been put on earth briefly to charm his readers and lengthily to torture himself. In the end futile literary promise had no greater anatomist, or his own promise no greater enemy, than Cyril Connolly.

Isaiah Berlin

A Charmed Life

I SAIAH BERLIN—with two long i's in the first name for the proper pronunciation, please—was a name that rang the gong in the best academic and intellectual circles for nearly half a century. "Isaiah"—I have heard that name roll off anglophiliac lips with no less pleasure than a wine connoisseur might say Château Le Pin. During the most radical days of the *New York Review of Books*, he helped sustain that journal's respectability. Conservatives were not displeased to quote him, either. In at least three countries—England, the United States, and Israel—the name Isaiah Berlin held its own special juju or magical ability to summon significant meaning.

A philosopher by training who later became an historian chiefly of political ideas, a figure and fixture at Oxford, where he spent the better (and best) part of his life, Isaiah Berlin was an international intellectual celebrity. He had a way of showing up in the best places—not least among them, in the indexes of books by or about Virginia Woolf, Igor Stravinsky, Evelyn Waugh, Joseph Alsop, and Katherine Graham. "I know the difference between Irving Berlin and Isaiah Berlin," the public relations man and consummate name-dropper Ben Sonnenberg Sr. said, "and I know them both."

Berlin's chief form was the biographical essay in which he traced the course of ideas through the lives of such writers as Vico, Machiavelli, Tolstoy, Turgenev, and others. (His one continuous book, a slender volume on Karl Marx, is disappointing.) In other, more purely political essays, his tendency was to argue against single-idea or "Great System" thinkers, and he became *the* philosopher of political limitation: against historical inevitability, for the liberty of the individual against that of the state, of two minds about the quality of progress represented by the Enlightenment. Liberals, he felt, were insufficiently impressed by the tragic quality inherent in life. Among his most often used quotations was Kant's remark: "Out of the crooked timber of humanity, no straight thing was ever made."

THE LABELS "PHILOSOPHER" and "political thinker" never seemed quite the right fit for Berlin. His talent, his propensity, and his instincts always seemed at least partially artistic. His biographical essays are those of a man who seeks to understand life as an artist does—which is why many of the essays have a continuing life and can be read, with intellectual profit, more than once.

Until the middle 1970s—when he acquired the services of a highly conscientious volunteer editor named Henry Hardy who offered to round up Berlin's various essays and lectures and see them published in book form—one had little notion of Berlin's writing constituting a genuine oeuvre, a body of work coherent within itself and carrying cumulative meaning.

I wrote that the essay was Berlin's chief form; more precisely, his true form was the extended, impressive, torrential schmooze. One of the most interesting revelations of Michael Ignatieff's biography of Isaiah Berlin is that Berlin did not write his essays—he dictated them to a secretary, polishing them later. People who spent time with Berlin have remarked on the striking similarity between his speech and his prose. Garrulity in speech, verbosity on the page, these, Berlin half-recognized, were his weakness.

Some among his critics felt this verbosity not an amusing but a serious flaw. A. J. P. Taylor told Edmund Wilson that when Berlin couldn't get into his subject, he "tried to carry things off 'with a burst of words.' " This quality in Berlin, subordinate clause lashed to subordinate clause, triplet after quadruplet of adjectives, gives many of his essays a shapeless quality, a feeling of overload, depriving them of the economy that is central to the essay.

ALL WHO KNEW, met, or merely heard Isaiah Berlin felt the need to describe him in verbal action, like so many pilgrims fresh from viewing one of the natural wonders of the world. "The first thing that everyone noticed about him," Berlin's friend Maurice Bowra wrote, "was the rapidity of his speech, which matched an equal rapidity in his thought. Some of us talked fast enough already, but Isaiah talked even faster, and at times I found it hard to keep up with him." Robert Wokler recently wrote that Berlin "was profligate with words; his knighthood, it was suggested, having been bestowed on him for services to conversation."

It was a show that no one, once having witnessed it, soon forgot. It swept people up; it conquered, it captivated. Edmund Wilson noted in his diary: "Isaiah Berlin affected me like nobody else I had known; though he was not particularly handsome, I tended to react to him a little as if he were an attractive woman whom I wanted to amuse and please: and this attitude on my part, evoked a kind of coquetry on his."

If Berlin seems to have given so much pleasure to friends over a long life, his own pleasures were seen to from the beginning of his life. Michael Ignatieff cites four significant facts connected with his birth in 1909: It followed that of an earlier, stillborn sister; he was the boy his parents longed for; he sustained a permanent injury to his left arm when the delivering physician too vigorously used the forceps on him; and he was to remain an only child. He was born a Jew in Riga, Latvia, to a lumber-merchant father who was sufficiently successful for the family to be able to move to St. Petersburg, usually out of bounds, or beyond the Pale, to Jews. His mother had a livelier mind than his father, and her love for her son was unstinting. The young Isaiah seems to have grown up under the reign of that "family egotism" in which, as Tolstoy put it, "parents decide that the rest of the world can go to hell as long as all is well with our little Andrei."

Although they survived the Russian Revolution, Berlin's father in 1921 wisely transported the family to England, where he had business connections and had stored up some £10,000. The money eased the exile, though there must have been difficult moments as what Michael Ignatieff describes as this "plump, unprepossessing Jewish child in a Gentile school, a bookish boy with a foreign accent and limp left arm" sought to win people over. But Berlin was to prove the consummate assimilationist, able to slide himself easily into any social circle he desired.

His entree, all his days, was his intelligence and his charm. The former was first put to service in gaining entrance to the best English schools. At St. Paul's his reputation as a charming talker—as a non-stop, talk-for-its-own-lovely-sake talker—began. He won through talk what others might win through athletics. His oddity seems never to have been held against him. Nor, apparently, was his Jewishness. His mother kept a kosher home, and Berlin throughout his life observed Passover and Yom Kippur as a matter of allegiance, though he seems to have been a skeptic, and religion scarcely figures in his writing.

BERLIN WAS VERY SMART VERY YOUNG—smart and savvy and subtle. In an essay on freedom written at St. Paul's at eighteen, he declared, "it hurts no man to conform if he knows that conformity is only a kind of manners, a sort of universal etiquette."

There was never any question of going into his father's profitable business; one of the things such a business makes possible, after all, is the maintenance of brilliant sons such as Isaiah. After failing to win a place at Balliol College, Oxford, he won a scholarship at Corpus Christi. He developed a love for the long, looping Victorian sentence—an early addiction was to the prose of Macaulay, another lord of loquacity—and tutors criticized his essays for rattling on at too great length.

Berlin's was the generation that entered Oxford just as Evelyn Waugh, Cyril Connolly, Harold Acton, and the other "Children of the Sun" (as Martin Green called them) were leaving. The great names of his own generation included Maurice Bowra, Stephen Spender, A. J. Ayer, R. H. S. Crossman, and Stuart Hampshire. Bowra, a rebel in those days, was known as leader of "the immoral front." Berlin, though part of Bowra's circle, was able to make himself welcome wherever he wished, without deeply committing himself to one faction or another. He had the reputation, rare among talkers, of actually listening, of expending genuine sympathy on the problems of others, of being able to put himself into the minds of others, which would later become one of his important traits as an analyst of the writings of men with whose ideas he disagreed.

He considered careers in journalism and in law. But he was also a most gifted student—gifted enough to win election to a coveted fellowship at All Souls College. Nothing could have suited him better, for he disliked the grind of teaching, and All Souls, a precursor of the Institute for Advanced Study at Princeton, had no students. It also carried enormous prestige. He was the first Jew ever to win a fellowship to All Souls. His election made him something of a celebrity within wealthier Jewish circles in England, and he found easy access to such homes as those of the Baron de Rothschild.

Berlin had an instinct for meeting important people. In 1938, he met Freud and, soon after, Chaim Weizmann. He became friendly with Elizabeth Bowen. He impressed Virginia Woolf, but not enough for her entirely to shed her anti- Semitism: "a Portuguese Jew, by the look of him," she wrote in her diary of Berlin, "Oxford's leading light." Berlin himself was a man without the least xenophobia. In Oxford, he was thought an insider, maybe an insider's insider.

BERLIN GRADUALLY DRIFTED AWAY from philosophy to do the history of ideas, for which he thought himself better equipped, if only because it was less open-ended. His line had been analytical philosophy, and he played the game well enough to give a lecture at Cambridge that apparently did not entirely bore Wittgenstein. Of his standing as a philosopher, Berlin said, "I knew I wasn't first-rate, but I was good enough. I was quite respected. I wasn't despised. I was one of the brethren." He also thought the logical positivism he had been practicing an intellectual dead end. "I gradually came to the conclusion," he would later say, "that I should prefer a field in which one could hope to know more at the end of one's life than when one had begun."

Berlin's own mind tended toward the historical, the exceptional case, the idea or cluster of ideas operating within a given time. He was not a pure thinker, but a reactive one who did better rubbing up against the ideas of others. Historical context became another crucial element in his thought. Stuart Hampshire felt all this so much twaddle, "period talking" he called it, vague and neither quite logical nor very positivistic.

Soon after England's entry into World War II, Berlin found himself in New York, where he had traveled with the Communist spy Guy Burgess (who planned to go on to Moscow, with Berlin serving as his unwitting cover). In the event, Burgess was called back to England, and Berlin stayed on in the United States. The British Embassy availed itself of his services in helping to get America into the war by influencing trade unions, black organizations, and Jewish groups to take up pro-British, anti-German positions. "America was," as Michael Ignatieff writes, "the making of him." With his talent for insinuating himself with important figures, Berlin soon became friendly with Supreme Court Justices Louis Brandeis and Felix Frankfurter, Charles Bohlen, Joseph Alsop, and the ineluctable Alice Roosevelt Longworth. He seemed naturally to gravitate toward power, toward establishments.

Liking Americans though he did, he found their talk dull. They found his talk scintillating. The Americans he encountered took great pleasure in his ironic descriptions of their country, delivered, as Ignatieff puts it, "in his rapid-fire semi-Martian vernacular."

PART OF BERLIN'S JOB was to send back to England summaries about America's readiness to enter the war. These were read by a very select audience, including the King, Winston Churchill, and Anthony Eden. He might have been described as an English purveyor of American gossip on the state of the world—for which years of Oxford gossip seem to have served him well. His audience sometimes found his dispatches too colored—a bit "too perfervid," said Churchill; perhaps, added Eden, with "too generous [an] Oriental flavor"—but they lent him cachet as a bright man with a penchant for making the best connections in the highest of places.

These dispatches were also responsible for a famous comic anecdote about the confusion between Isaiah and Irving Berlin. In the anecdote, Winston Churchill, at a dinner party, mistakes Irving for Isaiah. He asks the songwriter his advice on a number of political questions—when does he think the war will end, will Roosevelt run again—to which confusing answers are forthcoming. He then inquires what Mr. Berlin thinks is the most important thing he has written, to which the unhesitant reply is: "White Christmas." The story was too delicious not to get around—Churchill, when he discovered his faux pas, himself told it to his cabinet. As Ignatieff notes, Isaiah Berlin gained a celebrity through the story without having to do anything to earn it. But then things always had a way of dropping into his lap.

Berlin also had a knack for historical timing. He meets David Ben-Gurion as the state of Israel is forming. After the war, he travels to the Soviet Union and is put in touch with Boris Pasternak, who later asks his help in smuggling out *Dr. Zhivago*. Twice on trips to the Soviet Union, Berlin visited Anna Akhmatova, then in internal exile under Stalin. A great poet, she had a correspondingly great talent for self-dramatization, and lent to her two meetings with Isaiah Berlin vast historical import. He felt himself utterly mesmerized by her, thought himself in love with her. She wrote a poem, "Poem without a Hero," in which he figures as "the guest from beyond the looking glass."

This connection, too, added to Berlin's prestige in the social as well as intellectual realm. By his late thirties, Lady Sibyl Colefax, Lady Emerald Cunard, and the American Marietta Tree sought him out for their parties; he became a social collectible. Churchill asked for—and apparently accepted— his literary advice on *The Gathering Storm*, his memoir of the 1930s. Einstein was pleased to meet with him. Chaim Weizmann wanted him to write his biography; Ben-Gurion offered him the directorship of the Israeli Foreign Office. His annual pilgrimages to the United States became events among the more socially advanced American intellectuals. His became a good name to drop.

BERLIN ENTERED THE SEXUAL FRAY rather late in life. He was never greatly enamored of his looks or physical gifts; he had, from quite early in life, what seemed to be the gift of perpetual middle age. He thought he might live out his days celibate. In an otherwise handsomely proportioned biography, Michael Ignatieff reports in perhaps more detail than required his subject's rather inept sexual coming out at the age of forty-one. Berlin showed a small talent for picking the wrong women. But here, too, his good luck held, and in 1956, at the age of forty-seven, he pursued a married woman, the (eventually divorced) wife of a colleague. She was a woman with wide tolerance for his settled ways and sufficient wealth for him never to have to work again. Once more he had landed nicely on his feet.

THE LAST TWENTY YEARS of Berlin's life, his biographer reports, were the happiest. Talks delivered over the BBC made his reputation as a dazzling lecturer grow even greater. He was appointed head of Wolfson, a new Oxford college for the study of social science, a position he much enjoyed. He was elected president of the British Academy. Honorary degrees, festschrifts, literary prizes rolled in. He was awarded the Order of Merit, which somehow set the seal on his self-doubt. He lived out his days in good health, surrounded by music (his great passion), conscientious servants, an admiring family. After his death at the age of eighty-eight, Isaac Stern and Alfred Brendel—friends, of course— played at his memorial service. In Michael Ignatieff he found a sympathetic and properly suave biographer.

Yet even into the most charmed of lives, a measure of doubt must fall, and in Isaiah Berlin it was a fairly large measure. As an intellectual, Ignatieff reports, Berlin wished to occupy a firm middle ground. "He was looking for a path between heavy-going engagement and mandarin detachment. He wanted to be serious without being solemn, to defend beliefs without being dogmatic, and to be entertaining without being facile." This is nicely formulated, and Berlin seems to have achieved it. Still, it wasn't, one suspects, quite enough.

Berlin had won the regard of the world of the *New York Review of Books*, but, at the next rung up the intellectual ladder, among the serious players, his accomplishments were viewed more skeptically. Leo Strauss, Michael Oakeshott, Raymond Aron, the men whom he must have looked upon as his true peers, were not quite persuaded by Isaiah Berlin, not quite ready to grant him the serious intellectual status he craved, even though he shared many of their core beliefs.

Though a political philosopher, Berlin preferred not to speak on particular political questions. Instead he wrote on the need to tolerate a pluralism of human views and values—a pluralism, he rightly insisted, that did not need to dwindle into an empty relativism. He tried to keep his idealism in equipoise with strong skepticism, something he much admired in Alexander Herzen, the nineteenth-century Russian intellectual exiled to London, who was one of his great heroes. But in Berlin it didn't quite come off, perhaps because he was too chary of taking positions that might make him enemies.

In attempting to formulate Berlin's politics, Ignatieff at one point calls him "neither a conservative nor a laissez-faire individualist, but a New Deal liberal." At another point he writes that Berlin "was a liberal social democrat, but he was more comfortable socially among conservatives. He tried to have it both ways."

Ignatieff tells of Berlin's admiration for "Toscanini, Churchill, Weizmann—men whose vices he excused because they did not include a fatal eagerness to please." Ignatieff puts the best possible face on Berlin's apparent eagerness to please, writing that "all his life he was to be reproached for the freedom of his friendships, for his capacity to be relatively indifferent to someone's views, providing they had other redeeming virtues." One has to applaud this, if true, for no one should be reduced to and judged upon his opinions merely. Yet issues arise in which one is bound—almost as part of being engaged with one's time, almost as part of being human—to take stands and positions, to risk enmity.

Ignatieff reports that Berlin despised Herbert Marcuse and Hannah Arendt for their loftily theoretical and ultimately cold-hearted views about the nature of the German death camps. (Nor did he like professional Holocausters.) But he kept his contempt to his correspondence, never speaking out publicly. He had no difficulty in announcing himself anti-Communist, was even skeptical about the "thaw" that was said to set in with Nikita Khrushchev after the death of Stalin. But my guess is that even here he might have found overly strong anti-communism a bit excessive—that is to say, vulgar. He cannot have approved the student depredations upon the universities, both in England and America, but here, too, he was silent. "One of the last things that Berlin said to me, not long before his death," Ian Buruma recently wrote in the *New Republic*, "was that he wanted to fly to Israel just to shake the hands of his liberal friends who continued to believe that Palestinians no less than Jews had a right to feel at home and be free." I do not doubt he said this to Buruma. That he would have said it publicly is all but inconceivable.

T HE MOST REVEALING BERLIN ESSAY is the one adopted from his Romanes Lecture on Turgenev. It is about the great Russian novelist's inability, reflected in the murkiness of *Fathers and Sons*, to declare which side he was on in the struggle for Russia's destiny. The left thought Turgenev created his young nihilist, Bazarov, to be mocked, while those on the right thought he was mocking the Russia of tradition and aspirations toward European culture. "But it was the attack from the left," Berlin writes, "that hurt Turgenev most," and later in the essay, he adds: "He found the scorn of the young unjust beyond endurance." Finally, Berlin justifies Turgenev, implicitly rating him above Tolstoy and Dostoyevsky by crediting him with greater subtlety and appreciation for complexity:

> His very gifts, his power of minute and careful observation, his fascination with the varieties of character and situation as such, his detachment, his inveterate habit of doing justice to the full complexity and diversity of goals, attitudes, beliefs—these seemed to [his enemies] morally self-indulgent and politically irresponsible.

Anyone who has followed Berlin's career will find no difficulty in replacing Turgenev's name in this passage with that of Isaiah Berlin.

But was Berlin's thinking too complex for taking any determined position on the issues of his day at all? Or might it instead have been the all-too-cautious instincts of the outsider who has succeeded beyond all dreams in beautifully assimilating himself in the socially closed world of smart society, the reward for which was a lifelong fear of making waves?

MICHAEL IGNATIEFF asked the eighty-five-year-old Berlin what had most surprised him about his life. "The mere fact," he answered, "that I should have lived so peacefully and so happily through so many horrors." He neglected to mention that there is an art to achieving this—the art of careful detachment.

Yet detachment, too, has its limits. Without intellectual courage, even the most charmed of lives lose their allure; unwilling to declare their beliefs, even the most brilliant of men are in the end divested of their gravity. In a 1967 letter to his friend Jean Floud, Berlin wrote: "I always want everybody to be satisfied: the wolf, as the Russian proverb says, to be satisfied and yet the sheep to remain uneaten: which, I dare say, cannot be done in this world."

But his problem with speaking his mind may have run deeper. Perhaps more than any other figure of his age, Berlin forces one to consider the significance of intellectual courage in the life of the mind. In Isaiah Berlin, alas, it ran to short supply.

Hugh Trevor-Roper
Arrogance Intellectual Division

A S A YOUNG MAN who felt he needed to read everything, I read Hugh Trevor-Roper's demolition of Arnold Toynbee's ten-volume *Study of History*, in a 1957 essay in *Encounter* titled "Arnold Toynbee's *Millennium*," with a feeling of immense relief and gratitude, knowing that I should never have to slog my way through those turgid books. With a tweezer and a howitzer, Trevor-Roper dissected and blew apart Toynbee's work, leaving it in greater desolation than Carthage after the Second Punic War. Trevor-Roper called Toynbee "the Messiah" of his own concocted "religion of Mish-Mash." Of Toynbee, then a much-revered figure, he wrote: "In spite of its Hellenic training, his mind is fundamentally anti-rational and illiberal. Everything which suggests the freedom of the human reason, the human spirit, is odious to him." If Trevor-Roper had done to you or me what he had done to Arnold Toynbee, we should have been left with two choices only: the witness protection program or the razor over the wrists.

I discovered that Trevor-Roper had earlier savaged the work of a younger historian named Lawrence Stone, who had written on the

decline of the feudal aristocracy making way for the English revolution of the 17th century. Later, also in *Encounter*, he would do
similar jobs—shock and awe, no prisoners taken, with a good salt-
ing of the earth before departing—on A. J. P. Taylor's *Origins of the
Second World War* and E. H. Carr's *What Is History?* He was the
polemicist of the age, Trevor-Roper. But what else was he?

Hugh Trevor-Roper, we learn from Adam Sisman's excellent
biography, may have suffered, as he himself said of Lord Macaulay,
from "instantaneous success." As a boy he shone under the rigors of
England's examination system and waltzed into the better schools:
first Charterhouse, then Christ Church, Oxford's most aristocratic
college. He might have been among that once endless chain of
brightest young men who came down from Oxford—usually, let it
be said, to fail—except that he never came down, but stayed on for
what all assumed would be a smoothly successful scholarly career.

At 26, Trevor-Roper published a strongly anticlerical book on
Archbishop Laud, the archbishop of Canterbury in the reign of
Charles I, that everyone agreed was impressive in its learning and
penetration for a man so young. Brilliant was the word most frequently used to describe it, and brilliant the epithet most often
attached to Trevor-Roper. He possessed a highly polished English
prose style; was socially part of an Oxford elite inner circle that
included Gilbert Ryle, A. J. Ayer, Isaiah Berlin, and Maurice Bowra;
and at the relatively early age of 43 he was appointed Regius Professor of History at Oxford.

Yet a slight tinge of disappointment clung to Trevor-Roper's
career. He hadn't, the feeling was, got the most out of himself.
In a splendid essay on Jacob Burkhardt, the great Swiss historian,
Trevor-Roper set out the definition of a mastermind historian.
He must be professionally competent yet more than competent
merely; "He must be a general historian, and something of a philosopher." He must also show in his work a feeling for general
history, and with an understanding that one age stands for itself

alone, but every age is also "part of a continuum, is relevant to the past." His philosophy as a historian "must survive the criticism of later generations and be found illuminating even in a new and radically different age." By these criteria Trevor-Roper qualifies on all grounds but one: He seems to have neglected to get round to writing an actual history.

If Adam Sisman's lengthy biography has a purpose, other than fascination with its complex subject *per se*, it is to explain why this immensely talented man did not write the great book everyone expected from him. Trevor-Roper scarcely wanted for ambition. His hero was Edward Gibbon; more than once he stated his wish to produce a work that could be mentioned in the same breath with *The Decline and Fall of the Roman Empire*. His prose, *mutatis mutandis*, was modeled on Gibbon's, and one of the pleasures of reading Trevor-Roper is coming upon him fairly regularly striking off Gibbonian sentences, those lengthy, anaconda-like contrivances that slither down the page with a comical ironic bite at the tail.

HUGH TREVOR-ROPER was born in 1914, in Northumberland, near the border of Scotland, to a physician father who had, as Sisman writes, "contracted out of fatherhood," and a coldly snobbish mother interested chiefly in the social climb. Sisman's verdict is that Trevor-Roper's "childhood had been a form of prison," not an entirely exceptional English story. Not much love in the home, if it doesn't break one down as a result of it, can build strong character. In ways not easily calibrated, not much love in the home helped build the British Empire.

Life opened up to young Hugh Trevor-Roper in the classroom. He did (no avoiding the word) brilliantly at Charterhouse, his public school, and at Christ Church he earned Firsts. His only recorded youthful setback was that he did not win a fellowship to All Souls College. He had also acquired a reputation for flippancy. In one of the papers he wrote for the All Souls fellowship, he referred to Rousseau's *Confessions* as "a lucid journal of a life so utterly degraded that it has been a bestseller in France ever since."

If Trevor-Roper's home life was bleak and devoid of pleasure, he did his best to make up for it during his years as an undergraduate, and later as a tutor, where he lived the life of a Bertie Wooster but with brains added: drinking, gourmandizing, driving fast cars, roistering generally. He failed to enter the skirt chase, and his biographer suggests that the youthful Trevor-Roper was not certain of his sexuality, though there is no talk in Sisman's pages of homosexual dalliances, always a vivid option at the Oxbridge of that day.

Arrogance, intellectual division, soon became part of his *modus operandi*. But it was arrogance with a comic twist. After being interviewed by the Merton College electors for a junior research fellowship, he remarked: "I hope I impressed them more than they impressed me." He entered in a disputatious way into fields not his own; as a young man, he presented a paper before senior classicists at Oxford arguing that *Prometheus Unbound* was wrongly attributed to Aeschylus. "I am often astonished by the depth and extent of my learning," he wrote in one of his wartime notebooks. Lest he become overdeveloped intellectually, better (he decided) to "devote more time to beagling, foxhunting, drinking, fishing, shooting, talking; or, if one must read, read Homer, Milton, Gibbon, who cannot harm the brain."

Two of the young Trevor-Roper's close friends were Gilbert Ryle and A. J. Ayer, leading figures in analytical philosophy at Oxford. Ryle mocked Trevor-Roper's foxhunting, at which he on several occasions fell off his mount—once breaking his back—allowing Ryle to claim that Hugh had "a bad case of Tallyhosis." Ayer said he "admired his intellectual elegance, appreciated his malice, and was delighted to find that he shared my anti-clericalism and irreverence for authority." Not everywhere was the quality of malice so highly valued as it was in the Oxford of the 1930s.

With the onset of World War II, Trevor-Roper began as a lieutenant in the Territorial Army, but was soon transferred to the Secret Intelligence Service, where he worked, with considerable success, at breaking German radio codes. Ryle and the philosopher Stuart Hampshire were part of his Radio Analysis Bureau, later called the Radio Intelligence Service. Sisman devotes several pages to the bureaucratic infighting within the British intelligence services; Trevor-Roper's position in these matters was never conciliatory. One of his superiors claimed that his "passion for being different from ordinary mortals amounts to insubordination." He suffered fools not at all, and one had only to disagree with him to qualify as a fool. What must have made this all the more infuriating is that he seems to have been correct much of the time.

Reading this section of Sisman's biography, one is reminded how much more intellectuals, making use of their minds, contributed to the British war effort than did their American counterparts. Graham Greene, Malcolm Muggeridge, Isaiah Berlin, Ryle, Hampshire, Ayer, Trevor-Roper, and many other English intellectuals had significant jobs during the war. Let us not forget Kim Philby, who puts in a cameo role here and may, as a spy for the Soviet Union, have done the most significant work of all.

Trevor-Roper had "a good war." He ended it as a major, and soon after was given the authority of a major-general to interrogate Nazi prisoners for a report on the final days of the Nazi high command. The significance of the report was to put an end to wild speculation about the whereabouts of Hitler, and it established in hard fact that he was dead—of a pistol he shot into his mouth while, beside him, Eva Braun swallowed poisoned pills, their bodies both subsequently burned in the garden of their bunker in Berlin—and not off in South America, waiting to give world domination a second shot. Trevor-Roper is the man who, historically if not literally, buried Adolf Hitler.

This he did with a fineness of detail, a thoroughness of argument, and a Gibbonian majesty, writing contemporary history through the long-sighted but clear lens of the past. Toward the close of his book, apropos of Ribbentrop, Schellenberg, Schwerin von Krosigk, and others, living in their "intellectual fools' paradise," Trevor-Roper writes: "We are reminded of the court-parasites of the Roman Empire, of whom Juvenal wrote: the bad jokes of Fortune—village pierrots yesterday, arbiters of life and death today, tomorrow keepers of the public latrines." He subsequently turned his report on the final days of the German high command into a book, *The Last Days of Hitler* (1947), which became an international bestseller and established him as an expert on all things Nazi.

With some of the proceeds from *The Last Days of Hitler*, its author acquired and took to tooling around Oxford in a Bentley. He did all he could to fortify the reputation invested in the undergraduates' name for him of Pleasure-Loper. When George VI and the queen visited Christ Church on the 400th anniversary of its founding, Trevor-Roper, in a letter to his friend Solly Zuckerman, wrote: "I signalized Their Majesties visit by extreme intoxication. My hand still trembles, my mind is cloudy, and I am crippled by mysterious bruises."

Teaching undergraduates was not sufficient to hold a man of Trevor-Roper's ambition. He was in search of that book that might give him lasting fame. But on what subject, precisely? He had, in the meantime, begun to write his attacks on other historians, which gave him his reputation as an intellectual liquidator, a terminator, a historian killer, a reputation in which he exulted. He loved controversy, and with a sharp mind, vast learning, and a prose style that could function as a deadly weapon, he was handsomely equipped for it.

When Trevor-Roper attacked R. H. Tawney's theory of the progressive bourgeois giving rise to the Puritan revolution in England, one of the editors of the journal to which he sent his attack wrote to his coeditor: "I find it difficult to decide whether T-R is a fundamentally nice person in the grip of a prose style in which it is impossible to be polite or a fundamentally unpleasant person . . . using rudeness as a disguise for nastiness." Trevor-Roper in polemical mode is reminiscent of no one quite so much as Richard Montague, a henchman of Archbishop Laud, who had, as Trevor-Roper writes in his biography of Laud, "controversial dexterity," and whose "books which he hurled, like apples of discord, into an interested world, were weighted with massive learning and pointed with a stinging wit." Another figure of the time remarked on Montague's "tartness of writing; very sharp the nib of his pen, and much gall in his ink, against such as opposed him."

Well off financially, intellectually settled as an established figure at Oxford, Trevor-Roper's life was still missing two major components: work on the great book and family. The latter was to be put paid to when, at the age of 39, he began seriously to court a married woman named Alexandra Howard-Johnston, seven years older than he and with three children. (Maurice Bowra remarked that he "had never known adultery to do so much for a man.") She was the daughter of Field Marshal Haig of World War I fame, and her husband, a belligerent man known to beat her, was a rear-admiral. Sisman is especially good at the complications of the courtship and Trevor-Roper and his wife's far-from-easy relationship after they had settled into marriage.

Known as "Xandra," Mrs. Trevor-Roper was, as her first husband had warned him, a "luxury girl," for which read, in the parlance of our day, "high maintenance." She was also an aristocracy snob, as was Trevor-Roper. The combination, with three children added, was perhaps more family life than Trevor-Roper had bargained for. Certainly it put pressure on him to earn more money than a don might normally do; this meant doing lots of journalism, much of it for the *Times*, including lots of political reporting in foreign quarters. He had no aptitude for fatherhood, let alone the more difficult proposition of step-fatherhood, and living with so emotionally volatile a woman as Xandra did not represent a daily walk in the park. Yet Trevor-Roper was never other than a loyal, and almost always a solicitous, husband, which could not have been all that easy for a man who appears to have been one of nature's true bachelors.

Trevor-Roper at his most humane is available in his letters to Bernard Berenson, which have been printed as *Letters from Oxford* (2006). The letters, begun in 1947 and running until Berenson's death in 1959, are filled with rich gossip ("Now what new indiscretions can I offer you?"), and jolly malice is their reigning tone ("The new prophet of darkness is apparently a man called Oakeshott, who is alleged to advance his appeals to unreason with great brilliance; which however, having met him, I doubt.").

England had a richer cast of comic characters in those years, and Trevor-Roper makes splendid use of them. Here he is describing the social-climbing publisher George Weidenfeld's rich (Marks and Spencer heiress) wife leaving him:

> As she surveyed the debris of her husband's last party, at which she had carried round drinks, with ever-increasing ennui, to ever giddier groups of loquacious peeresses, gossip-writers, fashionable novelists, and professional party-goers, and saw the carnage of empty champagne bottles, crushed lobster-shells, and trodden caviar, she decided she could bear it no longer.

He recounts to the old man, B. B., locked in the fastness of his opulent Italian villa I Tatti, Oxford college elections as if they were battles upon the plains of Greece. After a full budget of gossipy news to Berenson's dear friend Nicky Mariano, he writes: "We shall have to confine our conversation, *faute de mieux*, to the Good, the True, and the Beautiful."

Trevor-Roper's self-appointed role was that of intellectual, with ties (through his wife) to the *beau monde*, always intellectually dazzling, immensely learned, never wrong. He made enemies quite as easily as he made friends, and seems to have cherished the two equally. One of the most relentless among his enemies was Evelyn Waugh. What set Waugh against Trevor-Roper was the latter's relentless anticlericalism, especially his anti-Catholicism, the church to which Waugh himself was of course a convert. A woman once remarked to Waugh that, though he claimed to be a Christian, he was one of the most unpleasant men she had ever met. Did he not, she asked, sense any contradiction here? "None at all, Madame," Waugh is supposed to have responded. "But just imagine me if I weren't a Christian."

WHENEVER POSSIBLE LARDING HIS PROSE with zingers to set what he invariably called "the papists'" tempers aflame, Trevor-Roper enjoyed (as he once put it) their "agonized and desperate writhings." He always saved a poisoned dart for Waugh, a convert, and therefore a member of "a tribe that distinguishes itself by doctrinal ferocity, not always accompanied by knowledge." Waugh made it a point never to call him anything other than "Roper," and let no chance pass without saying something damning about him and the paucity of his achievements. Trevor-Roper never granted Waugh intellectual respect, but did acknowledge that in face-to-face confrontations he could not win, owing to Waugh's superior rudeness.

A fairly regular refrain in Sisman has Trevor-Roper returning to his study to begin work on a new book: on Oliver Cromwell, on the English Revolution, on Scotland, on English Catholicism, and so many more. In his review of this biography in the *London Review of Books*, Neal Ascherson counted no fewer than nine such uncompleted books. Some of these were worked on extensively and a few made their appearance as extended essays. "Enchanted cigarettes" Balzac called those books authors dream of but never get around to writing; Trevor-Roper smoked enough of them to acquire the intellectual equivalent of lung cancer.

Was it perfectionism that stopped Trevor-Roper from writing his great book? Or was he guilty of the kind of sloth that goads a man to do fifteen other things in place of the one thing he should be doing? He certainly did the fifteen other things. What with lecturing at foreign universities, turning out lots of journalism and book reviews, maintaining a costly domestic establishment, bucking up an easily demoralized wife, continuing his wide reading, and indulging his never-slackening passion for travel, the great book somehow never got written.

One fine book did, though, and this is *Hermit of Peking: The Hidden Life of Sir Edmund Backhouse* (1976), his study of the English Sinologist, a charlatan and fantasist who was one of the great literary frauds of the modern era. With a novelistic feeling for pace and character, Trevor-Roper tracks down Backhouse (1873–1944), who was a British spy in China during World War I, negotiated fraudulent business deals, and collected Chinese manuscripts, vast quantities of which he donated to the Bodleian Library, hoping thereby to acquire a professorship until it was discovered that many among them he forged.

Hermit of Peking is a book in the tradition of, and of no less quality than, A. J. A. Symons's classic *Quest for Corvo*. Both are investigations of human nature at its oddest. Immensely readable as a work of detection of the highest order, *Hermit of Peking* is also a reminder that Trevor-Roper (as Sisman says) considered himself "a writer first, and an historian second."

In 1979, quite out of the blue, Trevor-Roper received an invitation to become Master of Peterhouse, the oldest and smallest of Cambridge's colleges. Earlier in the same year he had been made a peer, Lord Dacre of Glanton, an honor bestowed upon him by Margaret Thatcher. The two events conjoined made actual Evelyn Waugh's exasperated wish, in one of their exchanges, that Trevor-Roper change his name and move to Cambridge. Apart from the emoluments—a fine master's house, a famously good college kitchen, and an excellent wine cellar—Trevor-Roper took on the job because it extended his academic life by six years. He should have had to retire as Regius Professor in 1981 at the age of 67, but was allowed to stay on as Master of Peterhouse until 1987.

In the event, it wasn't a good move. Peterhouse turned out to be a hornet's nest of intramural controversy. So reactionary were the majority of fellows that the force of their general unpleasantness turned Trevor-Roper, who could never rest content for long in a condition of conformity, into a reformer. The most vicious academic squabbling set in, never to be resolved, and at the end of his term as master, Trevor-Roper allowed that his seven years at Peterhouse were wasted.

In 1983, in the midst of the Peterhouse years, documents claiming to be Hitler's private diaries surfaced, discovered by the German weekly *Stern*. If authentic, this would have been a momentous historical event, promising an extended gaze into the heart and mind of perhaps the most evil man in modern, if not world, history. Times Newspapers thought to buy English rights to the diaries, but they first wanted Trevor-Roper, who was at the time a director of the corporation, to authenticate them. Trevor-Roper's agent, A. D. Peters, was able to extract a handsome fee for him to do so. And after much last moment hesitation, authenticate them he did—wrongly.

Here was the former Regius Professor of Modern History at Oxford, the current Master of Peterhouse at Cambridge, zestfully spending much of his life pointing out the errors, the intellectual shortcomings, the slovenliness, if not outright fraudulence, of others who had now himself, at the age of 69, made the howler of howlers, and on the world stage. One has to imagine the family-values politician caught emerging from a male bordello, the menacing class bully wetting his trousers at the blackboard.

The sky darkened with chickens coming home to roost; deafening was noise from the licking of chops. A. L. Rowse, Conor Cruise

O'Brien, Bernard Crick, all Trevor-Roper's old enemies, lined up to hurl their brickbats at him. *Private Eye* ran a lengthy piece called "My Days of Agony by Lord Lucre of Glenlivet (better known as Sir Hugh Very-Ropey)." Auberon Waugh, standing in for his now-deceased father, suggested that Trevor-Roper change his sex and move to Essex. Columnists weighed in against him. Adam Sisman notes that Trevor-Roper took all this abuse without outward complaint. Nor did he allow his anguish to show, though Sisman recounts a lunch at which Trevor-Roper was late and his older stepson found him "lying in a foetal position on a bed in a spare room, his face turned to the wall." Sisman concludes that "the damage to his reputation was substantial and long-lasting." Not a few obituaries at his death led with this great embarrassing international *faux pas.*

Hubris, got up in the lifelong habiliments of flamboyant arrogance, met its just end—or so some might say. Yet Trevor-Roper rode out this major defeat and continued to write, turning out superior essays right up until his death at 89 in 2003. A recently (posthumously) published collection of essays, *History and the Enlightenment* (Yale), displays him at the top of his excellent game. The essays demonstrate what should have been evident all along: Hugh Trevor-Roper was a better historiographer, or student of the history and theory of history, than he was a historian. His contemporary, Arnaldo Momigliano, the great historiographer of the ancient world, also failed to write a great book. Perhaps what explains the inability of both men to write that single imperishable historical work is that they understood too well the many pitfalls of writing history.

Sisman ends by writing that Hugh Trevor-Roper's "work will continue to be read long after his blunder [with the Hitler diaries] has diminished into a mere footnote." Surely this is correct. Trevor-Roper deserves to be remembered as a devastating polemicist; an elegant prose stylist, one of the most suave of the past century; and an Oxbridge figure of the kind that, much to the loss of contemporary intellectual life, has now departed the planet, off not to a better world but perhaps to a place where the air is thick with the smoke of enchanted cigarettes, and playful malice is greatly appreciated.

John Gross

Gentleman of Letters

M Y FRIEND JOHN GROSS died on Monday, January 10, 2011. His son Tom, who sent out an email announcing John's death to a large number of his friends, noted that his father's death was caused by complications relating to his heart and kidneys. His health had been failing in various ways for quite a long spell. Tom Gross also mentioned that his sister Susanna, John's daughter, was reading to him from Shakespeare's *Sonnets* when he died. That is a proper touch, for John knew English literature, knew it with greater breadth and more deeply than anyone I have ever met.

If a decently educated person knows Shakespeare, and someone with a specialized interest in the theater also knows the plays of Marlowe, Beaumont and Fletcher, and Kyd, John knew Elizabethan playwrights at the next level down. The same was true of every other age or genre of English literature: obscure Romantic poets, unknown Victorian novelists, barely published critics of every age—John knew them all. As a young man, John wrote a brilliant survey of English criticism and reviewing called *The Rise and Fall of the Man of Letters, English Literary Life Since 1800* (1969). He also wrote *Shylock: Four Hundred Years in the Life of a Legend* (1992), a splendid account of the differing ways the character of Shylock has been presented on the stage, from utter fiend to sympathetic victim. These were subjects that a standard English or American academic could nicely kill, but John wrote about them with easy sophistication, brio, charm, wit, and his always present common-sensical intelligence.

Such fame as John enjoyed was, I suspect, chiefly English, though for a period he worked for the *New York Times* as one of its daily reviewers. He also wrote with some regularity for American journals, among them the *New Criterion, Commentary*, and the *New York Review of Books.* Unlike many English intellectuals, he was a man without the least touch of anti-Americanism, and in his memoir of the first 17 years of his life, *A Double Thread* (2001), he recounts how important American movies, popular songs, and comic books were to him when growing up:

> Not everyone approved. Objections floated down from the adult world—political criticisms from the left, disdain for American vulgarity from the right. But among children, if I am in any way representative, the image was overwhelmingly favorable. America stood for streamlining and the open road, for excitement and optimism.

John had a good run as an editor, both of intellectual journals and of anthologies. He was an assistant editor at *Encounter.* He was the literary editor of the *New Statesman* at a time when the so-called back of the book, where reviews of books and arts appeared, was easily the best thing about it. He later worked at the same job for the *Spectator.*

But John's great editorial contribution was as the principal editor of the *Times Literary Supplement*, from 1974 to 1981. As editor of the *TLS* he put an end to the paper's long tradition of anonymous reviewing, which too frequently resulted in the corrupt practice of puffing the books of friends and sneering at those of enemies. Quite as important, he widened the range of the *TLS*, making it less scholarly-parochial by opening it up to subjects of broader intellectual interest without in any way diminishing its seriousness.

His editorship at the *TLS* came at a difficult time. For one thing, the then very belligerent British printing union was menacing the paper, frequently threatening not to print the current week's edition or refusing to do the lithography that made possible the photographs and drawings accompanying an issue. (This belligerence was finally put down by the new owner of the *Times*, Rupert Murdoch, who built a new printing plant in the London district of Wapping, which kicked into force, with the help of the Electrical, Electronic, Telecommunications, and Plumbing Union, when the printing unions announced a full-scale strike in 1986.)

The *TLS* had the standing of a national paper, which meant it couldn't, like most American intellectual journals, comfortably hew to a political line. The time of John's editorship also saw the rise, in universities, of critical theory, academic feminism, and other university waste products, whose measure one may be sure John had taken but which he could not altogether ignore in the pages of the *TLS*. Although John had his own politics and his own strong views on all things literary, as editor of the *TLS* he had to walk a high and slippery tightrope. That he did so without ever undermining his own beliefs or surrendering his standards is a tribute to his tact, subtlety, and extraordinary intellectual balance.

I wrote for John before I had met him. For more than a year, in the days before email, our letters began "Dear Mr. Gross" and "Dear Mr. Epstein." Then one day I received a letter that began, "Dear Mr. Epstein, How I wish I could, as Henry James said on a similar occasion, leap the bounds of formality and address you by your first name." A perfect John touch, allowing me to begin my next letter to him, "Dear John, There, now the bounds of formality are leapt."

JOHN GROSS

At the *TLS* he gave me, then a youngish writer, plummy assign-
ments. I wrote about Maxwell Perkins, Edmund Wilson, and Walter Lippmann for him. He was an editor whose tolerance for the
slightly *outré* and distaste for received opinions one could count on,
so that, when asked to review a book on the Pulitzer Prizes, I knew
that in his London office John would be amused at my writing that
the Pulitzer Prizes tend to go to two kinds of people only: those
who don't need them, and those who don't deserve them.

After his seven-year stint at the *TLS*, John worked briefly for
the publisher George Weidenfeld and then took a job as a reviewer
at the *New York Times*. How one wishes that he had instead been

asked to edit the *New York Times Book Review,* for he would have made it, for the first time in its long history, serious and substantial. With his easy charm, he was a great social success in Manhattan. He never mentioned it to me, but I had heard that he led a book discussion club for Brooke Astor and her friends.

Working at the *New York Times,* which he did between 1983 and 1989, was something else. What it mostly produced was a fund of amusing stories about the ineptitude and fecklessness of the paper's editors, at all levels. I recall John telling me a story about his mentioning in one of his reviews the name Plekhanov, whom he described as "the father of Russian Marxism." One of the paper's copy editors wanted to know his authority for calling Plekhanov that. "It's almost a bloody cliché," John told me recounting the story, "like George Washington was the father of his country." But the copy editor wouldn't back down until John, exasperated, said, "Look. Why don't we compromise and refer to Plekhanov as the uncle of Russian Marxism."

John had a keen taste for the absurd behavior of intellectuals and the vanity of writers. He got a kick out of my calling the contributors of the *New York Review of Books* "mad dogs and Englishmen," and told me that the visits to London of that journal's editor, Robert Silvers, given the obeisance that English intellectuals paid him, resembled nothing so much as the return home of the Viceroy of India.

I didn't see the *Sunday Telegraph,* for which John became drama critic, but always thought it an amusing mating for a man with a taste for the absurd having to review so many plays that must themselves have been well beyond absurd. He was once seated in a London theater, watching a production of *King Lear* being done in mud, when he was attacked by severe angina. "Oh, Lord, I said to myself," he told me, "dear Lord, please don't let this be the last thing I ever see." Fortunately, it wasn't, though he went home afterwards and had a heart attack and, subsequently, bypass surgery.

John's sense of the absurdity of intellectuals was nicely conveyed in his letters, subsequently his emails, and his occasional phone calls to me. He was a wonderfully entertaining gossip with a large supply of artful indiscretions at his disposal. One day he would tell me about Harold Pinter sending out, in John's phrase, "one of his pukey little poems" to scores of friends and acquaintances, and sitting back to await their unfailing praise; another day he would ask me if I knew with what English left-wing adventuress Fidel Castro was sleeping.

I don't know when, precisely, John's health began to break down, but when it did the steps down the precipice were all serious. He had a heart attack, as I mentioned, and at one point he suffered a stroke that, he reported to me, left one of his arms temporarily dangling out of commission. After some hesitation, I took a chance and wrote to him to say that I hoped he would not take advantage of his bad arm to do imitations of Isaiah Berlin or George Steiner, who each had a withered arm. He thought it very amusing, or so he said.

Part of John's genius was for tact. He reviewed two of my books, praising them both, but in each case quietly getting in real criticisms, both of acts of commission and omission on the author's part. So suave a prose stylist was he that it might seem that John had, to use the music critic Sam Lipman's phrase, "no fist." In fact, when sufficiently aroused, John had a knockout punch. See his quietly devastating review of Stefan Collini's *Common Reading* in the (London) *Sunday Times* of May 21, 2008. John also had little use for dogmatic critics. Readers of *The Rise and Fall of the Man of Letters* will recall his attack on the still alive and then-highly influential Cambridge critic E. R. Leavis. In defense of the vigor of his attack, John wrote in an afterword to a republication of the book in 1992: "I still believe I was right to react as I did. Leavis attempted, as no one before him, to pronounce a death sentence on the entire man-of-letters tradition. He also set a precedent for trying to police literary studies and impose one man's will on them."

In the end I am not sure that it is as a writer that John will be best remembered. He wrote four books—along with those I have already mentioned, he did the *James Joyce* volume (1970) in Frank Kermode's Modern Masters series—all excellent of their kind. He edited a number of anthologies for Oxford University Press, among them *The Oxford Book of Essays*, *The Oxford Book of Aphorisms*, *The Oxford Book of Literary Anecdotes*, *The Oxford Book of Comic Verse*, *The New Oxford Book of English Prose*, *The Oxford Book of Parodies*, and *After Shakespeare: Writing Inspired by the World's Greatest Author*— quality goods, all these volumes, exhibiting John's immense range of reading in English literature, and books that will live on for many years. But he never thought to put together a volume of his criticism and reviews. *A Double Thread*, an autobiographical account of his early life, is, for an autobiography, written with an unusual tact and modesty. The truth may be that John hadn't the egotism and vanity, the pushiness and self-absorption, required of the true writer. (Please not to ask how I know about these requisite qualities.)

John may also have enjoyed life too much. He had a natural bonhomie combined with a winning detachment. Once, in Chicago, he told me that he was the next day to visit a woman (he did not vouchsafe her name), who now lived in the city, with whom he had been close during his years as a student at Oxford. "Pity we never married," he said, with his amused irony. "We could have caused each other much heartache." (John's one marriage, to the editor and writer Miriam Gross, ended in divorce, but the two remained good friends, and I never heard him utter a critical word about her.) He once took my wife and me round London, to the (in that day) with-it clubs and to the historical places only a born Londoner knew. His love of the city was palpable.

So John Gross is dead at 75. For me, he has left too early. But then I always felt John had left too early, which is another way of saying that I never got enough of him. During his last phone call to me, six or so weeks ago, we talked about a T. S. Eliot essay I had written; he told me about his own meetings with Eliot, and left me with one of his characteristic golden nuggets of gossip.

The last time I saw John in person was in Manhattan. We had breakfast together, and after breakfast we walked around the block, it must have been 10 times, trading stories, telling jokes, gossiping, laughing. At the end, I remember saying to him, "You know, John, if I were the sort of Jewish gent who went in for show-biz-like hugging, I should bestow upon you my best bear hug. But you don't seem to me a man in desperate need of a hug."

"Quite so," he said, and we shook hands and parted.

John Gross was my contemporary, the smartest literary man of my generation, a sweet character, and his death marks a genuine subtraction, not merely in my life, but in the life of the culture.

Popular Culture

Alfred Kinsey

The Secret Life

FAME, LIKE SEX, is all too brief—a proposition I recently kitchen-tested by asking a classroom of 25 intelligent undergraduates if they had ever heard the name of Alfred C. Kinsey. Only one had, and he was not exactly sure what it stood for. What it stood for, of course, was sex, neither pure nor simple.

Nearly 50 years ago, Kinsey's name was both a red and a white flag, a household word, an attention-getting device. With the publication in 1948 of *Sexual Behavior in the Human Male*, a book brought out by a scientific publisher that sold an astonishing 200,000 copies in hardcover in its first two months in print, Kinsey was declared (depending upon one's point of view) a hero of the modern day or the greatest underminer of traditional morality the world had ever known. His name was everywhere, from popular songs to church sermons, from limericks to newspaper editorials. He was on the cover of *Time*, profiled in *Life*, the subject of *New Yorker* cartoons. By his admirers his book was thought to be in the same class as *Principia Mathematica*, *The Wealth of Nations*, or *Das Kapital*; its author was often compared to Galileo, Copernicus, and

Freud, scientists who similarly had struggled against an obtuse and belligerent public to bring the truth to light.

The particular truth brought to light by Kinsey's book had to do with the wide discrepancy between official—which is to say, standard, middle-class— accounts of sexual behavior and what was actually going on in the sexual lives of American men. Resting his conclusions on a vast number of interviews, Kinsey was able to show that 90 percent of American men masturbated, 85 percent had had premarital intercourse, between 35 and 45 percent had had extramarital intercourse, 59 percent had engaged in mouth-genital contact, roughly 70 percent had had dealings with prostitutes, 37 percent had had at least a single homosexual encounter that ended in orgasm, and no fewer than 17 percent of farm boys had experienced bestiality. Or so the "Kinsey Report," as Kinsey's book came to be called, reported—scientifically.

66 THERE ARE A GOOD MANY FIELDS of investigation, particularly in the social sciences, where in fact if you say anything at all it will not be scientifically justified," Chester I. Barnard, president of the Rockefeller Foundation, wrote in 1951. "And yet in all the affairs of life this kind of investigation seems to be necessary, and I don't think it can be avoided." The subject of Barnard's comment was Alfred Kinsey's work at the Institute for Sex Research at the University of Indiana, which the foundation had been indirectly supporting for many years. Given its potential for controversy, the Kinsey connection was quite worrisome, all the more so because Kinsey, a brilliant man at public relations, had cunningly attached the prestige of the foundation to his own work.

Barnard was on to something, but, truth to tell—and now all of it has been told, in detail, in a massive biography of Kinsey by James T. Jones—he was not aware of a tenth of it. Jones's biography may not be, in a cant phrase of our day, a page-turner, but it certainly is, in the cant phrase of another day, an eye-opener. His lengthy portrait of Kinsey, marked by its own deep earnestness, reveals a man whom perhaps only his family and a few friends and assistants really knew.

"The man I came to know," Jones writes in his preface, "bore no resemblance to the canonical Kinsey." Instead of a cool scientist, Jones discovered a man of missionary zeal, "a crypto-reformer who spent his every waking hour attempting to change the sexual mores . . . of the United States" and who was perfectly willing to bend the canons of science to that purpose. More: while traveling under the flag of a disinterested researcher, Kinsey himself led a secret life as a voyeur, an exhibitionist, a homosexual, and a masochist. "I do not have the impression," wrote Alan Gregg, head of the Rockefeller Foundation's medical division, "that Kinsey or any of his associates have any morbid or pathological preoccupation with any particular aspect of sex." Dr. Gregg could not have been more wrong. In Jones's succinct words, "The beauty of sex research [was] that it allowed Kinsey to transform his voyeurism into science."

Social science is vulnerable to an examination of the lives of its investigators in a way that pure science is not. Newton's religiosity in no way invalidates the theory of gravity, nor does Einstein's rather soft liberalism vitiate the theory of relativity. But in the social sciences, "every idea," as Nietzsche somewhere says, "has its autobiography," and that autobiography can sometimes disqualify the ideas themselves. Although today Kinsey's predilections might help get a man a tenure-track job at an Ivy League university, in the 1940s and early 1950s, the years of his connection with Rockefeller, open knowledge of them would have been sufficient to detonate the Institute for Sex Research, the University of Indiana, and the Rockefeller Foundation in one compact hydrogen bomb of scandal.

ALFRED KINSEY was a man of more than ordinary contradictions. What we would nowadays call a "control freak," he had a strong need to oversee every aspect of his life and work and to dominate everyone around him. Yet he also took insane personal and professional chances in life, and his daily existence was marked as much by compulsion as by rationality. He voted Republican, yet was contemptuous of the middle class; he was in many ways conventional, yet also a genuine revolutionary, a moralist who in all matters relating to sex was very close to amoral; he was a devoted husband and father of three whose own deepest sensual pleasures were homosexual.

Where all this came from is the subject of James Jones's book. We learn from him that even as a child—he was born in 1894— Kinsey despised his father, a pompous, selfish, puritanical man who held a subsidiary teaching job at the Stevens Institute of Technology in Hoboken, New Jersey. His mother tended to be of no help: a submissive woman who was overprotective of Alfred and her younger son and daughter, she served mainly to reinforce her husband's many little tyrannies. The Kinsey family was religious (Methodist), struggled to appear middle-class, and was apparently quite without joy. In later life, though Kinsey kept up some small contact with the other members of his family, he would refuse to see his father.

When Alfred was ten, the family moved to South Orange, a prosperous bedroom suburb of Newark and New York. There, according to Jones, Kinsey caught fire; making "the schoolroom his arena of achievement," he graduated as high-school valedictorian, while also becoming interested in classical music and scouting. No athlete, he was by temperament a collector: of stamps, butterflies, bugs. As for sex, his father held him in close rein; Alfred was not allowed to go to movies or dances, and he had no real contact with girls outside the classroom.

Masturbation was said in those days and in those quarters to cause everything from madness to blindness to the mysterious growth of hair. Kinsey's biographer tells us that he went in for it in a prodigious, and exceptionally guilty, way. Given who his father was, his religious upbringing, and his habit of self-criticism, Kinsey, Jones speculates, must have felt the guilt much more acutely than most boys—so much so that to the practice of solitary sexual release he came to add a rather complex form of masochism, one expression of which was his habit of inserting objects in his urethra while masturbating. "In secret," Jones writes, "Kinsey found pleasure through pain."

After high school, Kinsey made it known that he wished to study biology, but his father insisted on a more strictly vocational training in mechanical engineering. After two mediocre years at Stevens, and very much against the wishes of his father—who later disowned him—Kinsey transferred to Bowdoin College in Maine. There he became a fraternity man and a leading figure in the debating club, and changed his religion from Methodist to Congregationalist. But his real conversion was to the divinity of science. As a son of the Progressive era, Kinsey, Jones writes, came to believe there were endless possibilities for improving the lot of men and women. Politics and religion were one means to this end; science, in his view, was another and much more efficient one.

Kinsey did his graduate work at Harvard, then a center for the "new biology," which aimed at rivaling the physical sciences in its power of formulating laws. He decided to specialize in taxonomy—a decision, Jones says, that "shaped his professional career"—and fell under the sway of one William Morton Wheeler, a high-rolling scientific operator in whom he also found a surrogate father. It was Wheeler who confirmed him in his ardor for the scientific method, helped land him an important post-doctoral traveling fellowship, and, subsequently, obtained a job for him in the department of zoology at Indiana University.

When Kinsey took up his job in Bloomington in 1920, he was twenty-six and still a virgin. There he met his future wife, Clara, an undergraduate chemistry major, and within two months he proposed. Jones reports that the Kinseys were unable to consummate their marriage on their honeymoon and for some while thereafter, owing to a physiological jigeroo in Clara that was later surgically corrected. In the end they would have four children, one of whom died before the age of four, and they seem to have had a genuine love for each other, if, to put it most gently, a less than ordinary sex life. Clara was herself quite a piece of work.

Prurience time: Kinsey, his biographer informs us, would in later years come to think of his Institute as a sexual utopia of sorts, in which no one would be "bound by arbitrary and antiquated sexual taboos," and he often used the attic of his home to stage little illustrative tableaux. The novelist Glenway Wescott, who used to visit the Kinseys in Bloomington, once confided to Kinsey that his own orgasms were so intense as to cause his body to jackknife at the moment of climax. Kinsey asked permission to film this event, and Wescott readily agreed, running a course on camera with his lover, Monroe Wheeler (director of publications and exhibitions at the Museum of Modern Art in New York). After the jackknife had been duly captured on film, "Clara popped into the room with a tray of refreshments, along with clean towels so they could freshen up." Paul Gebhard, Kinsey's successor at the Institute, reported that at the conclusion of still other filming sessions, Clara, the perfect hostess, "would suddenly appear, literally, with persimmon pudding or milk and cookies or something." Has social science ever seemed so, well, social?

IN HIS EARLY DAYS AT INDIANA UNIVERSITY, Kinsey was considered a good but not a popular teacher. He was strongly opinionated, not particularly collegial, impatient with dull students. Like all monomaniacs, he was essentially humorless. He took his greatest pleasure in scholarship, which in his case meant studies of the gall wasp, the subject of his award-winning dissertation at Harvard. He was relentless in his pursuit of these insects, for through them he hoped to transform taxonomy, as Jones puts it, "from a descriptive discipline into a science with a strong explanatory power." This, of course, would later become his mission with regard to human sexuality.

Having shed religion, Kinsey by now had also shed conventional views about sex and marriage. He encouraged nudism on field trips with young male graduate students, and later sent pornography to them. Like anyone beyond a certain age who is preoccupied with sex, he became a creep; the wife of one former student described him as "a dirty old man." Kinsey, Jones writes, "could be manipulative and aggressive, a man who abused his professional authority and betrayed his trust as a teacher." He also ran a serious risk of exposure, which could have put paid to his career.

Kinsey's interest in teaching revived when, in 1938, he organized and began to provide the pivotal lectures in a course on marriage and the family. He had been reading the sexologists of the day—Havelock Ellis, Richard von Krafft-Ebing, and the rest—and was singularly unimpressed. "You know," he told a colleague, "there isn't much science here." If the sexologists disappointed, neither did he put any trust in physicians, and he certainly had little use for Freud or psychiatry, whose mission he took to be the reinforcement of the social and sexual status quo. By now Kinsey had developed his own ideas about sex. He had come to believe that Christianity, with its denial of sexual naturalness, was responsible for "the breakdown of the modern family," and he thought "the great distortions" of the day were "the cultural perversions of celibacy, delayed marriage, and asceticism."

Kinsey had found his true subject—in fact, his life's work. Through his teaching and research on human sexuality, he could simultaneously do science, proselytize, and, with luck, bring comfort to people like himself who had suffered under the old regime of sexual reticence and repression. In connection with his course, Kinsey began to counsel students, and from these sessions to amass data on their sexual lives. He found he had an extraordinary knack for eliciting secret information, and soon was asking everyone who took his marriage-and-family course, and eventually others in the university as well, to fill in a lengthy sexual questionnaire. Most— in the name of science—agreed.

In his earliest researches Kinsey did not set out to interview homosexuals as homosexuals, but by the summer of 1939, when he took himself on a field trip to Chicago, he was telling the men he interviewed in the city's gay subculture that he was out to change social attitudes. He developed a taste for men on the margins of society, conducting interviews with male prostitutes, prisoners, and other odd and sometimes unsavory characters. He frequently corresponded with the men whose sexual histories he had recorded, letting them know that, though much of society might view them as deviant, he certainly did not. "Indeed," writes Jones, "anyone who did not know better would have thought Kinsey was socializing, not researching."

"In truth," Jones immediately adds, "Kinsey was socializing." He was also cruising. He spent a lot of time in gay bars in Chicago, where his assignations tended to be of the quick-hit variety. Closer to home, one of the first young men he hired full-time was a student named Clyde Martin, with whom he was in love. Even as he was pursuing Martin, he asked the young man to attend to Clara Kinsey's sexual needs, which Martin obligingly did. (He was not Clara's only extramarital lover.) Here again Kinsey was taking a big chance; in later years, aware of the importance of appearances, he would become more cautious, hiring as interviewers only married men with children, and eschewing anyone whose wife might have a drinking problem or who had an interest in left-wing causes.

For a long while, Kinsey financed much of his sex research out of his own pocket. But once his Institute was in place, and his Rockefeller connection established, he went to work in full earnest. He began to collect every kind of pornography he could find, depositing it in the Institute library. Booksellers began to put aside erotica for him; others sent things in the mail, which caused problems with US Customs and the post office. He became increasingly attracted to men with wild or twisted sex lives: masochists, sadists, pedophiles, sexual overachievers of any stripe. Normality, in regard to sex, was not a notion Kinsey recognized.

Prurience time again: one of Kinsey's discoveries was a sixty-three-year-old man whose history it took seventeen hours to record and who was a full-time, polymorphously perverse sex machine. "Mr. X" had had sex from the earliest possible age, and had kept files on his vast exploits. Among his claims was that from, so to speak, a dead start he could achieve ejaculation in ten seconds, and he proved this before Kinsey and his assistant, Wardell Pomeroy. So riveted was Kinsey by this man that he used his experiences in a chapter in *Sexual Behavior in the Human Male* on "Early Sexual Growth and Activity," conveniently overlooking the fact that Mr. X was also a predatory pedophile who, to quote Jones, "masturbated infants, penetrated children, and performed a variety of other sexual acts on pre-adolescent boys and girls alike." But then, as Jones also remarks, Kinsey, "in his eagerness to combat prudery and to celebrate Eros," was finding it "increasingly difficult to maintain moral boundaries."

WHEN FAME CAME IN 1948 with the appearance of *Sexual Behavior in the Human Male*, it was in part the result of careful orchestration. Kinsey put all his controlling impulses to work on the book's publication. He invited journalists to Bloomington for special briefings, and wherever possible lined up friendly reviews in both the scientific and the popular press. The book swept all boards, intellectually, socially, commercially. It was written and talked about—and purchased—at a rate akin to *Gone with the Wind*. Its effect was electric. Thanks to Kinsey, as the *New Yorker* writer Janet Flanner would put it some years later, "that powerful little crotched corner of the body, which religion, the Christian religion at least, had so long tried to keep covered up and quieted down, has suddenly swollen to a clitoris or penis the size of a mountain from whose height the view is extended all over the Western world."

Still, international celebrity though he was, Kinsey could not control everything, and attacks, too, came rolling in. His use of statistics fell under fire; so did his sampling and interviewing techniques. He was accused of being a crude empiricist, a blatant behaviorist, a coarse scientific reductionist.

Critics claimed he was ignorant of the complexities of culture, or that in neglecting the crucial element of love he had disqualified himself from speaking about sex. Finally he was assailed, in his biographer's summing-up, as "a crypto-reformer who promoted permissiveness under the guise of science."

These criticisms—by psychiatrists, anthropologists (Margaret Mead remarked that Kinsey's book "suggests no way of choosing between a woman and a sheep"), literary critics (notably Lionel Trilling), and theologians (Reinhold Niebuhr attacked him twice)—did not shake Kinsey. But they did shake the officers and trustees of the Rockefeller Foundation, who took steps to withdraw their support from Kinsey's Institute for Sex Research. This got to him, and he never quite regained his confidence. His second book, *Sexual Behavior in the Human Female* (1953), made nothing like the splash of his first, nor did it sell nearly so well. He was beset with financial worries, and those close to him said he was on the edge of a nervous breakdown. He died in 1956, at the age of sixty-two, believing himself a martyr to science.

"WE WILL PROVE TO THESE SOCIAL SCIENTISTS," Kinsey told a colleague early in his researches, "that a biological background can help in interpreting social phenomena." As a number of critics pointed out at the time, and as James T. Jones's biography now makes definitively clear, Kinsey's "interpretations" rested less on the findings of biology, or on science of any kind, than on his own social-sexual agenda. Rather than following where scientific methodology led, he simply reversed the process. He set out to prove, for example, that homosexuality was a good deal more common than anyone thought. Havelock Ellis had already declared that homosexuality was not a pathology but a statistical abnormality. Kinsey now undertook to show that it was not even a statistical abnormality. This he did by gathering a radically skewed sample, from which he then proceeded to extrapolate wildly and "interpret" freely.

As one who "loathed Victorian morality," Jones writes, Kinsey was "determined to use science to strip human sexuality of its guilt and repression." But even this was not enough. His real aim, according to his biographer, was to smash all accepted definitions of "normal" and "abnormal" in matters sexual, and thus to clear the field for a new dispensation. Jones is very frank about the nature of this new "moral calculus." As, in Kinsey's view, men were inherently more interested in sex than were women, and, among men, none seemed so interested as homosexuals, he came to believe that the key to sexual utopia lay in the "homoerotic model."

Alfred Kinsey was a moral revolutionary in scientist's clothing. The science was bad, even bogus; the man himself may now be forgotten; but the revolution came to stay, with a vengeance. Kinsey's message—fornicate early, fornicate often, fornicate in every possible way—became the mantra of a sex-ridden age, our age, now desperate for a reformation of its own.

At one point in this biography, Jones relates how Kinsey, in a black mood because the Rockefeller Foundation might not renew his grant, tied a rope around his scrotum, flipped the rope over a pipe, climbed onto a chair with the loose end in his hand, and jumped off, suspending himself in midair, no one knows for how long. There, hoist by Kinsey's petard, hang we all still.

Charles Van Doren

Robert Redford's Charlie & Mine

HEN I READ THAT ROBERT REDFORD was about to release a movie about the 1950s quiz-show scandals, my first thought was: poor Charlie, poor damned— possibly genuinely damned—Charlie. Charlie, of course, is Charles Van Doren, the central if by no means major figure in those scandals. I worked with Charlie between 1965 and 1970 in Chicago, where he was in effect in exile, and found him, and his position as a national pariah, of keen interest.

Charles Van Doren has had to bear a heavy load as a symbol for much that was wrong with America in the 1950s and, for those who like to push these things a bit further, for much more that would continue to go wrong later. The appearance of the Redford movie, *Quiz Show*, would mean, among other things, once more against the firing-squad wall for Charlie, who was then nearing seventy: an opportunity for every moralizing wiseguy to fire off a few more rounds of the journalistic equivalent of rotten tomatoes at him. Being a pariah in America is not only a full-time job but, apparently, one from which no retirement short of death can be expected.

Not many people under forty-five today can have much recollection of the excitement of the quiz shows of the 1950s and the immense stir that followed the revelation that most of these shows had been fixed, the contestants having been picked for their telegenic qualities and supplied with the questions and answers in advance, and the contests themselves being staged for the maximum dramatic effect. *Twenty-One*, on which Charlie would win $129,000—very serious bread in those days—was seen on Monday nights on NBC, going up against *I Love Lucy* on CBS.

In Redford's often cartoonish movie, people come thundering out of the subway, rushing home to watch *Twenty-One*, and even nuns are shown posted before their television set when it is on. True, the quiz shows—*The $64,000 Question*, *The $64,000 Challenge*, *Dotto*, *Tic Tac Dough*, *Concentration*, and *Twenty-One* above all—did seem, between 1955 and 1958, a dominating presence on American television and hence in American life. Charlie was on the cover of *Time* ("Quiz Champ Van Doren") on February 11, 1957—Leonard Bernstein was the magazine's cover subject the week before and Martin Luther King, Jr. the week after—and on the cover of *Life* on October 26, 1959, when the scandal broke.

The $64,000 Question, begun on CBS in June 1955 and sponsored by Revlon, preceded NBC's *Twenty-One*, which was sponsored by Geritol, a mixture of vitamins, minerals, and alcohol that claimed to be an antidote for "tired blood." *The $64,000 Question* was a more high-rolling version of the radio show known as *The $64 Question*. Unlike *Twenty-One*, which presumably tested generalized knowledge, *The $64,000 Question* tested highly specialized knowledge, and the odder the contestants, it seemed, the better the ratings: a shoemaker who knew opera, for example; a marine officer who knew French cuisine; or a woman psychologist (Joyce Brothers) who knew boxing. But technical differences between the two shows aside, there was, theoretically, no limit to how much money one could win on *Twenty-One*, whereas the limit on *The $64,000*

Question was set by the show's title. Both shows had booming ratings and sold their sponsors' products wonderfully well.

Set up to compete with *The $64,000 Question*, *Twenty-One* soon blew it off the court. It did so when Charles Van Doren, then a thirty-year-old instructor from Columbia University, appeared on the show to defeat a rather klutzy New Yorker from Forest Hills named Herbert Stempel. Charlie stayed on for 15 weeks, sweating and hesitating, palpably cerebrating before 30 or 40 million people, but finally always coming up with the correct answers. "Charlie," his mother wrote before the scandals hit, "turned out to have that mysterious chemical attraction which inspires multitudes." He was tall, just missed being good-looking, spoke in a cultivated accent, and gave off an aroma of learning and intelligence without any of the fumes of snobbery that in America so often seemed to go with it.

When Charlie appeared on *Twenty-One*, it almost seemed as if his family had gone along with him into the "isolation booth," as the glass cage was called where contestants stood awaiting their questions. And it was quite a family. Charlie's father was Mark Van Doren, who looked like nothing so much as an Americanized Mr. Chips and was a famous professor at Columbia, as well as a Pulitzer Prize poet and a prominent literary critic. (At Columbia, Charlie and his father shared an office.) Charlie's mother, Dorothy, who had been an editor at the *Nation*, wrote pleasant little books about the comic hardships of life in the country or of living with a professor. His Aunt Irita was something of a power in publishing as a literary editor at the *New York Herald-Tribune*. Perhaps most impressive of all was his Uncle Carl, a man of letters and the author of the best available biography of Benjamin Franklin (another Pulitzer Prize). The Van Dorens were not a patrician but a Midwestern family—Mark Van Doren had gone to the University of Illinois—and its intellectual members had achieved what they had not through social connections but through talent and hard work.

CHARLES VAN DOREN (right) with host Jack Berry and fellow contestant Vivienne Nearing on NBC's *Twenty-One*

When Charlie sprang into the national consciousness, that nice young man who seemed to have all the answers, it was as if he had been sent over by central casting. In a strong sense, he had. "The principle of careful casting," as one of the quiz-show producers once called it, was essential to their success. What was wanted was contestants who were brainy but not dull: bouncy young woman lawyers, like the one who ultimately replaced Charlie on *Twenty-One*, or interestingly odd people, or people who looked as if they were themselves of the people. When the producers saw Charlie they sensed they had glommed onto a Henry Fonda with the mind of an Einstein.

Although other contestants made more money than Charlie— a Columbia graduate student in sociology named Elfrida Von Nardroff, who appeared on the show after him, topped out at $226,500—none achieved anything near his celebrity. There was nothing nerdish, nothing Bronx High School of Science (where

Herbert Stempel had gone), nothing neurotic about Charlie. He was very American—he looked as if he could have played on our Davis Cup tennis team—except for his immense knowledgeability. Mothers, it was said, saw him as the answer to Elvis Presley. The Russians had launched Sputnik, the first satellite in space, the same year that Charlie was on *Twenty-One*; in some quarters, Charlie was thought to be our answer to Sputnik.

He was great copy. *Time*, in its cover story, noted: "Along with [his] charm, he combines the universal erudition of a Renaissance man with the nerve and cunning of a riverboat gambler and the showmanship of the born actor." Some *Time* editor must have enjoyed describing Charlie in his isolation booth: "Clamped in a vise of earphones, the eyes roll heavenward and squeeze shut, the brow sweats and furrows, the teeth gnaw at the lower lip." Faculty members at St. John's College, in Annapolis, where Charlie had been an undergraduate, pointed out, according to *Time*, that "Van Doren's mind comes through on TV not as a card-index file but as a reasoning instrument that explores a memory clearly embedded in taste." It was a complete fake, every moment of it, but a hell of a performance.

THE FIRST TIME I MET CHARLIE I had to shake off the red borders of an imaginary *Time* cover to get him into proper focus. He looked remarkably like himself, which is to say like the man I had watched all those Monday nights, marveling at his knowledgeability and his cool instincts ("I have always been a gambler," he told *Life*). This meeting took place at Encyclopaedia Britannica, where I had recently been hired as a senior editor, and where Charlie worked directly for the man who was to give the new Britannica its intellectual design, Mortimer J. Adler, in an office Adler called, with no mean pretensions, the Institute for Philosophical Research.

The Institute, among its other activities, planned to turn out books on each of the 102 "Great Ideas," the organizing principle of the "Syntopicon," which was itself an elaborate index sold with

Britannica's "Great Books"; this was an old Adler project that Dwight Macdonald once called "The Book-of-the-Millennium Club." Charlie was writing a book for Adler, to be titled, with (I thought at the time) more than a touch of irony, *The Idea of Progress*. The irony came with the fact that no one's progress had been stopped colder than Charlie's after what was already known to history as "the quiz-show scandal."

To be so famous, and yet to have one's fame take the character of pure notoriety, as did Charlie's, left him with a peculiar social burden upon meeting new people. He had to consider the possibility that the person before him might despise him. I met him in 1965, just six years after the scandal had blown Charlie out of the water. He could not, after all, pretend that his past did not matter.

Charlie handled our meeting beautifully, I thought. We were at lunch, with two other Britannica editors, and I mentioned that I had bought a house on which I was to close that afternoon. "Ah," said Charlie, with the smile that came so easily to him, "the last time I closed on a house, in New York, I had two jobs, one at NBC and one at Columbia, and the very next day I had neither."

After the scandal, Charlie had indeed been fired from his job as an assistant professor at Columbia, over the protest of many students, who felt he deserved a break. It seems unlikely that any teaching or other serious intellectual work was then available to him. Charlie got the job he now had thanks to Mortimer Adler's friendship with Mark Van Doren. Adler was part of a little network of men who had gone to or taught at Columbia, among whom were Mark Van Doren, Joseph Wood Krutch, and Clifton Fadiman.

Charlie remained in Chicago for twenty or so years. Chicago must, at times, have felt to him like being in Novosibirsk, in western Siberia. He had left the good life in New York, where he owned a red Mercedes convertible and a townhouse in the Village, and had a regular slot on Dave Garroway's *Today* show, for which he was paid the then-princely sum of $50,000 a year.

As befits an exile, Charlie lay low, never becoming a figure of any sort in Chicago. How could he have done? His position was still that of a major national phony. This man, who was supposed to bring renewed respect for learning to the masses through his television performance, had instead besmirched everything by partaking in the general fraudulence. I remember once getting into an argument with Charlie over some now-forgotten political issue; as it began to heat up, I realized that we would both do well to back away. Like almost everyone else in the country, I began with too great a moral advantage over him.

Charlie was not married when he was a contestant on *Twenty-One*, but not long after he married a Jewish woman, Geraldine or Gerry, whom it was said that Charlie's scandal had come near to crushing. Her Jewishness is worth remarking, for in *Quiz Show*, Robert Redford makes much of the Jewish-Gentile rivalrousness that his screenwriter, Paul Attanasio, has inserted as one of the main subthemes of the movie. The Stempel-Van Doren match-up is played in the movie as the aggressive Jewish neurotic *schlemiel* (to put it kindly) versus the cool WASP nonpareil. In reality, when Stempel was told he would have to take a dive and lose to Charlie, he begged that the two of them be allowed to play the game straight, no falsity whatever, a match between CCNY and Columbia, which in retrospect seems a sad little demonstration of school spirit.

WHAT ONE MAY BE PERMITTED TO CALL the Jewish aura of *Quiz Show* runs deep throughout the movie. It begins with Richard Goodwin (played by Rob Morrow), a young Harvard-trained lawyer working for the House subcommittee on legislative oversight, who picks up on the quiz-show scandals when stories about disgruntled contestants begin appearing in the press and decides to investigate them on behalf of the subcommittee, headed by Congressman Oren Harris of Arkansas. In the movie, Goodwin—a chapter of whose book, *Remembering the Sixties*, is the only work cited as the basis for the screenplay—is made to seem the man most ardently in pursuit of showing up the dishonesty of the quiz shows. In fact, the one who did the most to break the scandals was Joseph Stone, who worked for New York District Attorney Frank Hogan. But dramatic necessity, I suppose, required falsifying history, so that in the movie Charlie has only a single, obsessive pursuer.

The Goodwin character is portrayed as an aggressive Jew, first in his class at the Harvard Law School, formerly a clerk to Felix Frankfurter, scruffy, not from Boston but, as he at one point explains, from (Jewish) Brookline. With Stempel (played by John Turturro) wanting to bring Charlie down out of what is made to seem an almost racial envy, and with Goodwin after him out of a sometimes ambivalent but ultimately moral zealousness, poor Charlie (played by Ralph Fiennes) is made to seem rather a WASP sandwich.

Herb Stempel, who is a walking ADL nightmare—aggressive, crazed, showing a blackened tooth—at one point refers to Van Doren as "that big uncircumcised *putz*"; and, after he learns that he has to lose to Charlie, he responds to a television promo for the forthcoming *Twenty-One* show by muttering, "Tune in and watch Charles Van Doren eat his first kosher meal. . . ." As for Goodwin, when he shows himself soft on Charlie, his wife—a "*shikse*," as she is described in the screenplay—eggs him on by calling him a betrayer of his people, "the Uncle Tom of the Jews." That the producers of *Twenty-One* were also Jews, and fairly lubricious ones as portrayed here, makes the entire movie at times seem as if it might deserve the title, "Get the Goy."

ALONG WITH ITS JEW-WASP THEME, *Quiz Show* is intent on demonstrating the corruption of big-time capitalism. Robert Redford has said that he sees his movie as a "parable" of "the eternal struggle between ethics and capitalism." Let it be noted that in putting this parable on the screen, he does not at any time let the ethics of art get in his way. The characters in his movie who represent capitalism, from then-NBC vice president Robert Kintner to the producers of *Twenty-One* to a New York judge who does not release the findings of a grand jury inquiry into the quiz shows, range as human types from the greasy to the gross.

The larger implication of *Quiz Show* is that the fix is in, and we little people, none of us, has a chance against the big boys. The big boys are the capitalists, and they are insidious. The owner of Geritol (played in the movie by the director Martin Scorsese) directs the producers of *Twenty-One* to knock Herbert Stempel off the show because the ratings are slipping. The judge, in not allowing the grand jury's findings to be either officially filed or published, is implicitly in cahoots with the networks and producers. Robert Kintner plays golf with Oren Harris.

Everything, in short, is a done deal. True, maybe everything always was, but now the big boys have the ultimate weapon for controlling the nation—television. The last line of dialogue in *Quiz Show* goes to the Richard Goodwin character: "I thought I was gonna get television. The truth is, television is gonna get us." And that, as they say in the business, is a wrap.

Apart from the irony of making a movie, in some ways the quintessential capitalistic enterprise, to expose capitalism, the political naiveté, not to say pessimism, of *Quiz Show* is impressive. One has to be a fool to be unaware of the possibility of corruption in any enterprise where big money is at stake; and very big money hung on the quiz-show ratings. Even if the sponsors did go along with the cheating perpetrated by the shows' producers—and there is no conclusive evidence that they did—one may be outraged but one ought not be shocked. Behind every great family fortune, as Balzac reminded us many years ago, there is usually a crime.

But the larger point, it seems to me, is that the quiz-show scandals are today known as just that—scandals. And they are scandals because the legal system, and men of impressive integrity such as Joseph Stone and Frank Hogan, sensed their scandalousness and, under the existing capitalist order, shut them down.

A FINAL UNDERLYING THEME in *Quiz Show* has to do with Charlie and his once-famous father. In the movie, this story is toyed with but ultimately scamped as only a movie is permitted to scamp serious material. The intellectual distinction of Charlie's lineage is tricked out in italics. When Richard Goodwin first learns that Charles Van Doren is to be on *Twenty-One*, he asks his wife: "Van Doren like Van Doren Van Doren?" Mark Van Doren is played in the movie by Paul Scofield, and played, let it be said, magnificently: not a steely gray hair out of place, not a syllable mis-accented, splendidly distinguished and handsomely out of it, a combination only an Ivy League academic of a certain era could command.

In the movie, Charlie shows, as one critic has put it, "a fierce ambivalence about a powerful father." Charlie, we learn, at one point left Cambridge to go off to Paris where he wrote a novel about a patricide. But Mark Van Doren is not portrayed as a crushing father; instead he is an almost too-good father whose attention is nonetheless difficult to hold and whose respect is difficult to win. In actuality, with his gray hair, with a face craggy not through dissipation but through, one assumed, the wisdom that comes of intellectual effort, the real Mark Van Doren seems not only to have looked like but to have been a great many people's ideal father. (Considerable, I know, is the number of not very good student poets he encouraged while at Columbia who, alas, still walk the streets intent on a career in poetry.)

It must have been more than a bit tricky to have Mark Van Doren as one's father. His evident superiority could not have been all that easy to live with. Throughout the movie, Charlie, troubled by his cheating on *Twenty-One*, cannot seem to get his father's notice long enough to offer an explanation of his situation and perhaps fire off a confession into the bargain. When he brings up the possibility that there has been cheating on the shows, his father, mildly amused at the notion, retorts that cheating on a television quiz show is "like plagiarizing a comic book." In the movie, one has the sense that Charlie is not quite taken seriously—or seriously enough—by his father, whose main concern about his son's appearances on television is that it might detract from his commitment to teaching.

In Joseph Stone's excellent and thorough book on the quiz-show scandals, *Prime Time and Misdemeanors*, the producer Albert Freedman, when he finally confessed to having fixed *Twenty-One* by supplying the contestants with answers, was told by Charlie that "the impact of exposure would be disastrous—it would destroy his family, might even kill his father." But when Charlie himself finally confessed before the Harris subcommittee in Congress, Mark Van Doren reportedly said that it was the proudest day of his life. Even understanding fully the intention behind that sentence, one begs to doubt its truth. In any case, one has the sense that the relationship between Charlie and his father was vastly more complicated than is suggested in Redford's movie.

I WAS NEVER A CLOSE FRIEND OF CHARLIE'S, but during the years I was at Britannica I once had dinner at his home, where I remember him reciting a poem over the wine, an amusingly pretentious little touch. I also remember liking his wife, who I thought showed signs of psychological fragility but who obviously loved her husband. I once went to a small party where Charlie showed up wearing beads; the time was the sizzling 1960s, remember.

While at Britannica I spent hundreds of hours in a large conference room with ten or twelve other senior editors, of whom Charlie had become one; and I had a chance to watch his mind at work. It will seem a comically obvious thing to say about the world's most famous quiz-show contestant, but Charlie actually knew quite a lot. After his undergraduate education at St. John's, he had set out to become an astrophysicist, though somewhere along the line he reined in his intellectual ambition and settled for a master's degree in mathematics. Later he would do a PhD in English literature.

What I found impressive about Charlie was the range of his random information. He seemed to know a good deal about Indian tribes and geology and Boolean algebra; how deep his knowledge of any of these things went, I am not sure, but he could talk a decently good game. Perhaps this came from growing up in so intensely bookish a home.*

Yet, much as he possessed an impressive range of factual knowledge, nothing in Charlie seemed to tie any of it together. He was cultivated and knowledgeable without being in the least intellectual. If Charlie had any ideas, he kept them hidden. If he had any true intellectual passions, these remained his private possession. If he had any politics, he tended to keep these, too, to himself—though later, when the tumult of the late 1960s got well under way, I came across a pamphlet of political pieces by Midwestern academics and journalists on the Left to which Charlie had contributed a small bouquet of platitudes of the day. Charlie's mother and father, after all, had both worked on the *Nation*, and I have been told that Mark Van Doren went for Henry Wallace in the 1948 presidential election.

One of the reasons I never became closer to Charlie at Britannica is that he was too much Mortimer J. Adler's man. The other senior editors at the corporation were united by their mockery of the project for which they had been hired—a replanning of the entire encyclopedia, beginning with a Rube Goldberg-like index of world knowledge—and on which Adler, a kind of mad prince of

---

* Even this would never have been enough for Charlie to have come through as stupendously as he seemed to do on *Twenty-One*. As Edward Jurist, one of the producers of the 1950s quiz show *Dotto*, told Joseph Stone, the world of information is so vast that nobody could be expected to answer more than two of ten randomly asked questions: "You cannot ask random questions of people and have a show. You simply have failure, failure, failure, and that does not make for entertainment."

logic, rode herd. Charlie never disagreed with Adler, whereas disagreement with and behind-his-back disparagement of Adler gave the rest of us what camaraderie we enjoyed.

Still, I never noted in Charlie any resentment, either of his situation or of those colleagues whose contempt he must have sensed. (I am a little ashamed of my own failure of imagination in not taking into consideration Charlie's impossible position as a family man with no other work open to him.) If he had any side or meanness to him, I never saw or felt it. In *Quiz Show*, Ralph Fiennes has nicely caught the quality in the Charlie I knew of bemused self-contentment. It combines, this quality, detached curiosity about the world and yet absolutely no doubt concerning one's deserved place in it.

Charlie was resilient, a survivor. Richard Goodwin, in his chapter on the quiz shows in *Remembering America*, quotes a letter written to him by Charlie after the congressional guillotine had fallen. The final paragraph reads:

> There have been many hard things. But I am trying to tell you that we [he and his wife] will live and thrive, I think—I mean I know we will live and I think we will thrive—and that you must never, in any way, feel any regret for your part in this. Perhaps it is nonsense to say this, but I thought it might be just possible that you would.

Charlie did of course live, and, materially, he throve. He and his wife raised a family. He eventually became an important vice president at Encyclopaedia Britannica, Inc. He was a skier; he played tennis. He was a good-time Charlie. Some years ago, I believe I heard someone say that he bought a place in Italy, or Switzerland. He retired early to his family home in Connecticut.

The passage of years had assuaged Charlie's notoriety. Generations have come into being to whom the quiz-show scandals are not even a memory, and for whom the name Charles Van Doren does not mean much, and that of his once distinguished family even less. (Charlie has long been more famous than Mark or any other Van Doren.) Charlie could actually look forward to meeting people who had not the foggiest notion of his past. Until, that is, Robert Redford and Paul Attanasio had this bright idea for a movie that has brought it all back.

Looking at Charlie in those meetings at Britannica, I used to wonder what might have happened had the scandal never blown up on him. Difficult to fix the limits here. He could, when still young, have been made the editor of Encyclopaedia Britannica, or the head of the Book-of-the-Month Club, or some other highly profitable middlebrow institution. A university presidency was a distinct possibility. A political career was not, I suppose, out of the question. Had the blade not fallen, Charlie would almost certainly have been heard from during the 1960s. He might have stayed in television and become a major-network version of Bill Moyers, doing a kind of intellectual talk show.

By the same token, without Charlie, I believe, the quiz shows would not have been quite so popular nor the scandals have loomed so large. Although contestants on the various shows included Xavier Cougat, the eleven-year-old actress Patty Duke, and Joyce Brothers, although Leonard Bernstein's sister Shirley was one of the producers of *The $64,000 Question*, and although some contestants won a good deal more money than he, Charlie was nevertheless correct when, in his confession before Oren Harris's subcommittee, he said that he "was the principal symbol" of the entire extravaganza. When Richard Goodwin, in the hope of protecting Charlie, spoke with Felix Frankfurter about the possibility of excluding him from the congressional hearings, Frankfurter rightly retorted, "It would be like playing *Hamlet* without Hamlet."

Charlie Van Doren, a teacher at Columbia, our answer to Sputnik, a Van Doren Van Doren—as he once seemed the most admirable of Americans, so after the scandals he seemed far and away the most culpable. Yet Charlie was not alone in accepting help on these shows. According to Joseph Stone, Albert Freedman "could not recall any prospective contestant who flatly turned down assistance...." Howard Felsher, who produced the show *Tic Tac Dough*, claimed that "not one of the people to whom he proposed assistance turned him down," either. Richard Goodwin, in his investigations, found only one man, a Greenwich Village poet, who refused to go along with the fixers, but in his book Goodwin cannot recall his name—another honest man lost to history.

Yet the crushing opprobrium came down not only hardest but, it seemed, almost exclusively on Charlie. He, the argument ran, should have known better. He, given his natural advantages in life, was least in need of the superficial celebrity that winning on a quiz show had to offer. He was, moreover, a teacher, whose life was bound by the ethic of intellectual honesty.

W HY DID HE DO IT? According to most accounts, including *Quiz Show*, Charlie was seduced into cooperation by the producers. In the movie he is portrayed as initially gullible, half-convinced that his winning is somehow good for education and hence for the country. Then—in for a penny, in for a pounding—he discovers he is in well over his head and unable to get out gracefully.

The movie takes it a step further. In a notable scene between the Charlie and the Goodwin characters the latter suggests that Charlie would actually *like* to get caught, so that he could finally be free of all the pressures of deception. In this interpretation, Charlie was looking for full excoriation, leading to expurgation, ending in expiation.

Then there are those with a light taste for Freudian psychology, who favor the view that the tremendous publicity that came with his appearance on *Twenty-One* was the only way Charlie could surpass his father in fame. Deeper Freudians might argue the need for scandal as the only way he could bring his father down. (In a notable, passionate exchange between father and son in *Quiz Show*, Mark Van Doren says to Charlie, "Your name is mine," implying, besmirch yourself and you besmirch me.)

But was Charlie really an attractive *naif*, perfect for casting purposes but finally himself no more than a brainy rube? Or, once taken in, did he, deep down, want to be caught? I doubt it. I think Charlie—as he told *Life*, he was always a gambler—bet all, risked all, and finally lost all.

I do think Charlie wanted off the hook. The mad publicity, combined with the fraudulence that made his fame possible to begin with, must have been troubling to him; beyond a certain point, he did not want the charade to continue. But neither did he want to lose what it had brought him. As Joseph Stone notes, after Charlie had made yet another denial of guilt to him: "I was convinced Van Doren was lying and was not about to risk the comfortable niche of celebrity he had achieved."

And so, up till the end, he attempted to tough it out. When the hint of scandal first hit the air with Herbert Stempel's accusations, Charlie told the press, "It's silly and distressing to think that people don't have more faith in quiz shows." He later affected a shocked disbelief at the charge that he himself could possibly be among the culprits. He told Richard Goodwin that Albert Freedman was lying to the district attorney in saying that *Twenty-One* was fixed, and that Freedman had reasons for smearing him. He claimed innocence on the *Today* show.

At another point, Charlie did acknowledge that he had been offered help, which would mean that he knew the fix was in, but asserted that he had decided to turn it down. Finally, in the telegram that resulted in his being called before the Harris Committee, he claimed through NBC that "at no time was he supplied any questions or answers with respect to his appearance on *Twenty-One*," nor was he ever "assisted in any form and he has no knowledge of any assistance having been given the other contestants."

Joseph Stone, who does not seem a vindictive man, believes that Charlie did not even come altogether clean in his famous congressional confession, which began:

> I have learned a lot in these three years, especially in the last three weeks. I've learned about life. I've learned about myself. I've learned a lot about good and evil. They are not always what they appear to be. I was involved, deeply involved, in a deception. The fact that I, too, was very much deceived cannot keep me from being the principal victim of that deception, because I was its principal symbol.

We shall probably never learn why Charlie went on the quiz show and then agreed to go along with the prepared script. Could Charlie himself, after 35 years to think about it, say with confidence? Even if he could, my guess is that he is not likely to. I think he can never tell the truth because he was caught up in too many contradictions and lies. Coming completely clean might also catch up others in the scandal whom Charlie would not wish to hurt. Finally, there is the possibility that Charlie himself still does not have the answer.

WHICH LEAVES US WITH THE QUESTION of the deeper meaning of the quiz-show scandals. Not everyone, of course, agrees they have a deeper meaning: Terrence Rafferty in the *New Yorker* referred to *Quiz Show* as "a speedy, absorbing chronicle of a trivial show-business scandal of the 1950s." But too many people were taken in for it to be trivial.

The conventional reading is that the quiz-show scandals spelled the end of American innocence. Richard Goodwin takes up this line, claiming "we were more innocent then," and adding that "we had been mind-fucked on an enormous scale. And we didn't like it." Goodwin would not be happy to hear David Halberstam's reading of this same episode in his recent book, *The Fifties*; there, Halberstam suggests that Charlie's success in the new cool medium of television made way for the new television star of the early 1960s, John Fitzgerald Kennedy—Richard Goodwin's next boss.

The temptation is to take the quiz-show scandals as yet another of those defining moments in American history. But I am not sure I can make out what they defined. If they meant the end of American innocence, then good riddance to such innocence. If they showed human corruption—on the part of the producers, advertisers, network executives, contestants—such corruption is hardly a new story. Big money breeds corruption, always has and always will. That, as they used to say, is life in the big city.

Which brings me back to where I began, with Charlie. *Quiz Show* ends, like a Dickens novel, though not so happily, by telling what happened to the characters in later life. From a "crawl," or scroll of printed matter, we learn that Herbert Stempel finished his degree in social work at CCNY and now works for the Department of Transportation of the City of New York. Albert Freedman works at *Penthouse* magazine. The producers Jack Barry and Dan Enright, seventeen years after the scandals, scored with another television show, *The Joker's Wild*, which made them millionaires. In 1990, the three major American television networks had gross revenues of $6 billion. Richard Goodwin, after being a speechwriter for Presidents Kennedy and Johnson, left the White House during the Vietnam war, retired from politics after the death of Robert Kennedy, and now lives in Concord, Massachusetts, where, the crawl fails to mention, like all former Kennedy men, he awaits the second coming.

And Charlie? Charlie, the crawl informs us, worked for Encyclopaedia Britannica and now lives as a writer in Cornwall, Connecticut. It would have been closer to the truth to say that, since 1956, when he first stepped into an isolation booth at that NBC studio, Charlie has continued living in an isolation booth—a portable one, to be sure, perhaps even a fairly plush one, but still lonely and terribly cut off. He has spent 38 years there. As punishments go, it may not be as cruel as solitary confinement in a maximum-security prison, but neither can it have been any bed of roses.

W. C. Fields

Never Give a Sucker an Even Break

F OR A COMIC OR A WIT, the enviable thing is to be so celebrated that one is given credit for the humor, repartee,
and amusing anecdotes of others. Oscar Wilde was in this
splendid position; so, too, closer to our own day, were Dorothy
Parker and Oscar Levant. Outside the arts, Winston Churchill
was assigned the honor of many a brilliant remark he never made.
So, again, was W. C. Fields, the great American vaudevillian and
movie comedian.

Here, for example, is a story told about Fields on his deathbed.
Allow me to present it as a movie scene, the form in which he, a
scenarist himself, might best have appreciated it:

> It is a late winter afternoon. Fields is in bed in a New York
> hospital, under an oxygen tent and lashed to an IV. He is
> obviously in a very bad way. His lawyer, his agent, and
> his mistress sit in vigil. From outside one hears the sound,
> faint but distinct, of newsboys hawking the afternoon pa-
> pers. Fields signals the three to his bedside.

FIELDS: (*weakly*) Poor little urchins out there. No doubt improperly nourished, ill-clad. Something's got to be done about them. Something's got to be done.

He closes his eyes. His lawyer, agent, and mistress return to their chairs. Twenty seconds later, Fields, even more weakly than before, signals them to return. They lean in close to hear what figure to be his last words.

FIELDS: On second thought—screw 'em.

Almost nothing about this story turns out to be true. William Claude Fields died—on Christmas day, 1946, at the age of sixty-six—in California. He had lapsed into a coma roughly a month earlier. A nurse and his secretary kept the deathwatch. In his grandson's account, he regained consciousness for the briefest moment, put a forefinger to his lips, winked, and departed the planet.

The apocryphal version, if I may say so, is better—better because it is more in harmony with the way those of us to whom Fields has given immense pleasure tend to think of him. And the way we have tended to think of him, of course, is as the great American curmudgeon. He was the man who, when asked if he liked children, replied, "I do, if they're properly cooked." A gardener, Fields is said to have fastened a note to his rose bushes: "Bloom, you bastards! Bloom!" Will Fowler, the son of the writer Gene Fowler, remembers Fields chasing a swan off his property, calling out, "Either shit green or get off the lawn!" When a young man who claimed to be Fields's illegitimate son showed up at his home, the butler asked what he ought to be told. "Give him an evasive answer," Fields said. "Tell him to go fuck himself."

Will Rogers, a contemporary of Fields, famously said that he never met a man he didn't like (causing George Jessel to say that he once had a wife who felt the same way, and it turned out to be no bargain). With Fields it was just the reverse—at least if his public persona can be believed. But the gap between the private and public Fields, between his personal life and his show-business life, is a complicated subject. Happily, it has been untangled for us in *Man on the Flying Trapeze*, a recent biography by Simon Louvish.

Louvish goes through what he calls the "Fields legend" in the spirit of a fact-checker *extraordinaire*. Some of the corrections he enters into the record cause, at least in me, a brief stir of regret. I did not enjoy learning, for instance, that Fields is not, after all, buried under a tombstone that reads, "I'd rather be in Philadelphia." Others range from the relatively inconsequential to the genuinely substantive. We learn from Louvish that Fields did not leave home at age eleven, as he claimed, but at eighteen; he did not deposit money in different bank accounts all over the world, but managed his finances quite sensibly; instead of hating children, as his movie roles often called upon him to do, he was a devoted grandfather; no misogynist, he found women delectable and was able to make himself charming to many; far from being a pinchpenny or stingy, he was something of a sport.

But it is not as if Louvish has discovered the real W. C. Fields to be a pussycat, a bird-watcher, or a teetotaler. Even in this account, he remains a pretty wild old boy: a skirt-chasing, heavy-boozing, lyrically profane man. Nor, in other respects, is the general effect of *Man on a Flying Trapeze* deflationary. Far from it. For what Louvish is really at pains to demonstrate in this book has less to do with the private W. C. Fields and more to do with the performing one: a highly self-conscious entertainer who carefully developed his skills to the point where they became art.

FIELDS, WHO WAS BORN IN 1880, liked to pretend in later life that he had grown up in a Dickensian atmosphere, mistreated and manhandled by a father who forced him to leave home as a child and scrounge a livelihood in the streets of Philadelphia, where he engaged in petty crimes and wild escapades. Simon Louvish tells

W. C. FIELDS

us otherwise. Fields's father, whose name was Dukenfield, worked as a commission merchant for fruits and vegetables, and although he drank his share, he and his son went at each other less violently than the son would later claim. Still, the household—"poor but dishonest," in Fields's characterization—was at least verbally pugnacious; his mother in particular was known for mumbling sarcastic asides in a manner her son would later adapt to brilliant comic effect.

Fields left home not in discouragement but for a life in the theater. As a boy, he had begun to juggle, and he worked hard at this charming, strangely elegant, and utterly useless art. He had fine eye-hand coordination, could do trick shots in pool, manipulate cards, and juggle just about anything less than his own weight. To innate talent he added powerful discipline. The mature Fields told a story—not refuted by Louvish—of working at home on a trick until the man who lived downstairs came to complain about the ceaseless din of falling objects, at which point Fields put him off by telling him about a little trick with paring knives that, if executed as prescribed, would have resulted in fairly serious injury.

Jugglers were then a standard act on the bills of every variety theater, and one had to carve out one's own niche, find a specialty within the specialty. Fields's first attempt along these lines was to wear a tramp's outfit and do a fine turn with five cigar boxes which a reviewer described as setting at "naught all laws of gravity." In the verbal byplay accompanying his juggling, he reacted with puzzled comments to the miscreant behavior of his recalcitrant hats, boxes, and canes. In the words of a British vaudevillian quoted by Louvish, Fields "would reprimand a particular ball which had not come to his hand accurately, whip his battered silk hat for not staying on his head, . . . mutter weird and unintelligible expletives to his cigar when it missed his mouth."

The climb of the young W. C. Fields was steady and not all that slow. A watchful caretaker of his career, he was soon able to get himself booked into better and better theaters, and his biographer is able to supply us with some of the great show-biz names who appeared on the same bills with him: the Keatons, Fanny Brice, Sarah Bernhardt, Harry Houdini, Maurice Chevalier, Ed Wynn, the Marx Brothers, and Eddie Cantor, the last of whom became a fairly close friend. Touring abroad before World War I, where the fees were especially good, Fields played England, Germany, the *Folies Bergère* in Paris, and Australia.

His only serious miscue was an early marriage, which produced a son from whom he would become estranged. His wife's name was Harriet Hughes, and she claimed to be related to the aristocratic Lees of Virginia; Fields's riposte was that she was really from the Levys of Brooklyn. Although he would later be reconciled with his son—a grandson, Ronald J. Fields, would even assemble a book, *W. C. Fields by Himself,* that attempted to rescue Fields from the self-created legend of his misanthropy—he divorced his wife and never remarried. One of his great comic subjects, in fact, became the nightmare of domesticity. Wives in Fields's routines do not get off lightly.

His life was in any case hardly set up for marriage. Regularly on tour during the early years of the century, he played the then-famous Keith circuit and later became one of the comic stars of the *Ziegfield Follies.* As time went on his verbal comedy came to occupy as large a share of his act as his physical comedy. Louvish reports that in those days he never repeated jokes—something not true of his later career, when he became an assiduous recycler of his own material. "It is hard to say which we admire most," a reviewer of the day noted, "his remarkable skill [at juggling] or his irresistible drollery." Another reviewer, in the *San Francisco Chronicle,* averred that Fields possessed "more of the real spark of comic genius than almost any who styles himself so in the legitimate field." Heywood Broun and Alexander Woollcott both praised him in print. The word, in short, was getting around.

By 1920, Fields was earning big money, a grand a week, and a few years later he left Ziegfield to join the *George White Scandals.* He had long before begun to write his own scripts, and he even made a single silent movie, a muddled and chaotic effort called *The Pool Shark* (1916). In it he wears a hopeless mustache—his "third eyebrow," he called it—and cannot be said to have established anything resembling a memorable character. Yet, with his fine weather eye, he had sensed that the action—which also meant the money—was henceforth in movies. He aimed to score big in Hollywood.

Sound, the talkies, is what made W. C. Fields. His voice—
that fine con-man drawl, "nasal and grating," as Louvish
describes it, "with that know-it-all tinge coupled with an eternal
ennui"—was the most potent single weapon in his arsenal. Splendidly rhythmic, absolutely distinctive, capable of providing exactly
the effects he required of it, his was one of the great comic voices
of all time. Many explanations have been offered for its origin: the
legacy of years of devoted boozing and smoking, the product of
cold Philadelphia winters, and so forth. Louvish argues, convincingly, that it was a work of pure invention, like Fields's walk, looks,
gestures—the whole package.

Little that Fields did was without calculation, either in his stage
and movie performances or, for that matter, in the creation of his
own legend. Although he was capable of shenanigans—including
drinking on the set—he was, Louvish writes, "the most disciplined
of actors when he was working for those he respected," among
them the directors D. W. Griffith, Joseph Mankiewicz, Leo McCa-
rey, and George Cukor. For an actor, he was also fairly well read;
he had a special love for Dickens, from whom he happily stole the
use of comic names and broad-stroke caricature. He understood,
with genuine intellectual precision, the mechanics if not the well-
springs of comedy. In a magazine article of 1934 he noted that "you
usually can't get a laugh out of damaging anything valuable," and he
also believed that "it's funnier to bend things than to break them."
With perfect pitch and timing, he bent them just about as far as
they could go.

Fields's voice was the ideal conveyance for the kind of highly
verbal comedy in which he came more and more to specialize. To
begin with, there was his rich and ornate vocabulary. (Whenever
I read H. L. Mencken, Fields's exact contemporary and another
brandisher of an ornate vocabulary, I always hear a Fieldsian into-
nation.) Fields loved language, juggled it as expertly as he did his
cigar boxes and hats, played it not only for laughs but for sheer

sensuous pleasure. He cared enough about language to compile a now-lost dictionary of his own neologisms, which included the word "philanthroac" (one whose mission in life it is to take care of drunks who do not desire his care).

In *My Little Chickadee* (1940), which Fields wrote with his co-star Mae West, he refers to her character, whose name is Flower Belle Lee, as "yon damsel with the hothouse cognomen." Later in the movie he tells her that she is "the epitome of erudition," adding, "a double superlative. Can you handle it?" (Miss West replies: "Yeah, and I can kick it around, too.") There is even in this movie an example of what I believe academic literary critics nowadays call "intertextuality": "Come up and see me sometime," is Fields's final utterance, echoing the most famous of all Mae West one-liners; to it, she replies, "Yeah, I'll do that, my little chickadee."

Fields was especially good at delivering innuendo, those comical asides and afterthoughts in which all his movies are rich. "I've never struck a woman in my life," he claims in the short film *The Golf Specialist* (1930). Hold one full beat. "Not even my own mother." More than just an instrument for conveying words, however gaudy, Fields's voice aimed at projecting something larger—a fully developed persona.

The great early movie comedians all had their own imprint: Charlie Chaplin's ability to wring pathos out of a charming underdog resilience; Buster Keaton's passive melancholy with its high threshold for frustration; the Marx Brothers' let-'er-rip anarchical zaniness. Fields's comic character may have been the most highly formed of the lot. When he was in control of a movie—he often wrote his own material, or used writers who knew his character the way a bespoke tailor knows his customer—then, as Louvish says, "the comic business, the gags, always illuminate[d] character, and all comedy stem[med] from the character, not from some mechanical plan."

ACTUALLY, THERE WERE TWO FIELDS CHARACTERS. The high-toned, often grouchy con man was one; the greatly put-upon husband or "sucker" was the other. From movie to movie he could slide easily from one to the next, and he could also play his con man for pathos, as in his brilliant portrayal of Mr. Micawber, the sesquipedalian optimist, in George Cukor's version of *David Copperfield* (1935). But there was no doubt in Fields's own mind about which was the harder trick to pull off. He once told a journalist: "Making you laugh at the hard-boiled three-card-monte man who is trimming a sucker is one thing—and not so easy—but making you laugh at the sucker is something else."

Of the two chief Fieldsian characters, the con man and the degraded husband, my own preference is for the latter. *My Little Chickadee* and *Never Give a Sucker an Even Break* (1941) have their fine moments, but I like Fields when he is less snarly, less frightening, less likely to cuff a child too enthusiastically; when he is not adding to the world's anarchy but is instead—like the rest of us, if to a much higher power—a victim of it.

In most of the movies in which Fields plays the chump, his character is locked in a hideously mistaken, a completely disastrous, marriage. He does not ask much—a drink with the boys, a night at the wrestling matches—but even that turns out to be too much. His wife is inevitably a harridan in a print dress, and sometimes there is a pompous and contemptuous stepson or a hopeless older daughter going with the wrong young man; added to the mix is often a younger son or daughter who is the Platonic ideal of the brat.

The put-upon husband is seen to best effect in *It's a Gift* (1934), about the Bissonette family—needless to say, the wife in the movie insists on pronouncing it Bissoné. Simon Louvish claims *It's a Gift* as his own favorite, and it is also mine. Among its riotously funny bits is an extended scene in which the grocery store of Harold Bissonette, the character played by Fields, is nearly destroyed by the maunderings of one Mr. Muckle, a blind man whom Fields implores to remain seated ("Take it easy, Mr. Muckle, honey, just stay seated, Mr. Muckle") while a bullying customer keeps yelling that he needs ten pounds of kumquats. The whole thing amounts to a form of juggling by other means, and at scene's end all the balls are on the floor. As the blind Mr. Muckle leaves, Fields reports: "He's the house detective over at the hotel."

I DO NOT MEAN TO SUGGEST that Fields's movies are all marvels of compression and wit, or without their longueurs. Sometimes they almost seem to go into slow motion. In two different movies there are checkers games in which the Fields character waits what seems like forever before giving advice that will result in a player's being quintuple-jumped. Fields can take endless amounts of time wriggling his golf club before striking a ball, or standing in the door to announce, "Ain't a fit night out for man or beast"—hold for three full beats—before getting a blast of snow in the puss.

Of greater interest is the world view that underlies and provokes the laughter. The chief subject in Fields's best movies is false respectability. His is a world where dysfunctionality and viciousness rule—where everyone tries to do in everyone else, and meanness and stinginess abound. Many of Fields's movies also provide an implicit critique of small-town America in the 1920s and 1930s, and especially of its narrowness and puritan hypocrisy; they are, in effect, Sinclair Lewis with laughter added.

The Bank Dick (1940), for example, is set in the town of Lompoc, with its three paved blocks and its many busybodies. Living with four women—a wife, the standard brutal mother-in-law, and two awful daughters—Egbert Sousè ("accent *grave* over the e," he invariably adds), who is not permitted to smoke in the house, takes refuge in the Black Pussy Café and Snack Bar, where he tanks up every chance he gets. In a nice Fieldsian bit, he fussily uses his water chasers as finger bowls.

In Fields's small town, respectability is all on the surface. "I shall make it my business to see that the Lompoc Ladies Auxiliary will be informed," an old biddy tells the manager of the hotel in which Sousè has stowed a bank examiner he has gotten drunk. Meanwhile, not very far beneath the surface, corruption is the order of the day. "We have three drugstores," notes the Fields character. "One actually sells medicine." Dr. Stall, the town physician advises an emaciated patient to "cut out all health foods for a while," bidding him farewell with the words, "That'll be ten dollars. The nurse will return your clothes with a receipt."

In each of these movies, the improbable demystifier of society's false surfaces turns out to be the character played by Fields himself. I suspect that this is what lay behind the revival of interest in him that took place in the late 1960s and early 1970s. Suddenly, posters, T-shirts, and coffee mugs began showing up bearing his great red-nosed likeness. In the eyes of a rebellious generation, Fields was an anti-establishment man. The old iconoclast had become, posthumously, an icon.

Sorry, wrong, anti-hero. ("Icon," one can almost hear the comedian drawling, "sounds awfully like I con.") In life, Fields was a Republican and a great contemner of Franklin Delano Roosevelt, not to mention an isolationist who disapproved of US entry into World War II. In his public persona, he was not only anti-establishment, he was anti-everything. As he wrote in a book of only faintly amusing essays, *Fields for President*:

> And when, on next November fifth, I am elected chief executive of this fair land, amidst thunderous cheering and shouting and throwing of babies out the window, I shall, my fellow citizens, offer no such empty panaceas as a New Deal, or an Old Deal, or even a Re-Deal.
>
> No, my friends, the reliable False Shuffle was good enough for my father and it's good enough for me.

Certainly no one could have been more politically incorrect than Fields, either in his art or in his life. He would say that he was "impersonating a Ubangi," or slip in the occasional reference to an "Ethiopian in the fuel supply." Of the ten items for which the con man J. Effington Bellwether (in *The Golf Specialist*) is wanted by the police, the final one is: "Revealing the facts of life to an Indian." He liked to make jokes about women's bottoms. (In *The Dentist*, 1932, a woman is bitten in the ankle from behind by a small dog. "You're fortunate," Fields ripostes, "that it wasn't a New-foundland.") Although many of his show-biz friends were Jewish, Hollywood producers drove him, as Louvish puts it, close to "tipping over into anti-Semitism." Planning to leave the majority of his estate to found an orphanage for black children in Philadelphia, he became offended by the behavior of a black servant and changed his will to restrict the orphanage to whites. When his friend Gene Fowler told him he was making a mistake and was bound to be misunderstood, Fields replied: "I've always been misunderstood."

The misunderstanding matters little now. The movies remain, and they are still very funny—some of them, for me, falling-off-the-couch funny. Over the years, the heavier he grew, the redder his nose became (he suffered from a skin disease called rosacea), the sourer he seemed, the more pleasure he gave and the greater artist he became. He was not everyone's cup of cognac. But for those of us whose cup he is, he continues to contribute, quite substantially, to the gross national comedy.

Irving Thalberg

Prodigy in Pictures

E ARLY ONE MORNING IN 1970, at my desk at the now long
defunct Chicago publishing firm called Quadrangle Books,
the receptionist called to say that a man had arrived with
a manuscript he would like to leave with me. The man, smallish,
handsome, with delicate features and light red hair, entered without saying a word, set on my desk a manuscript in black binders,
with the title *Enigmas of Agency* on a white label on its front cover.
I opened it to the first page, where I noted the author's name. I
looked up. "Yes," the man said, "I am his son."

His name was Irving Thalberg, Jr., and the manuscript was a
work of technical philosophy. He was, I now realize, 40 years old
and taught at the University of Illinois at Chicago. "Look," he said,
"I'm not trying to buy you off or anything of the kind, but if you
want to publish this book, and the cost of publication is a problem,
I have a fund out of which I can defer the expenses. But only, you
understand, if you really want to publish the book."

No one at the firm, it turned out, thought the book was for us—
it was eventually published in England by Allen & Unwin—but I
have always regretted not having invited its author out for coffee or

436 ■ Essays in Biography

a lunch. So many things I should have liked to talk with him about. His mother was Norma Shearer, a great beauty and one of the few movie stars to make the transition from silent to talking movies with her popularity increased. Irving Thalberg Jr. died of cancer, in 1987 at 56, living 19 years longer than his father, who pegged out at 37 in 1936, the most famous and by all odds the most talented producer in the history of American movies.

What exactly it is that a producer does has never been altogether clear. As much as he can get away with is, I suppose, one answer. For the producer usually represents "the money," and money, as the saying has it, talks, too often ignorantly and vulgarly—that is, if one is to listen to directors and writers. The problem is that, without producers, movies don't get made, nothing gets done, and all one is left with is the sound of no hands clapping to the accompaniment of a chorus of vastly overpaid and highly articulate bitching.

No ordinary producer, Irving Thalberg was the man on whom F. Scott Fitzgerald modeled Monroe Stahr, the hero of his final and uncompleted Hollywood novel *The Last Tycoon*. Fitzgerald was among the scores of writers Thalberg hired while chief of production at Metro-Goldwyn-Mayer. Ardently though Fitzgerald wanted to succeed at the job—he needed the money and, down on his luck, was looking for a victory of any kind—he couldn't bring it off. As a screenwriter, he saw words when pictures were wanted; he wrote dialogue when action was called for. But he also saw in Irving Thalberg a genius of a rare kind, a high-level artist who produced no art of his own but bent all his efforts at releasing and orchestrating the talent of others. Beyond counting are the number of movies Thalberg helped get made, improved, burnished from pure dross to high and entertaining gloss and, sometimes, a little more than mere entertainment.

While alive Irving Thalberg never allowed his name to appear in the screen credits for a single film. He may not have craved fame as it is usually packaged, but he was far from self-effacing. "I, more than

IRVING THALBERG

any other single person in Hollywood," he declared, "have my finger on the pulse of America. I know what people will do and what they won't." Making decisions was for him never a problem. He told Fitzgerald that "when you're planning a new enterprise on a grand scale, the people under you mustn't ever know or guess that you're in any doubt, because they've all got to have something to look up to and they mustn't ever dream that you're in doubt about any decision." He never bullied anyone under him but was not to be fooled with.

The word "filmmaker" has been much bandied around in recent decades, usually applied to directors sufficiently modest to eschew the more pretentious "auteur." But in the history of American movies, there may have been only one true filmmaker: a man whose hand and mind were there from inception through conception of hundreds of movies, seeing to each detail and without whose behind-the-scene participation the movie would fail to exist—and that man was Irving Thalberg.

Born in 1899, growing up in a period before people wasted four to six years going off to acquire so-called higher education, Thalberg began young. His first job was with Universal City, where, by the time he was 20, he was made general manager, at a respectable salary of $450 a week, with the responsibility of running daily operations. He was small—5' 6", 122 pounds—but from the first possessed of a quiet authority. When he attempted to hold the line on Erich von Stroheim's outrageous spending on a movie, von Stroheim, with characteristic modesty, said: "Since when does a child instruct a genius?" Not long thereafter, Thalberg fired von Stroheim, an act, according to David O. Selznick, that "took guts and courage," and it also changed power relations in movie-making forever, with the producers now being understood ultimately to rank above the directors of films.

Courage, confidence, cool executive ability of the highest order, none of this, for Irving Thalberg, was in short supply. What was in short supply was time. From a very early age, he knew he was going to die young. He was a "blue baby," born having a poor supply of oxygen to the blood and given a medical prognosis calling for him not to last much beyond the age of 30. The dark prospect of early death, some say, gave Thalberg especial clarity about his own life and what he wished to do with it of a kind unavailable to those who wait until 80 to begin to believe that there is an odd chance they could possibly die. He had a strong mother; his father, like that of George Gershwin, another contemporary Jewish genius, seemed, as the old joke about Jewish husbands has it, not to have had a speaking part. Henrietta Thalberg, Mark A. Vieira, Thalberg's excellent biographer, writes, "had given her son a sense of self—his poise, his impatience with mediocrity, his need to achieve success within a limited time."

Vieira's *Irving Thalberg, Boy Wonder to Producer Prince* is the third biography of Thalberg, and far and away the most thoroughly researched, comprehensive, and penetrating. The book follows from, and carefully fills out, the biographical essay that Vieira wrote for his sumptuous but serious coffee-table book called *Hollywood Dreams Made Real*, about Thalberg and the rise of Metro-Goldwyn-Mayer. In the new work Vieira recounts what Thalberg accomplished, how he was able to achieve what he did, and over whose live bodies he brought it all off. This book is as close to definitive as any biography of Irving Thalberg is likely to get.

On the first page of *The Last Tycoon*, the novel's female narrator remarks of the Stahr/Thalberg hero that "not half a dozen men have ever been able to keep the whole equation of pictures in their heads." (*The Whole Equation* is the title that the English movie critic David Thomson gave to his recent history of Hollywood.) Thalberg quickly picked up on the equation, and could manipulate it brilliantly. He thought, really, of little else but movies; on his wedding day, while dressing, Vieira reports, he was discussing scripts.

What Thalberg understood is that movies are not merely primarily but entirely about storytelling, and, though he could not himself write stories (or movie scripts), he had a fine understanding of why some stories worked—and quite as important, why others did not. Every good movie requires at least one unforgettable scene, he held. Character is key, he believed. Thalberg it was who came up with the notion that the Marx Brothers would be a lot funnier if they played their exuberant zaniness off rigid social institutions: the opera, the university, diplomacy, thoroughbred racing, high society. He never wrote any of the Marx Brothers' scripts, but without this central idea, the genius of the Marx Brothers would never have come to the glorious fruition that it did.

One of Thalberg's obsessions was to try to comprehend, as one of his screenwriters put it, "why some films could tune into an audience and others could not." He once told Charles McArthur that his own "tastes are exactly those of the audience. What I didn't like, they won't like." He was enormously patient, prepared to have scenes shot and reshot as often as required. Movies are not made, he held, but remade. He was a surgeon, one of his screenwriters remarked, "who cut to heal." One of his sub-producers, Lawrence Weingarten, remarked: "Thalberg directed the film on paper, and then the director directed the film on film." Here, in a single sentence, is Irving Thalberg's philosophy of filmmaking: "The difference between something good and something bad is great, but the difference between something good and something superior is often very small." That small but crucial difference was, of course, a large part of the whole equation.

F. Scott Fitzgerald said that the sign of high intelligence resides in the ability to keep two contradictory ideas in one's mind at the same time and still function. Thalberg seems to have been able to keep as many as 50 movies in his mind at once, and through subtle but firm indirection, also keep any number of egomaniacs on the job, fend off the Hays Office on censorship, satisfy a difficult Louis B. Mayer and money-minded partners in New York— in short, keep an entire studio functioning without ever seeming in the least ruffled.

Only a monomaniac could bring this off, a man with a wide but deeply grooved, single-tracked mind. Ben Hecht, who worked with Thalberg and whose abiding, sometimes hyperbolic, cynicism about the movies is never wholly out of order, wrote of him:

> He hadn't the faintest idea what was going on anywhere
> in the world except in his office. He lived two-thirds of
> the time in the projection room. He saw only movies.

He never saw life. He had never noticed life. He was a
hermit. He hadn't the faintest idea what human beings
did—but he knew what their shadows should do.

Irving Thalberg was the founding father of the studio system, a
movie-making assembly line that made it possible to turn out as many
as 50 or so movies a year. This system, responsible for so much trash
and not a few gems, required the regular turnover of what nowadays
would be called product: movies to feed the many movie chains—
MGM had a partnership with Loews—during a time when more
than three-fifths of Americans saw at least one movie a week. So good
was Thalberg at running this monster machine that, during 1932, the
worst year of the Depression, MGM showed a profit of $8 million.

The studio system was famously hell on talent, especially literary
talent. Among the more glittering literary names Thalberg brought
to MGM were Anita Loos, William Faulkner, Dorothy Parker,
Robert Benchley, James M. Cain, P. G. Wodehouse, George S.
Kaufman, Sidney Howard, and S. N. Behrman. In *The Last Tycoon*,
Fitzgerald has Monroe Stahr remark that he hires good writers,
"but when they get out here, they're not good writers—so we have
to work with the material we have." Thalberg worked writers in
pairs; sometimes, as Fitzgerald has Stahr say, "I've had as many as
three pairs working independently on the same idea," without one
set knowing what the others are doing.

Individual talent never came close to taking precedence under
the old studio system, with the exception only of actors, whom
Thalberg largely considered a species of children. Thalberg was
excellent at choosing, cultivating, and caring for stars. He wrote:

> In pictures, the actor, even more than the play, is the
> thing. He, more than the author, even more than the
> director, must hold the mirror up to life. By his ability
> to convey the author's and the director's ideas to the
> screen and to the people out front, he must transport
> his audience into a dream world.

Thalberg was not without his blind spots. Vieira notes that he was initially wrong about sound movies, thinking they would not soon (if ever) fully replace silent movies. He was wrong, too, about Technicolor, and had to be pushed into it. He was not without standard Hollywood greed, though this can be explained by his understanding that, in Hollywood, you are finally measured by what you are paid. Nor was he above engaging in ego wars with Louis B. Mayer.

THALBERG BEGAN AS MAYER'S GOLDEN BOY. In time, though, Mayer seems to have been made nervous by the younger man's mania for control. The two men's tastes in movies differed widely, with Mayer's running to the sentimental and prudish, never crossing the line of the middlebrow. He also did not appreciate that Thalberg made sure that he received the salary and rewards coming to him, every penny and every perk. Thalberg's wanting control and money, too, was, according to Vieira, the cause of the breakdown between them. At one point, Mayer brought in his son-in-law David O. Selznick to undermine Thalberg's authority. Eventually Thalberg's empire at MGM was broken up, leaving him in charge only of something called "the Thalberg unit," no longer the entire studio, and feeling, as he told colleagues, betrayed. As Vieira wrote in *Hollywood Dreams Made Real*: "Mayer wanted to be appreciated. Thalberg wanted to make films his own way. Neither would acknowledge the other's needs." In the end, Mayer won because he, with his partners in New York, controlled the money—and in Hollywood, then as now and now as forever, the money wins.

The theme of Irving Thalberg's life, in Vieira's recounting, goes beyond the extraordinary level of his odd gifts for organization, the freakishness of his youthful accomplishments. The theme of Thalberg's life was his pure love for making movies. He was always ready to spend more money to get things right; MGM in his day was known as "Retake Valley." He was not opposed to experiment in movies, and thought it good for the industry. No matter how many poor movies were made, he insisted on emphasizing the good ones. He devoted himself to legitimizing movies in the mind of the American public. Behind all this was Thalberg's belief that movies, surpassing the stage, the novel, and all else, were "the greatest form of expression yet."

He was, alas, wrong in this judgment, but far from wrong in trying to raise the level of movies as the great American—and eventually global—art form. In a scene in *The Last Tycoon*, Monroe Stahr is walking the beach near an ocean-front home he is building, when he encounters a black man collecting grunion. They get into conversation, and the man asks Stahr what he does. When he tells him that he works for "the pictures," the man replies that he never goes to the movies—"There's no profit" in them, he says— and he tells Stahr that he "never lets his children go, either." The following day, when he returns to his office, Stahr tells himself that the black man was wrong, and determines that "a picture, many pictures, a decade of pictures, must be made to show him he was wrong." Stahr straightaway cancels four borderline movies he has in the works, and puts back on the front burner a difficult movie he earlier decided not to do. "He rescued it," Fitzgerald writes, "for the Negro man."

Fitzgerald did not get far enough with his novel to bring Monroe Stahr/Irving Thalberg to his death. Life, as the physicians of his infancy had promised, took care of that detail, when Thalberg's heart, after a number of earlier attacks, gave out in 1936, at the age of 37. "Thalberg Dead!" ran the headlines on the day he died.

Thalberg's deft hand made possible many swell movies—*Mutiny on the Bounty, Grand Hotel, The Good Earth, Marie Antoinette, A Day at the Races, A Night at the Opera, Goodbye, Mr. Chips,* and several more—and many entirely forgettable ones among the roughly 400 he worked on. His heritage, in Mark Vieira's view, is in his aspirations for movies as popular but still complex art, movies that could be quirky, took chances, were made without formula, and for grown-ups. Through the painstaking working-out of detail, Irving Thalberg more than anyone else before or since was able to pry magic from film—the same magic that keeps many of us going back to the movies week after week, even though by now we should know that the odds against our finding more of that same magic are considerable.

George Gershwin
Rhapsody Imbued

ALL GENIUS IS INEXPLICABLE, but some kinds of genius are more inexplicable than others. George Gershwin falls into the latter category. The second son of a Russian Jewish family in New York, he was a genius of the natural kind—his mother had no special interest in culture or talent for music; his father ran bakeries, Turkish baths, a cigar store and a pool parlor, and was briefly a bookie—but Gershwin had only to sit down at a piano in his boyhood to realize that in music lay his destiny.

Like many vastly talented people, he could not be accommodated by school, so he dropped out at 15 and went to work plugging songs to vaudeville for a music publisher. Soon he was writing them. At age 21 he had his first hit, "Swanee," with lyrics by Irving Caesar. The song's sheet music "sold in the millions, as did Al Jolson's recording of it," writes Walter Rimler in *George Gershwin*. Rimler's book is an "intimate portrait" that tells the story of its subject's life and career with an admirable economy, showing an impressive feeling for the complexities of Gershwin's character and the twists in his fortunes.

The variety of Gershwin's work, from his early tossed-off Tin Pan Alley songs to his classical compositions, is inexhaustible, yet all the music is unmistakably his. Random and easy though he made it look, Gershwin was never without a plan. "There had been so much chatter about the limitations of jazz," he wrote, recalling his early days as a composer. "Jazz, they said, had to be in strict time. It had to cling to dance rhythms. I resolved to kill that misconception with one sturdy blow." The blow, successfully administered in 1924, was "Rhapsody in Blue."

Throughout his brief life—he died in 1937 at age 38—Gershwin had the golden touch. The phenomenon of George Gershwin astonished everyone—not least Gershwin himself. He was famous for his immodesty, except that in him it came off as something else, self-amazement perhaps. "You know the extraordinary thing about my mother," he once said, "she's so modest about me. . . ." When a friend in Hollywood was driving wildly, Gershwin alerted him: "Careful, man, you have Gershwin in the car." Listening for the first time to a full orchestral rendering of the opera *Porgy and Bess*, he exclaimed: "This music is so wonderful, so beautiful that I can hardly believe I wrote it."

Not F. Scott Fitzgerald but George Gershwin may have been the reigning figure of the Jazz Age. Gershwin holding forth at the piano at parties in Manhattan, everyone gathered around as if by magnetic force—these scenes were among the symbolic tableaux of the 1920s. Samuel Behrman, the playwright and memoirist, described his reaction when he first heard Gershwin at one such party: "I felt on the instant, when he sat down to play, the newness, the humor, above all the great heady surf of vitality. The room became freshly oxygenated; everybody felt it, everybody breathed it."

Gershwin did everything with the throttle all the way out. As a golfer, he is said to have run between holes. He could compose intricate music in a crowded room; in fact, he preferred to do it that way. His being less than conventionally handsome—he had a

GEORGE GERSHWIN

chosen nose and a pendulous lower lip, with an early receding hair-
line—did not get in the way of his notable success with women.
Money from his music royalties rained down upon him, and he
spent it lavishly on clothes, townhouses, dashing cars.

More thorough biographies than Mr. Rimler's slender volume
exist—Edward Jablonski's *Gershwin* at 436 pages, Howard Pollack's
George *Gershwin: His Life and Work* weighing in at 882 pages—
but for those of us interested less in the technical details of Gershwin's music and its performance than in the comet called George
Gershwin that blazed briefly across American skies, Mr. Rimler is

the astronomer of choice. He writes well, is quietly authoritative (he is also the author of *The Gershwin Companion*) and, while discriminating in his selection of details, never loses the larger subject, which is the trajectory of George Gershwin's extraordinary life.

Mr. Rimler remarks in an author's note that Gershwin's was "as personal and original a musical voice as Chopin's" and that the question about his career was not whether he would "choose between jazz or classical, songs or concert works"; rather, the conflict "was about whether he could make full use of his powers." By this Mr. Rimler means how deeply could he develop his astonishing musical gift.

Three stories play through Mr. Rimler's book: one is Gershwin's lengthy love affair with a brilliant woman named Kay Swift; another is his relationship, musical and personal, with his brother, Ira; and finally there is Gershwin's travail in getting *Porgy and Bess* composed, launched, and properly appreciated as a great American opera.

Kay Swift, when Gershwin first met her, was Katharine Swift Warburg, married to James Warburg, a scion of the famous banking family and a man who longed for a life in art. The mother of three daughters, Kay was bright and attractive, a talented musician, in fact a composer herself—she was the first woman to write a successful Broadway musical, *Fine and Dandy* (1930)—and thus well-positioned to understand Gershwin's achievement. Mr. Rimler nicely conveys what kind of woman Kay Swift was by quoting her on whether Gershwin knew he had a masterpiece in the works while composing *Porgy and Bess*. It was like "watching a pitcher who has a no-hitter going for him," she said. "He knows it and you know it; and, in the case of George Gershwin, as in that of the pitcher, nobody mentions the fact at the time."

Their love affair was an entirely open secret, a fact far from painless to her husband. When the Warburgs divorced, Gershwin, who valued his freedom perhaps too much, did not step forth to marry

Kay—probably, Mr. Rimler suggests, a mistake. Unlike tennis, golf, and gin rummy, monogamy wasn't Gershwin's game.

Ira Gershwin was George's older brother and in every way different from him. Where George was brash, Ira was bashful; where George was free-spirited, Ira was under the control of his strong-willed wife; where George was a full symphony orchestra of self-esteem, Ira refused to blow his own piccolo. They meshed beautifully, though, in the realm of talent. Ira Gershwin may have been the greatest lyricist in the history of American popular song, a man born to translate his brother's joyous music into words. He played an essential role in *Porgy and Bess*, George Gershwin's big gamble, in which he set out to stake his claim to being a great American composer.

With a few exceptions, Gershwin had always been treated as a bit of an interloper by contemporary classical composers. Prokofiev spoke slightingly of his piano concerto in F major. At Yaddo, Aaron Copland excluded him from a festival of the works of modern composers. Virgil Thomson wrote crushingly of *Porgy and Bess* that "it is clear, by now, that Gershwin hasn't learned the business of being a serious composer, which one has always gathered to be the business he wanted to learn," though Thomson spoke more kindly of him off the record. Ravel, one of the exceptions among serious composers, delighted in Gershwin's music and recommended him to the great classical music teacher Nadia Boulanger. She claimed that she had nothing to teach Gershwin, a remark that Mr. Rimler holds is "open to interpretation." Did it mean that he was too advanced to require her aid, or did she instead think him hopeless?

While the premiere of *Porgy and Bess* in 1935 marked the zenith of Gershwin's musical accomplishment, the work also signaled the beginning of his fall. To begin with, confusion set in over whether the work was meant to be a musical or an opera; that it carried the subtitle "a folk opera" served only to confuse matters. The reviews, led by that of the *New York Times*'s Olin Downes, were unenthusiastic. Crowds stayed away even when ticket prices were lowered. "There was no need," Mr. Rimler writes, "to spend one's dollars on what had been deemed a pretentious hodgepodge."

The show ran for 124 performances on Broadway—not a catastrophe but certainly not what Gershwin had dreamed of. In a state of depression, he fled, along with Ira, to Hollywood in 1936. They had a 16-week, $55,000 contract with RKO to write music for Fred Astaire and Ginger Rogers—and the charming *Shall We Dance* (1937), with the song "Let's Call the Whole Thing Off," was the result. Gershwin never gave up the hope of a *Porgy and Bess* revival, but such was the elasticity of his musical talent that he could go from writing serious formal music to movie music without a hitch. He had also knocked off the song "Nice Work If You Can Get It" for the Astaire musical *Damsel in Distress* (1937) soon after the debacle in New York, and Mr. Rimler claims that "just about everything he had written since beginning work on *Porgy and Bess* had been a masterpiece."

With his characteristic *joie de vivre*, Gershwin enjoyed Hollywood—the weather, the golf, the women. He had an earnest flirtation with the actress Paulette Goddard. Only the work was dreary, especially after he was hired by producer Samuel Goldwyn, who foolishly failed to appreciate Gershwin. Goldwyn, that philistine of philistines, instructed him to "write hits like Irving Berlin."

All this while a tumor—technically, a "malignant glioblastoma"—was growing in Gershwin's brain. Earlier he had begun to sense the smell of burning garbage; horrific headaches soon set in. His omnipresent energy drained. Several authoritative medical misdiagnoses didn't help. Gershwin began to despair—over his health and his career. Sam Behrman, an old friend, knew the game was up when he visited Gershwin in Los Angeles. "I asked him if he felt like playing the piano. He shook his head. It was the first such refusal I'd ever heard from him."

Why a man whose music has brought so much pleasure to so many people should have spent his last days in wretched pain, certain that his life had been a failure, is one of those sad puzzles for which neither Mr. Rimler nor anyone else has a solution.

Joe DiMaggio

Where'd He Go?

HE BEST CRITERION OF FAME is when a crazy person imagines he is you. In his full-court-press biography of Joe DiMaggio, Richard Ben Cramer does not say whether this ever happened to his subject, but it is difficult to think that it did not. DiMaggio had, after all, first-name fame—fame of the kind that exempts headline writers from even mentioning your last name, like Frank (Sinatra), Johnny (Carson), Barbra (Streisand), Marilyn (Monroe), Michael (Jordan), Jerry (first Lewis, now Seinfeld). It is a small club, and Joe DiMaggio was a charter member.

Fame was DiMaggio's portion, and it was served to him early, often, and throughout his long life. He received it in all its forms, high, mass, and squalid. No doubt he loved it, but it also made him, quite properly, paranoid. "Even paranoids have real enemies," the poet Delmore Schwartz insisted, but it is their friends of whom the immensely famous must really beware. Fame can easily be coined, and, though DiMaggio himself proved excellent at this, turning his mere presence into cash, his signature into gold, he was always leery of others trying to make a buck off his name.

Joe DiMaggio was what is nowadays called an icon. (Once understood to mean a small religious painting, the word "icon" has been called into service in recent years to accommodate the national language inflation, which finds mere "superstar" insufficient.) One of the best reasons *not* to be an icon is that it brings out iconoclasts, often in the disguise of biographers. "The story of DiMaggio the icon [is] well known," writes Richard Ben Cramer. "The story of DiMaggio the man has been buried." His self-appointed task is the indelicate one of exhumation, and his *DiMaggio* leaves plaster shards and shattered glass all over the joint.

Cramer begins his story in 1930, when Joe was fifteen. He was one of nine children, the fourth of five sons, born to a Sicilian fisherman, illiterate in both Italian and English, who lived in the North Beach section of San Francisco. He was, in Cramer's telling, an oddly detached boy, the sort who was not in need of the approval of his pals. People, somehow, came to him. He also had none of the standard marketable skills. He did not want to work on the fishing boat with his father and older brothers; he hated, in fact, the smell of fish. He had no interest in school, and dropped out at fifteen (his elder brothers had done so even sooner). Instead he hung out, scuffled for a few bucks a week selling newspapers, playing poker, finding something that could be resold.

But there was one thing Joe could do: he could hit a baseball, really cream it. Whence this talent? Cramer does not, probably really cannot, say. What can be said is that it did not come from relentless early training or deep determination. DiMaggio entered baseball many decades before Little League came along with its early coaching, which is to say long before play for children, for better and worse, was organized. Kids just met on the playground, chose up sides, had established positions, and played the game. Joe played it supremely well and without great effort.

As a boy, he apparently had no special passion for baseball. He became more interested later when he discovered he could make a few dollars playing on semi-pro teams. At eighteen, he signed with the minor-league San Francisco Seals, where his brother Vince played. (A younger brother, Dominic, also played for the Seals and, later, for the Boston Red Sox.) That first season with the Seals, he had a 62-game hitting streak, batting .340 for the year.

He broke into baseball as a shortstop, a position at which he was not much good. The Seals also tried him at first base, at which he was not much better. After joining the New York Yankees in 1936, he would eventually become, along with Willie Mays in the National League, the greatest centerfielder to play the game, Mays having a flair for the dramatic, DiMaggio a flair for making every catch look as graceful and as easy as a thoroughbred trotting into the winner's circle.

Joe DiMaggio's competence at baseball touched on the profound. He could do six of the seven things required by the game: run, throw, field, hit, hit for power, and—here the sixth, magical quality entered in—do all of the above at times of maximum pressure, "in the clutch," when the game was on the line. The only aspect he never mastered—chiefly because he was never called upon to do so—was pitching. (Babe Ruth began as a pitcher, and, during his years with the Boston Red Sox, was a good one.) DiMaggio also had great sports intelligence, intelligence of a kind that, in my experience, is connected to no other, and which entails the instinctual certainty that prevents one from ever making the kind of mistakes that other players make fairly regularly.

At the plate, DiMaggio was a classic of quiet elegance. "The guy was a *statue*," Lefty Gomez, his Yankee teammate, once said. Tall (6' 2"), smoothly muscled, he stood, stock still, all concentration, fearless during an age when the vocabulary of pitchers included such happily menacing phrases as "a little chin music" and "smoke him inside." He had the sweetest stroke in the game, and was often photographed—as he is on the back cover of *DiMaggio*—at the end of that great follow-through that left him, stride complete, weight on the left foot, bat on the left shoulder, ball (one assumes) either rolling away out of reach in one of the power alleys or in the delighted hands of a fan in the stands at Yankee Stadium.

JOE DIMAGGIO

A DiMaggio strikeout was a rarity—the New York saloonkeeper Toots Shor, one of his pals and hangers-on, said Joe looked better striking out than other men making a hit. In more than 6,000 times at bat over his career, as we learn from Cramer, he was two-and-a-half times more likely to hit for extra bases than to strike out. On the subject of his superior hitting DiMaggio was not much of a theorist; he believed it came from the same place that Aristotle thought the power of making metaphors derived: God.

In his era—roughly from 1936 to 1951, with two years out for stateside service in World War II—DiMaggio's only rivals as pure hitters were Ted Williams, Stan Musial, Hank Greenberg, and, later, his teammate Mickey Mantle (to whom DiMaggio rarely spoke, telling another teammate, "He's a rockhead."). He was especially rivalrous toward Williams, who may have been the better pure hitter and who was the last player in the major leagues to bat .400 in a season. (DiMaggio probably would have matched it in 1939 if he had not been forced to play the last three weeks with an eye infection, which caused his average to drop 30 points to .381.) "He throws like a broad," DiMaggio said of Williams, "and runs like a ruptured duck." Besides, he would add later, Williams never won anything.

DiMaggio won everything. In his thirteen seasons in the majors, the Yankees were in ten World Series, and victorious in nine of them. He was among that small number of athletes who, through the main force of ability combined with attitude, can make a team produce winners. Others have been able to do this in basketball—Michael Jordan most recently—but basketball involves only five men on the court at one time. In football, a quarterback—Joe Montana comes to mind—can sometimes do it, but since there are two separate teams in football, offense and defense, the feat is highly unlikely. It is rarest of all in baseball, where nine men are on the field and no one but the pitcher dominates, and pitchers work only one game in five.

DiMaggio seems to have accomplished it not only through amazing play but also through an Olympian contempt for anyone who contributed to his team's defeat or failed to meet his personal standard. His teammates were in awe of him, in awe of his skill, and no less in awe of his determination to play even when in deep pain. In 1949, he led the American League with 39 home runs, had 155 runs batted in, hit .320, and was in the lineup in 153 of 154 games—playing, as Cramer reports, "hurt in almost every one of them."

A lonely man with no gift for gregariousness, DiMaggio always kept apart from his teammates. Occasionally he would take a young player in hand—the relief pitcher Joe Page is an example Cramer mentions—and build up his confidence. But he dressed for the field in a corner off by himself and spent the half-innings in which he would not be batting near the tunnel to the locker room, alone with a Chesterfield and half a cup of coffee. (A reserve outfielder named Hank Workman had the job of lighting DiMaggio's cigarette just before he arrived in the dugout from centerfield.) He usually made the trip back to his hotel with a friend who was not a team member. A measured aloofness was everywhere part of his style.

Great timing marked not only DiMaggio's playing at the plate and in the field but his larger career. He started with the New York Yankees a year after the great Babe Ruth retired, which seemed to put him in a direct line of succession as the greatest player in the game. When he arrived, the Yanks had gone four years without a pennant; in his rookie year he helped take them to the World Series, which they won.

John Gregory Dunne was no doubt correct to observe in the *New Yorker* that DiMaggio would not have achieved the same fame had he played for St. Louis, Cleveland, or Detroit. New York had its own cachet. With its heavy concentration of high-powered sports-writers working the then more than twelve city dailies, DiMaggio's every move was chronicled in highly colored prose. Besides, television was not yet on the job when DiMaggio entered the majors, exposing players day in and out, subjecting them to inevitably dis-appointing interviews, everywhere erasing whatever aura their on-the-field performance might bring. The burden of description was left to sportswriters and radio announcers, who could make a duel between, say, DiMaggio and the Cleveland fastball pitcher Bob Feller seem like a battle between Achilles and Hector.

Along with all this, DiMaggio had somehow, as Cramer notes, "grown into his face." He became—with his gap-toothed smile and wide nostrils—if not handsome, then, in a masculine version of the *jolie-laide*, a "beautiful-ugly" man. In the realm of sobriquets, he also had two of the best: Joltin' Joe (for his hitting) and The Yan-kee Clipper, which felicitously suggested his stately presence in the ocean that was centerfield in Yankee Stadium. A great sobriquet requires a definite article—Red Grange had The Galloping Ghost; Ted Williams, The Splendid Splinter; George Herman Ruth, The Babe—and The Yankee Clipper seemed a perfect fit.

Raw to the point of being a rube when he came up, DiMaggio did not take long to learn how to fulfill the role of a quiet hero, the epitome of grace under pressure. Although he played as hard as anyone going, he never caused consternation afield by arguing with umpires, badgering opponents, or getting into fights. When an otherwise obscure Brooklyn Dodger outfielder named Al Gionfriddo made an amazing catch on a ball DiMaggio expected to be a World Series home run, DiMaggio, already rounding the bases, kicked the bag at second, an incident so out of character that it is remembered even now. In press interviews he gave little away, and if he had any secrets, the press was not yet devoted to uncovering and exposing them. His taciturnity translated itself as reticent dignity. He came off as a gent: a Hemingway hero in Yankee pinstripes.

Such, at any rate, did The Clipper appear from the outside.

Richard Ben Cramer proposes to show us the less than elegant inside. Not to put too fine a point on it, *DiMaggio* makes Joe out to be a drip, a jerk, a bore, and a creep, with nothing good to be said about him off the baseball field. At one point, early in the book, Toots Shor, whose most honored customers included Jack Dempsey, Ernest Hemingway, and Joe DiMaggio, is quoted offering a definition of class—"a thing," says Toots, "where a guy does everything decent." In Richard Ben Cramer's pages, Joe DiMaggio does almost nothing decent. He is a bad father, a worse husband, a poor friend, a cheapskate, selfish, humorless, a prude operating on a sexual double standard, a solipsist of the highest order.

In his bachelor days, Cramer tells us, DiMaggio was happy to dance between the sheets with any woman who was ready and willing; and, fame being a great aphrodisiac, more than a few were. He was a guest (nonpaying, surely) at the cat-house of Polly Adler, *madame extraordinaire* and author of *A House Is Not a Home*, where he complained that the shiny sheets did not allow him to get enough traction. As did most bachelors of the day, he referred to women as "broads," though in their company he tended to be quite formal. In later years, he was known (here comes the double standard) to send male friends home for a change of clothes if they showed up in mixed company at restaurants neglecting to wear a jacket and tie.

That Joe was not much of a husband also appears on the bill of complaint. What he was, was a husband on the Sicilian model. He married his first wife, an actress named Dorothy Arnold, in 1939, in a wedding in San Francisco that required police crowd control. They had a son, Joe, Jr. Conflict did not take long to get under way. The new Mrs. DiMaggio wanted both her marriage and a career in the movies. Joe did not see much point in the latter. Something had to give, and soon enough the marriage did.

In the middle of this marriage, DiMaggio had his 56-game hitting streak, still unsurpassed in the majors, which ran from May 15 to July 17, 1941, when it was stopped in Cleveland by a negligible pitcher named Al Smith. (The next day he began a streak that lasted for an additional fifteen games.) Once under way, the streak put him in the headlines every day, taking people's mind off the war in Europe. His teammate Lefty Gomez said, "He seemed like a figure, a hero, that the whole country could root for." And they did, except at home; in 1944 his wife sued for divorce, charging mental cruelty. Translation: indifference.

DiMaggio's second marriage, to Marilyn Monroe, has been more exhaustively chronicled than the relationship between Romeo and Juliet. When they first met, she, sweet ditz, was perhaps the only person in the country who had never heard of him. He had been out of the majors for a few years, and their courtship put him back in the headlines. "They are folk heroes, Marilyn and Joe," wrote the sports columnist Jimmy Cannon, "a whole country's pets." They were the best athlete and the sexiest girl, the king and queen of the prom, with the whole nation as high school. They married in 1954, when she was twenty-seven, he thirty-nine. They had only their fame in common.

The marriage was unrelieved hell. She thought he did not care enough about her career; he was jealous and discouraged by her willingness to play the national bimbo. On their honeymoon in Japan, she went off to entertain the troops in Korea. Lots of other men were always sniffing around. She was rumored to wear no underwear, and then, in the famous photograph of her skirt blowing up while she stood on an air grate for the movie *The Seven-Year Itch*, she showed the entire world that this was not so. Joe was on the set the day the scene was shot. Cramer quotes the director Billy Wilder, who recalls "the look of death" on his face. Murder may have been more like it. He roughed her up that night, and three weeks later she filed for divorce. The marriage lasted nine months. "I suppose no one," Oscar Levant quipped at the time, "can be expected to excel at two national pastimes."

The children of the famous do not, for the most part, have uncomplicatedly joyous lives, and Cramer, by more than implication, accuses DiMaggio of making things even worse for his son by being an indifferent father. To be the child, especially the son and namesake, of Joe DiMaggio, and not oneself a good athlete, was to draw a very difficult card in life. Joe, Jr.'s second bad card was being the child of divorce. Prep school, Yale, the Marines, businesses his father set him up in, connections he made for him—nothing seemed to work. He lapsed into drink and drugs, and ended up a middle-aged man with a gray ponytail and false teeth. Left an annual stipend of $20,000 in his father's will, Joe, Jr. died of an overdose of heroin and crack cocaine six months after his father's death in 1999.

That $20,000 stipend leads inexorably to the subject of DiMaggio's cheapness, about which Cramer rattles on endlessly. We are told about the hanger-on who gave him a free Cadillac, to which his response was, "Did you fill it with gas?"; about his habit of carrying his wash to a local laundromat because the machines were fifteen cents cheaper than in the building where he had a free condominium; about how, apart from a single check for $100, he never gave anything to the Joe DiMaggio Children's Hospital in Hollywood, Florida, where he lived out his last years; and, especially, about how he was disinclined to pick up any restaurant check—he was after all known as The Yankee Clipper, not The Yankee Tipper—or in fact pay for anything, even though he had millions tucked away, including a safe-deposit box jammed with $100 bills.

The final major item Cramer puts on DiMaggio's rap sheet is his connection with the mob. The Boys, as we used to call them in Chicago, cultivated the great Italian hero. Every time he went into one of the Boys' restaurants or nightclubs, which in those days included most places in New York, they put a couple of hundred dollars in a special account for him in the old Bowery Bank. One of Joe's greatest patrons among the Boys was not an Italian but a Jew named Abner "Longy" Zwillman, who, Cramer claims, gave DiMaggio three boxes of cash to stash for him before he was murdered—money that DiMaggio later rescued from his house in San Francisco during the earthquake of 1989.

When material of this kind comes up in *DiMaggio*, one especially feels the want of footnotes. Where did Cramer get all this dish? Pete Hamill, the veteran New York journalist, has suggested in a review that Cramer probably got it from third-level mafiosi, adding that "mob guys, particularly low-level hoodlums, are notorious bullshit artists." But even if it were all true, it is unclear how else DiMaggio was supposed to behave. Tell Longy Zwillman and the others that he was too high-principled to accept their kindness? Nothing, after all, was ever asked of him, nor does Cramer claim that DiMaggio was ordered to appear in mob-owned places, let alone do anything that was against the law. Was he supposed to have been saintly enough—or perhaps brave enough—to turn down the money, which was not even handed over directly?

The fact seems to be that the Boys were no less caught up in the mystique of Joe DiMaggio than everyone else. Whenever he flew, American Airlines upgraded him into first-class, assigning him a seat, D5, corresponding to his initial and his old Yankee uniform number. Throughout his life, DiMaggio had guys to run his errands, do his bidding, smooth the way for him. He never asked favors; he didn't have to. Toots Shor, Jimmy Cannon, a man-about-town ticket agent named George Solotaire, a foot surgeon named Rocky Positano, and others rushed to do them for him. They did so not because he commanded or conned them, but because they wanted to—because their friendship with The Clipper came to seem the most significant thing in their lives.

As for his cheapness, even Cramer does allow that DiMaggio picked up checks when out with his teammates. So if any principle was in operation here, it would seem to be that he let people pay who were themselves making a profit by being with him, of whom there were more than a few. If Joe DiMaggio ate in your restaurant, lived in your condominium complex, wore the clothes you manufactured, such would be the rush of other people wanting to do likewise that it all meant money, fairly serious money, in the bank. Because of the magic of his name, and the even greater magic of his presence, he was visited by a plague of leeches all his life. The last seventy or so pages of *DiMaggio* showcase the work in this line of a Florida attorney named Morris Engelberg, who eventually sold, through Sotheby's, DiMaggio's canceled checks, license plate (DiMag5), MasterCard, driver's license, hundreds of signed baseballs, shirts, and other paraphernalia, and just about everything but the tumor in his lung that killed him.

"I'm not great," DiMaggio told the writer Gay Talese in 1966, attempting to put off a request for an interview, pleading to be left alone. "I'm just a man trying to get along." Years later, when first acquainted with the lines from Paul Simon's song "Mrs. Robinson"—"Where have you gone, Joe DiMaggio?/A nation turns its lonely eyes to you"—he is supposed to have responded, "I haven't gone anywhere. I'm employed." Yet if he was not the deep creep presented by Cramer, neither will it do to make him out to be just a dumb jock. He was more complicated than that.

Although a lousy husband, for example, DiMaggio proved an excellent ex-husband to Marilyn Monroe. He looked after her as best he could, coming to her aid whenever needed. This was fairly often, for she needed a lot of looking after, not least when she landed in Payne Whitney for mental problems and he bailed her out. He always despised Frank Sinatra and Peter Lawford for pimping her, and the Kennedy brothers, John and Bobby, for treating her like a whore. Cramer reports that Joe and Marilyn planned to remarry, and when she was found dead in her apartment in 1962 an unfinished letter to him lay beside her body. He went to his own grave believing they—"the fucking Kennedys," as a friend reported him calling them—had killed her.

Nowhere did DiMaggio seem so gallant, or so tragic, as in the aftermath of Marilyn Monroe's death, when he stepped in to take care of all the details of the funeral, seeing that it was conducted in dignified privacy and arranging that fresh roses be sent to her crypt every two weeks "forever." At the time, I remarked on the impressiveness of this to Saul Bellow who knew Arthur Miller, who was Monroe's husband after her divorce from DiMaggio. According to Bellow, Miller had said DiMaggio used to beat her up fairly regularly.

Only two beatings of Marilyn Monroe by DiMaggio are recorded in Cramer's biography, however. I say "only" and "however" because, such is the relentlessness of his attack, if he had known about more he would surely have reported them. Nor, for all his digging in secret sexual places, is Cramer able to report any instances of DiMaggio fooling with another man's wife. Monroe herself, when asked later if Joe hit her, said, "Yes, but not without cause." And she is not the only one who has ever wanted to come to DiMaggio's defense, or to find extenuating circumstances for his behavior. Any reader of *DiMaggio* will feel much the same way.

Henry Kissinger, whose admiration for DiMaggio began at age ten, when he watched him play in Yankee stadium, and who later became a friend, has said: "If you had told me in 1938 that I would be Secretary of State, and I would be friends with DiMaggio, I would have thought that the second was less likely than the first." At *Time* magazine's 75th anniversary dinner, when they wanted DiMaggio to sit at the head table with President Clinton, he refused. He despised the Kennedys as sexual predators, and he despised Clinton on the same grounds. He sat instead with Kissinger and his wife.

In most contests between a biographer and his subject—and contests they often come to seem—it is difficult not to find yourself rooting for the subject. The reason is that the contest is an inherently unfair one, for the biographer has not only hindsight but can bring virtue—if he pretends to it—to bear on his side.

Richard Ben Cramer, cool and with-it though he strains to be, plays the virtue card throughout. If DiMaggio uses the word "broad," or cannot make a go of marriages to two very difficult women, he is a misogynist (a touch of political correctness thrown in at no extra charge). If he fails to tell members of the mob to stick it in their ears, he is practically a member of the mafia himself. If his son does not turn out to be an astrophysicist, he is a rotten father.

In scoring off DiMaggio in all these various ways, in smoking him inside, Cramer's own position is implicitly one of moral superiority. But if the biographer is the morally superior man, why does he seem so much less interesting than his subject and finally so unconvincing? The short answer is that his moral superiority exists only on paper.

Michael Jordan

He Flew through the Air

"Forget it. It'll be close at the end, and then with about twenty seconds left, Michael will have the ball and he'll keep his eye on the clock, and then with a few seconds left he'll go for a jumper and hit it. The Bulls will win, and the legend will live. It's who he is and it's what he does."

—CHUCK DALY, NBA coach

W HEN I WAS THIRTEEN, my father allowed me to put up a wooden backboard and basket in our backyard in Chicago. The yard was small, mostly grass, the only concrete being a narrow sidewalk leading to the alleyway. I used that basket in all seasons, including insultingly cold Chicago winters when I would daily shoot a hundred free throws with my gloves on. At other times, I would play fantasy games. Since I have always been of the realist school, in personal life as in literature, I would limit my scoring to somewhere between 24 and 33 points a game, usually winning for my team by popping in two free throws after the clock had run out. Not in my sweetest fantasies could I ever imagine myself doing what Michael Jordan, the retired star of the Chicago Bulls, would do in actuality some 40 years later. If I was a realist even when grounded in fantasy, he, Michael Jordan, was a magic realist, soaring in life.

In *Playing for Keeps*, his book about Michael Jordan, David Halberstam uses the phrase "Jordanologist" to describe close students of the great player, marketing phenomenon, and international celebrity. Only now do I realize that, since 1984, when he left the University of North Carolina after his junior year to play with the Bulls, Jordanology has been, as the professors say, my subspecialty. Over this period of time I must have seen Michael—as we in Chicago refer to him—play perhaps a thousand games; even though I watched most of them on television, I feel that I know his facial expressions, his moods, his verbal responses at least as well as I do those of most members of my own family. When I acquired cable TV, I did so not chiefly but exclusively in order to see more of Michael before he closed out his career. The prospect of seeing him at night could lift my spirits during the day; actually watching him play—even through the cool medium of the screen—brought me the kind of ephemeral but never-to-be-gainsaid pleasure of a fine meal or a lightish aesthetic experience.

Maybe not so lightish as all that. Having had the chance to observe so much of Michael Jordan in performance may be the equivalent, in sports, of having had tickets to the early years of George Balanchine's New York City Ballet. If this reference to Balanchine seems too elevated, the law of carefully measured accolades has long ago run out on Michael Jordan. By now he has been compared with nearly every genius the world has produced, with the possible exceptions of Goethe and Proust. In many quarters, he has become the standard by which genius in *other* fields is measured. "Frank Galati," I heard a former president of Northwestern University say about a theatrical director who happens to teach there, "is the Michael Jordan of the contemporary theater."

When Michael retired, Jerry Sloan, coach of the Utah Jazz, whom the Bulls twice defeated in the NBA finals on their way to winning six championships in eight years, said that he should be remembered "as the greatest player who ever played the game." Sidney Green,

MICHAEL JORDAN

a journeyman player and briefly a teammate, asserted that Jordan "was the truth, the whole truth, and nothing but the truth, so help us God." Jayson Williams, the power forward for the New Jersey Nets, called him "Jesus in Nikes." Bobby Knight, the coach of Indiana University, once remarked that we would not see his equal in our lifetimes and neither would our children or our grandchildren in theirs. Later he pushed things up a notch by stating that Michael Jordan was the greatest player of all time, not just of basketball but of any sport. My own view is that in Michael we had the reincarnation of Achilles, but without the sulking and without the heel.

CHICAGO HAS NOT BEEN NOTABLE for its winning teams—the Cubs, the stale joke has it, are now going into the 112th year of their rebuilding program. But we have had a splendid run of gentleman black athletes, beginning with Ernie Banks and moving chronologically through Gale Sayers, Walter Payton, André Dawson, and Michael Jordan. These are men who, like a much earlier generation of black jazz musicians, have brought a high degree of quality to their craft and much dignity to their personal bearing. Alas, with the exception of Michael, all have had to settle for playing on losing teams, while Michael, by contrast, after a few early years in the NBA desert without capable teammates, triumphed with an astonishing completeness.

In part because I grew up in Chicago, in part because of the mysteries of temperament, I identify in sports almost exclusively with the losers. The poor guy who misses a crucial field goal that costs his team the Super Bowl, the pitcher who allows a game-winning home run late in the World Series, the nineteen-year-old kid who blows two free throws and knocks his team out of the Final Four—these are the athletes whose long, melancholy off-seasons I ponder, not those who, champagne dripping from their hair, announce they are off to Disney World. Having an athlete like Michael in my life, an athlete who is so clearly a winner, has been a switch, and of a radical sort. Yet in retrospect even Michael's winning has seemed of the dramatic sort, that is, winning against the odds, coming from behind, pulling it out of the fire—which was, of course, his specialty.

I am a Jordanologist of sufficiently long standing to have seen Michael actually *not* come through, even to see him blow a few games with poor passes or by having the ball stolen from him. But the more lasting impression is of the surging Michael, the Michael who could put together a dazzling 24-point fourth quarter before a television audience of twenty million. Even in 1995–1996, when the Bulls won 72 of 81 regular-season games, more than any other team in the history of the National Basketball Association, it seemed—

whether true or not—that the vast majority were won by coming from behind, as often as not with Michael scoring at the buzzer.

IN THIS, AS IN MANY OTHER RESPECTS, Michael Jordan was very much a basketball player of the modern era. As a fan, I myself go back to the game in its medieval phase, being old enough to remember when Jews were still a strong presence. I recall the elegant Dolph Schayes, of the Syracuse Nats; and Nat Holman and, later, Red Holzman, two of the great names in coaching; and Abe Saperstein, the founder and original owner of the Harlem Globetrotters. In the Chicago Public League of my youth, there were coaches named Bosco Levine and Sid Novak, and many of the All-City players had names like Irv Bemoras, Harvey Babetch, and Eddie Goldman. One of the great annual sports events in the city was the game between the Catholic Youth Organization and the B'nai B'rith Youth Organization.

The best athlete in my own neighborhood, Ronnie Rubenstein, a kid two years younger than I, was good enough to start at Louisville, then as now a big-time basketball school; in Louisville, local Jewish businessmen would take the Rube to their tailors for bespoke sport jackets. Sports-minded Jews of my generation and slightly older had a special love for basketball, which may perhaps explain why so many NBA franchises today have Jewish owners. A man named Jerry Reinsdorf is the principal owner and managing director of the Chicago Bulls, and David Stern, the commissioner of the NBA, grew up basketball-crazy in New York.

As for the game itself, when I first came to it the great offensive weapon was the two-handed set shot, and free throws, more often than not, were still made underhand. The set shot elided into the one-hander, the one-hander into the jump shot. The slam-dunk would come later—specifically, with the extraordinary and sudden advent of excellent coordination in large men, which seemed to have happened, quite mysteriously, in the late 1950s.

But the really dramatic change occurred with the integration of black players into big-time college programs and the NBA. As late as the 1950s, Harry Coombs, coach at the University of Illinois, and Branch McCracken, coach at Indiana, did not trouble to recruit blacks; and Adolph Rupp, at the University of Kentucky, was said to have no compunction about expressing his own racist sentiments. The first black in the NBA was Nat (Sweetwater) Clifton, a former Globetrotter who played for the New York Knicks. As everyone knows, basketball turned out to be a game at which blacks excelled and soon came to dominate. A black comedian, when asked why, replied, "It's our golf."

The game has been further jazzed up in recent years by such innovations as the outlawing of the zone defense, the installation in 1954 of the 24-second clock, and the three-point shot. The NBA has also lost the scruffiness that old-line fans like me used to love. I recall seeing a player named Togo Palazzi play a game, on national television, wearing shorts of the wrong color, which suggests not only that he was a careless packer but that NBA teams in the 1950s operated on a very slim budget. Between then and now, the really huge difference has been made by money. In his last season, Michael Jordan's salary was $36 million, and he is said to have earned another $40 million or so through endorsements—for McDonald's, Gatorade, Hanes underwear, Nike, etc.—as well as from royalties and personal contracts.

PROFESSIONAL BASKETBALL has run in waves of success and failure, athletic and commercial. When I first began to watch, the Boston Celtics, with players such as Bob Cousy and Bill Sharman and then later Bill Russell and John Havlicek, were indomitable, magnificent to watch, and downright irritating in their refusal to lose championships. A new phase set in with the sleek New York Knicks of Willis Reed, Earl Monroe, Walt Frazier, Bill Bradley & Co. and the Los Angeles Lakers of Jerry West, Elgin

Baylor, and Wilt Chamberlain. But then the play dipped badly. I recall going to a Bulls-Knicks game at some point in the mid-1970s with Jerome Holtzman, the sports columnist for the *Chicago Tribune.* "They need four or five more balls out there," he remarked as we watched the two teams pound drearily up and down the floor. "One ball isn't enough for these selfish creeps."

Things picked up again with the entrance into the NBA of Larry Bird of the Celtics and Magic Johnson of the Lakers, two players who revitalized the game. Others worthy of a connoisseur's interest—Pete Maravich, Julius Erving, Isiah Thomas, Paul Westphal—came on the scene. Michael Jordan arrived toward the close of Bird's and Johnson's careers, and he clearly represented something new. He took things to a higher level, and brought an excitement of a kind the game had never quite known before.

Power in the NBA is demonstrated in a number of ways. But only a very small number of stars have had the authority, in effect, to appoint their own coaches. In practice, this has meant the power to fire any coach who does not run the team the way the star wishes. Magic Johnson, for example, was able to have Paul Westhead canned because his run-and-gun offense was not Magic Johnson's kind of offense. Larry Bird might have been able to do the same, though under the strong management of Red Auerbach it is unlikely he would have tried.

But Michael Jordan outdid them all: he was able not only to insist on the retention of Phil Jackson, the Bulls' coach during their championship seasons, but to elevate Jackson into serious money—roughly $7 million—during Michael's and Jackson's final year. The alternative was watching Michael retire early or otherwise take his golden-egg-making apparatus away with him, and there could be no mistaking the goldenness of those eggs: David Halberstam reports that, in 1993, with Michael playing, the NBA finals for the first time achieved higher television ratings than the World Series—and when he was not playing the audience dropped by eight million viewers, or roughly a third. In June 1998, *Fortune* estimated the reverberating effect of Michael on the national economy, including tickets, merchandising, television revenues, endorsements, and the rest, at "just about $10 billion—and still counting."

A S FOR WHAT GAVE MICHAEL JORDAN all that allure, commercial clout, and bargaining power, it was, to begin with, his performance on the court. He was a natural—with preternatural strength and speed, huge hands, astonishing leaping ability, amazing stamina. Adding to Michael's leaping ability was his capacity to maintain himself in the air; "hang time" is the term of art here, and at moments—when leaving from the free-throw line for a slam, say—he did seem as if attached to an invisible hang-glider. When Hersey Hawkins, another player, asked him how he executed a certain shot, Michael replied: "When you get up, you hang for three seconds and let the defender fly by and then you release it."

If Michael was a natural, he was a natural who worked hard to improve his game, and who possessed, along with great court savvy, an indomitable, a really quite fanatical, will to win. He began as a slashing, driving player, able to elude defenses and then arrange to score in some inventive way. Later in his career he developed one of the game's great jump shots, which he released high in the air and fading away—a thing of beauty and a joy, if not forever then till the next time he did it. In *The Jordan Rules*, a more critical book than Halberstam's, the journalist Sam Smith records Phil Jackson's continual amazement at Michael's ability to score pretty much at will against even the best players in the world: "It was a curse in some ways to be a comet racing across the game with everyone light-years in your wake."

On the court, finally, Michael was the complete player—as brilliant on defense as on offense. Led by Michael and two teammates, Scottie Pippen and Ron Harper, the Bulls had what was known as the Doberman defense. That is exactly what it must have felt like to play against these guys—as if one were being pursued by a pack of lean, mean Doberman pinschers.

David Halberstam argues that the great NBA players over the past twenty years have not only had a will to win but have been able directly to transfuse this will into their teammates. Not *all* the great players have been able to accomplish this: Julius Erving, one of the most elegant offensive players in the history of the game, could light a fire only under himself; Kareem Abdul Jabbar, one of the most consistently efficient players, could not lead; Wilt Chamberlain, one of the strongest athletes in any sport, was so lacking in this capacity that it seemed a team could not hope to win *with* him (though the Philadelphia 76ers did, once, in 1963). But three players who did have it—and of whom Halberstam provides lengthy accounts—were Magic Johnson, Larry Bird, and Isiah Thomas.

Did Michael? He certainly had the will to win, and to the highest power. But sometimes this worked to the detriment of the team itself. He practiced so hard that he often tended to wear his teammates out. He was a specialist at baiting other players on his own team. If he did not think a newly arrived player fit, he would stay on the guy's back until he either remade himself to Michael's specifications, asked to be traded, or simply disappeared from the league. He had a nice taste for vengeance, never forgetting either a slight or an injury.

BASKETBALL BEGAN AS A NON-CONTACT SPORT, but it has not been one for decades. So violent can the rebounding become that the area around the basket is known among the players as the alligator-wrestling pit. Everyone in the NBA now does weight training. Superior coordination and endurance and style are important, but, at the highest level, without the muscle to back it up they do not come to much. The Detroit Pistons, who dominated the league before the Bulls, did it on sheer physical intimidation; the New York Knicks, under the coaching of Pat Riley, attempted the same thing, though without comparable success.

When Michael Jordan first came into the league it was understood that his then-teammate Charles Oakley was his bodyguard. Anyone roughed up Michael, Oakley would find a way to repay him later in the game. It is dangerous out on an NBA floor, where one's masculinity is regularly tested. Michael himself eventually muscled up. He came into the league at 6' 6" and 185 pounds; he ended his career 30 pounds heavier—all of it muscle, carefully acquired with the help of a personal trainer so that the added weight would not slow him down.

But the largest problem that Michael presented, especially to his own team, derived not from his weight or his manners but from his extraordinary ability, with which he dominated every game. One of his teammates, a now-forgotten center named Dave Corzine, complained that when the team won it seemed it was Michael's doing but when the team lost it was everyone else's. A man with so much talent tends to render the concept of teamwork beside the point, if not wholly to derogate it.

When the Bulls first attempted to install their complicated Triangle offense, which would, among other things, have taken some of the pressure off Michael's having to score so frequently, he described it derisively as "an equal-opportunity offense." In *The Jordan Rules*, Sam Smith reports that once, during a time-out, Phil Jackson was designing a complex play in a tight spot. Cutting him short, Michael told him, "Give me the fuckin' ball." The temptation to do just that in each and every tight spot had to be great. Basketball writers took to calling the Bulls "Michael and the Jordanaires," and Michael himself referred in a press conference to his teammates as "my supporting cast"—not a smart move in a man who made few bad moves, on the court or off.

OFF THE COURT, one of the reasons Michael was able to garner so much endorsement money is that he gave off the solidest of vibrations. Bill Russell, the great center of the Boston Celtics and then for a few years coach of the Seattle Supersonics, is said to hold a low opinion of most contemporary professional players. Yet he thought Michael an exception, a young man of good character. Halberstam notes in him "an innate elegance and coolness." He could make baldness look good, he wore clothes splendidly, and if there are still best-dressed-men lists he must be atop most of them. "I wanna be like Mike," was the tag line from his Gatorade commercial, and many people did.

He also had a way of making people forget about race. "As Jordan smiled," Halberstam writes, "race simply fell away." In good part this was owing to his absolute refusal to whine, complain, or show moodiness of the kind too many black athletes are susceptible of whenever things do not go their way. Unlike many of them, Michael never fell back on white racism as an excuse to justify poor performance or broken contract negotiations. No less impressively, he kept himself well away from the drug and easy-sex scenes that in recent decades have been part of the world of NBA players, young men with the dangerous combination of too much money and too much free time on their hands. The closest he came to scandal was when he lost serious-sized bets to a golf hustler with a criminal record.

Michael has also kept himself free from politics. When the Nike company was found to be manufacturing its products at low wages in southeast Asia, columnists in the *New York Times* proclaimed that Michael ought to denounce the practice and perhaps threaten to break with the company. But he chose not to speak on the matter—or on any other, similar matter. After one of the Bulls' championships, he even declined to attend the team meeting at the White House with George Bush, preferring to play golf. Whether he thinks politics bad for business, or just does not care, nobody knows for certain; perhaps a combination of the two keeps him apolitical.

Halberstam refers to Michael as "very well-spoken." I disagree. I would say he is half well-spoken. Certainly he has mastered the jock jabberwocky that passes for analysis in post-games interviews: "I thought we had a nice flow of energy out there, especially in the second half, when the momentum seemed to shift. But it was a question of whether we could keep our focus down the stretch and if our bench could step up, which they were able to do." He can also do the false-humility bit as well as anyone: at his retirement press conference, with journalists from all over the world gathered in a huge hall, he began by reminding everyone of a recently murdered Chicago policeman, whose funeral was taking place the same day, noting that this was the real story of the moment.

Michael is more believable when his natural and controlled—and, I would add, earned—arrogance shows through. The genuine Michael is the man who replied, when asked what advice he might give to his then-teammate Dennis Rodman, who had taken to having himself photographed in a wedding dress: "I'd advise him to wear pants as often as possible." This is also the Michael who is said to have regularly driven the better part of the 30-mile trip from his suburban home to Bulls games in Chicago on the shoulder of the Kennedy Expressway. Typically, the police, if they stopped him, would recognize him and let him go; when necessary, he gave them tickets to the game or a signed basketball before driving off.

UNE SAISON EN ENFER, Arthur Rimbaud titled one of his two books of poems, but Rimbaud did not know the half of a season in hell of the kind Bull's fans are currently undergoing without Michael Jordan. The team is currently in last place in its division in a season truncated by a long strike, and we figure to undergo many a sad *saison* more.

Without Michael, professional basketball itself has come to seem, at least to this fan, flat, devoid of drama, without magic. Still, one counts one's blessings. Having spent too many hours watching boys and men hit, kick, and throw balls, and having been born too late for Babe Ruth or Bobby Jones or the prime of Joe Louis, I am grateful that I was around to see my share of Michael Jordan. A fine rousing spectacle, watching this magnificent athlete who turned his sport into an art—the art of coming through in the clutch, which he did, splendidly, time after time after time.

James Wolcott

The Voyeur

I N *LUCKING OUT*, James Wolcott's memoir of the 1970s, one
learns that its author is a man of humble origins. He was born,
he reports, into a drab working-class family in Baltimore:
"socially corner-pocketed," as he puts it in one of the many phrases
he avails himself of that have more flair than precision, "and Beauty
deprived." He began his professional life even humbler, as a rock
critic for *The Village Voice*. In the hierarchy of arts criticism, that of
rock ranks just a notch above the criticism of marbles.

Rock music, like sex, doesn't really require being written about
it. Best to enjoy it if you can and shut up about it afterward. But
this doesn't stop its critics from taking up the old air guitar—once
in the form of a typewriter, today in that of a laptop—and stompin'
away. An early critic of rock, my friend the late Albert Goldman,
who wrote iconoclastic biographies of Elvis Presley and John Lennon, many years ago sent me an essay he wrote on The Doors—
"C'm on baby, light my fire" and all that—which caused me to buy
the group's most recent album. When I told him I had done so, he
asked me what I thought of The Doors. "Al," I replied, "they should
have sung your essay."

Beginning as a rock critic explains a lot about James Wolcott's overwrought prose—that old air guitar—which he slathers lavishly on all subjects. "Being glib is harder than it looks," he writes. To which I would reply that finding a paragraph in his memoir free of heavy injections of false energy and sloppy phrasing isn't any easier. Wolcott will strike off a straight arresting sentence, then follow it up with two or three clotted ones, usually larded with sexual metaphors, similes, and allusions. "I had too much the altar boy in me to seize the bitch goddess of success by her ponytail and bugger the Zeitgeist with my throbbing baguette," is but one example among scores. In writing about punk rock, he alerts us that this was a time before "the gold medallions and furry testicles of disco descended." (Get that metaphor to a urologist.) "A date movie for the damned, *Looking for Mr. Goodbar* looked as if it had been coated from floor to ceiling with contraceptive jelly. . . . " "Niche journalism hadn't yet whittled too many writers into specialty artists, dildos for rent." Such prose is beyond mere editing; it requires Drano.

"Our idols are our instructors," writes Wolcott, and his own idols have been Norman Mailer, Seymour Krim, John Leonard, Marvin Mudrick, Alfred Chester, and above all Pauline Kael. What these writers have in common is that—with the exception of Mudrick, a literary attack specialist—they all vaunt and themselves went on instinct, and had no great regard for intelligence. Pauline Kael once remarked in Wolcott's presence of the movie reviewer David Denby: "All that boring intelligence." If a porn movie, a rock performance, a book feels good, it must, *ipso facto*, be good. Feeling, which must never be betrayed, is all.

Lucking Out includes chapters on Wolcott's days at *The Village Voice*, his friendship with Pauline Kael, his fascination with Punk Rock as he encountered it at the CBGB (Country, BlueGrass, Blues) bar in the Bowery, his interest in pornographic movies, and his discovery, the illegitimate child at this family reunion, of the burnished beauty of the New York City Ballet.

The book begins with Wolcott's dropping out of a college called Frostburg State in Maryland during his sophomore year and taking his chances on a career in New York. The goad for Wolcott's leaving school and making a raid on Manhattan was a letter from Norman Mailer. Watching Mailer's antics one night on television while he was under attack from Gore Vidal and Janet Flanner and Dick Cavett, Wolcott wrote an article for his college paper on the melee—a tempest, more precisely, in a demitasse—in defense of Mailer. When he sent the article to Mailer, the novelist responded by suggesting that Wolcott apply for a job at *The Village Voice*.

Wolcott was eventually given a menial job at the *Voice*—first in the circulation department answering phone complaints, then as a receptionist of sorts—from which he was able to jump himself up through writing brief entries, then longer pieces on rock concerts and other popular culture oddments. Charm, one gathers, has never been even Wolcott's short suit, and his failure to please his boss at the *Voice*, the city news editor, a woman named Mary Perot Nichols, resulted in his being fired.

"From that point onward," he writes, "I never worked a regular office job again, solely writing for a living, something that would have been impossible if New York hadn't been a city of low rents [in the 1970s] and crappy expectations that didn't require a trust fund or a six-figure income for the privilege of watching everything fall apart before your eyes." *Lucking Out* is as much a book about New York in the 1970s as it is about James Wolcott. No one would argue that the 1970s in New York was a golden age, unless one's taste ran to grunge, graffiti, unorganized crime, aggressive begging, and ubiquitous squalor.

In one of his dreary Greenwich Village apartments, from which the view presented on the streets below was of muggings and sexual exhibitionism, Wolcott one day received a phone call from the movie critic Pauline Kael. She liked an article he had written about stand-up comics, and now invited him, in effect, to join the cult devoted to her and become, as the various young men in the cult became known, one of the Paulettes. (The names of some of the other Paulettes are David Kehr, Michael Sragow, Joe Morgenstern, Terrence Rafferty, Owen Gleiberman, and, mentioned earlier, David Denby, who published an essay in *The New Yorker* in 2003 called "My Life as a Paulette.")

In his lengthy chapter on Pauline Kael, Wolcott records several of her more wickedly amusing remarks about John Simon, Joyce Carol Oates, Joan Didion, and others. (A shame Kael, who always mocked Didion's stylish despair, wasn't alive to comment on Didion in her current professional-mourner phase.) She was death on Neil Simon and Mike Nichols ("God, the shit he gets away with!" she said of the latter). William Styron and Gore Vidal were also on her black list. She sniffed, then snuffed out, pretension, which in the making of movies there is never a short supply. Of the movies of John Cassevetes she wrote that he exhibits "the kind of seriousness that a serious artist couldn't take seriously." She was not much taken with Woody Allen, and thought even less of him after he became a genius.

Kael never allowed herself to see a movie twice, lest thoughtfulness kick in, eliminating feeling, and ousting original gut instinct. "One thing I learned from Pauline," Wolcott writes, "was that when something hits you that high and hard, you have to be able to travel wherever the point of impact takes you and be willing to go to the wall with enthusiasm and over it if need be, even if you look foolish or 'carried away,' because your first shot at writing about it may be the only chance to make people care."

Wolcott's exact relation with Pauline Kael isn't entirely clear. Was he her Boswell and best imitator, or merely her Jerome Zipkin, the man known for walking fashionable women in Manhattan. He notes that she would sometimes read her *New Yorker* movie reviews to him over the phone. He was among those invited to join her for screenings of new movies, where her most glancing comments could gravely upset producers of the movies. Friendship with Pauline Kael came at a price; it was said that one was allowed to disagree with her about three movies—but no more. Wolcott claims no influence upon Kael, and, rather the reverse, feared her influence upon him, or at least feared her wanting to control his life by choosing not merely his opinions but also his lady friends.

"In a sense," Wolcott writes, "we would all fail Pauline because none of us would surpass her defiant nerve, her resounding impact." Certainly no critic stirred up more talk about his or her subject than did Pauline Kael about the movies during her years, 1968–1991 (minus the time she spent on a failed excursion as a producer and consultant in Hollywood), at *The New Yorker*. Her opinions on movies were far from conventional: she didn't care for Charlie Chaplin, she disliked *Chinatown* and *Butch Cassidy and the Sundance Kid*. She raved about *Last Tango in Paris*, comparing its historical importance to the night of May 29, 1913, that Stravinsky's *Le Sacre du Printemps* was first performed. She was always brilliant but frequently wrong. She could treat a throwaway movie like *Popeye* as if it were Pindar. Moral seriousness in movies seemed to infuriate her; she would supply that on her own.

Pauline Kael's style could be imitated—contemporary slang, kitchen confidentiality—but not her passion. Passion is what one feels missing from James Wolcott's writing. In an author's note to a collection of political pieces published under the title *Attack Poodles and Other Media Mutants*, Wolcott wrote: "Don't fake what you don't feel is an adage I try to live and write by, because the piece that means the most to me will mean the most to the reader as long as the emotions behind the arguments run true." But behind his bloated prose, his relentless with-it-ness, his slashing insults, one doesn't finally know what James Wolcott stands for, what truly matters to him.

In *Lucking Out*, Wolcott refers to his own sense of detachment as a young man and writer:

But this hanging-back business was more than precedence and habit. It betrayed my reluctance, my fear of
getting too close to anybody or anything; my preference for maintaining detachment, distance, for avoiding
involvement and allowing myself a quick escape route
from where I found myself. I wanted to take everything
in, from safe afar, through a panoramic lens.

Yet the line between being detached and being a voyeur can be
blurry, and Wolcott, man and critic, frequently smudges it.

What Wolcott claims changed all this was his engagement with
punk rock. This began with his untrammeled admiration for the
singer Patti Smith. The pages on punk rock in *Lucking Out* are perhaps the most embarrassing in Wolcott's memoir. Wolcott sets off the
full lawn-assortment of fireworks in describing how it first hit him:

The band wasn't as tight and motoring as it would become
(especially after Jay Dee Daughtery joined on drums),
but it also wasn't the Fugs futzing around, and Patti already had her stage persona pencil-sharpened into a self-
conscious, couldn't-care-less wild child, playing with her
zipper like a teenage boy with a horny itch, pistoning her
hips, hocking an amoeba blob of spit between songs,
scratching her breast as if addressing a stray thought,
and, during the incantatory highs, spreading her fingers
like a preacher woman summoning the spirits from the
Pere Lachaise graveyard where Jim Morrison and Oscar
Wilde were buried to rise and reclaim their former glory.

Punk rock is, I suppose, an acquired taste, like that for arsenic. If
you don't have it, sentences such as the following aren't magically
going to infuse you with it:

The band called the Sic Fucks—whose backup sing-
ers, Tish and Snooky (the Laverne and Shirley of the

East Village), dressed onstage in nuns' cowls and Bettie Page lingerie, were the entrepreneurial founders of the St. Marks Place landmark store Manic Panic—endeared themselves with such plainly felt sentiments as "St. Louis sucks" and "Chop Up Your Mother," the lead singer, Russell Wolinsky, doing a hilarious running patter between numbers like some Catskills emcee, mocking punk pretenders and crusaders (he could be scathing about the Clash and their commando attitude), the scene has evolved far enough to burlesque itself.

Perhaps, like the Spanish Inquisition or the Great San Francisco Earthquake of 1906, you had to be there.

Of his enthusiastic if not entirely decipherable advocacy of punk rock, Wolcott writes that "it was nice not feeling like the bad guy in print for a change." Praise does not come easily to Wolcott; nor, when he attempts it, does it persuade. In what he calls "my ruthless climb to the top of the middle," Wolcott, as he writes, "developed a reputation for being 'a smart-ass' in print." I have myself always thought of him as a hit man, with no mafia behind him, a man who killed for the sheer pleasure of expressing his free-floating hostility. "When I flick back at the book reviews I did in the seventies, I sometimes wince at the nasty incisions I inflicted on writers when I crossed the line between cut and cutthroat (I won't quote examples—no need to inflict wounds)." One of my books in those days was so inflicted; the experience resembled going to bayonet practice, with your book serving as the straw-filled bag.

Wolcott doesn't have much of interest to say about porn movies in the 1970s, though it does allow him to crayon in some of the scuzziness of Times Square in those days. His introduction to porn movies began with a *Village Voice* assignment. Porn had in common with punk, he writes, that both "were amateur uprisings from below deck, ragtag operations of low production values and high casualty tolls where fame was sought under an assumed name." Describing the crowd at porn movies, Wolcott writes:

> Porn hobbyists and rapid rejaculators with dark circles under their eyes and dull hair never reap the benefits of the dramatic gutter romance of alcohol or drug addiction, the binges and blackouts and bleary dawns in strange beds, the Christly withdrawal convulsions of the racked flesh and the beatific predawns that lead to the resurrection of recovery, reentry into society.

Fun.

When he encountered Balanchine's New York City Ballet, which he began attending with some regularity, Wolcott was staggered. Witnessing high art in pure form after years of playing exclusively in the grimy grey sandbox of popular culture—writing about punk, porn, television, the whole shabby works—blew him away. "Ballet," he writes, "was nearly everything I wasn't, and what I wasn't was what I must have wanted most." The New York City Ballet, then still under the direction of George Balanchine, the last living hero of high modernism, "remained a pennant-bannered Monaco moated and aloof from the nagging needlings of the Zeitgeist to be relevant, socially concerned, hip, happening, and in harmony with the vibrating moment . . . ." Perhaps slides would help such overheated prose.

Still, to be "relevant, socially concerned, hip, happening, and in harmony with the vibrating moment" remains the name of Wolcott's desire. Whether he is writing about the media, popular culture or politics—on politics he eschews analysis and plays the insult comedian, a Bill Maher with a gaudier vocabulary—Wolcott is intensely, relentlessly, hopelessly with-it, breathing heavily in the attempt to stay twenty minutes ahead of the loop. Always a mistake, this venture, because with-it-ness does not comport well with getting older, and Wolcott, who will be sixty this year, is no longer a kid. Unless he is up for wearing one of those depressing grey ponytails, James Wolcott, clearly, needs a new style—in fact, he needs an entire intellectual makeover.

Malcolm Gladwell

Jack-out-of-the-Box

M ALCOLM GLADWELL is a slender man, still youthful-looking, sporting an afro gone haywire, as if he had just put his finger in a live electrical socket. The effect is to make him resemble nothing so much as a Jack-in-the-Box. Like a Jack-in-the-Box, he pops up here (on C-SPAN), there, (on You Tube), and everywhere (giving, it is reported, talks to corporations for impressively large fees). Yet Jack-in-the-Box isn't quite right. What Gladwell, whose stock in trade is to challenge what he takes to be received opinions and conventional wisdom, prefers to present himself as is, in one of the reigning clichés of our day, an "out-of-the-box" thinker. He is, one might say, our very own Jack-out-of-the-Box.

A Village Explainer par excellence, Gladwell will tell you how Hush Puppies shoes came back into style, why Korean airline pilots had such a dismal flight record, what causes policemen to lose it and shoot innocent men, and ever so much more. A strong appetite must exist for such explanations as he provides, for all three of his books—*The Tipping Point* (2000), *Blink* (2005), and now *Outliers* (2008)—have been immensely successful, lounging for weeks and weeks atop the *New York Times* and other bestseller lists. Perhaps it requires another Village Explainer to account for this remarkable success.

Explanation of the kind that Malcolm Gladwell specializes in is evidently reassuring. The point of explanation is to make the world seem more intelligible. T. S. Eliot said that humankind cannot bear too much reality, but in a secular age it seems able to stand mystery even less. In his books Gladwell nicely eases the mystery out of life by informing his readers how, as he understands it, the world really works: And it works, if he is to be believed, quite rationally, if one will only stop and think about it. The happy news is, if you find Gladwell's various explanations persuasive, not only are the clouds of mystery gone but the sunshine of infinite promise glows in the sky high above. Everything depends, of course, on whether you find his explanations genuinely persuasive.

The Gladwellian method is by now well established, if not formulaic. He takes a received opinion—the superiority of young Chinese at mathematics, say—sets out the conventional wisdom on the subject, and then refutes this wisdom with the aid of anecdotes backed up by one or another social-scientific study. Gladwell does social science—second-hand social science, really—with a twist: The twist is that he uses it inevitably to supply happy endings. Attend to his instruction and you, too, can spot trends, think more clearly under pressure, and now, with *Outliers*, increase your chances to achieve an impressive success.

"In *Outliers*," Gladwell writes, "I want to convince you that . . . personal explanations of success don't work." People who enjoy resounding successes, he holds, "are invariably the beneficiaries of hidden advantages and extraordinary opportunities and cultural legacies that allow them to learn and work hard and make sense of the world in ways others cannot." In the understanding of what lies behind success, Gladwell's position is that nurture (the social

MALCOM GLADWELL

conditions surrounding one) is much more important than nature (one's intrinsic, or God-given, talents and character).

Gladwell's methods in this book remain much as in his two earlier books. He tells anecdotes supported by social-science research, all written up in prose that Richard Posner, in a devastating review of *Blink* in the *New Republic* that demonstrates the thinness of Gladwell's use of social-science research, characterized as "for people who do not read books." Gladwell's is a prose accessible, mildly charming, with all sense of intellectual struggle or conflict neatly removed: a good read, in the cant phrase.

Gladwell often sets up his reports on psychological or social-scientific research with piquant thumbnail sketches. Tall, wearing three earrings and a metal plate in his head, availing himself of profanity of a kind that would make an Algerian camel driver blush, Zack Zipperman, PhD has for the past 26 years, in his windowless laboratory at MIT, been teaching white mice to dance the cha-cha-cha, with interesting results for those who can't comprehend why men born after 1942 never carry handkerchiefs. I parody, but not that wildly.

The true target of attack in *Outliers* is the notion "that success is a function of individual merit, and that the world we all grow up in and the rules we choose to write as a society don't matter at all." (I don't, incidentally, know anyone who would say that the context of individual success, the environment in which it takes place, is negligible, but let's allow that straw man to stand.) "The closer psychologists look at the careers of the gifted, the smaller the role innate talent seems to play and the bigger the role preparation seems to play," Gladwell writes. When one was born, into which ethnic group or social class, and under what cultural conditions, in Gladwell's pages everywhere trumps any natural aptitude or extraordinary savvy a person might have. "Outliers," according to Gladwell, "are those who have been given opportunities—and who have had the strength and presence of mind to seize them."

GLADWELL ARGUES, FOR EXAMPLE, that Bill Gates wouldn't have been the success he is today if he hadn't been born wealthy and sent to a private school that could afford him unlimited time to work on a mainframe computer, where he learned and mastered his trade. Yet Steve Jobs, if I have his biography correct, came from a broken home, grew up with adoptive parents, and scored a success quite as considerable as Gates's by hanging around nearby Hewlett-Packard where he attended lectures and got a summer job and managed to learn from fellow employees.

No one would argue that when a person was born is unimportant in determining his career. But in *Outliers* Gladwell makes it seem crucial. (I should say where one was born might be even more significant: Had Steve Jobs been born in Detroit, he might today have been an automotive designer; had I, whose birth date is 1937, been born in Europe I should, like as not, have gone to the gas chambers as a child.) *Outliers* begins with a consideration of the fact that so many successful Canadian hockey players seem to have been born in January, February, or March. The reason is that, in the Canadian equivalent of Little League, the early deadline for players is January, and those born nearer to the beginning of the year have, in the early years of life, a distinct advantage of physical maturity over those born later in the year. Gladwell contends that this advantage aggregates over the years, and on a chart—he tends to be big on charts; they give that old secure social-science feel—shows that a large number of Canadian professional hockey players were also born early in the year of their respective births.

Something to it, perhaps, but not all that much. Athletic ability tends to even out over time, and in my experience, talent will show, and so will physical gifts. Michael Jordan, who came into his full height relatively late in his youth, could see the entire basketball court more clearly than any player of his or perhaps any other time; the quarterback Brett Favre has physical courage of a kind that date of birth, culture, or anything else can't explain; the pitcher Greg Maddux has the gift of athletic intelligence (he doesn't make mistakes) that has more than compensated for his less than astounding physical attributes; and for all I know all three of these magnificent athletes may have been born on the eve of Yom Kippur.

Gladwell notes that people born between 1935 and 1945—before, that is, the Baby Boom—were fortunate in belonging to the 20th century's smallest birth cohort, owing to the Depression. The advantage in this is that college admissions were easier for them, fewer people being around to apply for the many openings available. Yet for all its advantages, I would add, this generation, of which I happen to be a member, has never put a president in the White House. Go figure.

Gladwell also remarks on the advantage of New York Jewish lawyers born around 1930 who, because anti-Semitism kept them out of white-shoe firms, turned their attention to cases entailing proxy fights with hostile takeovers and the litigation that followed from them. These cases later became among the most lucrative in legal work. Date of birth, once again, if Gladwell is to be believed, is destiny.

But long practice at one's line of work is no less important. The chief reason for the Beatles' smashing success, Gladwell holds, is that, when they first set out, they worked in the strip joints of Hamburg, where they played six- and eight-hour stretches every day, strumming and drumming their way to international success. No doubt, all this time that the Beatles had to work up their songs, to meld their various talents, was a great help. But they also happen to have had, in Paul McCartney and John Lennon, two immensely gifted songwriters along with a fortunate—and no doubt fortu-itous—combination of personalities and talents who, together, comprised the astonishingly successful group. Eliminate Lennon, eliminate McCartney—poof! The Beatles are just four more work-ing-class kids hoping to win the rock 'n' roll lottery.

With his penchant for precise formulation, Gladwell sets out the 10,000-Hour Rule required for success in any field of endeavor, be it computer programming, hockey, classical music, mathematics, what have you. His false precision aside, who would argue against the notion that practice, if it does not always make perfect, helps? But what Gladwell leaves out are the elements of passion and desire that sustain an athlete, an artist, a scientist in the loneliness of his relentless practicing.

For three decades I taught courses in prose style to students who, by taking the course, had in effect announced their interest in becoming writers. Some were immensely impressive in their talent—much more talented than I at their age. Yet many of the most talented among them washed out, drifting off, perhaps happily enough, into other kinds of work, settling for the consolations of security, marriage, family life, for all I know excessive venery. Why? Not, I think, for want of practicing—for failing to put in Malcolm Gladwell's requisite 10,000 hours—but for want of desire. They didn't want to be writers strongly enough. Whence does desire derive? I don't know, and neither, I venture to say, does Gladwell. Nor would a full battalion of scientists or social scientists in white coats armed with plush research grants be likely to find out. In the realm of desire, we are in the presence of a mystery and have no choice but to live with it.

Cultural background is another crucial determinant in Malcolm Gladwell's kit of handy explanations. Nobody doubts that being Jewish, French, Chinese, Mexican, Swedish, Indian, etc., brings with it its own rich mental cargo. A person's ethnicity and nationality are always worth inquiring about, and are often of the greatest interest. The tendency is to dismiss such inquiries, because their history has been fraught with prejudice, treating the inquiries themselves as potentially dangerous.

Gladwell, understanding this, suggests that we need to get over it if we are to recognize that taking cultural background into consideration can be of the utmost importance. His first example of this is the deference culture of Koreans, which he believes was for many years responsible for the poor record of Korean airline pilots. Co-pilots were too deferential to their superiors, the pilots, and they were also too deferential in dealing with control tower personnel, often noted for their no-nonsense aggressiveness, at such places as LaGuardia Airport, for example.

Through reprinting snippets from the recovered black-box conversation of a Colombian airlines (Colombia is another deference culture) co-pilot with both his pilot and the LaGuardia control tower of a plane that went down near New York, Gladwell shows that what the psychologists call "mitigated speech"—speech that is not direct and straightforward, owing to deference—had a great deal to do with causing the crash. Gladwell even goes so far as to write that, where mitigated speech prevails, "Planes are safer when the less experienced pilot is flying, because it means the second pilot isn't going to be afraid to speak up."

All this is belied, of course, by the experience of the US Airways Flight 1549 plane captained by Chesley B. Sullenberger III, whose perfect landing, under conditions of maximum stress in the Hudson River, saved 155 passengers. Captain Sullenberger, a veteran pilot, in his first interview, claimed that he knew that nothing less than a perfect landing—wings exactly level, nose slightly up, at a descent rate that was survivable, landing at just the right speed—would do to bring the plane down without destroying it. "I was sure I could do it," he said afterwards, without the least braggadoccio. No explanation for this—in birth date, cultural conditioning, even practice—for the saving of the lives of the passengers of Flight 1549, except bloody wonderful good luck in having so fine a pilot in charge.

When it comes to the question of why Asians, and in especial Chinese, tend to excel at mathematics, Gladwell upholds the "importance of attitude in doing mathematics." He then sets out a claim for the Chinese cultural inheritance of patience and scrupulous attention to detail required by the cultivation of rice paddies, which involve relentless long days of work every day of the year. (American farming, by contrast, as he informs us, is merely seasonal.) Such work is part of the cultural inheritance of the Chinese, we are told, and the care and patience that go into the cultivation of rice are useful in the cultivation of mathematical skills, for patience is of the highest value in doing math.

Something to it, perhaps, but, again, not all that much, or at least not enough to persuade. In the same cultural vein, Gladwell remarks that many Jews do well in business because their parents and grandparents, as immigrants to the United States, started out in the needle trades, often working on their own at home at the end of the factory day. This, and a taste for work that they could throw themselves into, encouraged entrepreneurship in their children. Hold the cultural interpretation, hold the secondary social science. In their place, I submit a rough Jewish aphorism, which runs, "Only a schmuck works for someone else," the short interpretation of which is that, insofar as possible, it is good not to have one's fate in the hands of anyone but oneself.

In *Blink*, Gladwell wrote that "there are times when we demand an explanation when an explanation isn't really possible." But such modesty isn't really what his books are about. Nor are all his explanations disappointingly thin, half-convincing at best. In *Blink* he includes a section on how auditioning classical musicians' performances from behind a screen has, over the years, eliminated the prejudices against women in classical music, so that today most symphony orchestras, once male-dominated, are roughly half-female. Jumping out of the box, as is his wont, Gladwell suggests that it might make sense to have defendants in criminal trials also behind screens, so that jurors will not convict them on their looks or manner. Like George Costanza in *Seinfeld*, Malcolm Gladwell tends to go too far.

In another instance, Gladwell compares the fortunes of a man with a very high IQ named Chris Langan, who has not had the success his raw intelligence would seem to deserve, with that of J. Robert Oppenheimer, the Berkeley physicist who headed the program to develop the atomic bomb. He concludes that Oppenheimer succeeded because he came from a wealthy and cultivated family, with all that implied in natural advantages in education and culture, where Langan came from a violent, dysfunctional one, and that, consequently, Oppenheimer was never daunted by the kind of minor setbacks that cost Langan the chance of a brilliant career. He caps this by saying that Oppenheimer had "a sense of entitlement" unavailable to poor

Langan; backed up by a sociological study done by someone named Annette Lareau, he claims that "this is the advantage that Oppenheimer had and that Chris Langan lacked."

J. Robert Oppenheimer, permit me to suggest, was a man of such suavity, subtlety, and layered complexity as to be quite beyond Malcolm Gladwell's ken and comprehension. One cannot say about such a man that the secret to his complicated and, in many ways, tortured life was that his birth bestowed a sense of entitlement in him. One can say it, of course, but in so saying one is dealing in the grossest caricature—social-science cartooning, really, nothing more—and has vastly distanced oneself from reality.

Too frequently one reads Gladwell's anecdotes, case studies, potted social-science research and thinks: interesting if true. Yet one feels naggingly doubtful about its truth quotient. So much Gladwell writes that is true seems not new, and so much he writes that is new seems untrue. Preponderantly, what he reports feels more like half- and quarter-truths, because they do not pass the final truth test about human nature: they rarely, that is, honor the complexity of life.

Only in *Outliers* has a political note sounded clearly in Gladwell's writing. The problem with life, it turns out, is an environment problem. All that is required to make life better, fairer, sweeter in every way, is to change the environment. "To build a better world we need to replace the patchwork of lucky breaks and arbitrary advantages that today determine success—the fortunate birth-dates and the happy accidents of history—with a society that provides opportunities for all," Gladwell writes. "The world could be so much richer than the world we have settled for."

The first step in the bestseller formula is to tell people something that they want to hear. Gladwell tells his readers that, with a few sensible alterations—a nip here, a tuck there in society's institutions, throw in a bit of persistence and lots of practice—everyone has a shot at success such as that achieved by the Beatles, Bill Gates, J. Robert Oppenheimer, you name him. In prose that never lingers over complication, he explains that life is fairly simple; no great mystery about it. Nothing cannot be explained, nothing not changed, nothing not improved. Knowledge is ever on the march. Life need no longer be unfair. Utopia is at hand, ours, with the aid of social science, to seize.

If you believe all this, do let me know, because I would like to sell you, at a very reasonable price, three only moderately marked-up books by the most popular out-of-the-box thinker of our day.

And Others

Erich Heller

1911–1990

I FIRST CAME TO KNOW ERICH HELLER through his sometimes dark and always majestic essays—the essays in *The Disinherited Mind* and in *The Artist's Journey into the Interior*. One had only to read a few of these essays to recognize that he, Erich Heller, was one of those critics who was himself something of an artist. In his criticism he wrote a species of poetry—poetry in the sense in which, in his preface to his Lord Northcliffe Lectures, he himself defined poetry: "any configuration of words such as have been written by Nietzsche or Thomas Mann, verbal compositions that, even without their aspiring to verse or rhyme, bear witness to the poetic faculty of man."

I first read those essays of Erich's roughly fifty years ago and was immensely impressed by them: by their elegance, by their learning, by their power, by the excitement with which he was able to imbue his dramatization of the ideas that stirred and shaped the writers who most interested him: Goethe, Nietzsche, Rilke, and Thomas Mann as well as Schopenhauer, Karl Kraus, Wittgenstein, and T. S. Eliot. It is perhaps only criticism of the kind Erich wrote, criticism that itself tells a story and is done in the spirit of the artist, that has any chance of attaining the standing of literature. Fifty years later, these essays of Erich's still seem immensely impressive.

Soon after I began teaching at Northwestern, in 1974, whenever a student would ask my advice about what courses to take, I would generally suggest a course by Erich Heller. One reason for this was that European teachers had been an important part of my own education at the University of Chicago, and I suspected that Erich would provide students with a substantial notion of the style and erudition of a European scholar and intellectual. In making these recommendations over the years, I never had an unsatisfied customer. The last student I know who took a course by Erich, a young man named Jason Karlawish, who went on to medical school, wrote to me:

> The passing of . . . Erich Heller caused me much grief.
> I shall never forget the man and his course [Introduction to European Literature, I believe]. He was one of those teachers who exerted influence that will last forever upon me. I miss him.

I did not myself meet Erich Heller until a year or so after beginning to teach at the university. A friend brought us together for lunch. Erich was most sociable, full of laughter and good will, and I noted the contrast between the darkness of the vision often implicit in his essays and the winning, quite cheerful quality of their author. Yet somehow no sparks of friendship ignited between us. It was only some years later, when we would occasionally meet at parties or events at the University of Chicago, that our friendship began to develop.

IT WAS ON THOSE TWENTY-MILE RIDES from Hyde Park to Evanston that I began to discover that Erich was a very witty man, an amusing (and much amused) observer of American academic manners, and a man who loved to hear a joke and also loved to tell one. We discovered, too, that we, Erich and I, had a few things in common: a love of literature and a fascination with the biography of writers, a shared politics (we both thought Communism a very bad thing, a somewhat heretical view in American universities over the past decades), and a skeptical yet comic view of life. I also learned that Erich had genuinely elegant manners. He was, for one thing, a good listener, which is rare for a professor (among professors, a wag once remarked, there is no listening—only waiting). He was, for another, very generous in praising. He once told me in this connection that Thomas Mann, in his diaries, refers to praise as Vitamin P, and that Mann preferred to take it in large doses. It was a small point of very real pride with Erich to learn that Mann himself praised—in his diary—Erich's own writing about him in *Thomas Mann, The Ironic German.*

After his retirement from teaching, Erich and I used to lunch together every two weeks or so and he would sometimes dine at our apartment. By this point in his life, his body was beginning to close in on him. He had emphysema, problems (as he once put it to me with his customary delicacy) with his "internal arrangements," serious loss of hearing, and his eyesight had begun to fail, so that, I am told, he could not read for more than ten-minute stretches. These various illnesses greatly shrunk Erich's world: first he discovered that he could no longer take the European and Irish holidays he so much loved; then he discovered that, such was his body's need for steady medical surveillance, he had to move out of his apartment and into a retirement home where medical help was available on the premises but which was itself in many ways depressing; then it became clear that plans even for journeying out for an evening with friends had to be tentative at best, for he could not count on his health holding up for four or five days in a row. Although he was never a complainer, the penultimate time I was with Erich, when he lay in a hospital bed lashed to oxygen and intravenous-feeding machines, much fatigued by the incursions of his emphysema, he remarked to me, contemplating life without health, "I suppose it's not really worth it." But then, the student of German philosophy right up to the end, he added, "Yet I suppose Schopenhauer was right." By this I took him to mean that, however unreasonable the project of living might seem, the will overrode the capacity for reasoning, and so one lived on.

The sadness of Erich's having his world so drastically shrunk is that he was a most worldly man with a marked sense of *joie de vivre*. He was a man of London and New York, Weimar and Florence, Dublin and Cambridge, Mass. Among his dear friends were Hannah Arendt, Isaiah Berlin, Stephen Spender, worldly characters all. He had grown old enough to have influential and famous—even infamous—students: Martin Peretz, publisher of *The New Republic*, was one of Erich's students; so, too, was the late Paul de Man, whom Erich had taught when at Harvard. Harvard, the colleges of Cambridge and Oxford, the intellectual Upper West Side of New York, such places constituted Erich's favored milieu, or, as the novelist Josephine Herbst kiddingly used to call it, *maloo*.

Yet if Erich was in one sense worldly, in another sense there was something slightly Pninish about him. Like Vladimir Nabokov's memorable character Professor Pnin, Erich, one felt, was far from entirely at home in this country. I recall his once telling me about the horrific fear with which, as an émigré in the late 1930s, he faced the challenge of learning English. That he became the brilliant English prose stylist he soon became is testament to his intellectual power. I have even heard him accused of being a "popularizer," that most admirable of putative academic put-downs; what it really means, I have come to believe, is that one writes extremely well, which Erich of course did.

Although he used English elegantly, Erich never lost his accent, even after fifty years in England and America, and it remained strong until the end. This and his loss of hearing served to increase his Pninishness. Invariably, my telephone calls to him began thus: "Erich, it's

Joe." "Tank you, tank you, tolerably vell," he would reply, guessing (wrongly) that I had inquired about his health, and we would be off on the wrong foot.

Hearing aids were a mixed blessing to Erich. He required them, but, when he wore them, some rooms were acoustically painful to him in their din. We used to look for restaurants where the food was good but that were not too noisy, not a combination easily found. We finally settled on one called Va Pensiero, across the street from his own residence. One o'clock, after the restaurant began to empty out, was our preferred time for meeting.

WHAT DID WE TALK ABOUT during those leisurely lunches? We talked a good deal about writing and writers. I had begun to reread the novels of Thomas Mann, which were a subject of unending interest to Erich, who, in *The Ironic German* and elsewhere, had written so well about them. (When one goes into the hospital, one takes along only those books one truly loves: on two different occasions when I visited Erich at the Evanston Hospital, his bedside books were much-used and badly battered German editions of *Joseph and His Brothers* and *Doctor Faustus*.) At these lunches we thoroughly analyzed the characters of colleagues as well as conjectured about the social relations of the intellectually famous. The vulgar might refer to this as mere gossip, and the vulgar would be right, except that it was fairly rich gossip. Erich much enjoyed gossip, and one of the memories I have of us together, before we had discovered the quietude of Va Pensiero, is of my almost yelling gossip to him in crowded restaurants.

I think that Erich enjoyed what I shall call here my forthrightness on the subject of writers, intellectuals, and academics about whom we were both equally dubious. It was always a point of pleasure to me, after having finished a fairly furious attack on some well-known intellectual's malfeasance, to hear Erich reply, tersely but reassuringly in accented English, "Qvite so." His own style in these sessions was not to show anger but to express puzzlement. How could it be that X could write such frightful gibberish? Why should Y wish to publish it? Can W not have known that this was the most patent nonsense? Who needs this sort of thing anyway? And then he would sometimes end by exclaiming, "Monstrous!" or "Fantastic!" Of most criticism written in the mode of the day, he would note, "Unreadable, of course. Absolutely unreadable."

As an unattached homosexual bachelor, Erich dined out a good amount. The best of guests, he repaid hospitality with attentiveness and exuberant charm and in the coin of superior jokes and lovely anecdotes. One of his anecdotes that I have found myself appropriating since his death is about the day in his early boyhood in Prague that a gang of toughs set upon Erich and his younger brother Paul. "Why are you doing this?" Erich asked. "We're beating you up because you killed Christ," one of toughs said. "Wait a moment," Erich replied. "We didn't kill Christ. The Cohen brothers killed Christ."

BUT IF ERICH HAD TRUE *JOIE DE VIVRE*—loving companion-ship, literature, food, contemplation of the endless odd angu-larities of human nature—if he was a worldly man, in the best sense of the word, there was another sense in which he was not quite at ease in the world. Those who read his obituary in the *New York Times* might have noted that Erich had all these years retained his British citizenship. He once mentioned this to me, though he said nothing more about it. I have the suspicion that it had to do with his having been a refugee from the Nazis. To be a refugee, to be forced to seek refuge can never be easy, but my guess is that perhaps the most psychologically difficult position of all was to have been forced into this condition by the abominable Reich that claimed it would last a thousand years. To have been chased from one's home by the Nazis was to be rendered, in some part of one's soul, perma-nently nervous, always awaiting the knock on the door, the return of the brutes. One sees evidence of this in the behavior of the most worldly people. Even a woman supposedly as politically sophisticated as Hannah Arendt was said to have been sufficiently terrified by the prospect of the Republican Party nominating Barry Goldwater for president in 1964 boding the advent of fascism in America that she began searching for a new home in Switzerland. A good friend of mine, another refugee from the Nazis, though otherwise utterly at ease with his Jewishness, decided, when his first and only son was born, not to have the boy circumcised at birth— the idea here being, well, you can never tell what test the boy might someday be put to. And Erich kept his British passport, which just might at some future time come in handy.

I think that when Erich was with his dearest friends, the handful of students who loved him and with whom he stayed in touch, or his brother Paul (the only member of his family who survived the Nazi death camps), he was at home in the world. I know that, viewed from the other side, the effect of being with him was to make the world always seem a more interesting, vivid, pleasurable place.

BUT I DON'T WISH TO CLOSE on a dark note, for Erich Heller, as I knew him, was a fundamentally bright and sunny man. A skeptic, true enough, but a laughing skeptic, much more in love with life than dubious about it. He was a kind and charming man, and his death marks a sad and serious subtraction from the richness of the world to those of us on whom he bestowed the generous gift of his friendship.

Aleksandr Solzhenitsyn

A Conrad Hero

FOR THE LEAST FAIR, but most penetrating, analysis of Russian character, one can do no better than to consult Joseph Conrad. The great novelist was a Russophobe. Little love is lost between Poles and Russians generally, but in Conrad's case there was added ground for animus: Russia orphaned him. Owing to the efforts of his father, a literary man-of-all-work, in behalf of Polish freedom, his family was exiled to Siberia in 1863. There, Conrad's mother became consumptive and died, and four years later his father died of the same illness; the novelist-to-be was then eleven.

Conrad's grievance was not quite in the class of an obsession, but it was there, ready for service when needed. Russia, he wrote in "Autocracy and War," a 1905 essay ostensibly about the Russo-Japanese war, was "this pitiful state of a country held by an evil spell," a "bottomless abyss that has swallowed up every hope of mercy, every aspiration toward personal dignity, toward freedom, toward knowledge, every ennobling desire of the heart, every whisper of conscience." Not even revolution could save it: "In whatever form of upheaval Autocratic Russia is to find her end, it can never be a revolution fruitful of moral consequences to mankind. It cannot be anything but an uprising of slaves." Of course that is just what the Russian Revolution of 1917 turned out to be—an uprising of slaves that enslaved the rest of the country, and most of Eastern Europe along with it, for more than 70 years.

For Conrad, Russia was another heart of darkness, this one in a cold climate. In *The Secret Agent*, it is the Russian embassy in London that puts the novel's central figure, Verloc, to the job of blowing up the Greenwich Observatory, which results in the killing of his own poor imbecile brother-in-law and sets in motion the book's nightmare logic. And in *Under Western Eyes*, not his most famous or even his most successful novel but among his most brilliant, the astounding human spectacle that is the Russian character became Conrad's true subject. According to the novel's *faux-naïf* narrator, an Englishman teaching English to foreigners in Geneva, Russian simplicity is "a terrible corroding simplicity in which mystic phrases clothe a naïve and hopeless cynicism"; in Russia, it is all but impossible to "tell a scoundrel from an exceptionally able man." (One immediately thinks of Mikhail Gorbachev, or of Boris Yeltsin.)

When *Under Western Eyes* was published in 1911, Edward Garnett—husband of Constance Garnett, the great translator from Russian, and a friend and long-time supporter of Conrad—accused him of prejudice. Conrad shot back that Garnett was "so russianized . . . that you don't know the truth when you see it—unless it smells of cabbage soup when it at once secures your profound respect." And indeed there are certain Russian characters in *Under Western Eyes*—as it happens, all are women—whose general views Conrad derides and in one instance despises, but whose seriousness, even heroism, he nonetheless freely grants. These characters are all able to live outside themselves, to give themselves to really quite hopeless causes, like the reduction of suffering in a merciless world or the recounting of truth in an undeserving one. Only Russia, one senses in reading this novel, is able to produce people ready to pit themselves against the world's great gray disregard and dark evil—only Russia, out of the depths of its barbarity, is able to produce moral giants.

JOSEPH CONRAD would not only have understood Aleksandr Solzhenitsyn but would, I believe, have been tempted to insert him into a novel. Solzhenitsyn has the scope, the depth, the moral grandeur that stimulated Conrad's imagination to its highest power. He is Conradian, too, in passing what, for Conrad, is the test of authenticity: the willingness to live one's ideas, to sacrifice for them, to make them indivisible with one's very being.

All the great Conradian heroes are isolates, men who have chosen either an occupation or a philosophy that carries with it the condition of apartness. No one could have felt lonelier than Aleksandr Solzhenitsyn during his more than twenty years as an underground writer in the Soviet Union—unless it was Aleksandr Solzhenitsyn during his eighteen years living in a compound outside Cavendish, Vermont, after being expelled from the USSR. In both places, he worked at his self-imposed task of bringing down the Soviet Union—a task whose successful achievement would, I suspect, be beyond the imagining of Joseph Conrad or any other novelist or poet. Even the word "heroic" does not seem quite adequate to describe this accomplishment.

Born in 1918 near Rostov, Solzhenitsyn was arrested and sentenced in 1945 to eight years in a labor camp, presumably for making disparaging jokes about Stalin. After an early release—thanks to the Khrushchev reforms—he was diagnosed with a supposedly terminal cancer, which he conquered. In 1962, during a rare period of cultural thaw, he was allowed to publish, in the Soviet journal *Novy Mir*, his taboo-shattering account of the slave-labor camps, *One Day in the Life of Ivan Denisovich*. Other works, including the novels *Cancer Ward* (English edition 1968) and *The First Circle* (also 1968), followed—but only in the West. In the West,

ALEKSANDR SOLZHENITSYN

too, appeared *The Gulag Archipelago,* his monumental three-volume exposé of the Soviet slave-labor system which single-handedly destroyed what remained of Western illusions about the great Communist experiment.

In 1970 Solzhenitsyn was awarded the Nobel Prize, but was refused permission to travel to Stockholm to receive it. Always in a relationship of the greatest strain with Soviet leaders, always a thorn in their sides—"This hooligan Solzhenitsyn is out of control," Leonid Brezhnev once said of him—in 1974 he was finally sent into exile.

Fortunate to have survived the war, the slave-labor camp, cancer, and many skirmishes with the KGB, Solzhenitsyn had come to think of himself as God's vessel. In *Invisible Allies*, a book written in 1975 but published much later, and dedicated to the small army of anonymous Russians who helped him during his years as an underground writer, he has this to say about *The Gulag Archipelago*: "It seemed as if it was no longer I who was writing; rather, I was swept along, my hand was being moved by an outside force, and I was only the firing pin attached to a spring." And in *The Oak and the Calf* (English translation 1980), an account of his battles with the Soviet cultural bureaucracy, he writes: "I had learned in my years of imprisonment to sense that guiding hand, to glimpse that bright meaning beyond and above my self and my wishes."

If God was guiding his hand, the mission on which Solzhenitsyn had embarked, at divine bidding, was to bear witness on behalf of his fellow *zeks*, as he refers to the countless prisoners in the Soviet gulag. In *Invisible Allies* and *The Oak and the Calf* he speaks of carrying "the dying wishes of millions whose last whisper, last moan, had been cut short on some hut floor in some prison camp." And again: "My point of departure [was] that I did not belong to myself alone, that my literary destiny was not just my own, but that of millions who had not lived to scrawl or gasp or croak the truth about their lot as jailbirds."

Having been a *zek* himself, Solzhenitsyn identified completely with his fellow prisoners. One sometimes gets the feeling in reading Solzhenitsyn that, in the terrible morality of Stalinist totalitarianism, to have been a *zek* was a mark of the highest distinction, while not to have been a *zek* was to have been on the one hand wondrously lucky, but on the other hand in some sense spiritually deficient. Nadezhda Vasilyevna Bukharina, a woman who helped Solzhenitsyn in storing, reproducing, and smuggling his manuscripts out of the Soviet Union, once told him: "Before I die I have to make up for the fact that I never saw the inside of the camps."

For Solzhenitsyn, the *zeks* were Russia's saving remnant, and he was their voice. But he also viewed himself as speaking for something else: the entire tradition of Russian literature. Not *Soviet* literature—that was permanently in thrall to ideology, to supporting the state, the party, the full grotesque apparatus of Communism. By contrast,

Russian literature, represented by Tolstoy, Dostoevsky, Chekhov, Pasternak, and others, was in thrall to nothing but its own freedom of spirit, hostage only to the truth of human complexity. This was a distinction that Solzhenitsyn insisted upon during his days as an underground writer. Of his falling out with Aleksandr Tvardovsky, the editor of *Novy Mir*, he writes: "The Soviet editor and the Russian prose writer could no longer march side by side because his literature and mine had sharply and irrevocably diverged."

THESE, THEN, WERE THE TWIN POLES of his mission—to give voice to the *zeks*, and to reclaim the heritage of Russian literature. In *The Oak and the Calf* at one of many points when he recalls thinking the game might be up for him, Solzhenitsyn writes: "Why must this work be brought to nothing? It was not just that it was my work; it was almost the only work that had survived as a monument to the truth." Whether or not it was "just" his work, Solzhenitsyn certainly felt that the fate of the truth, and perhaps even of Russia itself, was all on his shoulders. Anyone coming after him would find it "still harder to dig out the truth, while those who had lived earlier had either not survived or had not preserved what they had written."

Was he correct, or did he overdramatize? On the merely mechanical level, what Solzhenitsyn achieved—the writing of his books under the most difficult of conditions—is astounding. While, in effect, in hiding, he produced before his fiftieth year an entire *oeuvre* of stories, novels, poems, a history, memoirs, and a vast historical novel (later to be completed in the United States). In a minuscule handwriting, leaving no margins lest he waste precious paper, he scribbled away at a fantastic clip. In *Invisible Allies* he describes his daily regimen while working on *The Gulag Archipelago*: he would rise at 1:00 a.m. and work through till 9:00 a.m., then start on a second day's portion of work, quitting for dinner at 6:00 p.m., sleeping from 7:00 p.m. till 1:00 a.m., and then begin again.

All this was done while awaiting a knock on the door from the KGB. His manuscripts had to be kept hidden not only from the regime but from his own first wife, whose trustworthiness had been forfeited. He sometimes slept with a pitchfork beside his bed. Yet he continued, relentlessly, to work, without the aid of editors or publishers and without any certainty that the typed and retyped copies of his books which made their uncertain transmission through the underground railroad of *samizdat* would ever see the light of day.

As for the substance of his achievement, even though all sorts of people have scratched about for reasons to deny it, the plain fact is that "in terms of the effect he has had on history," as the journalist David Remnick put it in the *New Yorker*, Solzhenitsyn is "the dominant writer of this century." He has been something writers often wish to be but rarely are—what he called in *The First Circle* a "second government." One man alone, without aid of weapons, a party, or even a movement behind him, took on the most systematically brutal regime the modern world has known and, without even benefit of support in the realm of public opinion, brought it to its knees.

Given the astonishing clip at which he worked in his underground years, it is not surprising that Solzhenitsyn, in *The Oak and the Calf,* laments about the cost this exacted from him as a writer: "I never had time to look for the precise, the definitive word." True, living underground, he had absolute freedom, with neither an editor's nor a government's censorship to worry about. Yet in sheer literary terms there was an "inevitable drawback":

> When you have been writing for ten or twelve years in impenetrable solitude, you begin without realizing it to let yourself go, to indulge yourself, or simply to lose your eye for jarring invective, for bombast, for banal conventional joins where you should have found a firm fastening.

Because of the extraordinary conditions under which Solzhenit-syn's books were produced, it is difficult to enter standard literary judgments about them. Norman Podhoretz has declared that Solzhenitsyn's two major nonfiction works, *The Gulag Archipelago* and *The Oak and the Calf*, are "among the very greatest books of the age." But for him the novels and stories, though some are better than others, are finally stillborn: "Despite everything that is right about them, they always fail to live."*

This is a more stringent view of Solzhenitsyn's fiction than the orthodox one, which continues to rank *One Day in the Life of Ivan Denisovich* highly and regards both *The First Circle* and *Cancer Ward* as important works in the realist tradition. What is undeniable about them is that they reflect Solzhenitsyn's own constricted view of what literature is for. He has attempted to write Tolstoyan novels, but to do so under the moralizing code adopted by Tolstoy at a time when the latter's own best fiction was long behind him and he had all but disowned it. "You ought not to approach literature without a moral responsibility for every word you write," Solzhenit-syn told David Remnick, who adds that Solzhenitsyn "cannot abide experimentalism for its own sake, or pure pleasure as a literary end."

Every work of Solzhenitsyn's has a point, and the point is always political, from *Ivan Denisovich*, which set out to expose the brute fact of the slave-labor camps, to his attempt to tell the true history of the Russian Revolution in *August 1914* and the subsequent volumes of *The Red Wheel* (completed but not yet fully available in English translation). These works resist judgment on purely or even on largely aesthetic grounds. One would almost do better to judge them by how well they make their points—which is to say, by the degree to which they have fulfilled Solzhenitsyn's mission.

---

* "The Terrible Question of Aleksandr Solzhenitsyn," *Commentary*, February 1985.

HAT MISSION IS EVEN LARGER than one might have thought. Helping to destroy Communism, it turns out, was only part of it. As Solzhenitsyn writes in *Invisible Allies*:

> Beyond the immediate struggle with the Communist state loomed a greater challenge still: the Russian spirit lay comatose, as if crushed beneath a mighty rock, and this vast tombstone . . . must somehow be raised, overturned, and sent crashing downhill.

Here we enter the complicated—one might say Conradian— terrain of Russian mysticism. By mysticism I mean the notion, held by Solzhenitsyn, that in the Russian spirit lie secrets, and, just possibly, a remedy for the spiritual vacuity of the West. "I put no hopes in the West—indeed no Russian ever should," Solzhenitsyn writes in *Invisible Allies*. "If the 20th century has any lesson for mankind, it is we who will teach the West, not the West us. Excessive ease and prosperity have weakened their will and their reason."

This notion of the West as distinctly not the solution, but as part of the same problem of modernity that brought about the hideous excrescence of Communism, has deep roots in Russia's Slavophile past. But it also has roots in Solzhenitsyn's own intense distrust of Western leftists, who stood by for decades while Russians suffered. Throughout his books, he takes shots at "useful idiots" (Lenin's term)—"the anti-fascists and the existentialists, the pacifists, the hearts that bled for Africa [but] had nothing to say about the destruction of our culture, about the destruction of our nation." When Jean-Paul Sartre wished to meet with him, Solzhenitsyn felt honor-bound to refuse this particularly egregious "useful idiot." At one point in 1972, when the Soviet leaders were making it especially hot for him, Solzhenitsyn thought to stage interviews in the *New York Times* and the *Washington Post*; but their respective Moscow correspondents, Hedrick Smith and Robert Kaiser, appalled him with the triviality of their questions.

Solzhenitsyn has never been a public-relations man's dream. "On one score I was adamant," he writes in *Invisible Allies*, "fame would never win me over." It never came close to doing so. When, an exile from his homeland, he arrived in the United States in 1975, Solzhenitsyn promptly told off Americans for their ignorance, their weakness, and worse. He accused us of collusion with tyranny: in pursuit of profit, American businessmen were selling the latest detection devices to the KGB to help imprison Soviet dissidents. He attacked our foreign policy: Soviet dissidents, he reported, "Couldn't understand the flabbiness of the truce concluded in Vietnam," and the entire policy of détente showed nothing but a wholesale misunderstanding of Communism. As for our popular culture, it was beneath contempt. Americans, he declared, live behind a "wall of disastrous unawareness or nonchalant superiority."

"Being an émigré is the most difficult skill to master," remarked the Russian émigré Nikita Struve, head of a Russian-language press in Paris; it was a skill Solzhenitsyn showed no desire to learn. Attacks upon him now came not only from the Kremlin but from the West, including from anti-Communists and from his fellow émigrés. Disagreement soon merged into accusation: it was said of Solzhenitsyn that he wanted Russia to become a new Byzantium, that his favored form of government was theocracy, that he was an anti-Semite, and finally that he was nothing more than an ayatollah.

Solzhenitsyn soon decided that speechifying was not worth the energy and the emotional drain it exacted. In the eighteen years he spent in Vermont with his second wife and four sons, he worked on completing the various "knots" of *The Red Wheel*, and putting much of the rest of his enormous *oeuvre* in order. He predicted his own eventual return to Russia, and awaited the time when it would come about.

When it did, after the fall of the Soviet Union, things did not quite work out as he might have envisioned. Having fulfilled his literary duty, Solzhenitsyn now meant to fulfill his duty to society. His ambition, which had very little to do with power or politics in the normal sense, was to revive the Russian spirit, a task at least as hard to accomplish in post-Communist Russia as under the Communist regime, if not harder.

objecting to human nature?

In *The Russian Question at the End of the Twentieth Century*, Solzhenitsyn explains why that should be so. With an acidulousness of which Joseph Conrad himself might fundamentally approve, he surveys the many barbarities and betrayals of Russian history. He writes of Three Times of Troubles (the capital letters are his): the 17th century, when Russian despotism started in earnest; the year 1917, when the Bolsheviks sent the efforts toward reform that had begun under czarism crashing down; and today, when "we are creating a cruel, beastly, criminal society." If Russian population growth is now falling, and male life expectancy is at roughly the same point as it is in Bangladesh, Indonesia, and certain countries of Africa, all this is owing to the despair of the Russian people, a despair Solzhenitsyn understands better than anyone on earth.

WHAT, TO ASK THE QUESTION Chernyshevski asked more than a century ago, is to be done? For Solzhenitsyn, there is altogether too much talk in the new Russia about the economy; what such talk signifies to him is, after all, only a "new explosion of materialism, this time a 'capitalist' one," and another dose of materialism will hardly do anything to save the Russian soul. Characteristically, his point of attack is moral. "We must build a moral Russia, or not at all. . . . We must preserve and nourish all the good seeds which miraculously have not been trampled down." But in what soil are these seeds to take root? The character of the Russian people, "so well known to our forebears, so abundantly depicted by our writers and observed by thoughtful foreigners," has been all but killed off by the Bolsheviks, who "scorched out compassion, the willingness to help others, the feeling of brotherhood."

Solzhenitsyn's reception in his homeland has been decidedly mixed, at best. Although, as David Remnick reports, a large number of Russians have told pollsters they would like Solzhenitsyn to be their president, elsewhere "a more ironical attitude . . . has formed. I found the attitude ranging from indifference to mockery." Lots of people, one imagines, and not just in Russia, would prefer that he just go away. Even his American publisher has said that he does not anticipate a large sale for the next installment of *The Red Wheel*. "The interest is just not there anymore."

Aleksandr Isayevich Solzhenitsyn was a prophet without honor in his own country. "I feel sorry for Russia," says a character in *August 1914*. So did Solzhenitsyn, but neither his sorrow nor his patriotism ever got in the way of his extravagant idealism, or stopped him from telling his countrymen precisely what he thought. He was, in short, a fanatic, but of the kind of which true prophets are made. Only Russia could produce such a man—and only Russians could ignore him. Joseph Conrad would have understood.

V. S. Naipaul and Paul Theroux
Poison-Pen Pals

WRITERS CAN BE CORDIAL, charming, social ornaments, but their talent for retaining friends is, on balance, less than impressive. They are notable for touchiness, a want of reciprocity, self-protectiveness—qualities conducing less to the preservation than to the ruin of friendships, at least of the kind that endure. The degree to which these qualities derive from the fact that writers spend too much time alone, dwelling upon their fantasies and their failure to achieve them, or are inherent in the activity of molding the penury of their actual experience into publishable works, varies from case to case. And this is not, of course, to speak of the drunks, neurotics, and pure creeps who sometimes appear to preponderate among contemporary authors.

Not only do they seem unsuited for friendship in general, writers are even more lamentably ill-equipped when it comes to dealings with their fellow writers. "People can be friends," says a character named Izzy Thornbush in John Updike's recent *Bech at Bay*. "Writers, no. Writers are condemned to hate one another." Rival-rousness, envy, ideological argumentativeness, and *Schadenfreude* being their reigning emotional states, these nicely pave the way for inconstancy, infidelity, and straight-out betrayal. Having mastered the means of expression, and having at their disposal the modes of publication, writers differ from the normally irritable and resentful by being all too ready to go public with their spleen.

Exceptions have existed, large-hearted writers with a genuine gift for friendship: John Keats was one such, Chekhov another; Turgenev and Henry James also qualify. And one can also find discrete acts of unmotivated generosity or kindness on the part of writers toward other writers: Edith Wharton secretly slipping funds into Henry James's royalty account at Scribner's; Ezra Pound generously promoting the career of T. S. Eliot and, through skillful editing, helping to bring *The Waste Land* into print in its best possible form; F. Scott Fitzgerald going out of his way to get the editor Maxwell Perkins to take on the work of the young Ernest Hemingway.

Generally, though, the record is one of almost unrelieved unpleasantness. The causes of this unpleasantness, Norman Podhoretz shows in his memoir, *Ex-Friends*, can occasionally involve political or ideological conviction, as in the case of Podhoretz's own breaks with writers and intellectuals to whom he was once close, or their breaks with him. More often, the causes are petty and "merely" personal.

Bad feeling was first planted between Thackeray and Dickens, for example, when the latter chose not to use the former as his illustrator for *The Pickwick Papers*, and the bad feeling was exacerbated over Dickens's belief that Thackeray was spreading rumors of his love affair with Ellen Ternan. D. H. Lawrence, a man of nearly perpetual testiness, broke with nearly all his literary friends, perhaps with none more crushingly than Katherine Mansfield and her husband John Middleton Murry. Hemingway, in *A Moveable Feast*, lined up the various writers who had aided him when he was a young man in Paris and shot them down with the most vicious tales he could contrive about each of them: John Dos Passos, Gertrude Stein, Ford

Madox Ford, with Fitzgerald, whom he wrote off as a sexually insecure drunk, getting the roughest treatment of all. The critic Edmund Wilson, after being initially helpful to Vladimir Nabokov when he first arrived in this country, later had the temerity to question Nabokov's grasp of Russian (!) in so aggressive a way as to cause a permanent rupture in their friendship.

When two writers inhabit the same family, the unpleasantness is often only more intense: a vivid example is the critic and novelist Anthony West's book attacking his mother Rebecca for her selfish neglect of him—which must, for her, author of *The Meaning of Treason*, have given treason itself a whole new meaning. Fallings-out among brothers are especially common. There is reason to believe that so sterling a character as William James felt animosity toward his younger brother Henry: turning down membership in the American Academy of Arts and Letters, William offered, not altogether facetiously, the consideration that "my younger and shallower and vainer younger brother" was already a member. To balance this, there is evidence in his letters that Henry did not appreciate William's rather philistine views on his own exquisite literary art. The Mann brothers, Thomas and Heinrich, were divided by politics and Heinrich's envy throughout their professional lives.

A COUPLE OF YEARS AGO, the novelist Alexander Theroux wrote an article blasting his better known brother Paul, also a novelist as well as a travel writer, for, among other things, cowardice, pretentiousness, and celebrity-chasing. The following sentence conveys the scorched-earth quality of Alexander's treatment of his brother: "Paul has bowel worries and eats prunes for breakfast and once made inquiries of me about platform shoes." In his own words, or quoting others, he indicts Paul for snobbery, Anglomania, cheapness, idiotic opinionatedness, self-importance, prickliness, and betrayal: for being "a terrible enemy but ... much worse as a friend."

What is interesting about this catalogue of accusations is that it roughly parallels the one leveled by Paul Theroux himself against V. S. Naipaul in *Sir Vidia's Shadow: A Friendship Across Five Continents*. This book treats its subject to an act of personal scrutiny as sustained and punishing as any I know. *Sir Vidia's Shadow* has itself come in for its own share of punishment at the hands of reviewers, having been roundly attacked as an expression of bad temper, resentment, and deep envy. "Mr. Theroux emerges as a petty, vindictive man," runs a characteristic comment in a review in the *Wall Street Journal*. Yet I myself found Theroux's account convincing on various fronts, and never less than full of interest, even when dubious; perhaps most interesting when most dubious.

Paul Theroux is an American, born in 1941, who has lived the greater part of his adult life outside the United States. V. S. Naipaul, born in 1932, is of Indian heritage; he was raised in the former British colony of Trinidad in the West Indies, won a scholarship to Oxford, and has lived chiefly in England ever since. Both men are in the tradition of the restless writer who travels to find his subjects; in the modern era, this tradition is largely English, associated with such names as Graham Greene, Somerset Maugham, Evelyn Waugh, Patrick Leigh Fermor. Traveling has for the most part taken both men to third-world countries where the terrain tends to be exotic, the squalor quotient high, the indigenes not necessarily friendly, and the journey often a touch dangerous.

Africa, in fact, was the scene of their first meeting. The year was 1966, and Paul Theroux was a twenty-five-year-old teacher at the University of Makerere, in Kampala, Uganda—this was before the tyrant Idi Amin wrecked the country. Naipaul and his wife arrived for one of those teaching stints that serious but financially less than successful writers take on to make ends meet. At thirty-four, Naipaul was already a published and critically celebrated writer—his novel *The Mimic Men* would win the 1967 Booker Prize—and one painfully exacting in his standards and utterly confident in his point of view.

"I had never met anyone," Theroux writes, "so certain, so intense, so observant, so hungry, so impatient, so intelligent." And, miraculous as it seemed to Theroux—then still a yearning, would-be author who had composed only poems—this stimulating, difficult man not only seemed to like him, but thought he had in him the makings of a writer. Naipaul took him seriously and regaled him with advice. A friendship, though not one between equals, was under way.

One of the first things that impressed Theroux was Naipaul's utter independence of mind and opinion. In matters literary, he openly expressed distaste for the work of Jane Austen, Mark Twain, Henry James, Emily Dickinson, and George Orwell, not to mention most contemporary English and American writers then of high repute. He had his doubts about Camus. He thought contemporary African literature, including the novels of Wole Soyinka and Chinua Achebe, little more than acts of mimicry, saying: "You can't beat a novel out on a drum." He himself read the Latin poet Martial and the Bible.

Outside the realm of literature, Naipaul claimed to hate music, all music; he also hated jokes. He disliked flowers. He despised children, telling Theroux: "I do not want children. I do not want to read about children. I do not want to see them." The Kenyan politician Tom Mboya, then greatly admired among Western intellectuals, he referred to as "a fat thug." Of Ian Smith, the leading political figure in Rhodesia, he said that "he is qualified to mend bicycles in Surrey [England]. Nothing more than that." His word for the people he encountered in Uganda who had intellectual pretensions was "infies," short for inferior persons. But, then, most people for Naipaul were "infies."

Nor was Naipaul's outrageousness confined to his opinions. Complaint was his natural note, his sole melody. He caused difficulties wherever he went. He was cold to his wife, with whom, Theroux reports, he did not sleep. He was a vegetarian, but a vegetarian who refused to eat salad. He was merciless to the students he taught, telling one young woman that her work was hopeless but her handwriting very nice, and suggesting that a literary contest offer only a third prize since no one could possibly be worthy of first or second. He wrote harsh put-down letters, and in all relationships was touchier than an infected thumb.

Sir Vidia's Shadow is an attack, but it is one most artfully executed. Theroux slowly builds up to it. In the book's early chapters, Naipaul's reactionary opinions are shown to have a certain charm, deriving in good part from their outrageousness, which in turn derives from an absolute indifference to any sort of correctness, political or otherwise. Although Theroux records Naipaul's idiosyncrasies, early in the book it is left to others to say critical things about him. When Theroux tells a young writer named B. S. Johnson that he is staying with the Naipauls, Johnson replies, "Naipaul is a prick." As for Theroux, despite everything that seems rebarbative in Naipaul, he finds in him a quality of independence that he cannot but admire. "I don't have a country," he records Naipaul telling him at one point, and at another, "I have no home."

He also has gravity, particularly about art, which he feels must be difficult, a struggle. Naipaul, writes Theroux, was "brilliant, and passionate in his convictions, and to be with him, as a friend or fellow writer, I had always to be at my best." Later, when Theroux himself begins to write novels, "what mattered most was that Vidia, a brilliant writer, believed in me." A letter praising Theroux's novel *Girls at Play* "sustained me for the next two years." No wonder that, as Theroux writes, friendship with such a man became "as strong as love."

Soon, however, Naipaul's charming outrageousness starts to take, in the pages of *Sir Vidia's Shadow*, a more and more ugly turn. He is shown to be cruel to servants; never to pick up a check. He is tough on his younger brother Shiva—also a writer—because Shiva has long hair and is unpunctual. He expresses racist views: of

George Wallace, the segregationist governor of Alabama, Naipaul remarks, "He has an awful lot of common sense."

Subtly, the relationship between the older and the younger writer begins to shift. Theroux recounts how Naipaul, after setting up a grand lunch at the Connaught Hotel in London, stiffed him with the £20 bill. He makes him out to be a wine idiot: "I think you'll like this," Naipaul says, pouring a white burgundy. "It's balanced, it's firm, perhaps a bit fleshy, but smooth and, I think you'll agree, round." And he underscores his hypocrisy: Naipaul mocks the notion of a British knighthood, and the two friends share a joke about his changing his name to Sir V. S. Nye-Powell, OBE; but when knighthood is later offered, Naipaul of course accepts it.

At this stage in their friendship, things have not yet irreparably fallen apart. Although Theroux establishes himself as a frequently published novelist—eight books before he is thirty—he is not yet commercially or critically successful. He is still deep enough in thrall to his much-admired friend to publish, in 1972, *V. S. Naipaul: An Introduction to His Work.* He ends that slender volume by underscoring the integrity behind Naipaul's talent:

> He conceals nothing; his ingenuousness, his avoidance of sarcasm, and his humor—a delight that no essay can do justice to—make him very special among writers; there is no one like him writing today. . . . It is evidence of the uniqueness of his vision, but a demonstration of the odds against him, that no country can claim him.

When, in 1975, Theroux's travel book, *The Great Railway Bazaar,* becomes an immediate bestseller, a deeper change is registered. Asking Naipaul's help with a planned trip to India, he senses, for the first time, a reluctance. The days when, as Theroux says, "I listened: I was Boswell, he was Johnson," are drawing to an end. Though Theroux continues to feel "blessed for all [Naipaul's] good advice, cautioned by his mistakes, stimulated by his intellect, enlightened by his work"—and also "aware of his contradictions"—from here to the close of the book it is the darker side of those contradictions that gets emphasized.

Naipaul's attitudes are now made to seem less amusing, more vicious. Theroux quotes his response to an interviewer's question about the future of Africa: "Africa has no future." When the poet Derek Walcott calls Naipaul a bigot in print, Theroux does not rise to his friend's defense. He is particularly hard on Naipaul as a husband, portraying him as insensitive, demanding, bullying, the perpetrator of many mental cruelties. "Stop chuntering," he is always telling his wife Pat whenever she expresses unhappiness. Yet Pat Naipaul, Theroux informs us, is all the things Vidia is not: discreet, kind, generous, polite, grateful, magnanimous. When she eventually dies of cancer, one is somehow reminded that cancer was once called the disease of the disappointed.

For a good part of his marriage, Theroux reveals to us, Naipaul had a mistress, whom he not infrequently took along when doing the legwork for his travel books. This, for Theroux, gives those books themselves a strong taint of fraudulence. "What was the challenge in traveling with a loving woman?" he asks. "There were no alien places on earth for the man who had his lover to cling to at night and tell him he was a genius." This negative opinion spreads, causing Theroux to revise his overall judgment of Naipaul's literary gifts: the man who in 1972 was unlike anyone else writing today turns out to be "the monomaniac in print that he was in person." Theroux even confesses, dramatically, that by 1979 his was the deciding vote that prevented Naipaul from winning the Booker Prize for *A Bend in the River*, a novel about an African country under the sway of revolutionary corruption and violence.

After his wife's death, Naipaul marries again—not his mistress but a younger Pakistani journalist. The overbearingness of this woman, in Theroux's account, is the cause of the final rupture of his more than thirty-year relation with V. S. Naipaul. The first sign of the end comes when Theroux discovers three of his own books, inscribed to his friend Vidia, for sale in a bookseller's catalogue. When he queries Naipaul about this, he receives a harsh fax from the new Mrs. Naipaul making it plain that he, Theroux, can no longer expect to find himself welcome in Naipaul's company.

"She's crazy, I thought, and I began to laugh and crinkle the fax paper in my hand," is how Theroux reports his response. He sends back an equally harsh letter, and, one thing leading to another, breakup becomes inevitable. When, some while later, the two men encounter each other on a street in London, Theroux asks if there is anything left of their friendship. "Take it on the chin and move on," is all Naipaul can offer. "Before we got to the Cromwell Road," Theroux writes, "I had begun this book in my head, starting at the beginning."

A T SOME POINT in the course of this extraordinary work, one has to ask how reliable is Paul Theroux, not only in his general analysis of Naipaul's character but in the matter of the words he ascribes to him. What means do we have of judging? None, really, except for the internal logic, by which I mean the consistency—or credible inconsistency—of comments and details as they build up through the course of the book. My own view is that, on this count, *Sir Vidia's Shadow* passes the test. The V. S. Naipaul who appears in its pages is a marvelous character; I have by no means read all of Paul Theroux's fiction, but I do not believe he is a good enough novelist to have invented anyone quite so extraordinary.

Defending Naipaul, David Pryce-Jones, in a review of this book in the *American Spectator*, notes that "Theroux did not *witness* Naipaul's cruelties to publicity girls, waiters, and other defenseless bystanders, but he repeats second-hand gossip about them" (emphasis added). And Pryce-Jones adds that Theroux is foolish to take everything Naipaul said literally, "as if he weren't trying things on for effect or didn't himself suffer insecurity." Perhaps so. But Naipaul has said enough outside the pages of *Sir Vidia's Shadow*—

I recall an interview in which he allowed as how he thought all fat people were immoral—to convince me that nothing Theroux has him say inside the book is wholly invented or inconceivable.

Part of the glory of V. S. Naipaul as a writer has been, in fact, his willingness to speak his mind on subjects that in almost everyone else tend to cause cowering. As a "person of color," he was for quite a long time granted a rare license to speak with candor about dealings between the first and third worlds, and he made the most of it. In his novels, essays, and larger works of nonfiction, he exposes the deep fraudulence that has tainted both sides in these dealings: the gauzy unreality of the Western liberal Left, the readiness to con on the part of "natives" being sucked up to, and betwixt the two more than a sufficiency of bad faith to go around. In *A Bend in the River*, a French couple working in a newly independent African country relax by playing the recordings of Joan Baez. Naipaul's narrator acidly remarks:

> You couldn't listen to the sweet songs about injustice unless you expected justice and received it much of the time. You couldn't sing songs about the end of the world unless . . . you felt that the world was going on and on and you were safe in it.

Only Naipaul has had the intellectual courage to tell such home truths.

Theroux writes of Naipaul that "really there was not a living writer he praised or any dead ones he acknowledged as exemplars." But this is to overlook Joseph Conrad, about whom Naipaul has written in trenchant praise and whom he, at his best, can sometimes resemble. He is like Conrad in being a writer without one true society but who knows many societies very well from without. He is like Conrad, too, in seeming to speak on behalf of a wider, a larger, a higher civilization—what Naipaul himself, in a lecture in New York in 1990, called "Our Universal Civilization."

This larger civilization, as he describes it at the end of his lecture, "implies a certain kind of awakened spirit," containing "the idea of the individual, responsibility, choice, the life of the intellect, the idea of vocation and perfectibility and achievement." Coming from a peripheral Caribbean culture, Naipaul believes that he has "seen or felt" certain of the core qualities of this civilization "more freshly than people for whom those things were everyday," and in writing about "half-made societies that seemed doomed to remain half-made," he has emphasized the corruption that has kept them from attaining precisely the ideal of universal civilization. This great subject—an entirely modern and politically international subject—has lent Naipaul's writing much of its impressive gravity.

Paul Theroux picks up on this point, if indirectly, when, of Naipaul's conversation, he notes: "He had that disconcerting way of turning chitchat into metaphysics about the human condition." True enough. But that leads to a question: would Theroux allow that, between the two of them, Naipaul is the superior mind, and the superior writer? Not merely superior, but in another league, really? Theroux has undoubtedly had the greater commercial success—well-selling books, movie deals—but Naipaul has had the success of being taken with the greatest seriousness that has eluded Theroux just about completely.

He must feel this deeply—which may be the reason why, in my reading, at any rate, the one unbelievable character in *Sir Vidia's Shadow* is the man who wrote it. Paul Theroux begins as the earnest acolyte, serving at the altar of an older and wiser and better writer. He remains for a good part of the early portions a happy naïf, amazed yet impressed by the man he is delighted to call friend; after the death, by heart attack, of Shiva Naipaul, "it was," he writes, "as though I were the brother who survived." The first real turning point, we are told, comes only after Naipaul is knighted in 1990, when Theroux realizes that all these years he has served as a perfect squire to a very faulty lord.

It so happens we know a great deal about Theroux's own unpleasantness—not only from his brother Alexander but from the rather icily contemptuous self-portrait that emerges in many of his own travel books. Yet in regard to his friend Naipaul, we are asked to believe that Theroux's behavior is always honorable, moral, exemplary. A serious mistake, this—in literature as in life, imputing undiluted virtue to oneself is of course one of the first signs of falsity.

ACCORDING TO THEROUX, "most writers are cranks, so friendship among them is rare, and they end up loners." This may be even truer when there is a discrepancy in the literary reputation of the two writers. Theroux reports that in 1967 Naipaul asked him, as a favor, to read the galley proof of his novel *The Mimic Men* for typographical errors. If that was Theroux's favor to Naipaul, then being permitted to read the novel, from which he claims to have learned much, was supposedly Naipaul's favor to him. But why does this not seem quite the "reciprocal" transaction Theroux thinks it is?

I once had a friendship with a famous American novelist—a man, as I would one day learn, with a genuine gift for intimacy and none whatsoever for friendship—who treated me to a similar favor: he read aloud to me from a novel in progress. And I did at the time consider it a favor, though what I really felt, I now realize, was flattery at being thought perceptive enough to make this exercise worth his while. As for him, from my reactions he gained, aside from the occasional minor correction, perhaps a slightly stronger sense of what in his novel worked well and what did not. Again, who here was doing the favor for whom?

It is all too natural for the lesser party in such a friendship to get this element of power askew—which is why it can be so dismaying to learn how unimportant one's friendship is to the more powerful party. My friendship with the novelist fell apart when he attributed to me an opinion about his work that I had never held.

Paul Theroux's friendship fell apart at the end because of a woman, Naipaul's new wife, who rebuffed him—or perhaps really when he learned that Naipaul had consigned autographed copies of Theroux's books to a bookseller. When something like this happens, when one realizes how much a friendship has meant to oneself and how little to the other person, one feels a double damn fool, and one's resentment soon leads one to seek revenge. I tried to kill my man in a short story. Theroux, having had a much longer putative friendship and more vehement feelings about its sad conclusion, has allowed himself a full 288 pages for the job.

"The melancholy thing about the world," V. S. Naipaul once told Paul Theroux, "is that it is full of stupid and common people, and the world is run for the benefit of the stupid and the common." Perhaps so. But after reading *Sir Vidia's Shadow*, one feels that in the end this arrangement may well be for the best.

Xenophon

The Third Man

XENOPHON (CA. 430–354 BCE), son of Gryllos, Athenian of the deme Erchia, had the bad luck to write history directly after Thucydides and to chronicle the thought of Socrates at the same time as Plato, his almost exact contemporary. Compared with such unsurpassed intellectual figures one can scarcely avoid appearing dullish, without penetration, more than a touch second-rate.

And so Xenophon, as historian and as philosopher, has often been considered. Macaulay thought Xenophon's two main works—the *Antabasis*, his account of the retreat of the Greek mercenaries following Cyrus after their defeat in Persia, and the *Hellenika*, his history of Greece from where Thucydides left off in 411 BCE to the defeat of the Spartans by Thebes at the battle of Mantinea (362 BCE)—"pleasant reading," though "they indicate no great power of mind. In truth, Xenophon, though his taste was elegant, his disposition amiable, and his intercourse with the world extensive, had, we suspect, rather a weak head." J. B. Bury wrote that Xenophon's "mind was essentially mediocre," and that "he was as far from understanding the methods of Thucydides as he was from apprehending the ideas of Socrates." A dilettante, Bury calls him, with "a happy literary talent," a man who, in our day, would have been "a high-class journalist," nothing more.

On the other side of the ledger, Cicero, in his dialogue "On Old Age," has his mouthpiece Cato remark that "the writings of Xenophon are in many ways extremely informative, and I recommend that you read them carefully." Machiavelli cites Xenophon more than any other classical writer (with the exception of Livy), and quotes him more than he does Plato, Aristotle, and Cicero combined. Leo Strauss, in *Xenophon's Socratic Discourse: An Interpretation of the "Oeconomicus,"* reminds us that the great classical scholar Johann Winckelmann praised "the noble simplicity and quiet grandeur . . . of the unadorned great Xenophon," comparing him to Raphael (and Thucydides to Michelangelo). Strauss himself held that our age is "surely blind to the greatness of Xenophon," and that "one might make some discoveries about our age by reading and rereading Xenophon."

Born of the class of knights in Athens, which meant his family was wealthy enough to keep horses and thus qualify as aristocrats, Xenophon as a young man is said to have been less than enamored with Athenian democracy. After all, it was Athenian democracy that was responsible for the death of his teacher Socrates in 399 BCE; that called back Alcibiades from Sicily, ensuring the defeat of the Athenian fleet there; and under Athenian democracy, too, that the generals who led the successful naval campaign of Arginousai in 406 BCE were executed for failing to return to save those Athenians left on their wrecked triremes. After the defeat of the Athenians by Sparta in 404 BCE at the Battle of Aigospotamoi, marking the end of the Peloponnesian War, Xenophon is said at first to have been sympathetic to the oligarchs, known as the Thirty Tyrants, put in control of Athens by the victorious Spartans.

In 401 BCE Xenophon took up the invitation of his Boeotian friend Proxenus to join the Greek mercenary band fighting on behalf of

XENOPHON

Cyrus, who was mounting a campaign to unseat his brother Artaxerxes from the throne of Persia. Whether he did this out of a sense of adventure, or to replenish his family's depleted fortunes, or a combination of the two, is not known. But this action, along with his less than full sympathy for Athenian democracy, and his later fighting at the Battle of Coronea (394 BCE) with the Spartan mercenaries who had earlier joined Cyrus, was responsible for Xenophon's being exiled from Athens.

Xenophon spent much the better part of his life among Spartans. He sent his two sons off for a Spartan education; physically brutal and mentally severe though it was, he thought it the best available in Greece. For his services to Sparta, he was given an estate at Scillus, a few miles from Olympia. He lived for 30 years at Scillus where, it is believed, he wrote most of the works by which he is remembered today. In the end, Xenophon was more of a Peloponnesian than an Athenian, though his Athenian exile was repealed in 368 BCE. Accounts differ about whether he died in Athens or in Corinth. A prolific writer, Xenophon was especially fortunate in having the greater body of his work survive into the modern age.

The most important relationship of Xenophon's early life was with Socrates. The anecdote is told that the handsome young Xenophon one day came upon Socrates in a narrow street in Athens; the philosopher barred his way by putting up his staff and inquiring of him the whereabouts of various goods in the city. He then asked Xenophon where he might acquire virtue, and when he didn't know, Socrates replied, "Then follow me, and learn."

HOW MUCH TIME Xenophon spent with Socrates, what Socrates' opinion of him was, how accurate his portrait of Socrates is, none of these things is, or can be, known with exactitude. Xenophon wrote four longish Socratic treatises—"Socrates Defence," "Memoirs of Socrates," "The Dinner Party," and "Estate Manager," also often called "Oeconomicus"—which, along with Plato's more extensive Socratic writings and Aristophanes' satirical play *The Clouds*, furnish the most complete knowledge we have of the great philosopher.

Although recognizably the same man, the two Socrates, Xenophon's and Plato's, differ in intellectual character and temper. Scholars claim that the later dialogues in Plato, which are more concerned with matters metaphysical and the exhaustive definition of moral terms, are in fact more Platonic than Socratic—that in these dialogues it is Plato rather than Socrates who is speaking. Xenophon's Socrates is less subtle, not so aporetic—that is, he doesn't raise questions without answering them, or undermine confidence by incessant questioning—but instead supplies his knowledge to his pupils straightaway. Nor does Xenophon's Socrates proclaim his own ignorance, which is of course at the heart of Socrates' investigations in the dialogues of Plato, used as a device to deflate the other fellow's assumption of knowledge. The English scholar J. K. Anderson puts it nicely when he writes that "it may well be that Socrates did in fact prefer, in Xenophon's case, to confirm his beliefs rather than [as in Plato's] to dissect them."

The Socrates of Xenophon is also much more pious than the Socrates of Plato, not only regularly acknowledging the hand of the gods in the fate of men and their various endeavors but emphasizing the importance of good order in one's life so that the unpredictability of the gods does not undo all one's plans, though it is understood that even the utmost prudence will not always fend off the occasional arbitrariness of the gods. Plato's Socrates, then, turns out to be more like Plato, and Xenophon's more like Xenophon. Yet in the end, if one partially agrees with the Russian classicist Michael Rostovtzeff, that "Xenophon was a man of moderate ability and slight philosophic training, [and] Plato one of the greatest thinkers in the world's history," it would nonetheless be a mistake to take Xenophon's own Socratic contributions as negligible or without interest. Unless one has a strong taste for metaphysics, which is not everyone's cup of mead, Xenophon's Socrates, with his stress on the first principles of order, prudence, and good sense, provides many compensations.

Xenophon was less subtle than Plato and not so penetrating as Thucydides, but he was by no means unintelligent. His interest in historical causes may have been minimal, for he concentrated instead on great men and major events. He was pious in his belief that the gods needed to be consulted regularly through divination—which meant animal sacrifices and the investigation of entrails that followed—and tended to hold that, while the gods do not always reward virtue, they do punish wickedness. What one comes to realize in reading Xenophon is that his real subject, not only in his Socratic dialogues but throughout his work, is leadership. In Xenophon's dialogue "Oeconomicus," Socrates, professing to be discussing how best to run a household and thereby increase its wealth, is really (as Leo Strauss underscores) getting at how best to run an army and a state, and how, finally, to lead the good life.

Xenophon's own experience as a leader of men was acquired during the *Anabasis* (called *The Persian Expedition* in the Penguin edition), an account of the roughly 900-mile trek from Persia after the defeat of Cyrus at the Battle of Cunaxa (401 BCE) through the territory of hostile barbarian tribes, making his way with 10,000 Greek soldiers back to the Hellespont. After the Persians had killed first Cyrus and then the Greek generals who led the mercenary force, Xenophon, in his own version of events, stepped up and, with the Spartan Chirisophus, led the Greeks back to their homeland. The extent of his role as leader is sometimes disputed, as is much else in Xenophon: how close he was to Socrates, which parts of his various books he wrote at what age, where and when he died.

What isn't in dispute is Xenophon's close relationship with Agesilaus, who ruled Sparta as one of its two kings for the unusually long span of 40 years. Plutarch writes of Agesilaus' "early life having added to his natural kingly and commanding qualities the gentle and humane feelings of a citizen." Despite being small and having had a limp owing to one of his legs being shorter than the other, "the goodness of his humor, and his constant cheerfulness and playfulness of temper, always free from anything of moroseness or haughtiness, made him more attractive, even to his old age, than the most beautiful and youthful men of the nation." As late as his seventies, Agesilaus was still leading the Spartans into battle.

Xenophon first encountered Agesilaus at the Battle of Coronea. He somehow managed to insinuate himself with the Spartan king. This connection, which placed him in the inner circles of Sparta, gave him, in effect, a chair in the royal box for viewing the history of post-Peloponnesian War Greece—a history that ended with the ultimate subduing of once-mighty Greece, through endless internecine battles and disputes, by the Macedonian Philip II, father of Alexander the Great.

Agesilaus and Xenophon shared a belief in the need to destroy the Persian Empire and a hatred of Thebes. Always loyal to friends, Agesilaus arranged for Xenophon's retirement estate at Scillus. One of the chief criticisms of Xenophon's *Hellenika* is its author's too kind—which is to say largely uncritical—treatment of the Spartan king, and his partiality toward the Spartans generally throughout his history. So strong is this partiality that, for long spells in the *Hellenika*, one almost forgets that Athens exists. One of Xenophon's modern critics suggests that the title of the work would more accurately have been *Peloponnesiaca*. The great Theban general Epaminondas, the man responsible for defeating the Spartans at Leuctra (371 BCE) and Mantinea (362 BCE), has scarcely more than a bit part in Xenophon's history. Lysander, the rival of Agesilaus for Spartan leadership, also gets short shrift in the pages of the *Hellenika*.

A new edition of this history is now published under the general editorship of Robert B. Strassler, who earlier brought out Landmark editions of Herodotus and Thucydides. Strassler is what is today known as an independent, which really means amateur, scholar, taking the word amateur in its root meaning of lover. After a successful career in business—oil drilling—he retired, and soon thereafter devoted himself to ancient history, the love of which he acquired as an undergraduate at Harvard and never lost.

The result of this devotion has been Strassler's Landmark editions. These books print the central texts in solid new translations, with marginal notes and useful footnotes, introduced by scholars, with still other scholars writing upon specialized topics pertinent to the central texts. Perhaps best of all in the Landmark editions are the maps, which are clear, plentiful, and immensely useful. One can read Herodotus and Thucydides over and over without having such basic knowledge as how large Attica and the Peloponnese are, how far is the distance between Athens and Sparta, or Corinth from either. Robert Strassler is himself, one learns, without Greek, and he has devised books of immense aid for the Greekless Hellenophile, of whom I am one.

A Landmark edition is especially useful for Xenophon's *Hellenika*, for it is a work over which much controversy hangs. Until early in the 20th century, Xenophon's history was taken to be definitive. Then, in 1906, the papyrus of an incomplete manuscript since known as the *Hellenica Oxyrhynchia* was found in Egypt that contradicted Xenophon in many particulars. A later, Roman chronicle by Diodorus Siculus, who tends to agree with the Oxyrhynchia historian, has further reduced the reputation for accuracy of Xenophon's *Hellenika*. Yet another controversy has to do with when Xenophon wrote his history. Some scholars have him writing different parts of it at different stages of his life. One of Xenophon's strongest critics, the Oxford classicist G. L. Cawkwell, holds that the *Hellenika* isn't history at all but essentially memoirs, the memoirs written by an old man, and as Cawkwell notes, "old men forget." Yet, whatever his faults, however much he falls short of the precision required by modern historical scholarship, Xenophon remains immensely readable and instructive. Without Xenophon's *Hellenika*, as Robert Strassler notes, "we would know nothing or very little of many events and developments of that dynamic period" from the end of the Peloponnesian War through 362 BCE.

History, in its less technical but most attractive form is, as Macaulay had it, "philosophy teaching by example," which is history of the kind about which Xenophon cared most. Throughout the *Hellenika*, but also in the *Anabasis*, the virtuous actions of leaders are what

Xenophon highlights and extols. Noble deeds please him most. Leaders (and they are chiefly Spartans) who consult the wishes of the gods show good sense. Bad conduct finds its recompense. To violate an oath is to court disaster:

> Agesilaus, beaming with joy, told the envoys to announce to [the powerful Persian satrap] Tissaphernes that he was quite grateful, because Tissaphernes, by violating his oaths, now had the gods as his enemies and he had also, by this same action, made the gods the allies of the Greeks.

The gods may not always reward virtue in Xenophon, but they "are not indifferent to the impious and those who do wicked things." Courage, honor, sensible leadership, the orderly life—these are the virtues Xenophon most admires. *Contra* Gerald and Sara Murphy, not living but dying well is, in Xenophon, often the best revenge. Of the Battle of Mantinea between the Thebans, led by Epaminondas, and the Spartans, led by Agesilaus, and which wrote *fini* to Spartan hegemony, he writes about the Athenians who, out of hatred for the Thebans, came to the aid of the Spartans, joining in the fighting:

> Brave were the men among them who died, and it is clear that the men they killed were equally brave. For no one had a weapon so short that he did not reach his enemy with it. And the Athenians did not abandon the corpses of their own men but, rather, gave back some of the enemy dead under truce.

With remarkable restraint, Xenophon chose not to mention that both his sons took part in this battle, and that one of them, Gryllos, died bravely in this battle, being, one of the Landmark *Hellenika*'s footnotes reports, "depicted in the picture of the battle commissioned by the Athenians for one of their public buildings." For all that it wants in intellectual rigor, the *Hellenika* contains many fine novelistic touches. After the Athenian disaster of

the naval battle at Aigospotamoi, Xenophon recounts the reaction
when the news of the disaster reached Athens:

> The *Paralos* arrived at Athens during the night, bringing
> news of the disaster at Aigospotamoi, and a cry arose in
> the Peiraieus and ran up through the Long Walls and
> into the city itself as one man imparted the calamitous
> news to the next. As a result, no one slept that night
> as they mourned not only for the men destroyed but
> even more for themselves, thinking they would suffer
> the same catastrophes they had inflicted on others. . . .
> On the next day they held an assembly in which they
> resolved to block up all the harbors except for one, to
> repair the walls and place guards on all of them, and to
> prepare the city in every other way for a siege.

Who was it said that history begins in the novel and ends in the
essay? Xenophon, perhaps more the novelist and essayist than pure
historian, would have agreed.

Some of the most important historical events in Western history have wanted great writers to witness and record them. The
French Revolution came inconveniently after the death of the Duc
de Saint-Simon and before Benjamin Constant had come into literary maturity. No great writer was on the scene for the American Revolution, or for our Civil War. The history of Greece and
Rome was more fortunate: Herodotus was there to record battles
between the Greeks and the Persians, and Thucydides to record
events, many of which he personally witnessed, in the Peloponnesian War. In Rome, Livy and Tacitus and Suetonius were in the
same fortunate position. The existence of such writers makes history more vivid and ancient history itself perhaps of deeper interest than any other.

The endless making and breaking of treaties and busting up of
alliances and dishonoring of pledges among Sparta and Athens
and Persia, ending in the eclipse of all three, is the greater story of

the *Hellenika*. The prolific Xenophon was, as we should say today, on the case, embedded, capturing a goodly portion of the life of his time, "the only historian from antiquity," as Arnaldo Momigliano wrote, "to rival Tacitus in the range of writing that came from his pen."

Denigrate him though many historical scholars have tried to do, they have succeeded in little more than putting a few dents in his shield. In the end, Xenophon stands, half a historian, half a philosopher, and wholly a marvelous writer.

Matthew Shanahan

My Friend Matt

M Y FRIEND MATTHEW SHANAHAN, born in 1917, was eighty-eight when I first met him in 2005. He was one of those handsome bald men, with delicate, rather aristocratic features, high-colored skin with few wrinkles, and bright blue eyes through which he could make out only the dimmest shades of grey or glints of the most glaring light.

Matt was blind, the victim of retinitis pigmentosa, which ran in his family. The disease began to affect him in his fifties, leaving him with scarcely any sight by his sixties, and progressing to total blindness. Deaf in his right ear, he wore a hearing aid in his left. Slender, perhaps 5'10" or so before age had bent him forward, he nonetheless had a natural elegance, and wore clothes well; each day these were chosen for him by one of the attendants at Friedman Place, the Jewish home for the blind on the northside of Chicago into which he had moved a short while before I met him.

The meeting came about indirectly through my granddaughter, then a junior in high school, who was working as a volunteer at Friedman Place, in connection with a course at her school. Matt Shanahan was the first person she visited. Her assignment was to help him with his Braille, testing him on a deck of Braille playing cards. When he had more vision, Matt derived much pleasure from the game of bridge. His main pleasure now, apart from the company of family, was listening to books on tape, and of these he had listened to a vast quantity. Not long after we met, in fact, he turned in my direction and asked, "Do you have any notion why Hannah Arendt wanted to sleep with a creep like Heidegger?" An interesting question coming from a man who never finished high school.

Because getting from her school to Friedman Place required three different buses, and because from her birth I have dedicated myself to spoiling her, I picked my granddaughter up at her school every Thursday afternoon and drove her to Friedman Place. I waited an hour for her in the lobby, where, sitting on a couch before an aviary filled with small charming birds, I read a book.

Not every resident at Friedman Place was entirely blind; some had serious vision impairments but could still see. The spread of ages ran from the youthful to the aged. Having been born blind, or become blind at an early age, it was apparent from my vantage point in the lobby, often resulted in strange, rather Aspergian tics of behavior. Among the arbitrary dirty tricks played upon them, some of the blind residents talked very loudly, with no sense of modulation; a few others had psychological problems, evidenced by grimacing twitches or scowls; a small man named Stuart had the slightly alarming habit of staring at women at close range in a manner that was clearly not social scientific.

Roz Katz, who organizes cultural fields trips for Friedman Place residents and is in charge of volunteers and is a person of great energy and sweetness of character, after noticing me sitting in the lobby a few Thursdays, asked if I would be willing to spend the hour reading to residents. Since Mrs. Katz is a woman who could sell a freezer on the installment plan to a man on his way to the gallows, saying no was not really a possibility. I started the following Thursday, reading to perhaps twelve people. I began with a Chekhov story, which cut my audience down to nine; a Turgenev story I read the following week brought it down to six; stories by Somerset Maugham and Saki and myself—and here I felt I was going down market—left me with four, sometimes three auditors. I was not, to put it gently, a great hit.

Matt Shanahan was at all my readings, sitting to my right, the better to hear out of his still good left ear. From his concentrated look I could tell that he was listening to the stories at a higher level of understanding and enjoyment than other people in the room. We would sometimes talk for a few minutes after the reading. Apart from his Hannah Arendt-Heidegger remark, I don't recall his saying anything striking, yet he established himself in my mind as a serious man capable of subtlety and of its faithful companion irony.

Not long after my granddaughter's semester of volunteer work was over, I decided to stop my unpopular Thursday afternoon readings. I told Matt that I had chiefly continued the readings on his account, and would much prefer to spend the time taking him to lunch every other Friday, when we could talk by ourselves uninterruptedly. He agreed. And so we did for the next six years, with occasional breaks for travel on my part and illness on his.

Each second Friday Matt would be waiting for me on a couch to the left of the aviary in the lobby of Friedman Place. I would touch him on the shoulder and take his hand. "Joe?" he would say, without bothering to look up. "The very same, sailor," I would reply. As we walked out of the lobby, he would grasp my right arm with his left hand—he carried his white and red cane in his right hand—and we made our way to my car parked on the driveway. I always described the weather to him, including the quality of the day's light. He had to negotiate a curb to get into the front seat of my car. Once he had his hand on the upper part of the open door, guiding by it, he was able to slide himself into the front passenger seat. The first time I said, "There you go" when he had done so, he replied, "What do you suppose that means? Where is 'there' and why 'go.' " He was careful with language, and we often investigated the nonsense of stock phrases: food that "hit the spot," "get a grip on yourself," "oops a daisy," "everything's on the up and up," and many more. His blindness made him especially thoughtful about language; he saw the words and their comical illogic perhaps more vividly than people with sight might do.

At first we went to different restaurants on the northside of Chicago: Greek, Italian, German joints. (I paid the check one week, Matt the next, giving me his credit card, and having me to sign his name when the bill arrived.) Then we settled on a place called Taste of Heaven on Clark Street, in the Andersonville neighborhood. I could usually get a parking space nearby, the food was fresh and good, and they served locally famous Peterson's Ice Cream, notably a flavor called Mackinac Island Fudge, with which we often topped off our lunches. Usually we shared a large sandwich, served on sourdough baguette, but if Matt ordered pancakes or French toast, I would cut it up for him. A West Indian woman at Friedman Place used to do this for him, always saying, "I make pieces," which he reported to me with his wry smile. At the beginning of the meal, I directed his hand to his coffee mug, and might report that on his plate the pasta salad was at three o'clock, the sandwich at six.

We generally made rather clattersome entrances and departures, Matt bent over, holding onto my arm, his white-and-red-stick pointed outward, capturing perhaps too much attention in the restaurant's narrow aisles. As we left, I would sometimes make dopey jokes. "This guy isn't really blind," I'd say, "he just uses the cane to pick up girls." Or: "Excuse us, but his dog is on vacation in a condo he owns in Boca Raton, and the agency sent me to take him to lunch." He went along with it beautifully, adding amusing comments of his own. "The dog has much better manners than this fellow," he might say.

Matt had come into his full blindness too late to be adept at dealing with it. Not many moves came easily to him. Watching him try to establish himself in a restaurant chair could be a reminder of what a subtraction loss of sight was: he would feel the seat of the chair with his hand, place his cap atop it, his white cane beneath it, then arrange to seat himself fully three feet from the table or, occasionally, facing the wrong way. Sometimes returning to my apartment after lunch with him, I would close my eyes, pretending to be blind, and for five minutes or so try to put myself through the simplest exercises: finding a light switch, opening the refrigerator and attempting to locate the orange juice carton, making my way to the bathroom and finding the sink and toilet once there. I didn't do well.

By rough count, we had 600 hours of uninterrupted conversation, Matt and I. Sometimes I would remind myself that he hadn't the least idea of my appearance. The way I dressed, the color of my hair, my smile, my physical reactions to his jokes, whether I seemed old or young for my age, graceful or awkward in my movements. I could have closed my eyes while he was speaking, or yawned, or read a magazine through our lunches together, and he wouldn't have known it. I bring this up because I am myself attentive, as are we all, to the least physical reactions on the part of people to whom I speak, to sense whether what I am saying is understood, agreed with, enjoyed, going down well. Owing to his blindness, Matt traveled without such a social compass, though it didn't seem to bother him much, at least not in my company.

Neither Matt nor I were confessional, nor did we go in for instant intimacy. We did, though, have an immediate rapport—or, as I told him, we Jews called it, rappaport. We never talked about sex, except as comedy, and agreed that everyone else's sex was comical but our own. We rarely talked about money—he was a paying resident at Friedman Place—though he once told me that if he lived to one hundred he figured to run out of his savings. On fundamental things we were in agreement: on what was amusing, on who was impressive, on what constituted decency.

He talked about his blindness matter-of-factly. He was without self-pity. I never once heard him complain about the mean trick of blindness that life had played on him. His only physical complaints were about his various hearing aids, which sometimes went on the fritz, tending to give off odd sounds. The hearing aid could also make the din in noisy restaurants unbearable.

Slowly, over the early months of our lunching together, Matt filled me in on his biography. He was the youngest of nine children of Irish immigrant parents. His father, who worked as a bricklayer, was illiterate; his mother, who ran their home on the northside as a boarding house, was the brains of the outfit. Details of life in another era came through: his mother's economizing by buying day-old bread, the oddity of some of their male boarders, their German neighbors, Kogen the Jewish pharmacist who treated most of the minor ailments among neighborhood residents. From time to time he would report an incident about one or another of his brothers or sisters, with none of whom, my sense was, he was particularly close and whose destinies varied from being briefly successful to being bust-outs with alcohol problems.

Matt went of course to Catholic school, and did well there, a favorite of the nuns for his quick mind. He dropped out before finishing, because he was offered a job working in a grocery store, which, with the Depression raging, seemed too good to pass up. He married young, and fought in World War II with the Marines in the Pacific Theater. He never mentioned killing any of the enemy Japanese, but he did catch some shrapnel just below the clavicle, for which he was given a Purple Heart. He wrecked his hearing by being too near artillery fire, and suffered dizziness long after the war was over. He once recounted seeing piles of dead Japanese bodies on Guam, which shook him and, though he never said so directly, may have been in good part responsible for his having lost his religion.

Religion was one of the things about which we disagreed—never violently, never allowing it to distract us for long. I held that life's mysteries were too abundant to make atheism even mildly persuasive. Truth is, religion wasn't a subject that much interested him; he had closed the books on it. Sometimes, after lunch, back in his room at Friedman Place, as I shook his hand in a slightly lingering way before leaving, he'd say, in a perfectly pitched phony sanctimonious voice, "I'll pray for you."

We also disagreed about politics. Matt was a liberal of the old-fashioned kind, which meant he was always on the side of the underdog. I told him it wasn't all that clear any more who exactly the underdog might be. I quoted to him Orwell's line about when he saw a policeman beat up on a man his, Orwell's, not having to decide whose side he was on, but I added that perhaps one did better to wait to see—the guy, these days, could be a rapist or a terrorist. His liberalism didn't get in the way of his viewing all politicians, in the approved Chicago manner, as guilty until proven innocent.

Matt was never a rich man. But I learned from his son David that, during the years that he lived in retirement in South Haven, Michigan, when he would receive a tax refund of two or three hundred dollars, he would take the money to the local grocery store and ask the manager to give it to someone in true need. He was, in other words, a liberal who put his money where his mouth was—a phrase he would have enjoyed deconstructing.

He knew I wrote for conservative magazines, and sometimes made comments that assumed I had connections that stopped just short of the war room in Republican administrations, an assumption of which I'm not sure I was ever able to disabuse him. He was himself much interested in if not approving of William F. Buckley, Jr., a fellow Irishman, and every week read, or rather listened to, *The National Review*, not because he approved of it—he didn't— but because it was available on tape. In fact we didn't waste all that much time talking about politics, either.

Matt was lucky in his family, a son and two daughters, and lots of impressive grandchildren—one an attorney at City Hall, another an Olympic-quality speed skater until he decided to give up skating for a career in medicine—with a number of great-grand-children added. His daughters live in Chicago, his son in Wisconsin, and they were devoted to him. One or another would pay him visits during the week, take him out for lunch or dinner on weekends; he was with them on all holidays. Often we would return from lunch to find a voice mail message from one or another of them, David or Pat or Kitty, and sometimes from all three. They must have known that their father was an exceptional man, and none among them let him down.

Matt was grateful to the staff at Friedman Place, for their kindness and attentiveness to him. He did not complain about the food, with the exception of the turkey bacon (he preferred the real thing), which a Jewish institution was compelled to serve. What he missed was the company of fellow residents. "When I first moved in here," he told me, "I expected all sorts of Jewish men of my own age with lots of stories and jokes to tell." None, it turned out, were on the premises. He went to all of Roz Katz's outings—to the classical music concerts, to plays, to boat rides on Lake Michigan. He took such classes as were offered (exercise, the history of popular music, opera, and others), and this provided diversion, but it wasn't quite enough. What he was looking for were contemporaries with a high quality of schmooze—which is, I suppose, where I came in.

Matthew Shanahan was as Irish as Joseph Epstein is Jewish. He had never finished high school and I had taught (without advanced degrees of any kind) for thirty years at Northwestern University. He had grown up working-class and poor, I middle-class and comfortable. He was twenty years older than I, yet when with him I felt in the company of a contemporary and a peer, and I think he felt close to the same about me. What we had in common was the city of Chicago, a certain bookishness, and amusement at human foibles, our own included, and a set of standards and values bred by the Depression and World War II that seemed to be on their way out.

From the moment he latched his seatbelt in my car around himself until the time nearly two hours later when I left him in his room at Friedman Place, Matt and I kept up a continuous flow of conversation. The conversation may have been more nonstop than normal because his blindness precluded all other distractions. Sometimes I would fill him in on a detail or two in the restaurant: a staggeringly beautiful young woman who just walked in, a new tattoo on the forearm of our waiter, an obese couple at a small table clearly nuts about each other. "Love," I informed him a Rumanian aphorist named E. M. Cioran wrote, "is an agreement on the part of two people to overestimate each other." He smiled. "That's good," he said.

Once he was safely seated in my car, I ceased to think of Matt as blind, with a few notable exceptions. On one occasion, as I was taking him back to Friedman Place after lunch, driving along the southernmost outer wall of Rosehill Cemetery headed toward Western Avenue, who should come jogging past from the opposite direction, in shorts, with his soft face, heavy white legs, and impossibly perfect hair, but our honorable and now jailed governor, Rod Blagojevich. In the company of anyone with eyesight, this would have been a conversation stopper, issuing in fifteen minutes of talk about politics, corruption, and the Blagojevich family political connections. But if you didn't see it, as Matt didn't, it didn't really happen, and the event had no more significance than if a squirrel had crossed the path of the car.

The share of talk between us was roughly equal, though I believe Matt did a bit more of it than I, possibly because of his hearing aid difficulties. His wife Arleane, who died twenty or so years before I met him, came up for fairly regular mention in his conversation, always with great respect. She was a serious, even a formidable, person and a true partner in his life. He would often bring up people he had worked with at Kraft Foods or the Post Office, from which he retired with a decent pension and excellent health insurance.

He never told me this, but I later learned that after his wife's death he had lived alone, in near and then total blindness, for twenty years in South Haven, doing his own shopping and cooking and arranging bridge games.

We talked a fair amount about words. He once asked me if every word in Yiddish was critical. I told that I believe every one could at least be used ironically, including the prepositions. We used to fill each other in on the distinctions between such linguistic niceties as the difference between farther and further, each other and one another, nevertheless and nonetheless (of the latter, according to H. W. Fowler, there isn't any). If either of us came upon an interesting or comical new word, he would report it to the other.

Matt never found passion in his work, or so I concluded. I once told him that he was missing the ambition gene, and he didn't argue otherwise. Some of this may have derived from his missing out on a fuller education, which would have qualified him for such work; some of it may have resulted from his coming of age in the heart of the Depression, when a job with security mattered more than challenging work. Yet, as there was no self-pity in Matt, neither did I ever pick up the note of regret in him.

I wonder, though, if I wasn't wrong. I have since come to think that, had he grown up in a different world, Matt might have been a writer. His powers of observation were strong. He was keen on analysis of character. He could distance himself nicely even from people he loved to scrutinize their weaknesses and strengths, their motives and illusions. His love of language and skill at manipulating it—he was very well spoken—would have served him much better on the page than at the Post Office. Yet without formal education, and having to raise a family, then with the intervention of the war, the very notion of work without a regular salary had to have been beyond conceiving to him.

We talked a fair amount about books. One week he listened to *War and Peace* being read by the old Shakespearean actor Alexander

Scourby, and insisted that I hear a few paragraphs of Scourby's magnificent performance. He was an amateur expert in the works of Marcia Davenport, whose memoir *Too Strong for Fantasy* he thought a fine book. We used to joke about his being the only man living who had read—years before, while he still had the use of his eyes—the autobiography of Loyal Davis, the neurosurgeon, locally (in Chicago) well-known anti-Semite, and father of Nancy Reagan.

He listened only to serious books, and when something reputed to be serious didn't pass muster with him, he showed his dissatisfaction. With his natural highbrow taste, he wasn't a fit member for the book discussion groups he was sometimes asked to join. I always told him what I had been reading, and in some instances suggested he try to order it on tape. I put him on to reading Willa Cather, whom he came to admire. We never discussed what we read in any extended or analytical way. Our very last phone call— he was, alas, my call waiting, so our conversation was too brief—he told me that the library that supplied him with tapes had sent him the wrong ones, and he wanted me to suggest some titles to him for a quick reorder. I mentioned Isaac Bashevis Singer's *Enemies: A Love Story*, Vassily Grossman's *Life and Fate*, and Gregor von Rezzori's *Memoirs of an Anti-Semite*, and then, alas, rang off.

Not long after we started going to lunch together, I began bringing him a CD. I brought him Louie Armstrong and Ella Fitzgerald and Duke Ellington and Lee Wiley and Louis Prima and Blossom Dearie, which he enjoyed well enough. His true taste, though, ran to classical music, so I began to bring him Schubert sonatinas, Frescobaldi harpsichord pieces, Clementi piano works, the songs of Reynaldo Hahn, and other mildly off the war-horse beaten track. I would put these on the CD player in his room, and leave him listening to them. From my own selfish perspective, it felt better to me than leaving him alone in the silent dark.

Matt began to complain about his memory slipping from him. I found it still impressive to the last. Every so often he wouldn't be able to call up the title of a book or movie or once-famous athlete, yet not as frequently as all that; no more than was the case with me. Sometimes, he left me with an assignment to check, on Google, a song lyric or the name of an old baseball player, and report back to him. The last item for which I did so was for a Joni James song called "How Important Can It Be." He wasn't certain that the song really existed and, though the tune was playing in his head, if he wasn't making it up.

During our last year together Matt told me that he had begun seeing, in his mind's eye, cities of his own invention, entire urban landscapes filled in by his imagination. A sapient blind person would perforce live in his mind more than the same person with sight who has the visible world always before him for contemplation and distraction, but this creation of complete cities seemed to me a nice touch, and gave him much pleasure. He told me he was also struck by observations that, he felt, should have occurred to him decades before. He mentioned in this connection a boy he grew up with who was able to beat him at all childish and boyhood games: marbles, mumbly-peg, sprinting, wrestling, everything. In recounting the story Matt said that he didn't mind losing to him in the least; he merely presumed the other's superiority at games. (Competition, like strong ambition, apparently wasn't in his nature.) Then much later in life, he met this fellow, now a middle-age man, who showed no interest in him whatsoever. "I existed merely as someone for him to beat," Matt said, "and when the games were over, so was any interest he had in me. But why did it take me more than eighty years to recognize this?" he asked.

What did we get out of each other? I had over Matt a somewhat wider experience of the world, but he had over me a deeper experience of the great events of our time. He had directly known the Depression and World War II, each of which had permanently marked him, while I lived only in their shadows, feeling chiefly their after-effects.

He may have got from me authentificiation of a sort. He knew he was highly intelligent, but he hadn't run into many people who the world—that great ninny, as Henry James called it—agreed to certify as intelligent. As a former university teacher, the author of books, a contributor to intellectual magazines, I passed the certification test. And I always treated him as an intellectual equal, because he was.

What I got out of my lunches with Matt, along with much laughter, a nice feeling of comradeship, and bits of education about life in Chicago before my time, was a heightened sense of life's possibilities, even when the odds are stacked against a man. Matt played on through blindness, near deafness, old age, felt life closing in on him, and kept his poise, humor, high spirits. The plain fact is that I admired him, and was pleased to hear other people tell me that he looked forward to our lunches.

The last four months or so, we switched restaurants, leaving Taste of Heaven, which had become too noisy on Fridays, for a place three blocks to the south on Clark Street called Svea, which specialized in thin Swedish pancakes with lingonberry jam and the crisp bacon—spare the turkey—that was to Matt's liking. Two doors and a double stoop had to be negotiated to enter, and the waitress, seeing us coming, held the second, inner door, open for us. I sensed Matt weakening physically. It was tougher for him to emerge from the front seat of my car; his always faltering walk became even slower. I sensed his already limited hearing was getting worse. His enthusiasm for talk, though, was undiminished. Toward the end he more than once said to me that he wasn't sure how much longer we could count on going out to our lunches together. Nonsense, I told him, if need be we would come to lunch in an ambulance.

Matt died at 2:30 a.m., in his sleep, I hope. The only thing he ever told me that he feared was a stroke, and he had avoided that. When I received a call about Matt's death I was not shocked or even surprised—he was after all ninety-four—but instead disappointed. We had more to tell each other. The other day I came across the word "agnology," whose root is in the word agnostic, and whose meaning is the study of things that cannot be learned. Perfect item for Matt, I thought.

I think of myself about to leave his room. My hand is on the knob of the door; he is seated in his chair, facing a window out of which he sees nothing. Famous arias, or Mozart quartets, or Bach suites are playing on his CD machine. Matt Shanahan is alone in the dark, except that, with his mind, he was never alone, never in the dark, not really.

Index

C